The Aesthetics of Island Space

The Aesthetics of Island Space

Perception, Ideology, Geopoetics

JOHANNES RIQUET

OXFORD
UNIVERSITY PRESS

OXFORD
UNIVERSITY PRESS

Great Clarendon Street, Oxford, OX2 6DP,
United Kingdom

Oxford University Press is a department of the University of Oxford.
It furthers the University's objective of excellence in research, scholarship,
and education by publishing worldwide. Oxford is a registered trade mark of
Oxford University Press in the UK and in certain other countries

First Edition published in 2019

Impression: 1

Published in the United States of America by Oxford University Press
198 Madison Avenue, New York, NY 10016, United States of America

British Library Cataloguing in Publication Data

Data available

Library of Congress Control Number: 2019954844

ISBN 978-0-19-883240-9 (hpk.)

ISBN 978-0-19-883241-6 (pbk.)

DOI: 10.1093/oso/9780198832409.001.0001

Printed and bound by
CPI Group (UK) Ltd, Croydon, CR0 4YY

This work was originally accepted as a PhD thesis by the Faculty of Arts and Social Sciences,
University of Zurich in the autumn semester 2014 on the recommendation of the Doctoral Committee
consisting of Elisabeth Bronfen (main supervisor) and Christina Ljungberg

To my parents, Gilles and Juliane Riquet,
for their endless support

PREFACE

'Ready, I think I see something, but I can hardly tell what it is; it appears to be in the air, and yet it is not clouds....'

'You're right, sir', replied Ready, 'there is something; it is not the land which you see, but it is the trees upon the land which are reflected, as they call it, so as to appear, as you say, as if they were in the air. That is an island, sir, depend upon it....' (Marryat 1841, 46)

After the wreck of the *Pacific* in Frederick Marryat's island novel *Masterman Ready* (1841), the Seagrave family are desperately hoping 'to gain some island' (45); their expectations are shaped by popular castaway narratives like *Robinson Crusoe*, which is discussed on deck shortly before the shipwreck. Their hopes are soon gratified: after its entirely imaginary appearance in the castaways' desires, the island first emerges as an uncertain visual phenomenon on the horizon. Looking neither like solid land nor like insubstantial clouds, it refuses to be classified. Ready's convoluted syntax reinforces the visual confusion expressed by Mr. Seagrave; the delayed declarative 'That is an island, sir' sits uneasily with the complicated explanation preceding it.

This example from *Masterman Ready* is one of countless fictional and non-fictional descriptions of islands marked by perceptual, geographical, and linguistic uncertainty and disorientation. In many ways, a growing fascination with these uncertainties was the starting point for this book. When I began this project, I was strongly influenced by a tradition of scholarship that viewed literary islands—especially literary islands from the English-speaking world—as supreme figures of bounded space and the fictions of modern individualism, nationalism, and colonialism that accompanied it. These valuable analyses alerted me to the ongoing importance of islands in the Western imagination, and to the ideological functions they have served. But I have gradually come to understand that British and American island narratives challenge these ideologies as frequently as they consolidate them, and that they mobilize and destabilize space as much as they render it static and controllable. It is this neglected story of islands that I wish to tell in this book, which aims to reconsider the central role islands have played in rethinking space since the 'insular moment' (Conley 1996, 167–201) of early modernity.

The Aesthetics of Island Space: Perception, Ideology, Geopoetics discusses islands as central figures in the modern experience of space. It examines the spatial poetics of islands in literary texts, journals of explorers and scientists, and Hollywood cinema. It differs from and complements accounts of fictional islands as tropes for enclosed, autonomous, and static spaces by tracing the ways in which literary and cinematic islands have functioned as malleable spatial figures of geo(morpho)logical instability and poetic production. In different ways, the island narratives examined in this study generate perceptual struggles and mental cartographies, and stage aesthetic experiences of space that take their protagonists and readers to the limits of human perception. In addition to rethinking island fiction, then, this book is a contribution to recent theoretical approaches to space that explore the intersection of lived experience, perception, culture, and physical geography.

The works examined span several centuries, ranging from early modern texts to contemporary representations. Each chapter is attentive to the ways in which different conceptualizations of islands have travelled through time as well as space. Terrence Malick's *The New World* offers a representative example of this textual wandering of islands. At the beginning of the 2008 extended version, we see a quotation from John Smith's *A Description of New England* (1616): 'How much they err, / that think every one which has been at Virginia / understands or knows what Virginia is.' As we hear Pocahontas invoking the spirit of the land, the camera seems to move forward into a part of the water littered with floral debris from the trees, creating an image of arrival. However, the unchanging reflection of the trees reveals that the movement is illusory, and that the water is actually moving towards the camera. We then see the camera moving over a map by John White, engraved by Theodor de Bry ('The Arriual of the Englishemen in Virginia', 1590), approaching an island (Figure P.1). Before the shot fades out, a group of trees reminiscent of those reflected in the water is superimposed on the map. Like the John Smith quote, which is 'extracted from its context' in a passage where Smith is really 'venting his frustration about amateurish map-makers' (Nicol par. 4), the map has been tampered with. In the original engraving (which appears, in

FIGURE P.1   Still from *The New World* (Terrence Malick, USA/UK 2005)

fact, one minute later in the film), several half-sunk ships are visible in front of the islands of the Outer Banks, with two large ships sailing towards them (see Chapter 1, Figure 1.3). In the version shown in the film, no sinking ships are visible, but one of the larger ships has been moved and appears (back-to-front) very close to the island, in the same position as one of the shipwrecks on the original map.

The Smith quotation, the forward movement of the water, and the map jointly create an image of hopeful landfall. The superimposition of trees on the map and the seemingly repeated camera movement (across the water, over the map) construct a multilayered island arrival between text, image, and material space. But the manipulations of text and map as well as the *trompe l'oeil*-shot also point to shipwrecks, frustrated hopes, and arrested movement at the island gateways of the New World. In this, Malick's film repeats the rhetorical operations at work in many of the texts written by the early colonizers. It also conflates various island beginnings: although it recounts the early history of Jamestown, the map shows the islands in front of Roanoke Island, the site of England's first, failed colonial experiments in America. Most importantly, Malick's film demonstrates the continued after-life of earlier island representations; indeed, the remediation of written texts, maps, and drawings in its first minutes points to the intersection of these texts in the cultural imaginary, spanning the period and the range of text types covered in this book.

* * *

I could not have written this book without the support of colleagues, friends, and family. Many of the ideas developed here emerged in conversation with my fellow members of the Island Poetics project—Daniel Graziadei, Britta Hartmann, Ian Kinane, and Barney Samson—and they have offered invaluable advice on various chapter drafts. My understanding of island narratives would be much more limited without this exchange. I warmly thank my former colleagues from the University of Zurich, especially Antoinina Bevan Zlatar, Johannes Binotto, Nicole Eberle, Martin Mühlheim, Allen Reddick, and Ana Sobral, as well as Kevin McGinley at Tampere University; their comments and feedback on ideas and drafts at various stages of this project have been a great help. My thanks also go to the research group 'Space/Phenomenology and Embodied Experience', among others, Martin Heusser, Rahel Rivera Godoy-Benesch, Michelle Dreiding, Stefanie Strebel, and Martino Oleggini. The stimulating discussions with this group have shaped my understanding of the spatial and phenomenological perspectives I draw on in my analyses. I am grateful to Godfrey Baldacchino, Tom Conley, Elizabeth DeLoughrey, Sarah Krotz, Jonathan Pugh, Jean-Michel Racault, and Anna Zdrenyk for ongoing conversations on islands as well as their valuable input and encouragement. This book grew out of a doctoral dissertation, and I would like to thank my supervisors, Elisabeth Bronfen, Margrit Tröhler, and Christina Ljungberg, for their support and guidance. Special thanks go to Margaret Freeman and Peter Schneck for their greatly appreciated encouragement and advice. I also thank Ninni Varanka for her editorial assistance in the final stages of the project, and Charlotte Coutu for compiling the index. I am indebted to Jonas Bühler, Michi Mötteli, Gabriela Rösli, and Josine Zanoli for patiently listening to my thoughts and for their general support. A great thank-you goes to Gabi Neuhaus for designing the installation on the cover. Finally, I would like to thank Aimee Wright at Oxford University Press for her help and guidance.

* * *

Parts of Chapter 2 were previously published as 'Killing King Kong: The Camera at the Borders of the Tropical Island, 1767–1937' (2014) in *Nordlit* 31, pp. 133–49.

Chapter 4 contains revised sections from an article that was published as 'Islands as Shifting Territories: Evolution, Geology and the Island Poetics of Darwin, Wallace, Wells and Ghosh' (2016) in *Insularity: Representations of Small Worlds*, edited by Katrin Dautel and Kathrin Schödel, pp. 223–36 (Würzburg: Königshausen & Neumann). They are reprinted with the kind permission of Königshausen & Neumann.

CONTENTS

LIST OF FIGURES

Introduction

Towards a Poetics of (the) Island(s)

At the beginning of Clint Eastwood's *Letters from Iwo Jima* (2006), we briefly see a black screen before the opening credits appear. At the same time, we hear the sound of waves. After the title has faded out, an image emerges that looks like a nocturnal sky speckled with stars before the camera tilts upwards to reveal waves lapping against a black, volcanic beach. Only then does the camera also pan right, centring Mount Suribachi, the dormant volcano that produced the island and is its strategically most important point (Figure I.1). The film thus begins by evoking a space and time devoid of human presence. The island takes shape before our eyes against the backdrop of the sound of the ocean that preceded it, while the optical illusion of the star-speckled sky evokes a cosmic order. The tilt, rising out of the black particles of its volcanic genesis, corresponds to the rise of the island out of the water, to the emergence of form out of a cosmic night, and to the appearance of the image in the dark cinema.

The emphasis on the border of land and sea foregrounds the island as a site of erosion before the focus shifts to the mountain, its geological and symbolic centre. Site of the famous photograph of the raising of the American flag, it evokes American victory and superiority. The next shot, however, makes it clear that the focus will be on the Japanese: rather than the American flag, we see a monument to the dead Japanese

The Aesthetics of Island Space: Perception, Ideology, Geopoetics. Johannes Riquet, Oxford University Press (2019). © Johannes Riquet.
DOI: 10.1093/oso/9780198832409.001.0001

FIGURE I.1   Still from *Letters from Iwo Jima* (Clint Eastwood, USA 2006)

soldiers on the mountain. In another tilt, the camera rises above the monument to reveal a panoramic view. The shot parodies a scene common in desert island narratives known as the '"monarch-of-all-I-survey" moment' (Pratt 2008, 1–42; Weaver-Hightower 2007, 4), when the castaway climbs to heights and takes visual possession of the island, like Robinson Crusoe, 'surveying it with a secret kind of pleasure... that I was king and lord of all this country indefeasibly...' (Defoe 2001, 80). What is surveyed at the beginning of *Letters from Iwo Jima*, however, is an almost monochrome wasteland, and nobody is there to contemplate the scene. And yet, the hesitant forward movement of the camera, the tilt, and the lingering over the view of the island imply an observing consciousness. The camera takes the position of the dead soldiers, as if rising from the grave.

Making and Perceiving Islands:
Poiesis and *Aisthesis*

This sequence encapsulates what this book is about: it examines islands between geography and text. The first shot combines various forms of production. It draws attention to the geological and geomorphological (re)creation of the island through volcanic processes, oceanic denudation, and resedimentation. This material production is paralleled by the cinematic and aesthetic production of the island. Both are linked to the construction of the island as a space invested with ideology along the lines theorized by Henri Lefebvre in *The Production of Space*; this third form of production manifests itself in the tension between the island's function as a site of commemoration of the Japanese soldiers and a space affirming American superiority. If geomorphology is the study of the genesis and sculpting of the land into diverse forms through various processes and forces (Strahler and Strahler 2002, 304), poetics is the equivalent of these processes in the realm of textuality, especially when understood in terms of the Greek ποίησις (poiesis: creation, production). According to the *Oxford English Dictionary*, 'poetics' in its most general sense means '[t]he creative principles informing any literary, social or cultural construction, or the theoretical study of these; a theory of form' ('poetics, n.' 2018). The resonance between these two types of form-giving processes is of central concern throughout this study, most explicitly in Chapter 4, when I turn to the geopoetics of islands.

But as the title itself signals, *The Aesthetics of Island Space: Perception, Ideology, Geopoetics* is interested in *aisthesis* as much as in *poiesis*. According to the *OED*, *aisthesis* means 'sense perception, sensation, perception' ('aesthesis | esthesis, n.' 2018), and the English derivative either '[t]he philosophy of the beautiful or of art;... the distinctive underlying principles of a work of art or a genre...'; '[t]he (attractive) appearance or sound of something'; or 'the science of sensory perception' ('aesthetics, n.' 2018). The Greek term, then, refers to the appearance of the world through sensory perception. Like *aisthesis*, the second and third meanings of *aesthetics* listed by the *OED* refer to phenomenal experience, while the first meaning overlaps with that of *poetics* as a set of formal and creative principles and processes. The two shots from *Letters from Iwo Jima* point to the perception of the island as much as to its geomorphological and textual production. In the first shot, the sound of the waves lapping against the beach evokes the island as an aural experience, while its subsequent emergence as an image creates a visual experience as the island takes shape before the viewer's eyes. In the second shot, the island again appears as an object of visual perception, even while the identity of the observer remains uncertain.

If this study talks about both *aesthetics* and *poetics*, it is to signal this interplay between *poiesis* and *aisthesis*, between the production of islands and their phenomenal appearance. I follow Terry Eagleton's contention that aesthetics is both linked to ideology and can '[provide]

an unusually powerful challenge and alternative to...dominant ideological forms...' (1990, 3). I also follow Elizabeth DeLoughrey and
George B. Handley's emphasis on an aesthetic engagement with the
earth (2011, 1–40). While we cannot escape textual mediation, different
poetic constructions of islands will imply different spatial conceptions,
and an attention to the materiality of islands can have transformative
effects: first, in the *resonance* between the materiality of islands and the
materiality of their textual production, and second, in the *interference*
of the former in the latter; in the resistance physical islands offer to
their various figurations and ideological appropriations in fictional and
non-fictional discourses.

Production, Destruction, Sedimentation: Islands between Geography and Text

Islands are particularly potent landforms for a reimagination of the
earth and our relation to it, which is partly due to the imaginative
potential of their geo(morpho)logical instability (think, for instance, of
volcanic islands). Indeed, if islands lend themselves to a discussion of
productive processes, they can equally be mobilized to negotiate
destruction and dissolution. In her classic text 'The Birth of an Island'
(1951), biologist Rachel Carson comments on the fate of oceanic
islands, writing that 'islands are ephemeral, created today, destroyed
tomorrow' (84). Gilles Deleuze's 1953 essay 'Desert Islands' reads like a
response to Carson. For Deleuze, continental islands are 'separated
from a continent' and manifest 'disarticulation, erosion, fracture',
while oceanic islands are 'originary', born from the water (2004, 9).
For Deleuze, as for Carson, islands manifest a struggle between land
and sea: '...that an island is deserted must appear *philosophically*
normal to us. Humans cannot live, nor live in security, unless they
assume that the active struggle between earth and water is over....
Islands are either from before or for after humankind' (9; emphasis
original). For Deleuze, islands make visible a constant threat of efface-
ment, exposing the apparent permanence of continents as a false
security. Desert island fictions manifest this philosophical condition
because they point to the before and after of human existence. Indeed,

castaways in island fictions 'come and go' (Beer 2003, 42). As Gillian Beer points out, island literature often revolves around the difficulty of establishing a founding population. Furthermore, castaways almost inevitably encounter traces of previous visitors: the footprint in *Robinson Crusoe* (2001) is one of many examples. These traces hold up a mirror to the castaway's own imminent disappearance from the island. Nourishing dreams of possession and colonization, island texts often frustrate these desires and give shape to a threat of extinction (cf. Beer 2003, 40–2). Scattered with ruins, these islands easily become sites of abandonment.

In *Letters from Iwo Jima*, too, the island is marked as a site of abandonment and destruction. The initial sense of a ghostly presence continues as we see abandoned sites and war ruins; most striking are two shots taken from behind a cannon, with the camera taking the position of the soldier operating it. The destructive potential of the volcano is signalled in the main part of the film. As the Americans attack the island, it looks as though the volcano were erupting; the suggestion that the Americans are trying to sink the island, uttered by one of the soldiers, continues this association. War is figured as a self-destructive volcanic eruption as the island is shaken to its foundations. Along with it, the filmic image trembles and threatens to dissolve.

The island in Eastwood's film is thus linked to both production and destruction. But it is best examined as a site in perpetual *re*construction, a space formed and reformed by textual layers as much as by volcanic sediment. Near the end of the film, this capacity of the island to reform itself is made clear as the Japanese soldiers listen to a radio transmission that features a song about the island sung by children: 'On the waves of the Pacific . . . / A small lonely island floats / The fate of our Imperial country / lies in the hands of this island / . . . We shall fight with pride and honor at any price / Our proud island / Iwo Jima.' Here, the island is turned into a myth, a symbol of cultural survival. Personified first as a 'small, lonely island', then as a 'proud island', it is figured as an organism embodying Japan. During the song, we see a military map of the island three times. While the same map has highlighted the hopeless position of the Japanese throughout the film, this image is now challenged. Significantly, the general does not look at the map directly the first time it is shown; through the song, a new image of the island begins to form. When the map reappears, it is slightly blurred, and we see a young soldier facing away from it, as if looking at this imaginary island. The third time we see the map, it has become completely blurred, and the shape of the island is barely recognizable. Different images of the island here follow each other; the map itself is already an image and implies a particular construction of the island. From the beginning, then, the film produces various versions of the island. Resonating with the capacity of the volcanic island to produce and reproduce itself by accumulating layers of ash and lava, the film effects an imaginary reconstruction of the island, producing layers of images.

In the last shots of the film, the various (re)constructions of the island are linked as we return to the frame narrative, which shows us a group of Japanese archaeologists digging into the tunnels made by the soldiers. The archaeologists find hundreds of letters written by the soldiers; in a series of shots, we see the letters dropping to the ground in slow motion, gradually covering the soil, while we hear voice-over snippets of their contents. These shots are followed by a final image of the black beach, the ocean, and the volcano, returning us to the first shot of the film. The cut signals a link between the volcanic sediment on the beach and the textual sediment in the tunnels; indeed, the letters mingle with the very soil of the island. The island, then, is made up of various strata consisting as much of spoken words, images, maps, and letters as of sand, lava, and ash. If humans are viewed as geomorphological agents, the textual constructions of the island become part of a set of processes forming and reshaping it. Yet where does this leave us with regard to the last image? It differs from the opening shot: the camera position is static, and the earlier grey is replaced by a glimmer of rosy colours in the sky. The island itself, having been violently shaken, survives: it signals permanence as well as transience. But we cannot determine which of its many versions survives. Do we see the island of American triumph? Do we see the island of the children's song, signifying the cultural survival of Japan? Do we see the island as reconstructed by the archaeologists? Do we see the island as a commemorative site, or a space haunted by ghosts? Or do we return to the material island devoid of human significance altogether? With the cosmic implications of the first shot in mind, does the empty island signify a world without humans? Structurally, the pattern is that outlined by Deleuze: the island is 'from before and for after humankind'

(Deleuze 2004, 9). But the final shot resists easy solutions. Throughout the film, the island is constructed and perceived in various ways that are aligned with different ideological positions. As a conglomerate of sediments, however, it is never final, and cannot be definitively assigned to any of them. This is what I mean when I argue that the material production of the island resonates with and interferes with its textualization. The physical space of the island lends itself to various figurations, but it also has the potential to resist and undo these: one of the possibilities implicit in the last shot is that we simply see an island, and nothing else. Perception, ideology, geopoetics: in this initial example, the island comes into being at the intersection of phenomenal experience, ideological appropriation, and the physical production of the island. The engagement with these processes is what I call the aesthetics of island space.

Spatial Disorientations: Islands and Modern Exploration

The basic premise of this book is that the modern voyages of discovery posed considerable cognitive and perceptual challenges to the experience of space, and that these challenges were negotiated in complex and contradictory ways via the poetic and aesthetic engagement with islands. While scholarship has frequently emphasized the literary construction of islands as geometrical abstractions and easily comprehended spaces, *The Aesthetics of Island Space* argues that the modern experience of islands as mobile and shifting territories implies a dispersal, fragmentation, and diversification of spatial experience. Discussions of island narratives in postcolonial theory have broadened our understanding of the ways islands have been imagined as bounded spaces easily subjected to the colonial gaze and controlled by imperialist powers. There is, however, a second story of islands in the Western imagination which runs parallel to the colonial story, and which has been neglected in critical discourse. This second story runs counter to the story of abstraction, simplification, and visual control, and instead foregrounds spatial openness, precariousness, disorientation, and perplexity. In this alternative account, the modern experience of islands in the age of discovery went hand in hand with a *disintegration* of received models of understanding global space. Throughout the book, I will show how this disruption is registered and negotiated by both non-fictional and fictional responses. In the pages that follow, I will establish some of the theoretical premises that have shaped my approach. These fall broadly into two categories: interdisciplinary scholarship about islands and island representations on the one hand, and theories of spatiality on the other, notably phenomenological and geopoetic approaches to space. These two sections will prepare the ground for the two general aims of this book: to rethink the role of islands in Anglo-American texts, and to develop new perspectives on literary and cinematic space through a lens that combines perception, experience, and geography.

The Poetics of Watery Land: From Insularity to Islandness and Archipelagicity

Whatever the island *means* in the last shot of *Letters from Iwo Jima*, it signals a position that is both precarious and potentially powerful. Its instability emerges at the border of land and sea as the film empha-sizes the interplay of water and land. As Beer explains, '"[i]sle" in its earliest forms derived from a word for water and meant, "watery" or "watered". In Old English "land" was added...: "is-land": water-surrounded land' (1990, 271). Throughout this book, I will reflect on the implications of including water in a conception of islands. Too much scholarship has ignored the vital role of water in the engagement with fictional islands. Postcolonial theory has done much to increase our understanding of the ways islands have been imagined as bounded spaces subjected to the colonial gaze, but little to help us think about them as spaces where lithosphere, hydrosphere, and biosphere interact. Thus, Rebecca Weaver-Hightower discusses the figuration of islands as masculine bodies in colonial island texts (2007). Diana Loxley examines nineteenth-century island narratives as manifestations of imperial dreams (1990). Dorothy F. Lane, too, argues that 'the island figure encapsulates ideas of enclosure and control' (1995, 1). The idea of reduction is common to these approaches to the literary island; Lane contends that '[t]he coloniser's language easily constructs the island, maps it, and finally claims ownership of that territory' (2).

As Matthew Boyd Goldie points out, islands in Western representations tend to be 'thought of as opposed to the sea, isolated, delimited, conversely paradisiacal or hellish, enclosed habitats, fragile environments...' (2011, 4). Within this discourse, islands are typically viewed in binary opposition either to the sea or to continents. Deleuze, too, ultimately 'retains the traditional binary of island and sea' (Goldie 5) by examining islands as products of a 'struggle between earth and water'. The commonly noted binary between islands and continents is discussed by Nicholas Ruddick, who draws on Donne's famous dictum that 'no man is an island' (2000, 1278) to argue that in 'the modern consciousness, to be born is akin to being shipwrecked on an island' (Ruddick 1993, 56).

These critical positions draw attention to the discursive constructions of islands in Western thinking, but they sometimes reinscribe the oppositions set in place by the texts they examine and need to be supplemented by a perspective that includes water as a constitutive part of islands. The 'continental island discourse' (Goldie 2011, 4) has been challenged in various disciplines. Thus, historical anthropologist Greg Dening theorizes the beach as a zone of cultural contact, conflict, and exchange in his writings on the Marquesas Islands. For Dening, 'islands are never static and unchanging' (1980, 32), and beaches are spaces to be crossed rather than enclosing boundaries (2004, 13). Historian John R. Gillis traces the diverse ways Atlantic islands have been imagined and emphasizes the constitutive importance of water for a modern understanding of islands (2004, 84). He argues that in early modernity, it was the Atlantic 'sea of islands, not the continents, which was to become the prime object of scientific scrutiny and literary imagination' (2003, 28). Gillis is alert to the function of the water as a connective element as, by the eighteenth century, '[i]t was through the networks of [Atlantic] islands that capital, goods, and labor flowed in ever increasing volume' (29), equally facilitating 'an accelerated circulation... of ideas' (30). Much earlier, historian Fernand Braudel made a similar point about the Mediterranean islands: 'The islands lay on the paths of the great sea routes and played a part in international relations' (1995, 154).

In reimagining the Atlantic as a 'sea of islands', Gillis draws on an essay by Tongan-Fijian anthropologist Epeli Hau'ofa entitled 'Our Sea of Islands' (1993). In what may be the most powerful critique of Western conceptions of islands as small, remote, and enclosed, Hauʻof a attacks the neocolonial view of Pacific islands as tiny and dependent territories. Against this view, Hauʻofa argues that Pacific islanders have always included the ocean to figure their islands as an expansive 'sea of islands' rather than 'islands in the far sea' (152); he emphasizes the islanders' mobility, the complex networks of relations characterizing Oceania in both pre- and postcolonial times. Édouard Glissant's *Poetics of Relation*, Daniel Maximin's *Les fruits du cyclone*, and Antonio Benítez-Rojo's *The Repeating Island* have also stressed the water in their imaginative engagements with the Caribbean as an archipelago crisscrossed by multiple paths. Within literary studies, DeLoughrey's *Routes and Roots* discusses islands in Pacific and Caribbean literatures, emphasizing the importance of including the ocean in an analysis of islands as cultural and literary spaces:

> In order to recuperate the centrality of the ocean in island discourse, I turn to Kamau Brathwaite's theory of 'tidalectics,' a methodological tool that ... provid[es] the framework for exploring the complex and shifting entanglement between sea and land, diaspora and indigeneity, and routes and roots. (2007, 2)

Reimagining islands in terms of dynamic networks, DeLoughrey draws on the works of Caribbean and Pacific writers to offer a counter-model to Western island discourses.

The emerging interdisciplinary field of island studies, closely associated with the *Island Studies Journal* founded in 2006, has played an important part in challenging colonial and continental ways of thinking about islands and championed 'the study of islands on their own terms', or *nissology*, as conceptualized by Christian Depraetere and Grant McCall (Baldacchino 2008, 37). For Godfrey Baldacchino, the term *islandness* is preferable to *insularity*, 'since the latter comes along with so much negative baggage' (2007, 15), and views of islands as fragments or secondary spaces ought to make way for discourses that see islands as 'sites of agency' (17) and resourceful territories in a 'world of islands' (17–18). Implicit in this view is a shift from essentializing views of 'the island' towards an embrace of islands in their plurality and diversity, and a reimagination of the planet in archipelagic terms; *Island Studies Journal* 8 (1) featured a special section entitled 'Reframing

Islandness: Thinking with the Archipelago' (2013). Despite the inter-disciplinary orientation of island studies, literary scholars initially played only a minor role, though recent studies like Bénédicte André's *Îléité* (2016), Ian Kinane's *Theorising Literary Islands* (2017), Daniel Graziadei's *Inseln im Archipel* (2017), as well as Ralph Crane and Lisa Fletcher's *Island Genres, Genre Islands* (2017) have explicitly drawn on island studies for their analyses of island writing from former French island colonies (André), recent Robinsonades (Kinane), contemporary Caribbean island writing (Graziadei), and islands in popular genre fiction (Crane and Fletcher); conversely, DeLoughrey's *Routes and Roots* has become an influential book for island studies scholars from other disciplines.[1] Meanwhile, film studies have yet to discover the field.[2]

As a study of literary and cinematic islands, *The Aesthetics of Island Space* is inspired by island studies, though it does not aim to study islands exclusively on their own terms. It cannot do so because it does not discuss real islands, at least not primarily; or rather, my analyses are guided by the conviction that 'real' and 'fictional' islands are inextric-ably intertwined. I can, however, study islands on the terms set forth by the texts and the films themselves. In order to do so, I draw on the insights gained from the reimagination of islands in the work of scholars and writers like Dening, Hauʻofa, and DeLoughrey as much as on the attention to the complexity of islands as lived environments within island studies. Reading literary and cinematic islands in this way means paying attention to the water as much as to the land of islands, and to the various forms of life (human and otherwise) arriving in, departing from, and living on or around them. In this view, the textual construction of islands is part of their human inhabitation; however invested with ideology, poetic figurations of islands are a form of engagement with their spatiality.

---

[1] The island studies collection *A World of Islands: An Island Studies Reader* (2007), edited by Baldacchino in the early years of the discipline, does not feature a single chapter by a scholar working in the field of literary or cultural studies. Geographers are clearly in the lead, with contributions from a range of other disciplines like biology, political studies, sociology, and economics. Ten years later, however, literary scholars have become regular contributors to the *Island Studies Journal*.

[2] Jeffrey Geiger's *Facing the Pacific* (2007) is, to my knowledge, the only book-length study with a strong focus on cinematic islands. Kinane (2017) devotes sections of his book to cinematic and televisual island stories. A special issue of the journal *Post Script* on *Islands and Film*, edited by Ian Conrich et al., has recently been published (2018).

The study of literary islands in terms of a poetics of watery land has been advanced by scholars working on Pacific and Caribbean islands, but received little attention in discussions of Western island fiction; thus, Maeve McCusker and Anthony Soares's collection *Islanded Identities: Constructions of Postcolonial Cultural Insularity* (2011) mainly investigates cultural productions from and about postcolonial islands. The essays collected by Rod Edmond and Vanessa Smith in *Islands in History and Representation* (2003) form an important resource for this book because they include discussions of islands in the Western imagination that move beyond viewing islands as bounded and discrete and take account of their multiple and mobile spatialities (Edmond and Smith 2003, 12). The volume contains an article by Beer, whose analysis of *Robinson Crusoe* through biogeographical perspectives informs my own approach to islands; Beer examines Crusoe's island as a space that is both physical and textual. Graziadei's (2011; 2017) call for an engagement with the textual production of islands in their various geospheres (or *nissopoetics*) is closely related to Beer's approach, even while Graziadei focuses mainly on Caribbean literatures. Within French scholarship, the works of Jean-Michel Racault offer important insights into the links between geography and politics in literary island utopias and Robinsonades.[3] In *Le livre des îles*, Frank Lestringant examines the malleable topographies of islands imagined in archipelagic terms, with a particular focus on early modernity: 'Il... s'agit... de laisser l'initiative à l'accident topographique et aux résistances du relief, bref de se laisser conduire par les suggestions imaginaires de la topographie...' (2002, 31–2).[4] Lestringant's phrasing is relevant: talking of the imaginary suggestions of topography, he allows for a dialectic exchange between earth and text.

I draw on the insights from these discussions of literary island space as well as on current debates in island studies to frame my own approach to islands located between fictional and non-fictional discourses, between different genres, between geography and text, and

---

[3] See especially his book-length study of political insularity from More's *Utopia* to Tournier's *Vendredi* (Racault 2010). See also Racault (1989; 1996; 2007).

[4] 'The question is one of... ceding the initiative to the topographical accident and to the resistances of the relief, in short, of letting oneself be carried by the imaginary suggestions of the topography' (my translation).

between word and image. What, then, are the implications of developing a poetics of watery land that views islands as dynamically experienced and inhabited spaces? Politicians and policymakers have long been aware of the profound implications of how islands are imagined. Indeed, even a simple definition of what constitutes an island is fraught with countless difficulties and has been endlessly debated: if it is land surrounded by water, what about continents? If relative size in relation to a mainland is a criterion, what about mainlands that are also islands (cf. Baldacchino 2008, 37), and what about cartographic conceptions of a world island surrounded by the ocean?[5] If maritime climate is a criterion, what about large islands or islands in lakes? Are islands only islands when they are imagined as such? Is it legitimate to talk about the earth as an island in space, a notion that became popular in the late 1960s? When do islands stop being literal and start being purely metaphorical? What about floating islands, whether natural or man-made?[6] Do artificial islands like the Principality of Sealand, a self-proclaimed micronation on a concrete platform off the coast of England, qualify?

There is perhaps no better illustration of the difficulty of defining islands than Article 121 of the United Nations Convention on the Law of the Sea:

Article 121

Regime of Islands

1.   An island is a naturally formed area of land, surrounded by water, which is above water at high tide.

2.   Except as provided for in paragraph 3, the territorial sea, the contiguous zone, the exclusive economic zone and the continental shelf of an island are determined in accordance with the provisions of this Convention applicable to other land territory.

3.   Rocks which cannot sustain human habitation or economic life of their own shall have no exclusive economic zone or continental shelf. (1982, 63)

After repeated sessions between 1973 and 1982, the Convention on the Law of the Sea was finalized, becoming operative in 1994. In itself,

---

[5]   For a discussion of classical and medieval conceptions of a world island, see Cosgrove (2001).

[6]   For a comprehensive bibliography on floating islands, see Van Duzer (2004).

Article 121 looks harmless enough, but the documentation of the negotiations reveals the heated debates hiding behind the deceptively impartial legalese. Islands became a crucial issue for the 1973–82 conference after 'the attention of the [Sea-Bed] Committee was drawn to the "special importance" of marine resources to the islands of the South Pacific. At that time, many of those islands were under foreign domination and control...' (Nordquist et al. 1995, 321). The article underwent numerous changes, and national delegates submitted various suggestions for improvement and clarification before the final text was approved. The debates revolved around issues like fishing rights, artificial islands, and islands with no autonomous population; there was considerable nervousness about the possibility of states extending their territorial seas or exclusive economic zones by occupying a tiny, otherwise uninhabitable island. These political struggles to define islands, islets, and rocks show the profound implications of deciding what an island is, and what is considered to be part of an island. In the final article, the sea is treated as an integral component of islands, and the possibility of inhabiting them is a defining criterion distinguishing islands from rocks.

Fictional island texts offer many reflections on these problems of definition. Thus, in the First Folio edition of William Shakespeare's *The Tempest* (as well as in later editions), the location is specified as 'an vn-inhabited Island' (1623, 19). Yet how can the island be uninhabited if it is clearly inhabited by Prospero and Miranda, and was already inhabited by Caliban, his mother Sycorax, and the airy spirit Ariel before their arrival? On whose terms is the island classified as uninhabited? The play itself uses a variant of the term when Adrian states that the 'island seem[s] to be desert—.... Uninhabitable and almost inaccessible—' (2. 1. 36–9). 'Uninhabitable' is here mentioned in the same breath as 'desert'. According to the *OED*, a desert island is 'an uninhabited, or seemingly uninhabited, and remote island; also *attrib.* and *fig.*, esp. (of equipment, cultural objects, or behaviour) suited to the social isolation and limited baggage allowance of a castaway on a desert island' ('desert, n.2' 2018). The definition is puzzlingly vague. By stating that only *seemingly* uninhabited islands qualify, the definition suggests that the term does not refer to any physical and measurable reality; the *OED* uses the same terms as Adrian in *The Tempest*. The first example cited by the *OED* dates from 1607, a few years before *The Tempest* was written, and confirms the suspicion that the notion of the desert island refers to an expectation rather than an absolute condition: 'They were driuen to a coast vnnauigable, where were many desart Islandes inhabited of wilde men' (qtd. in 'desert, n.2' 2018). 'Desart Islandes inhabited': what seems like a blatant contradiction rests on the exclusion of the 'wilde men'. In this example, the islands 'seem' uninhabited because no white men live there.

But *The Tempest* has both white and non-white inhabitants. Who, then, wants the island to be uninhabited? I would argue that the stage direction reflects a long-standing Western cultural bias that islands—literary islands, anyway—are uninhabited and remote. But as Racault points out, the very notion of the desert island is flawed: '...c'est presque toujours par abus de langage qu'on emploie l'expression d'"île déserte", car il est impossible qu'elle le soit entièrement si elle est l'objet d'une description...' (2010, 13).[7] Accordingly, I do not look at desert islands in this study,[8] but at inhabited islands, although a number of the texts I consider belong to what is traditionally called the desert island genre. Like the exclusion of the sea, the idea that islands are uninhabited presents them as closed-off, bounded spaces: we want islands to be uninhabited, perhaps, because as lived and living spaces, they interfere with our fantasies about them. Indeed, as we will see in Chapter 3, the transition from water to land is problematic in *The Tempest*, although the play is permeated by images of water: the word 'sea' is used a total number of thirty-four times, even more often than 'island', which is used twenty-five times. In my understanding of islands, then, I follow the definition set forth by the United Nations. While the texts and films I discuss often present the inhabitation of their islands as precarious, they all gesture towards a heightened form of spatial experience. The literary and cinematic islands I examine all poeticize space, but they do so in different ways. They are linked to different forms of mobility—the protagonists' movements to, through, and from the islands, the movements of the sea, the movements of the imagination and, finally, the mobility of the islands themselves.

---

[7] 'It is always almost abuse of language when one uses the expression "desert island", for it is impossible that the island is entirely desert if it is the object of a description' (my translation).

[8] Barney Samson discusses recent desert island fiction in *Desert Islands and the Liquid Modern* (2020, forthcoming).

The ~~Meaning~~ of Islands: From Geometrical Abstraction to Material Interference

Examining how island narratives poeticize space has important implications for the relationship between islands and meaning. The problem is that islands generally mean too much. According to Judith Schalansky's popular *Atlas of Remote Islands: Fifty Islands I Have Never Set Foot on and Never Will* (2010), for instance, islands are paradise and hell, colonies and prisons, stages and objects of erotic desire. As her title indicates, Schalansky has no interest in islands as lived spaces: she needs them to be empty so they can be filled with meaning. Scholars frequently discuss islands as readable and particularly *meaningful* spaces. According to Chris Bongie, '[t]he island is a figure that can and must be read in more than one way' (1998, 18). For Loxley, '[t]o read the natural world...is also to achieve an annexation of its meaning and this is the primary significance of the supreme legibility of the literary island' (1990, 8). Edmond and Smith see the island as 'a figure for figuration itself' (2003, 5).

I am not primarily interested in what islands mean. I am more interested in the spatial energies they generate, and the ways in which they resist what they are made to mean. This entails taking their material dimensions seriously rather than viewing them as geometrical abstractions, even if this materiality is mediated by words and images. The cartographic impulse often associated with islands is illustrated in Jill Paton Walsh's 1994 novel *Knowledge of Angels*:

> Suppose you are contemplating an island....You are looking at it from a great height—you see fig orchards, vineyards, almond orchards, and apricot orchards....You see the wooded cliffs of the shore, the beaches of bright sand, the principal city....
>
> At this height your viewpoint is more like that of an angel than that of any islander. But after all, the position of a reader in a book is very like that occupied by angels....Hearts and minds are as open as the landscape to their view, as to yours; like them you are in the fabled world invisible. (9–10)

In this 'monarch-of-all-I-survey' scene, the angel's gaze is associated with that of the reader and the omniscient narrator. While the sea is given no consideration, the topography of the island is rendered with cartographic accuracy; the island is completely visible and geometric-ally transparent. This view, however, is only possible if the angel-readers are excluded from the landscape they observe. It denies islands their material existence. This denial characterizes a lot of island schol-arship, too, including Yi-Fu Tuan's reflections on islands in *Topophilia*:

> Unlike the tropical forest or the continental seashore [the island] cannot claim ecological abundance, nor—as an environment—has it mattered greatly in man's evolutionary past. Its importance lies in the imaginative realm.... In numerous legends the island appears as the abode of the dead or of immortals. Above all, it symbolizes a state of prelapsarian innocence and bliss, quarantined by the sea from the ills of the continent.   (1990, 118)

Tuan is curiously insistent on the unimportance of the island as a lived environment: he is even prepared to venture speculations on evolu-tionary history to support his point. He seems to require this disavowal to free the island as a realm for the imagination. Indeed, it seems appropriate that he evokes the legendary islands of the dead before moving on to the island's symbolic meanings. Tuan generically talks of 'the island' rather than islands in their diversity; his argument rests on the exclusion of lived and living islands in favour of what islands *mean*. Again, the material island makes way for an abstraction. Tuan is in good company: the stage direction in *The Tempest* and Schalansky's empty islands are two of countless examples of this impulse.

But a cartographic view of islands does not necessarily entail geo-metrical abstraction. As Denis Cosgrove points out, the well-ordered 'tricontinental world island' (2001, 97) of medieval cartography made way for a 'nonhierarchical conception of the world' (99), an island world, in the early modern *isolario*. As Lestringant points out, island books like André Thevet's unpublished *Le grand insulaire et pilotage* figured the discontinuous experience of modern space (153). Tom Conley similarly emphasizes the spatial experimentation in the *isolarii* and cartographic writings of early modernity (1996, 167–201). He argues that the manifold shapes and the mobility of these islands conveyed 'a sense of a world that is in congress, multiplication, and dispersion' (187). In this view, the materiality of text and cartographic image constitutes a counterpart to the vivid experience of space in flux: the *isolario* offers the reader an intense experience of textual space. In the experience of spatial indeterminacy and mobility, the modern subject is simultaneously confronted with uncertainty and offered a heightened experience of space. Living space and lived space here resonate with each other: the life *of* space is linked to life *in* space.

The cartographic analyses of Cosgrove, Lestringant, and Conley foreground the early modern islands' resistance to geometrical abstraction. *The Aesthetics of Island Space* is interested in the links between the life of its islands and the life on them, in the material bases of islands and their textual production. In D. H. Lawrence's short story 'The Man Who Loved Islands', the protagonist successively lives on three different islands, each smaller than its predecessor. Both the protagonist and the narrator have preconceived ideas of what islands are and mean:

> An island, if it is big enough, is no better than a continent. It has to be
> really quite small, before it *feels like* an island; and this story will show
> how tiny it has to be, before you can presume to fill it with your own
> personality.   (2007, 286; emphasis original)

The islander's insular desire is figured as a desire for geometrical reduction and abstraction: 'He had reduced himself to a single point in space...' (289). Yet the islands frustrate this desire. While the second island seems smaller than it is ('The small island was very small; but being a hump of rock in the sea, it was bigger than it looked'; 298), the third island tricks the senses in the opposite way: 'Then, in a light sea-mist, he landed, and saw it hazy, low, stretching apparently a long way. But it was illusion' (303). Throughout the story, the islands seem to have a life of their own, interfere with how they are imagined, and refuse to be absorbed by Euclidean space.

Reading islands in their material dimensions means giving up the knowledge of angels. It means giving up the desire to understand them completely, a desire characteristic of many protagonists of island narratives and frequently reinscribed by island scholarship. In a short essay, Andrew Wingfield rehearses some of the meanings conventionally ascribed to islands ('isolation', 'loneliness', 'obstacle', 'opportunity') only to question them: 'Finally, it's an island. An enduring piece of the physical world. A thing that exists well beyond the wide and tangled web of my mortal associations' (2005, 158). Giving up the knowledge of angels also means engaging with islands as non-transparent pieces of the physical world: less understanding here means more involvement. This does not mean sidestepping the imaginative appeal of islands. Indeed, Gaston Bachelard emphasizes that the poeticizing of space is a form of engagement with the lived environment (1964, 17). Bachelard's phenomenological interest in the resonance between the material and the poetic is an important inspiration for *The Aesthetics of Island Space*, as is John Wylie's more recent landscape phenomenology. For Wylie, landscape is animated by tension: 'It is a tension between proximity and distance, body and mind, sensuous immersion and detached observation. Is landscape the world we are living *in*, or a scene we are looking *at*, from afar?' (2007, 2). Wylie views landscape at the intersection of perception, ideology, material space, and art. He concludes by stating that '[l]andscape…is a perceiving-with, that *with which* we see, the creative tension of self and world' (2007, 217). I take my cue from Wylie to investigate the productive tensions in the islandscapes that are the object of this study, and the ways the texts ask their readers and viewers to 'perceive-with' these islandscapes.

Theoretical Perspectives on (Island) Space: Phenomenology, Geopoetics, Geocriticism

The starting point for each of my chapters is a cultural moment in which the lived experience of islands posed profound perceptual challenges to the experience of space in a global context. This calls for a phenomenological approach to space. Wylie's deconstructionist landscape phenomenology is part of a recent revival of phenomenological perspectives on spatiality. Theorists like Wylie have thereby responded to poststructuralist and Marxist critiques of phenomenology for its apparent bracketing of cultural, social, and political concerns in favour of exploring a unified human subjectivity and its immediate experience of the world (see Wylie 2013). These new approaches emphasize the political relevance of phenomenology on the one hand, and foreground discontinuity, disruptions, and uncertainty as constitutive of spatial experience on the other. A pioneering example is Paul Carter's *The Road to Botany Bay* (1987), which takes a phenomenological stance in its spatial history of Australia to challenge the ideological bent of imperialist accounts of settlement. In many ways, *The Aesthetics of Island Space* is, like Carter's book, 'concerned with the haze that precedes clear outlines' (xii), the disruptions of spatial, geographic, and cultural certainties connected to the experience of islands in both nonfiction and fiction.

I am also indebted to a set of more recent approaches by phenomenological or phenomenologically inspired thinkers like Wylie, Ted Toadvine, Timothy Clark, and Timothy Morton who, in the words of Clark, have developed 'a kind of post-phenomenology that is sensitive to the opacity and otherness of things and that does not excessively posit nature as continuous, homogenous, predictable and assimilable' (2014, 6). Wylie offers a concise account of this trend: 'This constitutes what Jessica Dubow (2010) terms a "negative phenomenology" of landscape, insofar as the focus falls upon the dislocated, de-centred and precarious nature of subjective experience and perception' (2013, 62).[9] This focus on the subject's precarious position in experiencing the world provides an important theoretical background for my own examination of the aesthetics of island space.

Studying islands in this way does not mean denying that Western discourse has constructed islands as idealized and abstracted worlds dissociated from the physical world. Tim Robinson's opening remarks about islands in his account of his first map of the Aran Islands responds to this impulse: 'So an island appears to be mappable. Already a little abstracted from reality, already half-concept, it holds out the delusion of a comprehensible totality' (1996, 1). Yet my aim is to offer an alternative account of the cultural and aesthetic impact of islands and their role in negotiating crucial experiences of modernity. Rather than focusing on simplification, *The Aesthetics of Island Space* discusses the tensions and frictions generated by the perceptual experience of islands as registered and negotiated by a range of literary and non-literary texts and fictions. *The Aesthetics of Island Space*, then, does not—or not primarily—consider islands as abstractions and

---

[9] See, among others, Wylie (2012), Morton (2007; 2014), and Brown and Toadvine (2003). Clark offers a useful overview of post-phenomenological positions (2014).

metaphors, but as lived spaces with their own distinctive materialities and dynamic processes creating, shaping, and undoing them—their sand, waves, waterways, beaches, coral, rocks, volcanoes, and trees—without forgetting their human and non-human inhabitants.

A focus on the poetic and aesthetic potential of these material properties and processes implies a geopoetic perspective. Going back to the work of Scottish poet and academic Kenneth White, geopoetics has become an important concept for a number of poets and critics interested in the interplay of material and poetic energies. Thus, the Caribbean poets and essayists Daniel Maximin (*Une géopoétique de la Caraïbe*, 2006) and Édouard Glissant (*Poétique de la relation*, 2007) have drawn on the geo(morpho)logical and geophysical processes shaping Caribbean islands to develop their own poetic practice and philosophy: '...the reality of archipelagos in the Caribbean or the Pacific provides a natural illustration of the thought of relation' (Glissant 34). Like Igor' Sid's geopoetic club in Moscow, these authors are invested in the poetic potential of dynamic physical energies as a counterforce to rigid ideological constructions and geopolitical regimes. For Rachel Bouvet and Myriam Marcil-Bergeron, geopoetics is tied to a lived and mobile experience of space, the pull of the material world that escapes and yet shapes language and representation (2013, 21). I will discuss geopoetic perspectives explicitly in Chapter 4, but they inform my approach throughout this book. Without subscribing to the Romantic idealism that sometimes characterizes White's writing, I use the concept of geopoetics flexibly to refer to a diversity of approaches that foreground the poetic potential of geography and trace an 'aesthetics of the earth' (DeLoughrey and Handley 2011, 1–40). Despite important differences, this understanding of geopoetics resonates with Bertrand Westphal's geocriticism, which advocates a 'geocentered approach' to space and 'places *place* at the center of debate' (2011, 112; emphasis original).

The present study thus combines an interest in perception with a focus on the material and poetic processes of creating islands. This implies reading the dynamic physical processes that make and shape islands in conjunction with the poetic production of and active perceptual engagement with island spaces. The islands discussed in this book manifest a challenge to perceptual certainties and allow the physical world, however mediated, to emerge and write itself into the text. Geopoetics as I understand it is linked to an opening up of thought through an exposure to the physical environment; grappling with a multiplicity of sensory stimuli and embodied experiences that cannot be fully grasped by their authors, protagonists, and readers, the texts and films discussed in this book indeed present islands as spatial figures to think with, about, or from—in the sense that they speak to and stimulate imaginative activity, open up thought, suggest possibilities and uncertainties, and encourage an interrogation of global space. In this, too, geopoetics resonates with geocriticism and its emphasis on a polysensory (Westphal 2011, 131–6) and multifocal (122–31) attention to space. For Westphal, examining multiple (material, cultural, textual) layers of space can challenge dominant spatial ideologies and weaken hegemonic discourse. In my readings in all four chapters of this book, the uncertainties of perception and the experience of the material world jointly destabilize the ideological constructions of Anglo-American island imaginaries.

Navigating a Sea of Literary and Cinematic Islands

A book about island narratives could be organized in various ways. Beginning with More's *Utopia* (1516) and ending with Michel Tournier's *Vendredi* (1967), Racault chooses a chronological approach. Other books engage with specific historical periods; thus, Loxley focuses exclusively on nineteenth-century islands in colonial texts. Gillis focuses on a specific region—Atlantic islands—in addition to a chronological organization. A related approach would be to focus on islands in different climate zones; tropical islands (think of *Gilligan's Island* or *Lost*) tend to be imagined differently than cold-water islands (like the ice-girt island in Georgina Harding's *The Solitude of Thomas Cave*). One could also follow Alfred Russel Wallace's geological classification of islands into oceanic islands (the eruptive volcanic island of Jules Verne's *L'île mystérieuse*, or R. M. Ballantyne's *The Coral Island*), continental islands (the small island off the coast of Devon in Agatha Christie's *And Then There Were None*), and ancient continental islands (Madagascar in H. G: Wells's 'Aepyornis Island').

Islands could further be classified according to size: the large and seemingly inexhaustible island of *The Swiss Family Robinson*[10] is a far cry from the 'few acres of rock' (2007, 303) that make up the third island in Lawrence's 'The Man Who Loved Islands'. They could also be placed along a continuum between 'real' and 'imaginary' islands, following the classifications of critics like Franco Moretti and Westphal, with Bernardin de Saint Pierre's *Paul et Virginie*, set in Mauritius, and the entirely fictional island of Neverland in J. M. Barrie's *Peter Pan* on opposite ends of the spectrum. The semi-fictionalized Marquesan island of Nuku Hiva in Herman Melville's *Typee*, the island of San Pedro off Seattle (a fictionalized version of San Juan Island, blended with Bainbridge Island in Puget Sound) in David Guterson's *Snow Falling on Cedars*, and the dinosaur island somewhere off the coast of Costa Rica in the *Jurassic Park* trilogy occupy intermediate positions.

The form of human settlement could be another criterion, ranging from the fully formed societies of utopian islands (Thomas More's *Utopia* or, in parodic form, Jonathan Swift's *Gulliver's Travels*) to islands inhabited by mixed populations like the island in Alex Garland's *The Beach*, and islands only temporarily inhabited as in Robert Zemeckis's *Cast Away*, or inhabited by pirates like Skeleton Island in Robert Louis Stevenson's *Treasure Island*. One could distinguish between natural, (semi-)artificial, and metaphorical islands, with examples ranging from the island of William Golding's *The Lord of the Flies* through More's *Utopia*, cut off from the continent by King Utopos, and the man-made island in Sam Mendes's *Skyfall*, to the metaphorical island in J. G. Ballard's *Concrete Island*, where protagonist Robert Maitland is cast away on a triangular traffic island. One could also examine islands in different genres or media.[11]

Rather than categorizing islands, however, the chapters of this book are arranged on the basis of different conceptualizations of (the) island (s). This sometimes means examining islands across geographical, temporal, generic, and medial boundaries. Indeed, island narratives

---

[10] Britta Hartmann (2018) argues that we never even receive proof that the family are actually shipwrecked on an island.

[11] For various island typologies and classifications from a geographical perspective, see Royle (2007) and Christian Depraetere and Dahl (2007).

themselves tend to exhibit a strong intertextual consciousness.[12] Like the elusive and wandering islands of early modern cartography, the islands examined in this study refuse to stay in place: they sometimes wander from one ocean to another, from written narratives to cinema, from non-fiction to fiction and back, from early to late modernity, from referential to imaginary space and vice versa; their movements are erratic and unpredictable. If I give equal weight to film and literature, it is because cinema draws on and develops literary figurations of islands. If I read journals of exploration alongside fictional accounts, it is because the genres borrow each other's aesthetic strategies and narrative patterns. Their referential basis does not mean that the islands in explorers' journals are not literary or even imaginary; conversely, their imaginary status does not mean that fictional islands do not offer ways of engaging with material space.

Nonetheless, the chapters are still structured by geographical and temporal continuities. The islands examined in the first chapter all lead to the New World. The islands discussed in the second chapter are all tropical islands. The third chapter focuses on the Pacific Northwest. Appropriately enough for its focus on archipelagic difference, the islands examined in the fourth chapter are scattered all over the world, but they are all linked to the scientific engagements with islands in the nineteenth century. The historical starting point is later for each successive chapter—early modernity in Chapter 1, the 1760s in Chapter 2, the 1790s in Chapter 3, and the 1830s in Chapter 4—but the chapters all extend into the twentieth or twenty-first century, thereby tracing four lines in a vast sea of mainly Anglo-American island narratives. This approach prompted the selection of primary texts: the texts examined in each chapter all respond to the encounters with islands in the voyages of discovery. It also guided the choice of theoretical approaches developed in each of the chapters, which largely emerge from the materials examined in them in the interest of advancing a decentred view of islands.

---

[12] See Chapter 1, note 30.

Overview of Chapters

Fortunately, the English language allows for multiple puns around the word 'island'; even more fortunately, they roughly correspond to the four main chapters of this book, and to the ways the texts examined in them conceptualize their islands.[13] In Chapter 1, islands are linked to arrivals and first landfalls in the New World: island becomes 'I *land*' (as in 'I arrive'). The chapter reads islands in relation to a modern 'migrant condition' (Cauchi 2002) by tracing the imaginative engagement with the multiple paths of migrational movements through the islands at the threshold of the New World. As such, the chapter is about various movements of flight to, through, and from islands, and about the poetic engagement with these movements. Lestringant contends that islands are linked to a rupture in the experience of space in early modernity (2002); this chapter argues that this rupture and its after-effects manifest themselves in various, often contradictory ways. Focusing on islands as sites of both arrival and departure for an imagined elsewhere, it examines the centrality of islands as gateways to the New World. The texts examined in this chapter poeticize the interplay of land and water in an island world. They construct an open sense of space, oscillating between a sense of emergence and possibility, and a corresponding fear of submergence and dissolution.

The chapter begins by discussing the figuration of American arrivals in the accounts of immigrants passing through Angel Island and Ellis Island in the first half of the twentieth century. These two islands epitomize hopeful arrivals (Ellis Island) and a sense of despair and blocked movement (Angel Island). They are read as spaces of transit, both physical and mental stepping stones (Gillis 2004) to an imagined America, and discussed in the context of a long tradition of real and imaginary voyages whose primal scene is Columbus's first arrival in a world of islands. The first part of the chapter thus maps the complex geographical and fictional archipelago of islands in the New World.

---

[13] To my knowledge, my island puns for Chapter 1 (I land) and Chapter 4 (isle/and) have not been deployed previously. Weaver-Hightower uses the eye-land pun in *Imperial Eyes* (9–14), but her use of it is different from my own in Chapter 2. The pun connected to Chapter 3, island as I-land, has frequently been exploited, though its implications are rethought here.

The second part of the chapter draws on the insights developed in the first part to offer a close analysis of two transoceanic island narratives. The first of these is Shakespeare's *The Tempest* (1611), which is read alongside accounts of England's colonial experiments on Roanoke Island in early Virginia. It discusses the ways Shakespeare's play and the historical documents negotiate an island arrival that both is fraught with uncertainty and offers a sense of promise. The last section of the chapter discusses Cecil B. DeMille's 1919 film *Male and Female*, which was made just before the United States put a curb on immigration. It is argued that in its mixed geography, the film reinvents the island of the play it adapts (J. M. Barrie's *The Admirable Crichton*) as a mental stepping stone, a sort of fictional Ellis Island, on the way to an America that can only be reached via a detour, and thus constitutes a twentieth-century response to a long line of island arrivals in the New World.

While Chapter 1 discusses the aesthetic engagement with islands as gateways to the New World, Chapter 2 examines islands as destinations in their own right. Its main interest is the mediation of perception across the border of the tropical island: the island is here an 'eye-land'. The chapter begins by discussing the descriptions of islands viewed from the water in the accounts of the early European explorers in the Pacific, and the ways they turned these islands into discrete, highly aestheticized images. It goes on to trace the paths along which this island-image travelled from the Pacific journals through a plethora of nineteenth-century texts and paintings into the cultural imaginary of the United States, as manifested by Hollywood's obsession with South Sea islands in the 1920s and 1930s. It argues that these films pick up on and transform the (proto-cinematic) visual strategies of the journals, allowing the island-image to travel into the twentieth century and beyond. While the chapter discusses the various ideological needs this Western island-image has been made to serve (first in European colonialism, then in the disavowed US imperialism in the Pacific), it is especially interested in the ways the texts and films resist the freezing of the island into a bounded image: the pre-colonial accounts are full of moments that critically reflect on the perceptual processes and cultural mechanisms by which their island visions are shaped.

A central premise of the chapter is that repeated viewing can go either way: as well as freezing an image, it can release it. It is argued, then, that these texts and films have the potential to ask readers and viewers to reflect on their own aesthetic experience of islands. Accordingly, the main part of the chapter seeks to complicate the cinematic gaze dramatized in *White Shadows in the South Seas* (1928), *The Hurricane* (1937), and, finally, *King Kong* (1933). If the Pacific journals register the perceptual uncertainty of their writers, the act of seeing is transferred to the viewer in these films via the self-consciously staged gaze of the camera. In the reading of *White Shadows* suggested here, the island-image crumbles upon repeated viewing, dissolving into dancing specks and lines. In the trembling graininess of the island as captured by the new medium, something of the uncertainty in the fresh gaze of the early accounts is reflected. *The Hurricane*, perhaps despite itself, exposes and dissolves Western conceptions of the island, potentially challenging the viewer's preconceptions; reading the film anachronistically through Hauʻofa's notion of a sea of islands reveals an uncertainty revolving around the film's own island constructions (1994). In *King Kong*, the cinematic gaze appears in its most violent form, annihilating and freezing the island. Yet this violence also masks the film's unexpressed engagement with another island (Manhattan/Mannahatta) in its pre-colonial guise.

While Chapter 2 discusses islands as bounded images available for aesthetic consumption, Chapter 3 examines a set of diaries and memoirs which express a more permeable conception of the islanded self—island as 'I-land'—and propose a different model for aesthetically engaging with islands. The chapter draws on (post-)phenomenology, ecocriticism, and Benoit Mandelbrot's fractal geometry to argue that opacity, disorientation, and incomprehension offer ways of thinking about islands in terms of a fluid and mobile spatiality rather than boundedness and immobility (1983). The texts examined in the chapter are mostly memoirs from the Pacific Northwest which create a world of islands where boundaries dissolve. The foundational text for this chapter is George Vancouver's journal of his exploration of the disorienting coastal archipelagos in Puget Sound and the Salish Sea in search of the Northwest Passage (1798b). Vancouver's diary is the beginning of a long tradition of poetic engagement with the islands of the region. Memoirs like Helene Glidden's *The Light on the Island* (1951), June Burn's *100 Days in the San Juans* (1946), and David Conover's *Once Upon an Island* (1967) imagine islands as spaces inserted within larger ecological and geological continuities. They include the water in their poetic construction of a fluid islandscape, opposing notions like 'island waters' (Tulloch 1978) and 'sea-lander' (Conover 2003) to insular visions of spatial autonomy and bounded subjectivity.

This reimagination of islands in multiple interconnectedness disrupts arbitrarily drawn political borders, and inserts the subject in a complex ecological islandscape. Yet the texts also have a tendency to recentre subjectivity by placing the subject in the midst of an expansive islandscape, thus decentring the island only to recentre a unified ecological landscape. While some of the memoirs actively seek to dissolve boundaries and ask the reader to revisit their conceptions of islands, Vancouver's journal and the geological diary of George Gibbs offer a more radical island poetics because they do so inadvertently as they struggle to order an intricate system of islands, waterways, and coastlines. The chapter argues that in these texts, the unfamiliar islandscapes aesthetically resist the cartographic drive to fix them. As such, the texts negotiate an intensive engagement with space precisely through the *failure* to comprehend it.

The final chapter, too, discusses islands as lived and living spaces. However, it goes further than Chapter 3 in that it discusses islands from a relational and archipelagic perspective: island is here 'isle/and'. The writers examined in Chapter 4 all portray islands in geo(morpho)logical space-time, and offer perspectives on the poetics of the material world. The chapter begins by examining how the spatial poetics of Charles Darwin's and Wallace's texts ask their readers to rethink planetary space as a discontinuous multiplicity of shifting island territories. It is argued that their challenges to received ways of thinking about space and the human and non-human life within it are brought about by a poetic response to the materiality of the islands they discuss. This notion of a geopoetic resonance between the material energies of the physical world and the poetic energies of language serves as the theoretical basis for the literary analyses in the second part of the chapter. There I discuss three literary responses to Darwin, Wallace, and their successors: H. G. Wells's *The Island of Doctor Moreau* (1896) and 'Aepyornis Island' (1894), and Amitav Ghosh's *The Hungry Tide* (2004).

The two texts by Wells negotiate the anxieties generated by the writings of Darwin and Wallace: they focus on single islands which function as beleaguered territories haunted by the spectre of human extinction. However, critical discussions of these texts fail to account for the geopoetic descriptions which suspend and textually interfere with the narrative, foregrounding the materiality of the island. In *Moreau*, this potential resides in the engagement with the volcanic forces shaping the island; in 'Aepyornis Island', in the imaginative fossilization of all living forms, including the coral skeletons forming the island itself. With a century of biogeographical thinking about islands in between, Ghosh's *The Hungry Tide* explores the poetic implications of Darwin's and Wallace's archipelagic thinking. In the novel, the human element intersects with other living forms, the physical geography, and textual spaces to form a landscape shaped by conflicts. This resonance between material forces (the archipelagic landscape always reconstitutes itself through tidal action) and poetic processes (the permanent reshaping of the archipelago through multiple cognitive operations on the part of both characters and readers) concludes the book as it offers a productive model of a geopoetic engagement with islands in their ungraspable multiplicity. In a study that focuses primarily on British and American texts, Ghosh's *The Hungry Tide* might be a surprising text to end on, but its exploration of a diversity of island conceptions tied to various characters of different nationalities (among others, British, Indian, and American) appropriately wraps up a chapter that has a global reach and explores the possibility of imagining a planetary archipelago.

Overall, the islands studied in this book are produced by geological and geomorphological forces as much as by textual dynamics. They are studied both in their geographical physicality (sand, water, volcanic formations) and in their textual materiality (words, images, sounds): they are produced geo(morpho)logically as much as discursively and poetically. They are invested with ideology, but they refuse to be absorbed by the fantasies and meanings they are encumbered with. They are living spaces, and they are lived in various ways. They offer vivid perceptual experiences, and are sites of spatial play and experimentation. Above all, they offer a geopoetic oscillation between the material energies of words and images, and the energies of the physical world.

From Island to Island, and Beyond

Arrivals in the New World

In the last shot of Orson Welles's 1947 noir *The Lady from Shanghai*, the camera follows protagonist Michael O'Hara as he walks towards the open sea. In the final seconds, the camera rises upwards in a crane shot to reveal a small island near the shore. The island is barely visible; it is little more than a blurry patch rising from the sea. Yet in its very insubstantiality, it materializes some of the central concerns of the film's imaginary geography. Having narrowly escaped from a web of intrigues that reached its tragic dénouement in a mirror maze on San Francisco's oceanfront, Michael seems to be stepping out of a meaningless world of images and illusions into a world that is both bleak and more material. Vast expanses of concrete and water dominate the image; both built and natural environments are reduced to their bare essentials, but they also emerge in their materiality, clashing with the phantasmagoria of the world Michael wishes to leave behind.

Yet the overall spatial design of the film forecloses any such simple reading. Westphal's call for a more sustained engagement with the complex relationships between real and fictional space under the banner of geocriticism (2011) is particularly pertinent to a film like *The Lady from Shanghai*. While *The Lady from Shanghai* clearly situates its

The Aesthetics of Island Space: Perception, Ideology, Geopoetics. Johannes Riquet, Oxford University Press (2019). © Johannes Riquet.
DOI: 10.1093/oso/9780198832409.001.0001

final scenes in referential space, it also produces an imaginary space, for the island suggestively blends various spatial orders. Like the sea and the pier, it is a pure surface, a mere rock. The shot was filmed on location on the northwest end of the San Francisco Peninsula, and the island is one of the Seal Rocks just off Cliff House. Some 200 feet in diameter and devoid of vegetation, it barely deserves to be called an island. Yet it resonates too strongly with the imaginary islands evoked at crucial moments in the film to be discredited too easily. The first of these appears when Michael asks Elsa, the young wife of Arthur Bannister, a rich but old and crippled lawyer on whose boat Michael served, to run off with him as they arrive in San Francisco Bay: 'You're going with me... . You think I'd be after running off with you to a desert island to eat berries and goat's milk?' The second reference occurs when George Grisby, Bannister's partner, explains his plan of faking his own death in order to disappear to the farthest recesses of a world he imagines to be threatened by nuclear apocalypse: 'They'll find you even on the smallest island in the South Seas. That's where I'm going to be, fella. On that smallest island.... But I wanna live on that island in peace.'

Both islands are linked to improbable fantasy scenarios. The first island parodies visions of insular self-sufficiency in castaway narratives like *Robinson Crusoe* (the reference to goat's milk is hard to miss); evoking a purely mythical realm, it underscores the impossibility of a common future for Michael and Elsa even while Michael himself uses it only dismissively. Grisby's South Sea island, in turn, can only function as a safe haven in the mode of irony in a world where there are no more unknown islands to escape to. Grisby can only resort to a remoteness produced by his own fictitious death. Paradoxically, the South Sea island setting becomes entirely superfluous in this stratagem. It survives as a mere rhetorical device; in fact, we later find out that Grisby's apparent plan itself was only a ruse. Yet the notion of hiding 'on the smallest island in the South Seas' to escape nuclear threat would have carried another, darker irony for contemporary audiences: *The Lady from Shanghai* was released just one year after the United States had started a series of nuclear weapons tests on the Bikini Atoll (cf. Scotte 2007, par. 8).

The film's imaginary islands can offer a promise of refuge ironically at best. They also undercut any sense of escape or freedom one might wish to read into the final shot of Michael walking towards the open sea: the island is both unmistakably referential (an insignificant but recognizable rock off the shore) and imaginary: its blurred appearance reinforces the potential of association with the other islands evoked by the film. The real rock's barrenness and proximity to the shore add to the irony pervading the film's island rhetoric: the freedom it seems to offer is a pure mirage belied by hard rock. The sea fails to offer any escape route because the protagonists have nowhere to escape to: they embody the transcendental homelessness Georg Lukács once saw as characteristic of the novel (1971). In the first shot of the film, the opening credits are superimposed on the restless waves of the ocean; the shot dissolves into a shot of Brooklyn Bridge and Manhattan at night seen from the water. It is significant that the film begins in New York and ends in San Francisco, the two gateways to the United States for European and Asian immigrants respectively, for Michael and Elsa are themselves immigrants from these two continents. While Michael is Irish, his question to Elsa as to her place of origin ('Where does the princess come from?') leads to a series of guessing games and further questions: 'Her parents were Russian' is her first reply, immediately qualified by 'You never heard of the place where she comes from.' Michael's response allows for further deferral: 'I bet you I've been to the place you were born.' Cheefoo on the Chinese coast is the answer, with the additional information that she used to work in Macao and Shanghai. The lady from Shanghai, we can infer, is not really *from* anywhere. The two protagonists of the film are global migrants. This is what the opening shot signifies: showing only waves, it cannot be placed geographically. Both Elsa and Michael, the sailor, are associated with the sea and perpetual movement, which is why the open sea at the end cannot signify freedom and escape: Michael merely returns to the element he was associated with from the start. Showing Brooklyn Bridge, a boat, and the island of Manhattan, the second shot of the film combines three signifiers of arrival in the United States, and of the promise associated with it.

New York, San Francisco: in order to arrive there, Michael and Elsa would quite possibly have passed through two small islands that served as immigration stations for innumerable Europeans and Asians and still have a firm hold on the national imaginary. Ellis Island and Angel Island: the film does not show them directly but cannot fail to evoke them. The island at the end of *The Lady from Shanghai* is thus also associated with the famous island in San Francisco Bay where an estimated 300,000 prospective immigrants were detained before being admitted into the country or, very frequently, sent back home between 1910 and 1940 (Lee and Yung 2010, 17–20). A virtual prison to countless immigrants, it resonates with that other famous island in San Francisco Bay, Alcatraz, a federal prison from 1933 to 1963, another rock in the sea evoked by the film's final image. All these resonances further underscore the thoroughly ironic deployment of the island as a trope for escape in the film. The immigration station on Angel Island closed its doors after a fire in 1940 but was used to detain German and Japanese prisoners of war and house American troops during the Second World War, and to process Japanese prisoners and repatriates as well as American troops on their way home after the war (Lee and Yung 301). The island was finally abandoned in 1946, one year before *The Lady from Shanghai* was released.

A similar development was taking place on the East Coast: while Ellis Island did not shut down until 1954, the flow of immigrants had dwindled drastically since the introduction of quota regulations in 1921 and 1924 and become almost negligible during the Depression years and the Second World War (cf. Bell and Abrams 1984, 92–101; Berman 2003, 109–25; Bustard 2012, 70–1; Foner 2000, 24; Hillstrom 2009, 59). By 1947, Ellis Island was palpably on its last legs. The *New York Herald Tribune* of 25 May 1947 featured a long article entitled 'Drab Ellis Island Has Fulfilled Elysian Dreams of 30,000,000'[1] that announced the imminent closing of the station. The article reads like an elegy to the island, commemorating the years when 'immigrants poured through the island gateway to the land of plenty'. It juxtaposes these bustling years with the island's spectral appearance in 1947: 'The once roaring babel has become a ghost town, and its personnel now wander forlornly about the silent grounds, the vast dormitories and the immense empty eating hall. In more recent years the island facilities . . . are used chiefly for speeding grim deported undesirables to their homelands.' The imagery used in the article is revealing, for it follows a tradition of representing Ellis Island as a gateway to paradise, here expressed in terms of the Elysian Fields of Greek mythology. At the same time, the

---

[1] This figure is a massive exaggeration; about 12 million immigrants passed through Ellis Island between 1892 and 1954 (Berman 9).

almost abandoned island already becomes an island of memory, a *lieu de mémoire* in the sense of Pierre Nora, 'moments of history torn away from the movement of history, then returned; no longer quite life, not yet death, like shells on the shore when the sea of living memory has receded' (2007, 149). Like Nora's figurative shells on the shore of what might indeed be an island of memory, the pieces of history on Ellis Island are represented as not quite, but almost dead. No longer properly alive, Ellis Island is turned into a national myth that already anticipates its present-day function as an official commemorative site attracting thousands of visitors every day.

It is rather ironic that the article powerfully evokes the masses of hopeful and expectant immigrants at the same time as it asserts the closing of the gate and even the reversal of the flow of people; America's immigrant history is celebrated at a moment when immigration is at its lowest and Ellis Island is no longer a stepping stone to America. The lesser-known Angel Island had never been a stepping stone in the same way, and therefore offers more resistance to the mythical construction of the United States as a nation of immigrants. For Lee and Yung, Angel Island facilitates an understanding of the ambivalent status of immigration in US history: 'Situated at the edge of the United States, the Angel Island Immigration Station was a place where global forces clashed with American national interests and identity. People from around the world were on the move as part of the era of global mass migration' (2010, 6). Michael and Elsa in *The Lady from Shanghai* embody this era of global migration, but they fail to make America their home: Michael, the European immigrant, walks towards the western edge of the country, towards the ocean that presumably carried Elsa to America. If *The Lady from Shanghai* evokes the closing island gateways to the United States, it also draws attention to some of the contradictions of the American project. For Lee and Yung, Angel Island makes these contradictions visible: 'The migration histories and experiences of the one million people who were processed through San Francisco and Angel Island reveals a world on the move and the making of America as both an inclusive nation of immigrants and an exclusive gatekeeping nation' (6).

This chapter is not about islands in the open ocean, although like *The Lady from Shanghai* it may at times appear to be about them. It is not about islands as destinations seen and imagined from a distance, like the islands that will be discussed in Chapter 2, but quite the reverse: it is about islands as spaces *from* which something else can be imagined. More specifically, it is about islands where an idea of America takes shape. Islands have functioned as both literal and, in Gillis's phrase, mental stepping stones to America (2004, 45–64). I am interested in the historical and fictional journeys where America is reached via a detour that is both geographical and imaginative. A stone's throw from the mainland, yet separated from it by a sometimes unbridgeable gulf, Ellis Island and Angel Island epitomize this trajectory.

In his last seminar, *The Beast & the Sovereign*, Jacques Derrida linked islands are to experiences of movement and flight:

> Why do some people love islands while others do not love islands, some people dreaming of them, seeking them out, inhabiting them, taking refuge on them, and others avoiding them, even fleeing them instead of taking refuge on them?
>
> But fleeing them, as much as taking refuge on them, presupposes a movement of flight. One cannot dissociate the figure of the island from the experience of flight. (2011, 64)

This chapter is about various movements of flight to, through, and from islands. Some of these movements are voluntary, others forced; some are marked by hope, others by fear, and many by both. Some of them are successful; others are interrupted, delayed, or arrested. It is about arrivals in the islands of the New World, or the New World as a world of islands, or maybe as islands without a world: 'There is no world, there are only islands' (Derrida 2011, 9). We will return to this statement in Chapter 4; for the moment, let us note that for Derrida islands disrupt the continuity implied by 'world'. Lestringant (2002) and Gillis (2004) contend that islands are linked to a rupture in the experience of space in early modernity; as I will argue, this rupture manifests itself in various, often contradictory ways. Focusing on islands as sites of both arrival and departure for an imagined elsewhere, I will examine the centrality of islands as gateways to the New World.

In *Writing Across Worlds: Literature and Migration*, Paul White states '[w]e live in what has recently been termed "The Age of Migration"' (1995, 1). As Eleftheria Arapoglou et al. point out, 'radical mobility is not a phenomenon of the twenty-first century alone'

(2014, 2). While migration has been 'a key constituent element of human life in virtually all periods' (Arapoglou et al. 2014, 2), Stephen Castles and Mark J. Miller point out that it 'took on a new character with the beginnings of European expansion in the sixteenth century' (2009, 2). This chapter, then, will read islands in terms of this modern 'migrant condition' (Cauchi 2002, 6) by tracing the imaginative engagement with the multiple paths of migrational movements through the islands at the threshold of the New World. In *Routes and Roots*, DeLoughrey offers a sustained discussion of 'island migration as a vital narrative trope' in the 'transoceanic imaginary' (2007, 20) of Pacific and Caribbean peoples. She draws on Kamau Brathwaite's concept of *tidalectics* to emphasize the importance of the interplay of land and water in this imaginary: 'Where the desert-isle genre emphasizes the boundedness of islands, tidalectics engages with their watery surroundings, foregrounding the routes of the oceanic imaginary' (20). Focusing on the island routes leading to America, we will engage with a different transoceanic imaginary.

I have opened this chapter with *The Lady from Shanghai* to prompt a reflection on the various movements of flight to and from islands hinted at by Derrida. We will begin our voyage through these island gateways by discussing the figurations of American arrivals in the imaginative accounts of immigrants passing through Angel Island and Ellis Island. We will then move back in time to the foundational moment of these recent migrational movements by discussing Columbus's first letter about the New World. Columbus's expectations were shaped by the travel narratives of Marco Polo and John Mandeville as well as the Irish *immrama*, notably the *Voyage of Saint Brendan*. I will briefly address these texts because they are important predecessors for the modern mobilization of islands as playgrounds for the imagination and as embodiments of a malleable spatiality. In the second part of this chapter, I will draw on the insights developed in the first part to discuss two transoceanic island narratives. The first is Shakespeare's *The Tempest* (1611), which I will read alongside accounts of England's early colonial experiments on Roanoke Island to show how the play and the historical documents negotiate an island arrival that is fraught with uncertainty even while offering a sense of promise. At the end of the chapter, I will return to the twentieth century by discussing Cecil B. DeMille's *Male and Female* (1919), filmed just before the United States put a curb on immigration. I will offer an unconventional interpretation of this film by reading it alongside a history of geographical and mental islands on the path to an America that has to be imagined before it can be reached—or rather, this America is in a sense never reached at all. It can only ever be glimpsed from the islands just off its shores.

In juxtaposing various ostensibly unrelated works, I do not suggest that they should be treated as direct responses to each other. Rather, I am interested in tracing the structural and aesthetic parallels between them to examine how the figuration of islands as gateways to the New World has circulated in the cultural imaginary. Following Stephen Greenblatt's discussion of the circulation of social energy, I would maintain that these exchanges and parallels are 'partial, fragmentary, conflictual; elements [are] crossed, torn apart, recombined, set against each other' (1988, 19). Reading them in conjunction will mobilize the texts' potential to shed light on each other while allowing for the diversity of paths they trace. What they share, however, is a poeticizing of space through the figure of the island as an ambivalent gateway to a world not yet reached. With this in mind, we will now embark on our own journey across texts, travelling from island to island, and beyond.

Interrupted Journeys and Island Prisons: The Angel Island Poems

Ellis Island and Angel Island are linked to an imaginative and aesthetic construction of America. Both islands gave rise to hopeful and despairing visions of America, but the latter predominate in the case of Angel Island. If the majority of prospective immigrants on Ellis Island were processed within a few hours (Werner 2009, 2), many immigrants passing through Angel Island, especially if they were Chinese, were detained on the island for weeks, months, and sometimes years (Lai et al. 1980, 22). With the Chinese Exclusion Act of 1882, which banned the immigration of Chinese labourers, it had become extremely difficult for Chinese people to enter the United States. Many Chinese came to America via a 'crooked path', i.e. with false papers that would either testify to their merchant status or assert their American citizenship;[2] their claims were often hard to validate or disprove (84–95). As a provisional in-between space where detainees were caught between the homeland and the 'land of the flowery flag' (cf. Lai et al. 40–6) or 'Gold Mountain' (cf. Lee and Yung 70–6), Angel Island literally produced poetry: many of those detained or awaiting deportation wrote or carved calligraphic poems on and into the back walls of the shabby barracks where they resided. One hundred and thirty-five of these poems have been recorded and collected in a beautiful volume by Him Mark Lai, Genny Lim, and Judy Yung, all descendants of immigrants detained at Angel Island.[3] The collection is entitled *Island*, which is how the Chinese detainees referred to Angel Island. As Lai et al. explain, most poems are written in the classical Chinese style, consisting of four lines with seven characters each. In their content, too, the island poets referred to classical Chinese poetry and especially to historical or mythical Chinese figures in adverse situations (1980, 23–8).

But the poets also read and cited each other's poems and thus developed specific imageries and associations revolving around the island experience. Some of the characteristics outlined by Lai et al. include feelings of hope and despair, frustration, loneliness, and home-sickness; other poems bespeak an 'increasing national consciousness' and even a 'recurrent defiant wish for China to become powerful enough one day to wreak vengeance on America' (1980, 25). For Lai et al., these poets 'unconsciously introduced a new sensibility, a Chinese American sensibility using China as the source and America as a bridge to spawn a new cultural perspective' (28), a perspective that expresses both the dreams of a golden land and their frustration, a sense of being stranded in a country where they were considered an 'inferior, undesirable race' that was to haunt Chinese American identities for decades to come (28).

Many of these Angel Island poems poeticize the island through a specific spatial imagery of water, land, and wind to paint a transitional experience. Often melancholy in tone, they oscillate between memories

---

[2] According to Lee and Yung, an estimated 90 per cent of all prospective Chinese immigrants came to the United States with false papers (2010, 84).

[3] The majority of these were first copied from the walls by two detainees in 1931 and 1932 (Lai et al. 1980, 23).

of a past left behind and glimpses of a desired future. The island hovers over the poems as a limbo space in between past and future. The first poem in the collection epitomizes this poetic vision:

> The sea-scape resembles lichen twisting and turning for a thousand *li*.
> There is no shore to land and it is difficult to walk.
> With a gentle breeze I arrived at the city thinking all would be so.
> At ease, how was one to know he was to live in a wooden building?
> (qtd. in Lai et al. 1980, 34)[4]

In this poem, land and sea merge. The sea is figured in terms of lichens, land dwellers and composite organisms themselves, which are in turn depicted as 'twisting and turning' like waves. The sea thickens in this image, no longer functioning as a medium of transport. The poem hints at a shore and a city as the envisaged destination, but the glimpse of the future remains hypothetical and almost irritatingly vague ('thinking all would be so'—we need to ask: how?), and the poem creates a sense of distance ('a thousand *li*'[5]) that poetically belies the proximity of Angel Island to the American mainland. The impossibility of landing implies both an infinite journey and imprisonment; maybe walking is difficult because the speaker is no longer quite at sea, but also not yet on land proper, doomed to walk in circles in an island prison. If the poem begins with the open sea, it despairingly ends with the rigid, enclosing structure of wooden walls. The hopeful movement of sea and breeze is arrested before the destination has been reached; what remains is the poetic movement of language. Without using the word 'island' once, the poem constructs a gloomy poetics of the island, that space which is neither quite sea nor quite land.

Imprisonment is indeed the most frequent trope. One poem sets off the notion of a prison against the name of the island and its associations of angelic freedom and mobility: 'This place is called an island of immortals / When, in fact, this mountain wilderness is a prison' (60). But many poems also produce the island as a prison

---

[4] English translation by the authors of the collection. The following comments are all based on the English translations and are likely to miss some of the subtleties specific to the Chinese originals.

[5] A Chinese *li* corresponds roughly to a third of a mile (Lai et al. 1980, 34).

through an imagery of arrested or interrupted movement, especially of water and wind:

> I have infinite feelings that the ocean has changed into a mulberry grove.
> My body is detained in this building.
> I cannot fly from this grassy hill,
> And green waters block the hero.
> Impetuously, I threw away my writing brush.
> My efforts have all been in vain.
> It is up to me to answer carefully.
> I have no words to murmur against the east wind.

(60)

The image of the ocean transformed into a mulberry grove recalls the figurative depiction of the waves in terms of lichens; the green waters have become frozen and 'block the hero' rather than connecting him to the mainland. The colour green reinforces the solidification of water and associates it with the 'grassy hill'. Sandwiched between landscape descriptions, the reference to 'this building' imprisoning the poet's body carries a double meaning: it refers, of course, to the detention centre, but the syntagmatic alignment with the surrounding ocean and 'this grassy hill' also facilitates the phrase's metaphorical extension to the entire island as a space enclosing the poet's body. Writing itself fails as a means of relief: the poet's words cannot prevail against the wind, which significantly comes from the east, and thus from the American mainland. It immobilizes the poet even more and indicates the only movement that seems possible: the voyage back to China. In this striking image, even the poet's imagination cannot reach America any longer.

Other poems renounce dreams of America altogether and cast their gaze nostalgically back to the homeland. Even the latter can seem out of reach: 'I wish I could travel on a cloud far away, reunite with my wife and son' (qtd. in Lai et al. 58). The elements themselves seem to conspire against the prospective immigrants: 'Waves as big as mountains' (42) and the 'angry surf' (56) make for 'delayed progress' (62). One poet figures himself as a 'drifting leaf' subject to the play of wind and waves, and awaiting an 'uncertain future' (54); even the visual connection to America is troubled in another poem as the mountain-front is 'cloud- and fog-enshrouded' (54). 'Hoping to step ashore the

American continent is the most difficult of difficulties' (162): the very *hope* of reaching the near mainland becomes a near impossibility. In the Angel Island poems, the physical space of the island and its surrounding elements becomes an imaginative site, a 'topotropogra-phy' (Miller 1995, 4) of frustrated desire which translates into the entanglement and resistance of the different geospheres converging on an island that is both a geographical location and a state of mind.

Through the Golden Door: Imagining America from Ellis Island

On the opposite coast, some 12 million immigrants entered the United States through Ellis Island between 1892 and 1954, where they were thoroughly inspected and examined before being admitted into the country—or sent back home (cf. Berman 2003, 9–11; Werner 2009, xi–xiii). Like Angel Island, Ellis Island has a neighbour in the harbour. If Alcatraz is an uncanny double of Angel Island as a prison island, Liberty Island signifies the opposite: the freedom and promise of unbounded possibilities. Closely associated with each other—in fact, present-day visitors to one have to visit the other as well as there are no individual tours to only one of the islands[6]—Ellis Island and Liberty Island have become two potent symbols of the American Dream (cf. Reeves 1991, 9). The physical history of Ellis Island reflects its symbolic import: it was continually enlarged to ten times its original size with the ballast left by ships from all over the world. 'How appropriate', we read in a newspaper article from 1951, 'that Ellis Island has the soil of so many lands from which came the enormous tide of future American citizens' (Kreis 3–9, March 1951). In this view, Ellis Island represents a both concrete and symbolic site of nation building where the tide of the outside world washes up to form the America of the future.

The idea of America as a space in perpetual construction is deeply rooted in American thought. The ur-American idea of leaving behind

---

[6] Similarly, visitors can book combined tours to Angel Island and Alcatraz Island in San Francisco, although the islands can also be visited separately.

the (British/European) past, moving forward and continually reinventing self and nation was taken up by the transcendentalists in the nineteenth century. In *Nature* (1836), Ralph Waldo Emerson advocates a forward-oriented gaze that was already present in the rhetoric of the American Revolution:[7] 'Our age is retrospective. It builds the sepulchres of the fathers.... The sun shines to-day also.... There are new lands, new men, new thoughts' (2003, 35). Around the same time, the Frenchman Alexis de Tocqueville gave one of the most memorable accounts of the American Dream:

> Among democratic nations, men easily attain a certain equality of condition, but they can never attain as much as they desire. It perpetually retires from before them, yet without hiding itself from their sight, and in retiring draws them on. At every moment they think they are about to grasp it; it escapes at every moment from their hold. They are near enough to see its charms, but too far off to enjoy them.... (1840, 138–9)

With different agendas, both Emerson and de Tocqueville stress a forward-oriented American gaze. While Emerson emphasizes the value of the new, de Tocqueville describes an ideal vision always within view, but never fully reached.

Taken together, their visions are as close as it gets to the rhetoric of the well-known Ellis Island photographs in which groups of immigrants face away from the camera, gazing and pointing towards either Manhattan or the Statue of Liberty. In one of them (*Immigrant Family Looking at New York Skyline*, 1925), we see an immigrant family standing on the edge of the water. Manhattan is recognizable in the hazy background. The image is horizontally divided into three sections: the edge of the island fills the bottom part and Manhattan and the sky the third, with the water occupying the middle. The silhouettes of the parents stretch across the three sections, their heads just about reaching into the indistinct shapes of Manhattan. The photograph constructs the island as the space where America emerges into view, and emphasizes the water as a connective medium from the island to the mainland (or rather, to yet another island). It is appropriate that the immigrants' heads are visually already in Manhattan. In their minds,

---

[7] See for instance Samuel Adams: 'Let us not look back...' (1999, 234–5).

the composition suggests, they are already in (a hazy dream of) America. There are many similar photographs, and they have become ingrained in the cultural imaginary. One of them (*Immigrants Waiting to Be Transferred*, 1912) shows a larger group of immigrants on the ferry dock against the background of an equally hazy Manhattan (Figure 1.1). Most of them are standing on the edge of the water and facing away from the camera, either looking towards Manhattan or getting ready for the departure. In another variant, four immigrants are standing on the same dock. The son's right hand is placed above his eyes, which emphasizes his intense gaze. The father is standing on the raised edge of the dock, on the outermost fringes of the island; his outstretched arm points to an even hazier, barely recognizable Manhattan. These immigrants are indeed, in de Tocqueville's words, 'about to grasp [America]' and 'near enough to see its charms, but too far off to enjoy them'. But the America that draws them on is still a dreamy,

FIGURE 1.1 *Immigrants Waiting to Be Transferred, Ellis Island, October 30, 1912* (Underwood & Underwood, 1912), Library of Congress, Prints & Photographs Division (LC-USZ62-11203)

insubstantial vision. The most famous of all Ellis Island photographs has the same visual configuration, but the immigrants are gazing towards Liberty Island. The look away from the camera implies the leaving behind of a past life; the blackness of the silhouettes empties the immigrants out, readying them to be refilled with a new identity. Gazing across the water at Liberty Island, they quite literally do not see America, but an *idea* of America.

This view of America as a hazy image also appears in immigrants' accounts of their arrival. Edward Corsi, who became commissioner of Ellis Island in 1931, begins his *In The Shadow of Liberty: A Chronicle of Ellis Island* (1937) by recounting his own arrival in 1907, the year when immigration reached its peak (Berman 2003, 9). Like the photographs, his account is marked by a haze that is epistemological as much as visual:

> My first impressions of the new world will always remain etched in my memory, particularly that *hazy* October morning *when I first saw Ellis Island.* ... [H]appy that we had come through the storm safely, [we] looked with wonder on this *miraculous land of our dreams.*
>
> ...Mothers and fathers lifted up the babies so that they too could see, off to the left, the Statue of Liberty.
>
> I looked at that statue with a *sense of bewilderment, half doubting its reality. Looming shadowy through the mist*, it brought silence to the decks of the *Florida.* This symbol of America—this enormous expression of what we had all been taught was the inner meaning of this new country we were coming to—inspired awe in the hopeful immigrants....
>
> Directly in front of the *Florida, half visible in the faintly-colored haze*, rose a second and even greater *challenge to the imagination.*
>
> 'Mountains!' I cried to Giuseppe. 'Look at them!'
>
> 'They're strange,' he said, 'why don't they have snow on them?' He was craning his neck and standing on tiptoe to stare at the New York skyline....
>
> During this ride across the bay, as I watched the faces of the people milling about me, *I realized that Ellis Island could inspire both hope and fear....* Impelled they may all have been ... by a *single desire*—to *make a fresh start* in a free country; nevertheless they were a strange and motley company ... *as they peered over the rail toward the tiny island* where their fate would be decided....
>
> [Old and young] saw in the future, *through their shadowy dreams*, what they believed was an *earthly paradise.* (3–5; my emphasis)

Quite fittingly, the chapter is entitled 'I Behold America': America emerges as a 'half visible' object of desire. Yet it is precisely this 'challenge to the imagination' that accounts for its miraculous quality. Mistaking the skyline of Manhattan for mountains, Corsi turns America into a magical object emerging in an uncertain visual zone. Just visible across the water, still escaping the onlookers who have yet to pass through Ellis Island, this America comes into being as a 'shadowy dream', an idea of a future yet to be realized. Like de Tocqueville's America, it draws its energy from its quality as a fragile image, tantalizing but escaping its beholder. Corsi paints an intensely visual scene where the real and the imaginary intertwine. He begins by tying his first impressions of the New World to the sight of Ellis Island, yet in what follows he does not describe the island itself. The latter is not marked as the primary object of fascination, yet it conditions and frames the various gazes structuring Corsi's text. Right after the initial reference to Ellis Island, Corsi describes the storm as 'one of the worst storms in the captain's memory' (3). However accurate this claim may be, the storm also functions as a trope and resonates with the countless storms and shipwrecks marking both fictional and non-fictional narratives of arrival in the New World, where they commonly signify the leaving behind of the Old World and a rebirth in the New.

This rebirth, however, typically goes hand in hand with a loss of orientation and a perceptual and cognitive difficulty in coming to terms with a new space; *The Tempest* is a prominent example. The play of signifiers in the account of the passage through the bay creates such epistemological confusion: the word 'shadowy' is used to describe both the immigrants' dreams *and* the view of Liberty Island, also attaching itself syntagmatically to the 'mist' in the bay; the word 'dreams' is used to describe the *object* of perception, the 'miraculous land', and the *medium* through which the future is perceived as an 'earthly paradise'. The islands in the bay are both real and imaginary; the repetition of the word 'half' further underscores this blending of perception and imagination by doubling the uncertainty ('half doubting'). This perceptual uncertainty is linked to the immigrants' uncertain future; their 'approach toward the unknown' (Corsi 1937, 4) is marked by heightened imaginative activity. This activity unites the group in a 'single desire' despite their motley appearance. At the end, Corsi stresses the passengers' gaze towards Ellis Island as a place inspiring fear and hope.

But the gaze towards the island is at the same time a gaze *from* the island as a concrete and imaginative gateway to America.

In a 1940 lecture entitled 'Plymouth Rock and Ellis Island', the Slovene-American intellectual Louis Adamic constructs a similar vision. Worried about increasing hostility towards immigrants, he expresses his concern over their spiritual homelessness. Figuring immigration as an experience shared by all Americans, he represents Ellis Island as central to the idea of America, linking it to Plymouth Rock and Jamestown, the first permanent English colony in the New World, set on another island:

> And the beginning of [these new Americans'] vital American back-ground as groups is . . . the as yet unglorified immigrant steerage; not Plymouth Rock or Jamestown, but Castle Garden or Ellis Island or Angel Island. . . . (10)
> . . . I have been repeatedly impressed by immigrants telling me or writing to me how they felt when they first glimpsed the Statue of Liberty: how tears filled their eyes, how they wanted to fall on their knees. . . . These immigrants were Americans before they landed. They were part of the same movement, the same surge towards freedom, that brought over the Pilgrims. (12)

Adamic constructs a view of America as an idea formed *before* (and often frustrated after) landing. If he initially differentiates between 'old-stock Americans' and new immigrants, he later unites the disparate groups through a shared American idea. His oral history project stems from a desire to 'keep [the American Dream] from turning into a Nightmare' (16); concerned about recent developments in the United States and the war in Europe, he fashions America as an idea facilitating 'unity within diversity' (16). In his vision, one does not become American by living there; being American is a condition for arrival. This is why Adamic stresses the islands just off its coast, forging links between Ellis Island, Angel Island, and Jamestown.

Adamic does not mention Christopher Columbus and his islands in his mythical geography, but Corsi gives him a prominent place: 'New York, where I had spent all of my life since that October day when our family landed from Italy, is a city of islands. Had Columbus landed at Ellis Island on a summer day he would have found the braves of the Manhattan Indians fishing from its shores . . .' (57). The point is, of course, that Columbus never landed at Ellis Island—nor did he ever set foot on the North American mainland. Yet Corsi's conditional proposition testifies to the importance of Columbus for American foundational mythology.[8] Corsi also stresses the importance of islands for the American experience by pointing out that New York 'is a city of islands'. And islands, of course, were of central importance for Columbus as well.

On the Cusp of Modernity: The Islands of Columbus and His Predecessors

As Lestringant points out, Columbus did not discover (as much as he discovered anything) a continent but a world of islands:

> Birds, stars, drifting tufts of grass, those signs of land multiplied day after day are signs of islands. So many archipelagoes figured in the air, in the firmament and on the water must needs lead to a veritable archipelago. It's precisely an archipelago that the Admiral discovers one beautiful morning in October 1492, and not a continent....
>
> (2002, 11; my translation)

Indeed, Columbus's first written account of his travels to the New World begins with a description of a world of 'many islands thickly peopled' (1870, 1).[9] After mentioning a series of smaller islands, Columbus describes a large island (today's Cuba). Sailing along its shores, he was convinced he had reached India and only accepted that he was not on the continent when he was assured by the locals 'that this land was certainly an island' (3). At this point, there is no more talk of a continent. The mythical, often utopian geography of this early modern world of islands was closely intertwined with fantasies of power, easy conquest, and enrichment (see Gillis 2003, 26). But this experience of islands also went hand in hand with a new understanding of space:

---

[8] On the latter, see Paul (2014, 43–88).

[9] The quotations are taken from R. H. Major's 1870 translation of the Spanish letter addressed to Luis de Santangel.

> [T]he Age of Discovery ultimately expanded the boundaries of the
> known world, disrupting the medieval and Renaissance geocentric,
> anthropocentric geosophy by both extending the horizon and dis-
> connecting it from the heavens.... The old vertical scales were dis-
> placed by a notion of horizontal space that seemed infinitely
> extendable. Space was now open, its once fixed horizons transformed
> into moving frontiers that beckoned ever westward.   (Gillis 2003, 24)

Space, in other words, became less rigid and unfixed. For Lestringant,
the Atlantic islands epitomized this distinctly modern conception of
space: 'The island appears as the privileged element of a malleable
geography whose form and design can be indefinitely reconstructed
in accordance with particular political projects' (2002, 14; my translation). Lestringant is referring to concrete political enterprises as well as
projected ones like that of More's *Utopia* (1516), which he considers to
be intimately bound up with contemporary island discoveries and
conquests. For Lestringant, the early modern islands embody the provisional, the possibility of continually remaking space through concrete
action and in the world of ideas. The fantasies of conquest this gave rise
to are thus linked to a radical departure from the stable structures of
the medieval world to a more fluid oceanic world. For Lestringant, the
Atlantic islands epitomize 'un monde éclaté. L'humanité n'habite plus
un sol stable, mais un archipel à la dérive...' (13).[10] In this view, the
continental world of medieval times exploded into a fragmented world
of islands.

As Gillis points out, Atlantic islands soon became 'the center of
Europe's attention, arguably its most valuable economic and strategic
assets' (2003, 28). They were important outposts from which international trade began to develop. With the rise of capitalism, 'coasts
and islands were the core and the continents the periphery of
geographical transfers of capital, people, and knowledge' (29);
'[Islands] facilitated an accelerated circulation not only of people,
but of ideas...' (30). It is no coincidence that the 1507 world map
by Martin Waldseemüller, the first map to name America, blows the

---

[10] '...an exploded world. Humanity no longer lives on stable ground, but in a drifting
archipelago' (my translation).

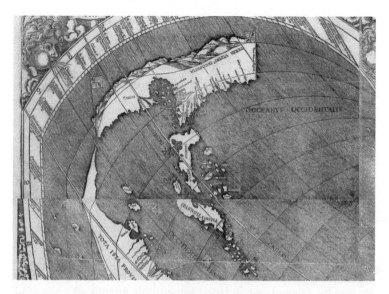

FIGURE 1.2   Detail from *Universalis Cosmographia* (map by Martin Waldseemüller, 1507), Library of Congress, Geography and Map Division

islands out of proportion while continental America remains small
and thin (Figure 1.2).[11]

As Christian Kiening (2006) argues, it took Europeans a long time to
understand the New World on its own terms and accept it as new. They
had not set out to discover a new world, but rather to reconnect with an
old world and tap into its riches. But Kiening is particularly interested
in the messiness of New World discourse as it blends old fantasies and
myths with new forms of representation emerging from the encounter
with unknown lands and people. For Kiening, what results is a myriad
of hybrid and unpredictable forms. Columbus's letter is such a textual
hybrid. It ends with the promise of further islands abundant in gold
and riches and inhabited by Amazonian women, people with tails,

---

[11]   Gillis points out that 'in the seventeenth and eighteenth centuries the role of islands
became so significant that maps exaggerated not only their number but also their size'
(2003, 28). The example of the Waldseemüller map demonstrates that this exaggeration
began much earlier.

cannibals, and other human curiosities. All of these visions of marvelous islands are already present in Marco Polo's late thirteenth-century account of his supposed travels to China and Japan, and in John Mandeville's fourteenth-century *Travels*. While Polo's historical existence is undisputed even if scholars disagree on how far east he really went, the real identity of John Mandeville is unknown, and we do not even know whether he travelled at all (cf. Moseley 2005, 11). Moseley cautions against anachronistic notions of truth and falsehood in judging the authenticity of these accounts, for Polo and Mandeville in turn relied on the classical tradition of Eastern monsters and marvels in authors like Herodotus and Pliny: in medieval times, 'no account of the East that omitted them could be held to be serious' (11).

What is certain is that Columbus was well acquainted with both Mandeville's and Polo's accounts and relied on them as sources of information (cf. Moseley 2005, 9; Kiening 2006, 215; Gillis 2004, 56–9). If Columbus partly reproduced their fantasies, it was also because his accounts might have aroused little interest otherwise and because he depended on his ability to convince his sponsors to fund further voyages (cf. Kiening 2006, 15). If he projects the mythical islands of previous travel accounts on the lands yet to be discovered, it is also to announce a gain that is both epistemological and economic: 'They assure me that there is another island larger than *Española*, in which the inhabitants have no hair. It is extremely rich in gold' (15). As Columbus's letter progresses, his islands become more and more marvellous, and the most spectacular fantasies are located just a step down the chain of islands he describes. Chet Van Duzer points out that 'in Marco Polo's narrative, the more distant the area he is describing, the more islands it has' (2006, 148); Polo and Columbus meet in an island world east of Asia and west of Europe that is textual more than anything else. Before America can fill this zone, these islands form a mental bridge connecting Europe with a very old world *and* imaginatively preparing the ground for a new world to come. America as a continent is not yet part of Columbus's vision. But he projects a promised land just beyond his last island, almost within reach. While the fantasies are old, Columbus's imaginary gaze looks forward to a land of possibilities.

The importance of islands as fictional and mental bridges to the New World (Gillis 2004, 51–4) cannot be overestimated. The fictional intersects with the real in complex ways: the 'most apparently fantastic of Columbus's ideas were *precisely* the ones which allowed him to make the most important of his real discoveries' (Valerie Flint, qtd. in Gillis 2004, 45; emphasis original). Kiening similarly argues that the New World emerged as the terrain of the imaginary (2006, 209); 'real' islands and invented ones, islands in travel accounts and literary islands like Utopia and the island in *The Tempest*, are part of the same discursive network. For Kiening, the New World is marked by movement, mingling, confusion, instability, and a plurality of references (220; 225; 235). The fashioning of the New World thus also tests and projects ideas; it is a site of literary conception, a notion Kiening finds epitomized by the Island of Immortality in Baltasar Gracián's *Criticón* (1651–7), an island in a sea of ink (231). Kiening is thus interested in the affective and literary potential of the island (217) as the prime site of what he calls the poeticizing of the New World (220).[12]

Significantly, Kiening begins by addressing the remarkable mobility of islands in early modern cartography (203; cf. also Gillis 2004, 51–4). Robert H. Fuson has published a book-length study of these wandering and phantom islands—Antillia, Brasil, and Thule are some of them—and the voyages of discovery they spurred on (1995). Fuson is occasionally a little too concerned with the real lands that may hide behind these famed islands, but his book demonstrates the imaginative and generative potential of islands. Columbus's American voyages took place at the end of a century that had seen the rise of the *isolario* genre (Van Duzer 2006, 151), island books containing maps and descriptions of real and legendary islands around the world.[13] These books became extremely popular in the sixteenth century, and testify to the centrality of islands in the imaginative engagement with the New World.

---

[12] For Greenblatt, an experience of wonder structured Europeans' engagement with the New World and was closely tied to, but not reducible to, desires to possess the marvellous other (1991, 22–3).

[13] Famous examples include Cristoforo Buondelmonti's *Liber insularum archipelagi* (1420), Benedetto Bordone's *Isolario* (1528 and 1532), and André Thevet's *Le grand insulaire et pilotage* (1586). On the *isolario* tradition, see Van Duzer (2006, 149–53), Lestringant (2002), and Conley (1996, 167–201).

Floating Islands and Spouting Volcanoes:
The *Voyage of Saint Brendan*

The narratives of Marco Polo and John Mandeville were important precursors of the *isolario*, but they were preceded by the Irish *immrama*, tales of sea voyages by Irish saints in the North Atlantic that were extremely popular from the eighth century onwards (cf. Van Duzer 2006, 145–7). Blending Celtic mythology of otherworldly islands with Christian geographies,[14] the *immrama* revolved around discoveries of islands in the west. They had a historical counterpart in the settling of North Atlantic islands by Irish monks until the eighth century AD (Gillis 2004, 36). The islands of the *immrama* were closely linked to notions of paradise on earth or, alternatively, the temptations of the devil and the torments of hell. Like the medieval *mappaemundi*, they mapped a 'biblical temporality and geography' (Gillis 2004, 37) rather than indicating 'precise locations or directions' (39). The most popular of these narratives was the *Voyage of Saint Brendan*, or *Navigatio sancti Brendani abbatis*.[15] The *Navigatio* chronicles the voyages of an Irish abbot in search of an island referred to as the Promised Land of the Saints; for seven years, Saint Brendan and his monks sail from island to island, often encountering the same island several times. The *Navigatio* is usually read as a religious text exploring a scriptural landscape; others have tried to link it to real voyages of discovery. Columbus himself was hoping to find Saint Brendan's island (McLeod 2009, 138); scholars have flirted with the idea of locating it in the Canary Islands, the Faroe Islands, Iceland, or even North America (cf. McLeod 2009, 136–8; Wooding 2002, 25; Fuson 1995).

In contrast to these approaches. I would like to read Saint Brendan's islands in terms of the poetics they deploy. While the islands of Marco Polo and John Mandeville are important precursors of the imaginative investment in islands in early modernity, they are not marked as

---

[14] As Elisabeth Frenzel points out, Celtic mythology was rich in islands of fairies, demons, and the dead (1980, 383–8).

[15] The author of the *Navigatio* is unknown, as is the date of its original composition; according to Wooding, the earliest manuscripts date from the 10th century AD, but earlier versions of the text might go back as early as the mid-eighth century (2002, 13–19). The Latin version referred to here was imitated in various languages.

islands; in fact, the illustrations of the medieval manuscripts of their narratives do not even make it clear that the respective places are islands (Van Duzer 2006, 148–9). Gillis makes a similar claim about the islands of the *Navigatio*: 'Nowhere in the account do we get a naturalistic description of the islands themselves. Their shape is invariably symmetrical, circular in the manner of the classical *omphalos*' (2004, 38). The overall spatiotemporal logic of the narrative is indeed cyclical; any sense of discovery is betrayed by the suggestion of predetermination present from the beginning. As Jonathan M. Wooding argues, 'the text is an allegory of monastic progression' (24); the overall organization of the eschatological narrative is episodic and symmetrical (19–22) and relies on monastic time, foreclosing any sense of progression by emphasizing the principles of *stabilitas* and *stasis* (24). This sense of predetermination is already set in place by the series of embedded narratives at the beginning of the *Navigatio*, when we learn about a certain Saint Barrind who visits Saint Brendan and recounts his own journey to the Promised Land of the Saints; he embarked on the voyage having in turn heard of his son's establishment on a certain Island of Delight. Saint Brendan thus does not set out to discover, but to recover; the very narrative structure displaces the original discovery of the island ad infinitum into an ever-receding past. The spatial journey is thus textually marked as a temporal journey, the recovery of an earthly paradise.[16] Structurally, nothing new awaits discovery: the destination is clear from the beginning, and the journey is one of revelation rather than of exploration. A number of prophetic figures (sometimes Saint Brendan himself) that regularly give the travellers precise information on the continuation of their journey reinforce the notion of a preordained spatial and narrative universe. At the end of the narrative, we return to its beginning as the description of the Promised Land of the Saints initially given by Saint Barrind is repeated. Or else, the narrative already begins with its ending, closing in on itself in a perfect loop.

And yet the predetermined circularity of the narrative is undermined by the description of the islands themselves. While Gillis rightly points

---

[16] As Gillis points out, '[b]ecause Europeans had set out to recover an old world it took a long time before the notion of a New World sank in and the idea of recovery was replaced by the modern notion of discovery' (2003, 24).

out the peculiar mixture of scriptural and pagan imaginaries in the description of the islands, he partly misses the geographical imaginary set forth by the text. The narrative is indeed cyclical and symmetrical, but many of the islands are, contrary to Gillis's assertion, irregular and shape-shifting. It is not true that there are no geographical descriptions of the islands; quite on the contrary, their spatial peculiarities are foregrounded throughout the narrative. Both aspects are central to the description of the *trompe-l'oeil* island that reveals itself to be a giant fish: 'The island was stony and without grass. There were a few pieces of driftwood on it, but no sand on its shore' (2004, 34). Albeit partly *ex negativo*, this description evokes the minimal geological and geomorphological elements required to make an island: a rock rising from the sea, an interior part with (or in this case, without) vegetation, and a shore where loose material accumulates from both inside (sand, here absent) and outside (driftwood) the island, where the island leaks into the ocean and the ocean adds material to the island in a dialectic exchange. Although it is not a proper island, the narrative insists on its physical characteristics. When the monks make a fire, 'the island began to be in motion like a wave', and finally 'moved out to sea' (35). Before we learn that the island is not an island, it embodies space at its most mobile.

This emphasis on the material and fluid characteristics of the island speaks to a sense of secular spatial wonder that accompanies and sometimes outweighs the religious wonder structuring the text. Lestringant's thesis is that the experience of island space in its morphological diversity shaped Renaissance thought, but antecedents of this primacy of space over narrative (2002, 30–1) can be found in the *Navigatio*. If there is an element of purely spatial *jouissance* to the cartographic fascination with islands and their extreme elusiveness and mobility on Renaissance maps, Saint Brendan's moving island embodies a forerunner of this impulse. Several other islands in the *Navigatio* have a similar function. One of them is described as 'very rough, rocky and full of slag, without trees or grass, full of smiths' forges' (54). When the monks flee from the island, the smiths throw lumps of slag into the sea after them:

> It looked as if the whole island was ablaze, like one big furnace, and the sea boiled, just as a cooking pot full of meat boils when it is well

plied with fire. All day long they could hear a great howling from the
island. Even when they could no longer see it, the howling of its
denizens still reached their ears, and the stench of the fire assailed
their nostrils. (55)

In the scriptural logic of the narrative, this island manifests a version of
hell, as Saint Brendan himself states. Yet the island cannot be fully
absorbed into the religious narrative. The unmistakable volcanic
imagery also makes it a very terrestrial island in constant eruption
and (re)production. As a manifestation of hell, it poses no real threat
to the scriptural symmetry of the text. As a manifestation of space in
flux, however, it marks a moment of narrative disintegration. Space
itself, as it were, comes to the fore, and is experienced in the full range
of sensory perceptions: the island initially offers a visual spectacle, and
continues to have aftereffects in the sounds and smells it produces. All
of these sensory impressions are extreme (fire, loud howling, and an
obtrusive stench). Space, as it were, attacks all the senses to the point
that it invades the monks' bodies, as when the stench is said to assail
their nostrils. The linguistic ambiguities in the slipping from literal to
metaphorical uses of both the infernal and volcanic imageries further
underscore the uncertain status of the island. While the description
initially refers to real forges, the later 'furnace' is merely figurative;
similarly, the imagery of hell is at first reinforced with a volcanic simile
('as if a volcano were erupting there', 55), before the blacksmiths from
hell disappear from view and the island presents itself in its volcanic
guise, which at that point is no longer figurative, or not only figurative.
Beyond their place in the text's religious geography, the islands of Saint
Brendan make for a heightened spatial experience.

The links between islands and an experience of space in flux can be
found in other medieval tales of exploration in the Atlantic such as 'The
Isle of Satan's Hand', Thomas Wentworth Higginson's late nineteenth-
century version of another legendary island that appeared on fifteenth-
century charts and was originally probably another *immram*
(Higginson 2006, 99–100). The tale explores various forms of spatial
mobility. The island extends outwards as a kind of hand reaches out
from it to crush the sailors' boats. Its spatial indeterminacy is further
marked by the 'chilly mists' (57) surrounding it and the fact that it
'constantly change[s] place' (57). Finally, the island itself topples over

like the icebergs surrounding it, 'and the whole water boiled for leagues around, as if both earth and sea were upheaved' (58). In an intriguing combination of the characteristics of very hot (volcanoes) and very cold (icebergs) islands, it becomes a site of maximum fluidity and commotion as earth and water mingle and boil over. Floating islands multiply in the tale: 'All around them dim islands seemed to float, scarcely discernible in the fog' (58). In the end, Higginson tells us of the island's final movement: its eventual disappearance from the maps. Like the infernal island in the *Navigatio*, the Isle of Satan's Hand only thinly masks its secular spatial appeal.

The notion of the floating island was to preoccupy the early modern imagination to such an extent that the German theologian and poet Georg Christoph Munz wrote a dissertation on floating islands in 1711.[17] The text is revealing as it offers a reflection on the place of floating islands in a worldview struggling to reconcile scientific investigations of geographic phenomena with the divine creation of terrestrial space:

> ... whether floating islands come to be, is indeed worth considering, for there are many objects in nature which have their genesis in the free and unstudied will of the Creator, and acknowledge no merely natural causes of their origin, while others now come into being, and now perish again, through the force of the laws of nature. Thus it bears asking whether floating islands belong to the first of these classes, or to the second. I answer that as it is held with good reason that all islands had their origin long ago in the Flood ... and as the same is indubitable and incontrovertible of many small fixed islands; so much the more is it true that floating islands, which because of their wandering motions are less durable, do not owe their origin to the Creation, but are born in time, and must be considered subject to birth and death through nature's various changes. (2004, 15)

For Munz, floating islands are secular islands: their existence is not divinely ordained but they come to be, change their shapes, and wander restlessly. Correspondingly, they are elusive and ephemeral. This also means that one can examine them through scientific lenses without risking blasphemy. They represent secular space in flux, not subject to

---

[17] Munz draws heavily on Athanasius Kircher's discussion of floating islands in his *Mundus subterraneus* (1665).

divine intervention. Munz's dichotomy of fixed and floating islands follows in the wake of a long line of texts and maps filled with islands surrounded by ambiguity and ontological uncertainty, from the *immrama* to early modern cartography and narratives.

Even the epitome of scriptural geography in the *Navigatio*, the Promised Land of the Saints, is not entirely free from this secular and indeterminate experience of space. To be sure, it is not a floating island, and a far cry from the bubbling and spouting infernal volcano, yet not only is the island enshrouded in fog like the Isle of Satan's Hand, but the text also constructs it through a curious double vision:

> When they had gone in a circle around that land, night had still not come on them.... for the space of forty days they reconnoitred the whole land and could not find the end of it. But one day they came upon a great river flowing through the middle of the island. Then Saint Brendan said to his brothers:
>
> 'We cannot cross this river and we do not know the size of this land.' (63)

The description of the island combines two incompatible spatial orders. On the one hand, the passage conveys a sense of spatial and temporal symmetry in line with the allegorical, schematic dimension of the island; the brothers walk in a circle for forty days, a scripturally significant number that recurs throughout the narrative,[18] and the island is said to be split in half by a river. This, indeed, implies the circular, geometrical island Gillis sees in all of Saint Brendan's islands. And yet, the text simultaneously asserts that the monks cannot find an end to the island and cannot determine its size, which we learn right after we have been told that the river splits the island in half. This discrepancy suggests dual focalization: the symmetrical view of the island in its totality represents divinely ordained, sacred space as seen by God. Conversely, the limited and indeterminate vision of the island represents an at least partly secular gaze. While the elusiveness of part of the island may point to the inaccessibility of paradise on earth, the text also suggests an immersion in an open space inviting exploration,

---

[18] Most importantly, the New Testament states that Jesus ascended to heaven forty days after his resurrection.

even if this exploration is foreclosed. The island is both bounded and open, both symmetrical and indefinite.

A similar form of double vision structures the frontispiece of the 1516 edition of More's *Utopia*, which combines two incompatible perspectives.[19] While the island is essentially flat and depicted in the God's-eye view of medieval painting, the landscape in the background is perspectival and three-dimensional, suggesting a human viewer immersed in space. But the island is also drawn in the style of contemporary maps; the pictogrammatically represented towns, accompanied by written labels, contribute to this effect. The God's-eye view that is present in the representation of Saint Brendan's island is here inherited by the modern cartographer. The *Utopia* map thus manifests a double impulse: the desire to explore space and an openness to the unknown at the expense of spatial certainty and control, and the reassertion of this control by fixing the newly explored space cartographically.

Emergence and Submergence in Modern Space: Multisensory Exposure in *The Tempest*

We may have strayed far from Columbus's islands and from the island as a site where America is imaginatively anticipated, yet it would be misguided to ignore the islands of the *immrama* and the narratives of Marco Polo and John Mandeville in a discussion of American island imaginaries. If the former prefigure the malleable space of early modernity, the latter establish the island as a playground of the imagination. The former tentatively offer a poetics of the island as a meditation on space in flux and a heightened spatial experience; the latter embody the movements of the mind, while largely unconcerned with islandness as a spatial phenomenon. As an idea, America gradually comes into being at the intersection of these two conceptual archipelagos. Around 1600, the island has become fully associated with both: with spatial indeterminacy and mobility on the one hand, and with a heightened imaginative activity on the other. This, at least, is its double function in

---

[19] Racault, 'Utopias, Travels and Insularity', workshop at the University of Zurich (9 May 2014).

Shakespeare's *The Tempest*, where the island also functions as a bridge between the Old World and the New. As Peter Hulme argues, the island has an ambiguous location: while ostensibly set in the Mediterranean, it also contains explicit references to the New World (1986, 106–9).[20] One way of reading this spatial indeterminacy is to see it in terms of Kiening's messiness in the representation of the New World; in this view, Shakespeare's island represents the New World partly in terms of the Old. And like Columbus's islands, the island of *The Tempest* enables the production of fantasies. It becomes truly an I-land: almost all of the major characters imaginatively turn it into their private kingdom. This may partly reflect the late medieval and early modern practice of European monarchs giving noblemen fiefdoms on Atlantic islands, often before their existence was even ascertained, to extend their dominions and rid themselves of political threats nearer home (Gillis 2004, 91). The colonization of the New World initially relied mainly on private initiative (Bauer 2003, 3).

The series of imaginary island kings in *The Tempest* includes Prospero himself ('This cell's my court'; 5. 1. 166) and several of the other castaways. Prospero's old counselor Gonzalo imagines himself as king of the island: 'Had I plantation of this isle . . . . And were the king on't, what would I do?' (2. 1. 140–2). The drunkard Stephano relishes a similar prospect, basing his vision on the apparent end of the old order through the supposed drowning of the rest of the group: 'This will prove a brave kingdom to me . . .' (3. 2. 139). Ferdinand imagines himself to be King of Naples, assuming that his father has drowned: 'Myself am Naples, / Who with mine eyes, never since at ebb, beheld / The King with my father wrecked' (1. 2. 438–40). Finally, the fratricidal plot devised by Antonio and Sebastian, brother to King Alonso of Naples, also casts Sebastian as the latter's successor. All of them wash up on the island as castaways, reaching it from the water and reborn on its shores; the imagery of birth is deployed repeatedly (cf. Weaver-Hightower 2007, 74). This sense of a fresh start is also evident in the perception of the island as an uninhabited *tabula rasa*. Thus, Adrian says to Gonzalo: 'Though this island seem to be desert— . . . . Uninhabitable,

<hr />

[20] Cf. Graves (1925, 191–232); Frey (1979); Hulme (1986, 89–134); Greenblatt (1988, 142–63); Skura (1989); Cheyfitz (1997); Barker and Hulme (2000); Brown (2000); Hart (2003); Kiening (2006, 217–30).

and almost inaccessible—' (2. 1. 36–38). The fact that the castaways' clothes seem to be 'as fresh as the first day [they] wore [them]' (2. 1. 99–100) confirms this sense of renewal.

If these fantasies are linked to the notion of (re)birth, a psychoanalytic reading can identify them as fantasies of completeness and omnipotence. Indeed, Meredith Anne Skura argues that Prospero displaces his own repressed childhood fantasies of plenitude, reversal, and revenge on Caliban (1989, 65). She points out that Caliban's trajectory is one of moving from being 'mine own king' (1. 2. 345) to the chastisement by a father figure (64). While Skura focuses on Prospero and Caliban, her claim that the New World was a site of golden world fantasies recalling childhood fantasies to many Englishmen (53–7; 67–9) can be extended to almost the entire group of castaways. Except for Gonzalo's, their fantasies all involve the death of a father figure. Although Ferdinand grieves over his father's death, he does not consider the possibility that he might still be alive, claiming that he saw him drown 'with mine eyes' (1. 2. 439). Since Alonso did not drown, Ferdinand's gaze can be read as a fantasized gaze of wish-fulfilment; Stephano as well as Sebastian and Antonio even plan the murder of the person still in their way. Yet it is in Gonzalo's vision that the link between seeing and imaginary completeness, between *eye* and imaginary *I*, becomes particularly apparent. Gonzalo links his vision to the golden age of Greek mythology (2. 1. 165). He places himself at the centre of his fantasy, as governor and king. As he rambles on about the life-sustaining quality of the island, he is mocked by Sebastian and Antonio:

GONZALO: How lush and lusty the grass looks! How green!
ANTONIO: The ground indeed is tawny.
SEBASTIAN: With an eye of green in it.
ANTONIO: He misses not much.
SEBASTIAN: No. He doth but mistake the truth totally. (2. 1. 53–7)

The figure of the 'eye of green' suggests that it is only in his imagination that Gonzalo perceives the ground as green. The *eye* that the trope places at the centre of the ground surrounding it, however, also puns on *I*, thus linking the central self and its sight. It is through an act of seeing, his *eye* being in the centre of the space he constructs, that Gonzalo constitutes his *I* in the centre of his imaginary kingdom.

In pointing to the imaginary import of Shakespeare's island, I am not primarily interested in the psychoanalytic implications of the castaways' fantasies. Nor is my present focus on the eventual ideological appropriation of these fantasies by Prospero, and the questioning of Prospero's own fantasy of power through the play's complex metatheatrical imagery and structure.[21] Rather, I wish to examine the island as an aesthetic realm of heightened imaginative activity and sensory experience. I have challenged Gillis's contention that the *Navigatio*'s islands are not physically described; the claim could be made with more validity for the island of *The Tempest*, at least at first sight. As I demonstrate in Chapter 3, we can indeed detect an impulse to produce the island as a circular, geometrical abstraction. Yet if the physical geography of the island itself is rarely present, its impact on the castaways' senses is all the stronger. So far, we have focused on sight, but the island impacts all the senses, often with the aid of the airy spirit Ariel: 'Then I beat my tabor / At which, like unbacked colts, they pricked their ears, / Advanced their eyelids, lifted up their noses / As they smelt music' (4. 1. 175–8). In an overflow of sensory stimulation, Ariel's music makes the castaways watch, listen, and smell at the same time, to the extent that the senses become confused and interchangeable. This sensory confusion is linked to the overall indeterminacy of the island. Prospero evokes yet another sense when he explains its peculiarities: 'You do yet taste / Some subtleties o' th' isle, that will not let you / Believe things certain' (5. 1. 123–5). Taste here becomes expressive of the castaways' sensory exposure to the island. Various senses are activated in the pageants staged by Ariel and his fellow spirits; the insubstantial banquet of Act 3, accompanied by music, teases hearing, sight, and taste. Caliban's famous speech in the same act is usually cited to demonstrate his poetic eloquence and native knowledge of a dimension of the island inaccessible to the colonizer (cf. Brown 2000, 224–5), yet it also establishes the island as a space of heightened sensory experience:

> Be not afeard. The isle is full of noises,
> Sounds, and sweet airs, that give delight and hurt not.

---

[21] On Prospero's theatrical power, see Orgel (1975, 44–8); Hulme (1986, 115–20); Barker and Hulme (2000, 236–42).

> ... and then, in dreaming,
> The clouds methought would open and show riches
> Ready to drop upon me, that when I waked
> I cried to dream again.   (3. 2. 130–8)

Again, the senses commingle in Caliban's description of a plethora of acoustic and visual stimuli. And again, ontological uncertainty is at the heart of the experience as Caliban's account marks the island as a dreamscape, or a space where dreams merge seamlessly with the reality of this experience; the space of the island itself is as uncertain as the multiple sensory impressions it produces.[22]

In *The Five Senses: A Philosophy of Mingled Bodies*, Michel Serres maintains that the senses flow into each other (2008, 305). For Serres, as Steven Connor points out, 'the senses are nothing but the mixing of the body, the principal means whereby the body mingles with the world and with itself, overflows its borders' (3). Serres is interested in moments when the body becomes aware of itself: 'You only have to pass through a small opening, a blocked corridor, to swing over a handrail or on a balcony high enough to provoke vertigo, for the body to become alert' (19). One of Serres's preferred images to describe this bodily alertness is that of the maze: providing 'a very long path within a short distance' (143), mazes enhance the body's exposure and receptiveness to a given space. The island in *The Tempest* is referred to as a maze several times. Thus, Gonzalo uses the trope of the maze to express his spatial confusion: 'By 'r lakin, I can go no further, sir. / My old bones aches. Here's a maze trod indeed / Through forthrights and meanders!' (3. 3. 1–3) Significantly, the image does not offer any description of the island per se, but registers a subjective and bodily response to it.

Yet the problem remains that the island itself is rarely described, and when it is, it is referred to as 'this bare island' (Epilogue 8), 'desert' (2. 1. 36), and 'uninhabitable' (2. 1. 39). The few descriptions we get, such as

---

[22] Numerous critics have pointed out the indeterminacy structuring the island, yet they tend to focus on linguistic uncertainty. Eric Cheyfitz's discussion of translation as a structuring principle of the play (1997), Russ McDonald's examination of deferred communication in *The Tempest* (1991), and Dorothy F. Lane's reading of the island as a 'place of conflict which resists efforts to own it linguistically' (1995, 24) exemplify this approach.

Gonzalo's reference to its greenness, are immediately discredited. This seems to sit uneasily with the intensified sensory experience just examined. Unless, of course, there is no island in the first place. Let me immediately qualify this statement: I am not suggesting that there is no island in the diegetic logic of the play. Rather, I am suggesting that the island is so indeterminate that it ceases to exist other than in the subjective responses it provokes. While the land itself remains elusive, the water around it is constantly referred to, and the play is pervaded by images of drowning. Indeed, *The Tempest* may well be the most watery of Shakespeare's plays, and it is full of visions of submerged bodies. Alonso acknowledges the primacy of the sea when referring to the apparent loss of Ferdinand: 'He is drowned / Whom thus we stray to find, and the sea mocks / Our frustrate search on land' (3. 3. 8–10). Yet bodies are not only threatened with submergence. They also emerge from the water, as Ariel points out when he says that destiny has caused the 'never-surfeited sea' to 'belch up' the castaways (3. 3. 55–6). The fear of submergence in *The Tempest* is closely linked to the possibility of emergence, and I would like to propose that the island embodies this possibility. How do we know, in fact, that the island is ever really more than the shifting sandbank Ferdinand finds himself caught on at the beginning of the play, barely emerging from the sea (see Chapter 3)? Who is to say that the island is ever more than thoughts and dreams emerging from water? How can we be sure that the island exists at all except in that most mobile manifestation of space, immaterial thoughts and dreams?

This coupling of the possibility of emergence and the threat of submergence is linked to a double-edged meditation on the subject's position in the world. Conley suggests that the insular imagination of the period, epitomized by the *isolario*, was tied to a new concept of the world based on 'subjective "singularities," that are fathomed in part by every individual's experience of the world' (1996, 169). This entails a 'productive fragmentation that momentarily allows various shapes of difference to be registered without yet being appropriated or allegorized' (169). It is also, however, a source of anxiety, as 'the displacement of the self...results from an increasing awareness of its entirely arbitrary presence in the world' (169). Conley emphasizes that this fragmentation is momentary; he does not assert an idealized form of pure subjectivity free from cultural constraints. Rather, he outlines an intense spatial experience that results from the crumbling of received ways of thinking about the world. The sense of possibility and the feeling of vulnerability are closely tied to each other; they both form part of an experience fraught with uncertainty. In *The Tempest*, the castaways do not really end up imagining anything new. Their fantasies are coloured by the political realities at home, and while they imagine alternative configurations of power, the structure itself remains unchanged; even Gonzalo's utopia simply inverts the familiar order 'by contraries' (2. 1. 144) and retains a model of kingship. But as I have argued, they do experience an abstract sense of possibility that is tied to their momentary dislocation and registers in their subjective and disoriented responses to the island. By the end of the play, this spatial uncertainty has been reabsorbed and neutralized by Prospero's authoritative narrative.[23] And Prospero himself has no more reason for staying on the island as his power is more firmly in place than ever. The island is a stepping stone for Prospero, but a stepping stone that returns him back home; what he imagines is not a space beyond the island, but a reconfiguration of his old dukedom. Viewed as a colonial venture, Prospero's project is a failure: the settlement on the island is unsuccessful.

'The mere worck of god flottynge of': *The Tempest* and the Roanoke Voyages

By the logic of the play, this argument must appear unsound; both Prospero and the other castaways arrive on the island involuntarily and depart purposefully. Yet in this, the play reverses the pattern of purposeful arrival and involuntary departure that marked the beginning of British colonial ventures in America. *The Tempest* is usually read in its immediate historical context, the 1609 shipwreck of the *Sea Venture*, one of a fleet of nine ships transporting supplies and 600 settlers to Jamestown, founded for the Virginia Company in 1607; the survivors

---

[23] Significantly, however, the resolution is deferred, as is the voyage home. Lane emphasizes the 'recurrent motif of "not yet"' in the play (1995, 27), drawing on the stylistic analysis of McDonald, who similarly argues that *The Tempest* is structured by a series of linguistic deferrals (1991).

lived in Bermuda for almost a year and reached Jamestown in 1610 (cf. Jarvis 2010, 12–16). Jamestown itself is an island, but it was preceded by another island 100 miles further south. Between 1585 and 1587, the English made several abortive attempts to start a colony on Roanoke Island in the Outer Banks of today's North Carolina under a patent granted to Sir Walter Ralegh by Queen Elizabeth. After a reconnoitring voyage in 1584, 108 men started a colony on Roanoke under the governance of Ralph Lane. Short of provisions, they hastily departed in June 1586 when Richard Grenville's supply ship did not arrive and Sir Frances Drake offered them a passage home. Three men were left behind; their fate is unknown. When Grenville's ship did arrive, he found Roanoke deserted and placed fifteen of his own men on the island, unwilling to leave it unoccupied. In 1587, a group of 113 arrived in Virginia to search for the fifteen men and start a new colony under the governance of John White, this time with women and children. White returned to England to procure further supplies. He would not live to see his colonists again: with the threat of the Spanish Armada in 1588, the priorities of the government lay elsewhere, and it was not until 1590 that another expedition could be dispatched to Roanoke. White and his men found nothing but two inscriptions indicating that the colonists had moved on to Croatoan, an island with whose indigenous population they had maintained friendly relations. They became the third lost colony of Roanoke: to this day, no conclusive evidence as to their fate has been found, although their story has inspired a number of speculations from both within and outside academia.[24]

My argument is not that *The Tempest* was based on the documents from the Roanoke voyages in any direct way, nor do I wish to suggest they should replace the Bermuda pamphlets as a source for the play. This is not the place for source criticism,[25] although Eric Cheyfitz's

---

[24] See, among others, Kupperman (2007); Horn (2010); Miller (2000). Historian David Beers Quinn compiled the historical documents from the Roanoke voyages into an extensively annotated two-volume collection (1955). He went on to write extensively about the Roanoke voyages (Quinn 1984; 1985). Even Quinn's scholarly rigorous writing is not free from extensive speculation, and has inspired fierce criticism by recent scholarship; see especially Cheyfitz (1997, 175–213) and Mackenthun (1997, 221–9).

[25] B. J. Sokol offers a discussion of *The Tempest* in its historical contexts. I subscribe to his view that 'many readings of *The Tempest* have overlooked aspects of the real experiences of the English in "Virginia" between 1584 and 1610' (1998, 22).

suggestion that Shakespeare probably 'knew the Roanoke voyages as well as he did the Jamestown documents' (1997, 196) is helpful. But I do want to suggest that *The Tempest* resonates with these voyages. It may be less interesting to settle on a single historical precedent for the play than to note that both the Roanoke and the early Jamestown documents are full of shipwrecks that compromised early English ventures in Virginia, and many texts are marked by an underlying sense of uncertainty and helplessness that is either openly expressed or glossed over. As Jeffrey Knapp points out, 'the English were in fact remarkably slow to colonize America, and their first attempts were dismal failures' (1992, 1). Indeed, the documents often convey the sense that the English were castaways in the New World; in his account of the arrival of the 1585 colony, Lane describes the near shipwreck of the *Tyger* in the treacherous shoals of the Outer Banks: 'ye Tyger lyinge beatynge vppon ye shoalle..., wee were all in extreeme hasarde of beyng casteawaye, but in ye ende by ye mere worck of god flottynge of wee ranne her agrounde harde to ye shoare, and soo with grete spoyelle of our prouysyones, saued our selfes and ye Noble shippe also' (1955b, 201). In Lane's account, the colonizers depend on chance to make the shore. The arrival in the New World is beyond their agency; it is the 'mere worck of god flottynge of'.

The abandonment of the first colony was propelled by another shipwreck as the *Francis*, the 70-ton ship stocked with provisions Drake had offered Lane, was lost in a hurricane; realizing 'the weaknesse of our companie' (1955a, 292), Lane made a hurried decision to abandon Roanoke. In the anonymous *Primrose* journal, written by one of Drake's men, Virginia is all storms: '[All the] Time wee weare in thys countrie, We had thunder [lightning] and raigne with hailstones as Bigge as hennes egges [There were] great Spowtes at the seas as thoughe heaven & [earth] woulde haue mett' (*'Primrose* Journal' 1955, 308). The stormy weather lost Lane's men a considerable part of their baggage: 'the weather was so boysterous, and the pinnaces so often on ground, that the most of all wee had, with all our Cardes, Bookes and writings, were by the Saylers cast ouer boord' (Lane 1955a, 293). Without developing the association further, Cheyfitz suggests that the 'scene of chaos aboard ship in the New World recalls the first scene of Shakespeare's *The Tempest*' (1997, 183). When White arrived at the abandoned settlement in 1590, he was struck by the destruction of his books: 'wee found fiue Chests, ... and my books torne from the couers, the frames of some of my pictures and Mappes rotten and spoyled with rayne, and my armour almost eaten through with rust' (1955, 615). White's choice of decayed and destroyed objects is significant, for all three carry symbolic force: while the books are associated with learning and epistemic power, the maps and the armour epitomize the spatial and military control of the New World. The decay of the latter, and the apparent destruction of the former by the locals, conveys an apt picture of the failure to arrive in and control the New World.

These narratives of failure are transformed into a success story in *The Tempest*. The initial storm turns out to be man-made, conjured, and fully controlled by Prospero. While Lane and White lament the drowning, decay, and destruction of their books, Prospero himself ritually drowns his book, key to his magic and his control of the island (5. 1. 56–7). For Cheyfitz, *The Tempest* represents a fiction of translation, an illusion of matching the terms of the New World seamlessly to those of the Old. I would like to suggest that the play itself also translates the unsettling texts of the New World experience: it translates the accidental loss of books into their willed renouncement, the incalculable contingencies of hurricanes into a carefully fabricated and calculated tempest, and the repeated abandonment of a small island into a willed departure for home. The play restores the threatened agency to the white colonizer: hurricanes can do him no harm, his power is so absolute that he no longer needs his books, and the New World is consciously left behind.

The island status of Roanoke is important in the early narratives' negotiation of the colonizers' fraught position in the New World, and we may well relate it to the suggestive potential of that other island of *The Tempest*, the sandbank on which Ferdinand is caught. Roanoke was full of sand: the colonizers had to face dangerous shoals, with shifting banks obstructing the passage of ships and boats. Furthermore, the sandy and swampy ground of Roanoke was not conducive to the erection of permanent structures. Sand is present in Arthur Barlowe's account of the first voyage of 1584, when the locals apparently tell the expedition of 'some Christian shippe' which was wrecked on the coast 'some twentie yeeres since' and 'cast vpon the sande' (1955, 104). It is also present in the caption to Theodore De Bry's engraving of

John White's pictorial map of the coast entitled 'The Arriual of the Englishemen in Virginia' (1590):

> The sea coasts of Virginia arre full of Ilands, wherby the entrance into the mayne land is hard to finde. For although they bee separated with diuers and sundrie large Diuision, whiche seeme to yeeld conuenient entrance, yet to our great perill we proued that they wear shallowe, and full of dangerous flatts, and could neuer perce opp into the mayne land, vntill wee made trialls in many places with or small pinnes. At lengthe wee … discouered a mightye riuer falling downe into the sownde ouer against those Ilands, which neuertheless wee could not saile opp any thinge far by Reason of the shallewnes, the mouth ther of beinge annoyed with sands driuen in with the tyde ….
>
> (1955, 413–14)

The caption stresses the difficulty of arrival in the New World. The coast only *seems* to 'yield conuenient entrance'; the difficulty of reaching the 'mayne land' is stated several times. In both map and text, islands block the way, and shifting sands frustrate further advance. Belying the title, the engraving and the caption suggest that the 'Englishemen' do *not* fully arrive in the New World; they are stuck amidst its sandy islands and banks (Figure 1.3). Sand appears again prominently in John White's account of the last Roanoke voyage in 1590 when he describes the Outer Banks islands (Low sandie Ilands', 1955, 608; 'narrow sandy Iland', 609) and their '[digging] in those sandie hills for fresh water' (611) on an island near Roanoke. It also appears on the deserted island itself: 'In all this way we saw in the sand the print of the Saluages feet of 2 or 3 sorts troaden y^t night, and as we entred vp the sandy banke vpon a tree, in the very browe therof were curiously carued these faire Romane letters CRO' (613). It is suggestive that the sand of the islands, along with their lowness and narrowness, is so visible in the account of the last Roanoke voyage. All White and his men encounter are traces: letters carved in a tree and footprints in the sand, soon to be erased by wind and weather. All of this is evocative of the early colonizers' tenuous hold in the New World; the islands have become a deserted landscape and a desert landscape at the same time.

Yet while it appears in the accounts of arrival in and departure from the New World, on the whole there is surprisingly little sand in the Roanoke documents. Instead, praise of the bountifulness of the land

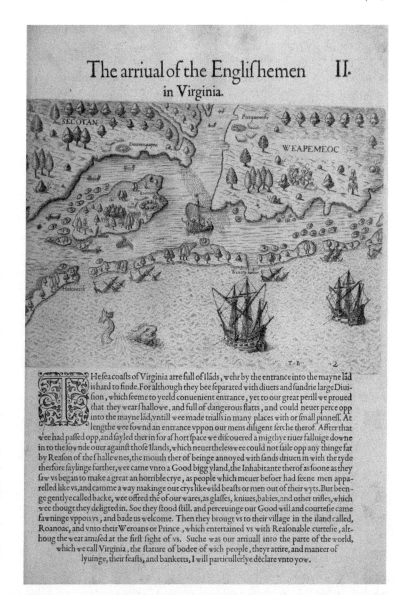

predominates in the official narratives. As David Beers Quinn points out, texts like Thomas Hariot's *Briefe and True Report* had to 'counteract impressions easily conveyed by those who had returned (and largely true of the immediate surroundings of Roanoke Island) that there were only sandy beaches and swamps, with little possibility of settlement' (1955, 325); Hariot explicitly attacks the 'slaunderous and shamefull speeches bruited abroade by many that returned from thence' (1955, 320). Figurations of Virginia as a 'delicate garden' (Barlowe 1955, 94) where Indians 'liued after the manner of the golden age' (108) already abound in Barlowe's account of the first voyage, which also praises the 'most pleasant, and fertile ground' (114) of Roanoke and confidently asserts that 'in all the word the like aboundance is not to be founde' (95). Intended to convince both investors and potential settlers of the profitability of the project, this 'conventional reworking of the age-old fantasy of Arcadia' (Horn 2005, 28) may ironically have jeopardized the enterprise as it 'left the first colonists dangerously unprepared for the conditions they would encounter' (29).

If many of the documents cannot quite gloss over the tension between a sense of inadequacy and an asserted 'promised land flowing with milk and honey', in the words of Richard Hakluyt (1955, 515), they attempt to resolve this tension by spatializing it. The promised land is located elsewhere, just beyond the colonizers' grasp—beyond the island, in a mainland that has not yet been fully reached. Thus, Hariot admits the absence of stones on Roanoke only to assert their varied existence elsewhere (366), ending the passage by speculating that quarries and limestone 'may bee in places neerer then [the Indians] wot of' (367). Time and again, the river is imagined as a route to an imagined elsewhere. A striking example occurs in Lane's *Discourse* after his description of a failed voyage up the river:

> for that the discouery of a good mine ... or a passage to the Southsea, or someway to it, and nothing els can bring this country in request to be inhabited by our nation. And with the discouery of any of the two aboue shewed, it willbe the most sweete, and healthfullest climate, and therewithall the most fertile soyle, being manured in the world.... (1955, 273)

Mary C. Fuller is quite right when she states that '[t]he passage leaves us dizzy' (1995, 53). It mixes not only observed and hypothetical spaces, but also maps these onto different temporal orders. Hidden in the passage, almost beyond recognition, is the statement that the country might not be worth inhabiting: 'nothing els' than a gold mine or a trade route to the Pacific can make the enterprise profitable. But with syntactic mastery, Lane turns the initial conditional proposition into a confident assertion of a certain future ('with the discouery . . . it willbe'). Although the existence of mines or a passage to the Pacific has nothing to do with the soil and the climate, the hypothetical discoveries are, rather absurdly, said to affect the climate and make the soil fertile; Lane here inadvertently lays bare the mechanisms of the discursive construction of an imagined America. As Fuller argues, a 'hypothetical voyage [substitutes] for . . . a real one not performed' (53) as Lane replaces his unsuccessful voyage with an anticipated future voyage; a vision of America comes into being through an 'invitation to suppose' (Fuller 51), activating the reader's imagination. This vision is spatially and temporally removed from the actual situation of the colonizers, but almost within reach: 'For this riuer of Moratico promiseth great things' (Lane 1955a, 273).

This imagined America is not entirely separate from what is seen and experienced at Roanoke; it enlarges and extends what is already within reach, which is why the river is such a potent trope. In his conclusion, Hariot writes that what he has mentioned 'doubtless and in great reason is nothing to that which remaineth to bee discouered . . .' (1955, 382). He justifies this assertion by drawing attention to the difference observed between the island and the land set back from the coast:

> yet sometimes as we made our iourneies farther into the maine and countrey; we found the soyle to bee fatter; the trees greater and to growe thinner; the grounde more firme and deeper mould; more and larger champions; . . . more plentie of their fruites; more abundance of beastes; the more inhabited with people, and of greater pollicie & larger dominions, with greater townes and houses.
>
> Why may wee not then looke for in good hope from the inner parts of more and greater plentie, as well of other things, as those which wee haue already discouered? (382)

Hariot's text here follows the logic of a crescendo. Starting from a minimal America on the coast, everything becomes larger, greater, or fatter; the word 'more' alone appears seven times, and there are sixteen comparatives altogether. The implication is, of course, that this expansive beginning will extend into the 'inner parts'; it is on this note of hope that Hariot ends, expressing the conviction that the land 'cannot but yeeld many kinds of excellent commodities, which we in our discouerie haue *not yet* seene' (383; my emphasis). Not yet: these two words epitomize the aesthetics of the Roanoke texts. They invite the reader to fill in what is still lacking, to imagine an America visible on the horizon, up the river, from the island: 'what hope there is els to be gathered... I leaue to your owne consideration' (Hariot 383).

Similar claims could be made about Jamestown, a swampy island full of mosquitoes; in the first year, countless of the settlers died from malaria, cold, or starvation. John Wood Sweet wryly notes that '[t]he settlement of Jamestown—however puffed up its prospects were in contemporary propaganda—was for its first two decades disastrously disappointing...' (2005, 5). Sand and swamps are imaginatively transformed by accounts such as Barlowe's, Lane's, and Hariot's. In *The Tempest*, the same transformations are at work: Gonzalo's description of the lush greenness of the island is corrected by Antonio's comment that '[t]he ground indeed is tawny' (2. 1. 54), and Adrian's assertion that '[t]he air breathes upon us here most sweetly' (2. 1. 47) is mocked by Antonio: 'Or as 'twere perfumed by a fen' (2. 1. 49). Adrian's statement evokes Barlowe's 'shole water, which smelt so sweetely... by which we were assured, that the land could not be farre distant' (93–4) in his account of the 1584 voyage. The latter may also, perhaps, be linked to Ferdinand's being lured to the island by another form of sensory stimulation, Ariel's music, and to the enticing food offered to the castaways by the spirits, which turns out to be insubstantial and vanishes as they reach for it. *The Tempest* is haunted by this sense that the island may be little more than an infectious swamp, or a tawny sandbank, a sandbank like the one where Ferdinand narrowly escapes drowning, cast away in the New World.

In both the Roanoke texts and *The Tempest*, this sense is counteracted in the construction of the New World as a multisensory realm of promises and possibilities. At its best, this takes the shape of a heightened bodily and aesthetic experience linked to an uncertain and disorienting spatiality; at its worst, it produces fantasies of conspiracy and fratricide. But *The Tempest* ultimately finds a different solution to negotiate the latent anxiety of the failure of the colonial project. The Roanoke texts offer the promise of a space beyond the island, reminiscent of Columbus's evocation of a large and bountiful island just out of reach. Conventional as many of these fantasies may be, their gaze is forward-oriented, and the island is a springboard for movements of body and mind. Focusing mainly on Jamestown, Sweet concludes that '[t]he great irony of this ambitious imperial vision was its fate always to be incomplete, compromised, transformed' (2005, 21). It is this sense of envisioning a New World despite, or maybe because of, a concurrent sense of incompleteness, precariousness, and failure that defines the early documents. America is an elusive object of desire in them, yet the vision itself is never given up. In *The Tempest*, the direction of the gaze is reversed: for the Italian characters, the object of desire is never the New World, but a reconfigured version of home. The mixed geography of the play supports this sense that the arrival in the New World is only partial and provisional; the failure to arrive in the New World is imaginatively transformed into the success of returning home.

Immigration with a Detour: Cecil B. DeMille's *Male and Female* (1919)

We have examined a number of islands, real and imagined, that serve as stepping stones to an America imagined but not yet reached. In various ways, these islands exemplify a condition of migrancy, a movement of flight—whether purposeful or forced by necessity, or both. They are not directly linked, and it would be unwise to claim any direct intertextual relations between the various configurations I have outlined. But they share a common origin in the voyages of discovery in early modernity and the imaginative voyages leading up to them, as well as in the secularization and subjectivization of spatial experience, and the corresponding malleability of geography (see Lestringant 14). They are, above all, linked to a poeticizing of space for the figuration of an experience of displacement in different registers—euphoric, despairing, possessive, anxious, or simply curious, and frequently a combination of these. These different poetic figurations of islands will inform my reading of the final island story discussed in this chapter: Cecil

B. DeMille's 1919 film *Male and Female*. This film resonates with all the other stories partially, and with none of them fully. When I speak of textual resonances in what follows, then, I do not claim any direct influence, let alone intention on the part of the filmmakers. Rather, I treat them as suggestive structural and aesthetic parallels in the figuration of America via a detour, coming into view on the islands just off its shores.

Somewhat surprisingly, *Male and Female* has received practically no critical attention. Based on J. M. Barrie's play *The Admirable Crichton* (1902), the film tells the story of an aristocratic London household shipwrecked on a South Sea desert island, accompanied by their butler Crichton and a maid named Tweeny. On the island, the hierarchies are reversed: Crichton, who turns out to be an expert survivor, asserts himself as king of the little community, and the women compete for his favours. Crichton chooses Lady Mary, but their wedding is interrupted as Tweeny, who is also in love with Crichton, spots a ship on the horizon. As the group returns to London, the old hierarchies are reestablished. If anything, as in *The Tempest*, they are even more firmly in place as the aristocrats go to great lengths to disavow the temporary shift in power. While *The Admirable Crichton* is a social satire about the rigid social hierarchies of Edwardian England, *Male and Female* reinterprets Barrie's British play by turning it into a film about America.

It does so by adding a short epilogue and an even shorter prologue to the main narrative; taken together, they construct America as a genuine alternative to the locked hierarchies of the Old World. Only three shots long, inserted between the credits and a series of vignettes of the different characters, the prologue establishes the film's New World poetics at or even before the beginning of the narrative. Or rather, it is a beginning about beginnings that questions the film's relation to its own origin. The first shot begins with a fade-in to an image of dawn, with the sunbeams emerging from behind the clouds. The image dissolves into a shot of waves in the ocean with the water filling the entire screen, very similar to the opening credits of *The Lady from Shanghai*. The shot dissolves into a North American canyon landscape. After a few seconds, a quote from Genesis 1:27 is superimposed on the landscape: 'So God created Man in His own image . . . Male and Female created He them.' This series of shots signals a fresh start through the image of dawn. The quotation from Genesis continues this emphasis on origins. Superimposed on the landscape, it establishes America as an originary landscape. Through the emphasis on light, the beginning also self-reflexively marks the beginning of the film, commenting on cinema's capacity to create fresh perceptions and Edenic landscapes. This sense of a fresh start is linked to an emphasis on fluidity, evident in the waves of the second shot. With the other shots in mind, the waves thus also signal the transport to a new space, with America as the destination of the voyage.

There is a self-reflexive dimension to this mobility, too, if the dissolves are read in relation to the water. Effecting transportation from one shot and one filmic space to the next, they comment on cinema's potential to bring about transitions and transformations, to transport the audience from one place to another. This general sense of renewal and mobility is also linked to the film's transformation of Barrie's play. Significantly, the Genesis quote contains the title of the film and thus points to DeMille's renaming of the source text. In a complex gesture, the film here reverses its own status as a supplement to the British play into an assertion of its originality, placing itself in a position of anteriority to the latter through the allusion to Genesis and the chronological primacy of the prologue with regard to the main narrative.[26] The prologue is not diegetically motivated, but it conditions the reception of the narrative that follows it.

The prologue intrudes into the narrative as the shot of the water is repeated to signal the arrival of the Loams' yacht on the open sea, with an intertitle reading 'Cross Currents' superimposed on the image. Again, the water signals both physical movement and a sense of possibility. Right after the shot, we see Lady Mary and her cousin reading a newspaper article that announces the marriage of a close friend of Mary's to her family's chauffeur. Mary reacts with scorn: 'The whole affair is ridiculous—it's exactly as if I were to marry Crichton', which provokes Crichton to turn around his head abruptly and close his eyes. For a brief moment, the possibility of contesting the social order emerges, even if it is dismissed as an improbable conditional proposition ('as if'). The mobility of the waves is here linked to a tentative unfreezing of rigid hierarchies; ideas are negotiated on

[26] My reading is here informed by Derrida's notion of the supplement as that which disturbs the self-presence of what would be 'the thing itself' (1974, 145).

water. Again, this scene is not present in Barrie's play. The shot of the water thus not only signals the juxtaposition of the diegetic voyage and the evoked voyage to America, but also the repeated intrusion of the film's American themes into the British plot. Robert S. Birchard seems to suggest as much when he argues that '[h]aving made the world safe for democracy, Americans were sympathetic to the themes of equality and the folly of class distinctions presented in the film' (2004, 149).

But Barrie's play is never really about equality. In fact, the social hierarchies on the island are reversed precisely because Crichton himself is a firm believer in the social order, and simply sees the island experience as a redistribution of roles according to changed conditions; the hierarchies themselves are firmly in place. The question of leadership is envisaged as natural, immutable, and beyond individual agency: 'It will settle itself naturally, my lord, without any interference from us' (2. 1. 427–8). *Male and Female* largely follows the same pattern, but not quite. As Simon Louvish points out, the social inversions in the film are different: 'Crichton in the film is no believer in the social order; he is rather an American-style democrat, a frustrated egalitarian who day-dreams about the very reversal of fortune that fate will soon bring about' (2007, 179). This is not entirely accurate. Once in place, the new order on the island is just as rigid and aristocratic as the one in England; King Crichton enjoys his elaborate dinner apart from everyone else, served obediently by the others, and he similarly invokes nature as an abstract force regulating hierarchies. But Louvish is not entirely wrong, either. In the film, Crichton's belief in the social order is less firmly drawn, and there are several moments where we see him and other characters envisaging the transcendence of the class-based hierarchies of England. In one scene, Mary looks out of the window to observe her friend flirting with her chauffeur and says: 'Rather democratic you servants are getting!', placing the film's transgressions within the frame of an American impulse to democracy.

Yet all of this merely prepares us for the truly utopian moment of the film: the arrival on the island. The chaos of the shipwreck has a levelling force like the storm in *The Tempest* (cf. Schenkel 1993, 43; Greenblatt 1988, 149). This becomes apparent when the dividing wall between the classes quite literally breaks down. Before the ship hits a rocky promontory, the spheres are neatly separated as the film cross-cuts between the interior of the yacht, where the aristocrats are leisurely reading and playing music (tinted in a warm, reddish colour), and the servants and seamen on deck (tinted in blue). The outside world abruptly intrudes into the seemingly protected aristocratic world as the water bursts through the wall behind the piano, that emblem of genteel idleness. In the ensuing commotion, books are drowned, furniture is shattered, and waves fill the shaky and canted images until the arrival on the island. As in *The Tempest*, there are several arrivals as the castaways are separated into three groups:[27] the majority escape in one of the boats, Lord Loam drifts off holding on to a box, and Crichton stays on the yacht because he does not want to abandon Lady Mary. Their arrival is important for the film's establishment of a utopian topography. As Mary clambers onto the rocky promontory, the scene reaches its maximum commotion. A shot of floating debris from the yacht signals the collapse of the symbolic universe; repeatedly attacked and partly covered by the waves, Mary has but a tenuous hold on the land. After a cut, we see Crichton entering the frame from the right. Significantly, the framing conveys the sense that they are caught on a tiny island as we see water washing around the promontory on all sides. This island is in constant danger of disappearing, periodically overflowed by the waves. The film here creates a separate island for Mary and Crichton on which their position is precarious, reminiscent of Ferdinand's sandbank in *The Tempest*. But in its precariousness, this island also creates a sense of openness and potentiality in the face of the dissolution of the old structures.

The cinematography conveys this utopian potential when we see Crichton carrying Mary onto the main island, filmed from the beach. Framed by a rocky arch, they appear as mere silhouettes against what looks like soft morning light when Crichton wades through the water (Figure 1.4). The shot is marked as the first landfall in a fresh space. As they emerge from the water, their old identities are cancelled out; like the silhouettes of hopeful immigrants in the Ellis Island photographs, they are emptied out and ready to be inscribed with a new identity. The intertitle confirms this sense of possibility: 'Suddenly— like mists melting before the sun—she was no longer a great lady to

---

[27] The seamen entirely disappear after the shipwreck scene. Irrelevant for the plot, they are excluded from the social reversals of the film, rather like the sailors in *The Tempest*, who are put to sleep by Ariel.

FIGURE 1.4   Still from *Male and Female* (Cecil B. DeMille, USA 1919)

him—but just a "woman"—a very helpless and beautiful woman.' These written words reinforce the image of dawn conveyed by the cinematography, further linking the shot back to the prologue. The image of mists dissolving in the morning sun suggests that the seemingly immutable structures of the Old World are contingent and illusory masks. In this fresh space, a relationship between Crichton and Mary suddenly seems possible. Although still imaginary, it is no longer dismissed but envisaged: 'as if' has become 'what if'. For a brief moment, people and objects are stripped of their symbolic investments and mobilized; a little later, the crystal from Ernest's watch is used to start a fire, fish bones serve as a comb, and Lady Mary's gold lace trimming becomes a fishnet. At the same time, the quotation marks around 'woman' in the intertitle inadvertently point to the fact that Crichton's fresh perception of Mary is already coloured by an ideology of gender, which replaces the ideology of class prominent earlier and casts him in the heroic role of saving a helpless woman. But the scene on the promontory makes it clear that Crichton does not in fact save her at all;[28] pure rock and waves, it is perhaps the most open moment of the film. Soon after these arrival scenes, the new order with Crichton as leader is established. As already mentioned, it is just as hierarchical and repressive as the former. The fact that this is a mere redistribution of power is also evident in the reversal of colour codes in the first night on the island: the shots of Crichton spooning his soup are now tinted in red and those of the hungry and shivering aristocrats in blue.

But in the moments of having just arrived, when everything is still uncertain, the provisional nature and potential transgression of all social orders is poetically envisaged. Dening views islands as potent images for culture in the making, always reshaped by what is washed up by the water and crosses the beach: 'Island identity, I suppose, is always in the Now and it is always in process' (2003, 206; see also Dening 1980, 158). In *Male and Female*, it is where land and sea meet that the permanence of the social order is put into question. Even if it is immediately reabsorbed, this utopian potential is present in the moment of arrival. On the aesthetic level, it never quite disappears: the frequent filming of the incoming tide serves as a constant reminder of it.

While the part of the island where Crichton, Mary, and the majority of the others wash up is all rocks and sand, Lord Loam seems to arrive on a different island. Where he arrives, the island looks like a tropical island is supposed to look, replete with palm trees, coconuts, tortoises, and monkeys. To be more precise, it looks like the tropical islands in nineteenth-century novels such as Frederick Marryat's *Masterman Ready* (1841) or Johan David Wyss's *The Swiss Family Robinson* (1812), taken up by Hollywood in the early twentieth century (see Chapter 2) and, later, by the popular television series *Gilligan's Island* (1964–7).[29] Indeed, characteristically of the island genre,[30] the film

---

[28] Despite his heroic refusal to leave the yacht, Crichton does little more than stumble around helplessly, watching Mary escape from the interior of the ship and swim ashore on her own.

[29] The first Pacific island film made in the United States was *Sailor in Philippines*, a short film produced by Kalem in 1908. The 1910s saw the production of numerous films set in the Pacific, mainly in the South Seas, but the genre exploded in the 1920s and 1930s. For an overview of Pacific islands films made between 1908 and the 1990s, see Langman (1998).

[30] Racault offers an insightful account of the sense of textual anteriority in many island narratives (1989, 121–3). The first sustained discussion of the intertextuality of

acknowledges this intertextual link: puzzling over how to reach the coconuts, Lord Loam remembers a trick from *The Swiss Family Robinson* (we see the corresponding passage in an intertitle).

But *Male and Female* was not filmed in the South Seas, but on Santa Cruz Island off the coast of Los Angeles. According to an article that appeared in the film magazine *Picture-Play* shortly before the film's release, entitled 'On a Typical, Tropical Isle', DeMille went to great lengths to bring the tropics to the island:

> In this case it was Howard Higgins, his production supervisor, who made geography and transplanted the tropics—a small matter of taking one hundred growing cactus palms, two hundred lemon and orange trees, avocados, sago palms, banana trees, and fifty crates of tropical rushes, and similar accessories from Los Angeles to Santa Cruz Island, one hundred miles away, landing them in a pounding surf on a rocky coast, and then making them look and feel at home. Several hundred sago palms were brought from Florida, and persuaded to grow in their new home. (1919–20, 43)

I draw attention to the film's production history because the younger castaways take a moment to arrive on this fabricated island. It is only after the arrival of Crichton and Mary that the tropical island comes into view. When the reunited group notices that Lord Loam is still missing, Crichton walks towards yet another rocky arch, which frames a view of the tropical landscape. As Crichton steps into this space, he pauses, raises his head and his arms, as if gazing in amazement, before the image fades out and a shot of Lord Loam arriving on his tropical beach fades in. The conventional, tropical island thus first comes into view as a framed image, a separate space whose artificiality is marked. For the remainder of the island episode, the island will remain in its tropical guise. Indeed, after the initial moment of openness and uncertainty, the island is doubly conventional both in its replaying of the class hierarchies and in its South Sea costume.

the island genre is offered by Pierre Macherey, who argues that the disturbance of the seemingly originary space of the island in Jules Verne's 1875 novel *L'île mystérieuse* (the semblance of naturalness on the island reveals itself as a production of Captain Nemo's) can be read as the intrusion of the text of *Robinson Crusoe* into Verne's narrative (2006, 177–277).

But what about the island *before* it becomes tropical? I would like to suggest that this first version of the island is at the heart of its utopian topography. Not yet filled with conventional fantasies, it is a space of possibility. While it may not be a 'bare island' or 'desert' (*The Tempest*, Epilogue 8; 2. 1. 35), it nonetheless resists its subsequent imaginary appropriation. I hesitate to call it empty or bare because it is, perhaps, its very barrenness that makes it tangible in its material existence. Within Western island imaginaries, sand and stone are harder to overlay with conventionalized imagery; while present in many island texts, they are typically linked to the difficulties of arrival before the island becomes its own imaginary self. The utopian moment thus conjoins a very material experience of space, a vulnerable position, and a mobilization of the imagination.

The delayed appearance of the tropical island also prompts me to include the profilmic reality of the island space, at the risk of being accused of a Bazinian belief in the realism of the image. Yet it is possible to allow the 'real' space in front of the camera to intrude into the diegetic world without naïvely asserting that film captures the world in its unfiltered reality (nor is Bazin's realism as naïve as is sometimes suggested[31]). Rather, in including the island where *Male and Female* was filmed I am following Westphal's geocritical call to engage with the various textual and material dimensions of any given space. Indeed, early discussions of the film were certainly aware of the suggestive history of Santa Cruz Island. The same *Picture-Play* article offers a colourful account:

> That's how he happened to select Santa Cruz, which, hundreds of years ago, was a Spanish prison island. An offender against the law was sent there with enough sheep, goats, and pigs to keep him alive. For a long time now it's been a desolate place, inhabited only by a few wild goats and hogs; not exactly a promising spot to turn into a vision of beauty! (1919–20, 43–4)

Edna Foley, who wrote the article, did not do her homework very well. Santa Cruz was indeed a prison at some point in its history. Yet neither

---

[31] See especially Bazin's essay 'Cinema and Exploration' in the first volume of *What is Cinema*, where he argues that it is precisely the apparent imperfections, failures, and faults of documentary film that constitute its witnessing character and realism (2005).

was this several hundred years before *Male and Female* was made, nor did Spain ever send any prisoners there. It was also not uninhabited when the film was made; it had been home to extensive ranching activities since 1855 ('Santa Cruz Island' 2016, par. 9–17). In the eighteenth century, there had still been several Chumash settlements on the island; due to missionary activities, the Chumash were removed to the mainland and the island was deserted by 1822 (par. 2–5). In his history of California written in the 1880s, Hubert Howe Bancroft writes that a group of eighty criminals were brought to California from Acapulco in 1830 (1886, 48). As California had no jails at the time, at least thirty of them were brought to Santa Cruz Island (48). Later that year, their camp burned down and the prisoners built rafts to reach the mainland, where they were eventually 'absorbed into society' (Redmon 2013, par. 9). The 1830 event was one of several attempts on the part of the Mexican government to send convicts to Alta California 'as a means for improving the morals of the convicts and for colonising California' (Bancroft 47). Hiding behind Foley's garbled version of the island's history in the *Picture-Play* article is a story of troubled immigration.

But Foley's article is not just bad journalism. Its shreds of Californian history are mixed with popular stories of survival on desert islands. Set several hundred years in the past, the story she tells is perhaps closer to that of Alexander Selkirk, who survived four years on a desert island in the early eighteenth century; his survival was aided by goats left on the island, presumably by a Spanish ship. Whether consciously or not, Foley seems to have had Selkirk's story in mind: a caption reads 'DeMille was the monarch of all he surveyed', quoting William Cowper's poem about Selkirk's experience.[32] Writing that Santa Cruz is 'not exactly a promising spot to turn into a vision of beauty', Foley paradoxically and unwittingly comments on the workings of her own text: the Santa Cruz she describes is *already* a version of the island transformed by romantic accounts of desert islands. Privileging myth over history, she excludes not only the island's Native American past, but also its grim history of convict immigrants—as well as the contemporary ranching activities. In this, she follows the film's own gesture of turning the island into a conventional fantasy.

---

[32] See Chapter 3, note 41.

In delving into the history of Santa Cruz Island, I have followed the film's call to engage with the openness of the island before it is reabsorbed and frozen into convention. What emerged was a moment of disturbance, an interference of the island in its subsequent figuration. If this has taken us astray from the path followed by the narrative, this is precisely the point. My argument is not, of course, that *Male and Female* is really a story about Mexican convicts in California (this would be an absurd claim). The point is rather that the moment of arrival marks an initial mobility, a movement of flight, which prompts the pursuit of various possible paths. I am more interested in this abstract sense of possibility than in its concrete realizations, for the latter—perhaps inevitably—lead back to an equally rigid order. But it is appropriate that what leads astray for a brief moment the film's trajectory of reestablishing the locked English hierarchies is a piece of American soil just off the coast. If this piece of soil has led us to a story of several migrational movements, part forced, part intentional, this is a fortunate coincidence. There can, however, be no doubt that *Male and Female* presents a story of immigration, a story that we shall now examine more closely.

Americans before They Arrive: *Male and Female*, Hollywood, and the Island

This story surfaces explicitly in the epilogue, which returns the film to its beginning about beginnings. Like the prologue, the epilogue consists of three shots and is very short, barely one minute long. After the last shot of the film's European story has faded out, a shot of Tweeny and Crichton happily working on an American ranch fades in. At the end of a second shot that shows them in a loving embrace, Tweeny bows slightly—ostensibly for Crichton, but as she is facing the camera, the bow is also for the audience; the circular framing underscores the sense of a final performance. The third shot shows Crichton and Tweeny walking towards the camera while the iris diaphragm encircles and frames them for a final vignette. The epilogue shows us that the voyage to America evoked by the prologue has been completed. The film does not show us this voyage; it offers a different voyage instead. But its framing by the prologue and the epilogue shows us that the latter voyage is a means to an end. The genuine alternative to the repressive social order of the Old World cannot yet happen on the island. It happens elsewhere: in an America that is envisaged as a land of possibilities. Structurally, then, the voyage to the island is a necessary detour to a destination that lies elsewhere. In Barrie's play, this destination simply does not exist; as in *The Tempest*, the voyage to the island takes its protagonists back home. In DeMille's film, however, the island becomes a site where the alternatives to the Old World order are glimpsed for the first time.

There are important historical contexts to the film's endorsement of immigration to America. When it was released in 1919, the United States was experiencing a new wave of anti-immigration feelings that led to the closing of the golden door in the early 1920s: 'When the United States entered the war in 1917, anti-immigrant sentiment intensified. The belief that immigrants represented a threat to American security and safety became widespread...' (Berman 2003, 109). The anti-immigrant voices continued to make themselves heard after the war as 'many Americans were eager to see the flow of immigrants severely restricted.... The war had rekindled a long-standing fear, even hatred, of foreigners' (92). In 1917, the United States passed a law that introduced several restrictions on immigration, including a literacy test, against the will of President Woodrow Wilson. Immigration had dropped to a minimum during the war. By 1919, numbers were on the rise again, and the realization that the Immigration Act of 1917 would not drastically curb the influx of immigrants led to the Emergency Quota Act of 1921, which limited the yearly number of immigrants from a given country to 3 per cent of the US population from the respective country in 1910. In 1924, the Johnson–Reed Act introduced even harsher quota regulations (see Schneider 2011, 53–60).

In this context, *Male and Female* advocates immigration by insisting on its central place in American identity. Still young in 1919, Hollywood itself had largely been created by immigrants, many of them from poor backgrounds (see Gundle 2008, 174–5; Cullen 2003, 173). DeMille himself was from an immigrant family: his Jewish mother had come to the United States from Liverpool at the age of eighteen (see Eyman 2010, 15).[33] Hollywood thus both exemplified the dream of America and represented it on screen.[34] Through Tweeny's bow and the iris diaphragm in the epilogue, *Male and Female* implicates its American audience by encouraging the viewers' identification with Crichton and Tweeny as Americans and former immigrants themselves. But the film's advocacy of immigration is ambivalent. By sending the most valiant of the European characters to America (Crichton's resourcefulness helps the castaways survive; Tweeny is loyal and hardworking), the film also picks up on the notion of the 'worthy immigrant' that played an important role in immigration debates (cf. Schneider 2011, 8). Also, British immigrants were not perceived as a threat to the same extent as immigrants from southern and eastern Europe.

The vision of an America invigorated by immigrants is thus not without its own exclusions: working on their ranch to feed Americans, Crichton and Tweeny are not exactly threatening immigrant figures. This in itself, of course, is significant. The film may privilege one form of immigration over others, but by doing so it also conveys a positive image of immigration in general. In fact, the vision of the worthy immigrant was also promoted by immigrants themselves. Orm Øverland maintains that homemaking myths claimed 'a deep spiritual and ideological relationship between the immigrant group and the American nation' (2000, 121). Thus, in his autobiography published in 1920, a Dutch immigrant wondered 'whether, after all, the foreign-born does not make in some sense a better American...' (qtd. in Øverland 2000, 142). Part of this discourse was the argument that immigrants already shared common ideals with Americans *before* reaching the United States: 'All immigrants, according to their leaders—their journalists, public speakers, and historians—were in many and important ways American before they came to these shores' (Øverland 2000, 140). Like Adamic in his 1940 lecture, then, Øverland views America as an idea formed before landing.

With these contemporary discourses about immigration in mind, we can say that it is the detour via the island that enables Crichton and

---

[33] DeMille's father, Henry Churchill deMille, was of Dutch ancestry.

[34] For a detailed account of the history of Hollywood as the creation of mainly Jewish immigrants who came to the United States with little means, see Gabler (1988).

Tweeny to become Americans before they arrive: they have to pass through a fantasy of America before they can land on its shores. Hollywood plays an important part in the production of this fantasy. Indeed, the island is closely associated with Hollywood as a space of transformative fantasies. DeMille's other major addition to Barrie's play is a lavish flashback sequence casting Crichton as a Babylonian king and Mary as his Christian slave. The sequence serves no narrative function whatsoever (cf. Eyman 2010, 157). Culminating in a shot of Gloria Swanson lying under a live lion in an extravagant costume, it stages her as a star and provides an opulent spectacle;[35] the scene thus self-reflexively performs the transformative glamour of Hollywood.[36] It is also explicitly associated with a desire to leave England behind. Just before the imaginary flashback, Crichton embraces Mary, whom he has just saved from a leopard, and says: 'That wonderful look of fear in your eyes makes me almost forget—England!' It is this desire which triggers the Babylonian fantasy. And again, a dissolve effects the transition as we see Crichton and Mary gazing at an imaginary scene. After the boat ride from London to the island, we are thus presented with a second voyage and a second transformation. This time, the voyage leads us into the glamorous world of Hollywood. Already in the prologue, the water and the dissolve were linked. This association is now consolidated. Both the boat ride and the dissolve enable a form of transportation and become metaphorically aligned; geographical desire translates into cinematic fantasy. In an article on the links between mass immigration to the United States and the development of cinema, Elizabeth Ewen points to the importance of Hollywood for the immigrant experience: 'In a world of constant language barriers..., [s]ilent pictures spoke primarily to urban immigrant audiences of women and children, themselves caught up in the social drama of transformation' (1980, S46). *Male and Female*, too, ties its story about immigration to a reflection about Hollywood.

---

[35] *Male and Female* was the first of four DeMille films that made Gloria Swanson 'one of the highest paid and most powerful stars of the 1920s' (Desjardins 2010, 112).

[36] In his history of glamour as a modern phenomenon, Stephen Gundle argues that '[t]he most complete embodiment of glamour that there has ever been is the Hollywood film star' (2008, 172).

Indeed, the second time England is explicitly blamed for the immobilizing rigidity of social hierarchies, it triggers the voyage to America. Crichton overhears Lady Eileen telling Mary that love across class boundaries is not possible: 'There is Heredity—and Tradition—and London!' This prompts Crichton to turn to Tweeny and tell her to join him, before he announces their marriage and departure for America. The substitution of Tweeny for Mary is appropriate: Tweeny may well be the most American of the film's characters. There is a subtle irony to the fact that Tweeny reacts with joyful surprise to Crichton's announcement, for she is ultimately responsible for their emigration. During the island wedding, Tweeny sits down by the open window and closes her eyes. When she opens them again and gazes out of the window, an expression of surprise and excitement enters her eyes, and we see a shot of the open ocean with a ship on the horizon. Joyfully turning around, Tweeny interrupts the ceremony at the last possible moment. The ship thus seems to spring right from her desire. As a point-of-view shot, the view is rather bizarre: showing only water and the ship, it appears curiously disconnected. The brightness of the shot also clashes with the blackness outside the window as seen from inside (the ceremony takes place at night). In fact, a first shot of the ship already appears shortly after Crichton's announcement of the wedding. In the general festivities, Tweeny remains seated at the table and closes her eyes in despair; right after she opens them again, a shot of the ship appears, framed by an iris diaphragm. The structural similarity to the second appearance of the ship and the subjective circular framing mark the ship as a product of Tweeny's imaginative activity.

If Tweeny's dissatisfaction propels the voyage back to England and the subsequent voyage to America, the same dissatisfaction already causes the shipwreck: distressed about the lack of attention from Crichton, she distracts the skipper by telling him of her sorrows. Significantly, Tweeny is the first character introduced to us after the prologue. Her imaginative capacities are signalled in the first shot, which shows her opening a window and looking out curiously and dreamily. Tweeny thus provides the link between the emphasis on mobility in the prologue and the rest of the film. From the beginning, she looks towards new spaces. It is her restlessness that opens and completes the film's cycle of voyages: she insists on looking out of windows, propels the action, and ultimately secures the passage to

America. As a scullery maid, Tweeny is lowest in the social hierarchy of the film; she has most to gain and best embodies the idea of America as a land of possibilities for anyone, regardless of social background. Tweeny's Americanness is located in the capacity to begin anew and imagine an America that does not yet exist.

Like Adamic's and Øverland's immigrants, Crichton and Tweenie can only get to America by becoming Americans before they arrive. I am not arguing that the film's island represents Ellis Island in any direct way. But it takes the structural position of Ellis Island in providing a mental stepping stone to a mythical America. As Schneider argues, '[i]n the American imagination, the history of immigration is always tied to the port of arrival: Ellis Island or Angel Island...' (2011, 61). Is no coincidence that Schneider begins her list of gateways to America with Ellis Island and Angel Island: it is these islands just off the shore that have captured the American imagination, with Ellis Island in the lead. And Ellis Island is the more appropriate structural analogue for the island in *Male and Female*. Despite its double image as an island of hope and an island of tears,[37] the story Ellis Island tells in the cultural imaginary is one of successful immigration. As such, it resonates with the film's successful completion of the voyage, a completion which is conditional on a geographical and imaginative detour. Yet there are other, displaced island stories linked to *Male and Female*. They are tangential to the film—indeed, they are probably located outside the film's boundaries altogether. They are the stories of the Mexican convicts forcefully brought to Santa Cruz Island and escaping to the mainland to be received with whips and imprisoned (Redmon 2013, par. 9), and of the Native Americans removed from the same island. They are stories of troubled immigration, and while they are not directly present in the film, we should not ignore them, for they resonate with the other stories of troubled immigration that remain untold: unlike the film's story of two vigorous and purposeful British immigrants starting a farm (an unlikely story in 1919), those are the stories of refugees, of uneducated workers, of people driven to the United States in despair and arriving in a climate of hostility towards immigrants if admitted into the country at all.

---

[37] Charles Guggenheim's 1989 documentary on Ellis Island is entitled *Island of Hope, Island of Tears*; see also Brownstone et al.'s *Island of Hope, Island of Tears* (1979).

Conclusion: Multiple Paths, Precarious Arrivals, Migrant Islands

These stories of perpetual or arrested movement return us to Michael and Elsa in *The Lady from Shanghai*, who fail to make a home in America. In one shot of the film, we see a view of the ocean with Bannister's yacht moving slowly on the horizon. Upon closer examination, we notice that the ocean is painted; the waves are not moving. This poetic freezing of the water offers an ironic comment on the restlessness signalled by the waves in the opening shot: always on the move, Michael and Elsa never arrive anywhere at all.

This chapter has looked at various island arrivals in the New World. Some of these island arrivals were successful, others disastrous failures; the juxtaposition of the poeticizing of Ellis Island and Angel Island exemplifies these two poles. In all of the texts I have discussed, the island is linked to a movement of flight, to mobility and displacement, whether purposeful or forced; it is not a destination, but a springboard to a new space not yet reached. The various historical and fictional navigators arrive at these islands only to depart again. The island prepares them geographically and imaginatively for a space beyond it. These movements originate in the age of discovery and the imaginative voyages preceding them. The poetic figurations of the island tied to these voyages are linked to a secular aesthetic experience of space as fluid and malleable, already hinted at by the trembling and floating islands of the *Navigatio Sancti Brendani* and the moving islands of early cartography. Approaching America from the other side, the wondrous islands of John Mandeville and Marco Polo helped to establish early modern islands as playgrounds of the imagination and points of departure for yet more fantastic worlds. When Columbus arrived among the islands of what was to become America, he may not have had a sense of the newness of the New World, but he certainly expressed a restless sense of moving ever onwards, from island to island. In various configurations, this sense of anticipation pervades all the texts examined in this chapter. Sometimes it is hopeful and optimistic, as in Corsi's account of his passage through Ellis Island; sometimes tied to frustration and despair, as in the visions of arrested movement in the Angel Island poems.

The early English arrivals in the New World are marked by both. As we have seen, both the historical documents and *The Tempest* bespeak an initial uncertainty in the exposure to a new space. In *The Tempest*, the initial precariousness in the castaways' subjective response to space is quickly superseded by conspiracies and fantasies of kingship and possession; these fantasies ultimately return their gazes back home. In the Roanoke documents, the tenuous hold on a sandy island is displaced by visions of a bountiful land beyond the island awaiting discovery. It is easy to overlook the sense of struggle in both the historical documents and *The Tempest*, but upon close examination both reveal a story of unsuccessful immigration; it is only with considerable effort that they turn the displacements they describe into accounts of purposeful journeys. They have to go to great lengths to transform the sense of being cast away in the New World into a story of success.[38]

Male and Female's successful story of immigration rests on an initial moment of fragility on the island and points to other, less successful stories. The detour via the island opens up possibilities, but it is also fraught with uncertainty. Crichton and Tweeny are model Americans, and their desire to move towards an as yet unrealized future makes them Americans before they arrive. They are shown to invigorate the United States. Their story is also a transformation of the accounts of immigrants as a threat to the country, abounding at the time the film was made.

With this in mind, the various figurations of islands as stepping stones may prompt us to reflect on more recent representations of American arrivals. If the rhetoric of *Male and Female* advocates immigration, some newer films have taken the opposite direction: thus, the first James Bond film (*Dr. No*, 1962) has the half-Chinese Dr. No prepare to disrupt the US space programme from an island in the

---

[38] We might remember this latent sense of failure in the islands of hopes and islands of tears at the threshold of the New World when reading accounts of present-day islands of hope and despair. In October 2013, *The Guardian* featured an article on the Syrian and Eritrean refugees arriving on the island of Lampedusa between North Africa and Sicily (Davies, 16 October 2013). Alluding to Ellis Island, the article is titled 'Why Lampedusa Remains an Island of Hope for Migrants'. It features three photographs: one shows a crowd of migrants on the dock of the island, the second a survivor from a calamitous shipwreck, looking off the island. The third picture shows a hangar full of coffins. Hopeful arrivals, immigrants looking away from the island towards an uncertain future, death by sea: they are familiar images to readers of the texts discussed in this chapter.

FIGURE 1.5   Still from *Superman Returns* (Bryan Singer, USA 2006)

Caribbean. In a sense, he represents the return of the repressed and almost fulfils the threat expressed in one of the Angel Island poems: 'The day our nation becomes strong / I swear we will cut off the barbarians' heads' (qtd. in Lai et al. 1980, 161). The figure of the immigrant preparing to conquer America on an island fittingly expresses Cold War paranoia. Similarly, *Superman Returns* (2006) plays on post-9/11 fears of a vanishing America as the villain Lex Luthor (though American himself) plants fast-growing crystals in the sea to create a new continent from islands and submerge the old America. He literally changes the map so that America shrinks once again to its size on the Waldseemüller map (Figure 1.5). The New World has become old; after the invasion of America by Europeans, European America is in turn under attack.

Discovery, displacement, exploration, conquest, homelessness, flight: these are some of the terms that intersect in the panorama of island arrivals I have outlined. They describe various paths leading through the islands at the threshold of the New World. The paths and the concurrent poetic figurations of islands are diverse, and this chapter has traced multiple and sometimes contradictory trajectories rather than trying to force them into a coherent narrative. These island stories have their place at the beginning of this study for two reasons: firstly, because their negotiation of arrivals and beginnings is an appropriate way to begin. Secondly, and more importantly, they have their origin in the migrational movements of early modernity, when islands suddenly moved centre stage in Western imaginaries as both geographical stepping stones and figurative sites to rethink received models of global space.

*   *   *

The second chapter also engages with arrivals, but its islands are no longer linked to a fundamental uncertainty about planetary space itself, nor are they stepping stones on the way to a world to come. Rather, they are destinations and objects of desire in themselves. Before we look forward to them, let us look back one more time. Like *The Tempest*, and like the Columbus letter, *Male and Female* offers a mixed geography in its engagement with America. I have read its island as a necessary detour on the way to America, but as we have seen, it is also shaped by conventional representations of tropical islands. Made in 1919, *Male and Female* is an early representative of a wave of Hollywood films set on tropical islands. As such, it offers a link to the discussion that is to follow. If there is a primal scene for the second chapter, it may well be the arrival of the *Dolphin* in the Tuamotu Islands and Tahiti in June 1767 after weeks of crossing the open Pacific. Captained by Samuel Wallis, the *Dolphin* was, as far as we know, the first European ship to reach Tahiti. This and subsequent voyages had a profound impact on the Western imaginary, shaping our fantasies of islands to the present day. It is to these islands in the Pacific that we shall now direct our gaze.

| 2 |

Islands on the Horizon

The Camera at the Borders of the Tropical Island

> It is the realisation of Arcadia, or what we had been accustomed to suppose had existence only in poetic imagination—the golden age; all living as one family, a commonwealth of brothers and sisters....
> Add to this ... their practical morality and strong sense of religion ... warm loyalty to their queen and attachment to the mother country; their only anxiety being the smallness of their island.
>
> (Walter Brodie, *Pitcairn's Island*, 1851, 32)

> Pitcairn seems to confirm Golding's dark vision. Like his unnamed island, it was a social laboratory, but a real one—the site of a unique experiment thrown up by a confluence of historical events. Put fifteen men, twelve women, and a baby on a rock, leave them alone for 200 years, then take off the lid.... Tiny, sealed, and cut off from the outside word: these are the perfect conditions for a *Lord of the Flies* scenario.
>
> (Kathy Marks, *Lost Paradise*, 2009, 272)

Reading the Pacific Island through Myth: The Case of Pitcairn

It was in January 1790 that a group consisting of nine British mutineers, six Polynesian men, twelve Polynesian women, and a baby arrived on Pitcairn Island under the leadership of Fletcher Christian, former mate of the *Bounty* under Lieutenant William Bligh. Two years

The Aesthetics of Island Space: Perception, Ideology, Geopoetics. Johannes Riquet, Oxford University Press (2019). © Johannes Riquet.
DOI: 10.1093/oso/9780198832409.001.0001

earlier, the *Bounty* crew had embarked enthusiastically on a voyage whose aim was to transport breadfruit trees from Tahiti to the West Indies to provide cheap food for slaves. The voyage was tightly bound up with the period's economic optimism and spirit of discovery, the expansion of the British Empire, and the eighteenth-century confrontation with racial otherness in the Pacific. The men were never to see their native lands again. Most of them were not to live very long, either. Within ten years of arriving on Pitcairn, the mutineers and the Polynesian men would murder each other; when Edward Young died from old age in 1800, he was the first of the mutineers to die a natural death, leaving John Adams the only surviving mutineer on Pitcairn, surrounded by nine Tahitian women, an eleven-year old girl, and twenty-three children born on the island. Until 1808, the settlement remained hidden from the world, when the island was rediscovered by the American sealing ship *Topaz*, captained by Mayhew Folger. The descendants of the mutineers and the Polynesian women have lived on Pitcairn Island to this day. The island has, at different periods of its history, entertained more or less intensive links with the outside world, but has been essentially remote and disconnected—until very recently: in 1999, a thirteen-year-old Pitcairn girl told a British policewoman who was staying on the island that she had been the repeated victim of sexual abuse. Within a few years, investigators unearthed a sexual abuse scandal that went back at least to the 1960s (possibly much further) and involved almost half of the male adult population and most of the island's young girls aged between ten and fifteen, sometimes younger.

The ensuing trials rapidly took centre stage in international news coverage. From afar, the world gazed at Pitcairn in horror and disbelief. While some newspapers and magazines rose to the defence of the accused men, others used titles like 'Island of the Damned', 'Trouble in Paradise' or 'Evil under the Sun: The Dark Side of the Pitcairn Island'. In her book *Lost Paradise* (2009), journalist Kathy Marks compared what had happened to William Golding's novel *Lord of the Flies* (1954, second quote above). The structure of the comparison shares an important point with the very different vision of Arcadian bliss expressed in the account of Walter Brodie, an Englishman who was stranded on Pitcairn for two weeks in 1850 (first quote above). While their statements are diametrically opposed, both Brodie and Marks evaluate Pitcairn after a detour, reading the island through myth. Their narratives become retellings of others: in Brodie's case, Pitcairn figures as Arcadia (and, implicitly, utopia) and is associated with the golden-age fantasies of pastoral harmony and human perfection that had high currency when Europeans started exploring the Pacific in the sixteenth century. For Marks, Pitcairn is associated with Golding's Freudian island fable of human evil. In both cases, the island is made to illustrate a mythic truth about 'human nature'. This is in line with K. R. Howe's claim that Pacific islands have functioned as 'allegorical sites' (2000, 11) ever since they were 'discovered' by Europeans:

> I suggest that all Pacific history, old and new, is an ongoing morality tale, fundamentally about the idea of Western civilization, its perceived rise and fall, its fears and triumphs, and its creation of a Pacific other onto which are projected and tested the West's various priorities and expectations. (3–4)

In Howe's view, Pacific islands were 'as much a rhetorical device, an intellectual artifact, as ... a physical or cultural location' (2) for European discoverers and travellers. Both Brodie and Marks tapped into a cultural discourse that was already established in the sixteenth century and in full swing when Bligh embarked on his voyage in 1787.

If early accounts of Pacific islands were dominated by visions of paradise and golden-age fantasies, the nineteenth century saw the rise of a different Pacific island narrative, one that spoke to fears of cultural degeneration and, at worst, the potential extinction of (Western) civilization. As Howe points out, these anxieties were related to an increasingly widespread opinion that 'culture was overdetermined by nature' (35), propagated by Kantian idealism, the theories of Karl Ritter and Alexander von Humboldt, and later bolstered by the evolutionary theories of Lamarck and Darwin: 'The added element of chance suggested that there was no certainty, *anywhere*, that "civilized" peoples might remain in control' (37; emphasis original). While the fantasies of Arcadia never disappeared, they were now supplemented by nightmarish visions of disaster and disease. Writing in 2009, Kathy Marks invented the association of a Pacific island with human degeneracy as little as Walter Brodie had invented its association with the golden age 160 years earlier. Pitcairn had been consistently associated with paradise since Mayhew Folger discovered the settlement in 1808, as his friend Amasa Delano's account makes clear: 'It reminded him of

Paradise, as he said, more than any effort of poetry or the imagination'
(1817, 144). The terms are almost the same as Brodie's: in both texts,
Pitcairn is explicitly associated with poetic fantasies. If unwittingly, the
texts point to the imaginary core of their visions. A zealously religious
model community of converted sinners, living without crime, in harmony with nature and each other: this was the representation of
Pitcairn the first visitors brought back to the world, which changed
little over the next 200 years.

In her travelogue entitled *Serpent in Paradise*, British writer Dea
Birkett, who spent four months on Pitcairn in 1991, begins by describ-
ing her own infatuation with the island. Reading her way through
Pitcairn literature, she found that

> [i]n whichever century the title I chose had been written, it told me
> the same appealing story:... While the rest of the world suffered
> revolutions, Pitcairn was unchanging. It was comforting to know
> that... there was always the constant rock of Pitcairn, harboring
> our hopes. Somewhere, far away, the garden of Eden flourished.
>
> (1997, 15–16)

Birkett's travelogue is keenly alert to the mechanisms of projection at
work in the construction of the Pacific island: 'An island, to be perfect,
to be paradise, ought to be empty.... Everything about an island
suggests a complete and private world, upon which you can make
your mark' (15). Birkett thus reaches the conclusion that the resilience
of Pitcairn as a desirable space ultimately resides in its character as a
pure idea: 'The fantastical tale of the mutiny of the *Bounty* and the
discovery of Pitcairn fulfilled our longing for perfection like no other
before it. Pitcairn soon became our island, everyone's island, anyone's
island' (15). In the account that follows, Birkett portrays her voyage to
Pitcairn as a disillusioning experience, a fall from imaginary paradise:
'We all hold a place within our hearts—a perfect place—which is in the
shape of an island.... My mistake was to go there.... By going to
Pitcairn, I had vanquished the perfect place within myself' (294).
When the sexual abuse scandal took the world by surprise a few years
after the publication of Birkett's book, reactions all over the world were
strong, but many of them were unexpected: 'Almost every news report
reproduced the Pitcairners' claims of a culture of underage sex, and a
plot by Britain to shut down the island. It was the mutineers'

descendants versus the big bad colonial power' (Marks 2009, 68). 'Experts' on Pitcairn such as Dr Herbert Ford, director of the *Pitcairn Islands Study Center* based in California, and communities such as the web forum *Friends of Pitcairn* and the international Pitcairn Islands Study Group, which publishes the quarterly *Pitcairn Log*, expressed their anger about what they perceived as a conspiracy against the island. These reactions betray a disillusionment like Birkett's; the real scandal of Pitcairn Island was not the sexual abuse scandal, but the shattering of the paradise myth of the island. In an article written in 2004, the year of the island trials, Birkett expresses the same notion:

> More than 200 years have passed since Fletcher Christian and his
> followers settled on this lonely speck of volcanic rock in the South
> Pacific, hoping to create a society free from any outside interference.
> This week, their dream of an unspoilt Eden—of simplicity, equality
> and perfect liberty—which has been reinforced over the years by
> countless books and by four Hollywood films, will be put on trial.
>
> (2004, par. 3)

For Birkett, then, what was really on trial in the improvised court room was not the sexual offenders, but a 200-year-old and very tenacious Pacific island myth.

What makes the case of Pitcairn so complex and revealing is that it is not just any Pacific island. When the settlement was discovered by Folger in 1808, the Pitcairners were doubly other: descended from Polynesian women and (mostly) British men, they embodied *both* the racial other and the other within the self; in the eighteenth century, mutiny was considered a threat to the Crown itself (cf. Dening 1992, 44). In following Fletcher Christian, the sailors had become outlaws, ranking on the same level as pirates (a term that was often used to describe them). Fletcher Christian knew that he would never again be able to resume life in England. When the group left Tahiti in the night of 22 September 1789, they left never to return. Christian was looking for an out-of-the-way and uninhabited island that would never be discovered. This was no easy task: between 3000 and 1000 BP, Polynesians had settled or visited practically every island even in the most remote corners of the ocean. They had originally come from Southeast Asia and, to simplify matters, gradually moved east, travelling hundreds of kilometres in canoes to reach ever more distant islands (Howe 1984, 3–68).

There was nowhere new for the mutineers to go; in their search for an island, they followed in the wake of both the seafaring peoples of the Pacific and the early European discoverers. It was in a copy of John Hawkesworth's popular account of the voyages of Byron, Wallis, Carteret, and Cook that Christian read about Pitcairn Island, which had been discovered by a midshipman named Pitcairn on Carteret's *Swallow*: 'I would have landed upon it, but the surf, which at this season broke upon it with great violence, rendered it impossible' (qtd. in Delano 1817, 135). It was Pitcairn's apparent inaccessibility that attracted Christian to the island. What the mutineers needed was an impossibility: an island so inaccessible that it could not be reached in the first place. The mutineers symbolically enacted their disconnection from the world by running the *Bounty* ashore and setting fire to it upon reaching Pitcairn. A conventional landing was, physically and symbolically, not an option.

In an article on the first encounters with the Pitcairners by British and American ships, Smith reflects on the symbolic geography of islands. She distinguishes between the spaces of the sea, the harbour, the beach, and the interior, arguing that accounts of island encounters tend to magnify the importance of the liminal spaces between sea and land by 'metaphoris[ing] the psychologies of arrival and departure more explicitly than do descriptions of cross-cultural contact in continental settings' (2003, 116). For Smith, the 'series of explicit crossings, staged traversals of distinct media: water, sand, land' (116) are both literal and metaphorical; crossing the beach of an island also means entering—and to some degree interacting or interfering with—a different culture. The notion of the island as both physical site and metaphorical location has been developed by historical anthropologist Greg Dening. Dening puts forward the thesis that history—Pacific history, anyway—is made on beaches, those 'marginal spaces in between land and sea... where everything is relativised a little, turned around, where tradition is as much invented as handed down, where otherness is both a new discovery and a reflection of something old' (1992, 177). For Dening, the beach is an intermediary zone where cultural contact is both enacted and metaphorized.[1] Mutual (mis)understanding and

---

[1] Dening's model is related to Richard White's notion of the *middle ground* as a zone where two cultural systems overlap, mix, and blend (1991).

(mis)interpretation in the in-between zone are central to Dening's models of culture and intercultural contact:

> A beach from the sea, from a ship, from a camera lens is full of fiction. The beach itself, however, is a much more marginal space where neither otherness nor familiarity holds sway, where there is much invention and blending of old and new. Tahitian beaches were special places of invention and discovery. (1992, 179)

In a literal sense, Dening's 'camera lens' refers to the fact that the beach of Tahiti's Matavai Bay was artificially produced for the 1962 Hollywood film *Mutiny on the Bounty*: while the actual beach is black, white sand was transported to the South Pacific all the way from New Jersey (Dening 1992, 179). Figuratively, however, Dening alludes to a larger phenomenon: 'The French had seen the whole island of Tahiti as New Cythera—Venus' birthplace. And the English, eyes blinkered by classical aesthetics, had seen Apollo and Hercules' (179). Looking at the beach from shipboard, Polynesians and Europeans gazed at each other in the 'titillation of a very mutual scopophilia' (Smith 2003, 117). A kind of cinematic fantasy was involved in the Europeans', and later the Americans', gaze at the beaches of South Sea islands. Crossing the beach meant entering an uncertain realm part reality, part fiction, and always potentially subject to effects of vision and processes of revision.

The problem with Pitcairn was that it had no beach. The whole point of Pitcairn was to prevent any exchange across its beach from taking place. When exchange, albeit rarely, eventually did take place, Pitcairn was immediately transformed into myth. Arguably, the visitors that carried this mythical image into the world, often having spent only a few hours or days on the island, never really stopped looking at Pitcairn through a camera lens. Pitcairn soon became one of the most fantasized-about of all Pacific islands, and its mythical image would prove extremely resilient. At the 2012 Bounty-Pitcairn conference in Angwin, CA, organized by the Pitcairn Islands Study Group and uniting ninety-five Pitcairn fans, among them philatelists and well-known linguistics professor Peter Mühlhäusler, the sexual abuse scandal was hardly even referred to, and the old mythologizing continued as if nothing had happened: 'Over 200 attendees felt the magic at Bounty-Pitcairn Conference 2012', wrote the *Pitcairn Log*. 'I've always had a fascination with faraway places, and I don't think you can get any farther away than Pitcairn,' were some of the first words in moderator Barbara Stein's introductory talk; and even Jacqui Christian, one of the victims who had spoken out in the Pitcairn trials, talked about her idyllic childhood of playing under the banyan trees and swimming in the surf.[2]

Islands in the American Imaginary: Tourism, Cinema, Fantasy

Pitcairn is not the only Pacific island invested with fantasies of paradise. One need only open any travel brochure to see that South Sea island fantasies of pristine beaches, coconut trees, and vast expanses of water still have high currency. If Fletcher Christian had a vision of Pitcairn as a place to escape to through reading Hawkesworth's hugely popular *Voyages*, the modern-day equivalent of those early journals are internet travelogues and travel brochures eagerly consumed by prospective tourists. David Vann's novel *Caribou Island* (2011) puts this modern-day island fantasy to striking use. The novel is about a couple trying to rebuild their failed lives and marriage by building a cabin on an island in Alaska, but the island turns into a nightmarish site as the woman first kills her husband and then herself. The novel ends with the daughter approaching the island, ignorant of what has happened. On the boat, she fantasizes about her wedding on a Hawaiian island although the relationship with her future husband is doomed to fail: 'A green, sunny bluff over blue ocean far away from here.... Walking the beach in her wedding dress, holding Jim's arm, her parents and Mark following behind... . A place carefree, a day she had dreamed of all her life, the beginning, finally' (293). As we learn earlier, Rhoda's dream is nourished by travel brochures promising Pacific bliss: '*As the sun kisses the horizon and you are bathed in golden light, your vows are*

---

[2] Christian's talk is entitled 'Pitcairn Islands: Back to the Future' (21 August 2012) and is available online at <www.youtube.com/watch?v=VKrol9oX530.>

lifted by eternal trade winds and scattered over a million miles of Pacific' (138; italics original). At the end of the novel, this fantasy reemerges, but its inaccessibility is even more pronounced in the ironic juxtaposition with the grim reality awaiting Rhoda: approaching a dismal island, she dreams of another, bright island, which provides a unifying fantasy in the face of a disintegrating family and death. Crucially, Rhoda is still at a certain distance from the island. Approaching its border, she cannot yet *see* beyond it in detail; the border becomes an aesthetic zone activating projective fantasies that mask a darker reality.

The South Sea island fantasy of *Caribou Island* is connected to an aesthetic tradition that goes back to the eighteenth-century accounts of European explorers in the Pacific and was adapted to specific American contexts by explorers, travellers, novelists, and filmmakers in the nineteenth and early twentieth centuries. In the 1920s and 1930s, American representations of South Sea islands gained new currency as American tourists trooped to the more and more accessible South Seas: 'The extreme popularity of the South Seas, which grows like a snowball from month to month, has, according to certain eminent authorities, brought the danger of congestion to those islands' (*The New York Times*, 21 August 1921). This development coincided with an explosion of travel accounts, novels, and films about South Sea islands. The historical reasons for this 'general exodus to Tahiti', as the same *New York Times* (*NYT*) article called it, were manifold. One of them was an escapist fantasy after the unsettling experience of the First World War; contemporary voices said that the South Sea islands were 'delightfully far removed from the atmosphere and the scene of the great war' (*NYT*, 25 April 1920). Jeffrey Geiger argues that the post-war period was a 'time of profound, collective self-interrogation for Europe and the US. In the wake of a brutal war, civilization seemed to signify the opposite of progress' (2007, 69). He goes on to argue that social changes like urbanization, fast transport, and modern communication also created a reaction against the perceived ills of civilization and a nostalgic desire for closer links to nature and a simpler way of life. The pervasive textual and cinematic fantasy of the South Sea island offered to fulfil these desires. A letter to the editor published in *The New York Times* in 1926 reads as follows:

South Sea Idyl.

To the Editor of the New York Times:

He was alone. He stepped softly to the porthole and peered out. All was quiet. An inky blackness met his gaze. As he strained his eyes for the first glimpse of light his patience was rewarded. Slowly a faint glow appeared directly in front of him. Gradually it spread and the sun crept over an island that seemed to be about two miles ahead.

Dawn in the tropics. He could almost hear the gentle wash of the waves on the distant beach. He had written so much of the South Sea Islands—and he knew dramaturgy. He watched intently for a few moments, then heaved a sigh of relief.

Everything was all right. Suddenly he cursed and turned to the machine at his side. The picture was out of frame again.

He was the operator in a movie theatre. (25 March 1926)

By tricking the reader into believing that it describes somebody's vision of a real island in the South Seas, the text points towards the visual dimension of popular conceptions of South Sea islands as aestheticized projections, cinematic or otherwise. Again, the distance from the island is crucial. The distance from boat to island is equated with the distance to the film screen; the gaze through the porthole is the gaze through the projectionist's own 'porthole', linked to the gaze through the lens of a camera that mediates perception. The island thus emerges as an initially uncertain visual phenomenon that gradually takes shape in front of the camera and the mind's eye; the 'dawn in the tropics' is associated with the light of film itself.

A similar fantasy appears in Frank Capra's screwball comedy *It Happened One Night* (1934). A rich girl escapes from her father and ends up travelling with a journalist; at nights, he erects a screen to divide the room for propriety. Towards the end of the film, the girl asks him about his ideas on love, which he answers with an idealized island vision. Crucially, he states that he '*saw* an island in the Pacific once' (my emphasis), not that he ever was on one, which makes it quite likely that he saw the island in a movie theatre. His vision is vague and generic but marks a turning point in the film: the girl crosses the boundary erected between them. The film was made shortly before the enforcement of the Motion Picture Production Code; it is clear what particular boundary is here metaphorically being crossed. The island fantasy is thus linked to illicit sexual desire, signalled by the violation of the 180-degree rule. This link had played an important role since the accounts of Polynesian sexual licence by explorers like Wallis, Bougainville, and Cook.[3]

As I will demonstrate, the mediation of perception across the border of the island has been a central part of Western island representations ever since the eighteenth-century accounts of European explorers in the Pacific. It finds both its epitome and transformation in Hollywood's island fantasies in the early twentieth century, surviving to the present day in the mythical accounts of Pitcairn and other tropical islands. My argument is theoretically informed by Howe's claim that Pacific islands have functioned as 'rhetorical devices' in the Western imagination (1), and Dennis Porter's analysis of the ways in which travel writing is haunted by the voices of previous travellers. In what follows, I will examine how a highly aestheticized image of the tropical island travelled from the eighteenth-century Pacific journals through a plethora of nineteenth-century texts into the cultural imaginary of the United States in the early twentieth century. The main part of this chapter will be devoted to three films which centre around imaginary tropical islands, and the different ways in which they negotiate the cinematic gaze towards the island: *White Shadows in the South Seas* (1928), *The Hurricane* (1937), and, finally, *King Kong* (1933).

Islands on the Horizon: The Journals of the Early Explorers in the Pacific

When HMS *Dolphin*, commanded by Samuel Wallis, emerged from the Straits of Magellan and headed for the open waters of the Pacific on 12 April 1767, it entered an area of the globe barely known to Europeans despite the fact that the Spaniards, most notably Pedro Fernandes de Queirós, had navigated these waters almost 200 years earlier. For weeks, Wallis and the crew sailed across wide expanses of water without knowing when and where they would encounter land. The journal of the *Dolphin*'s

---

[3] The escapist fantasy of the journalist's island vision is characteristic of Depression-era screwball comedies.

master, George Robertson, foregrounds this uncertainty: in a period in which very little happened at all, minor events such as sightings of flying fish, birds, or seaweed took on increased significance in potentially pointing to land and triggering hopes. The longer the journey continued, the more intense the hopes, fears, and wishes of the sailors became. In a revealing passage, Robertson describes their yearning for land:

> [A]bout Noon some of our Men Supposed they saw land but was Mistaken—at this time we was all Earnestly wishing to fall in with some well Inhabited Country...and Every man wishd to find what he liked most, some wanted to find Good Beef, others Sheep or Hogs...Oythers that was hearty and well wished for wild Game, Gold, Silver, Diamonds Pearls & some for fine young Girls. (1948, 113)

The account of the erroneous sighting of land is here directly followed by a description of the various fantasies the sailors projected on the horizon. The frustration of perception is replaced by an imaginary gaze, and the apparent sighting of land itself takes on the status of a mirage produced partly by the desire to see itself. Crucially, the fantasies commonly associated with the European explorers of the Pacific—fantasies of fertility, abundant riches, and sexual fulfilment—emerge even before the first landfall, which corroborates Howe's point that these were a 'rerun of a very old Western theme' (2000, 14); as he points out, these visions of paradise go back to early Indo-European golden-age fantasies present in Indian mythology, Greek myths of Arcadia and Elysium, and the Judeo-Christian myth of the Garden of Eden (2000, 8–14). In Robertson's diary, these fantasies are activated at the very moment when the possibility of land beyond the horizon becomes possible, but when perception is still uncertain. In his philosophical treatise on the horizon, Didier Maleuvre discusses the importance of this zone 'where perception fades off' (2011, 2) in Western cultural history. Part of the fascination of the early Pacific journals resides in the entanglement of perception, expectation, and imagination that marks these journeys as both intense and profoundly uncertain visual experiences. Islands occupy a central role in this, and the most vibrant and spectacular parts of the journals are often those that describe them from the water, from a distance.

There is an intimate connection between the perceptual uncertainties arising when it is not clear whether a blurry patch on the horizon consists of clouds or of solid land, and the projective investment in islands whose existence is already established. The Pacific journals abound in the former; both low-lying coral islands (like the Tuamotu Archipelago) and high volcanic islands (such as Tahiti) are known for visually deceiving sailors, and the countless mythical or phantom islands appearing in explorers' accounts and contemporary maps played their part in producing uncertainty and structuring perception. In Robertson's journal, the first appearance of Tahiti is marked by uncertainty: '... we saw the Appearance of a very high land to the Southward but the weather being so thick and hazy we could not see it plain Enough to know it for certain' (130). As the existence of the land is ascertained, the sailors are 'fild ... with the greatest hopes Imaginable' (135), but their perception is simultaneously mediated by myth and desire: 'we now suposed we saw the long wishd for Southern Countinent, wich has been often talkd of, but neaver before seen by any Europeans' (135). A similar uncertainty relating to the first sighting of Tahiti is reported by Sir Joseph Banks, naturalist on board James Cook's *Endeavour*, which entered the South Pacific two years after Wallis in 1769: 'At this time it remain in dispute whether what had been so long seen to the Westward was realy land or only vapours' (2006, 69). Not having perceived any land himself, Banks is forced to admit in the next day's entry that the more numerous 'non-seers' (69) had been wrong: 'I found the fault was in our eyes yesterday' (69). Conversely, Louis-Antoine de Bougainville describes several apparent sightings of islands that turned out to be a mere 'land of clouds' (2002, 85) in his *Pacific Journal*, which details his voyage from 1767 to 1768.

The initial descriptions of islands viewed from the water, across a distance that is cultural as much as physical, bespeak an even more pronounced epistemological uncertainty. Discussing the ways in which Western perceptions of Pacific islands have always been mediated by specific 'cultural lenses' (Howe 2000, 1), Howe begins by asking a question: 'How do we know what we see?' (1). In many ways, the early Pacific journals pose the same question. When Banks describes the first island of the Tuamotu Archipelago in the *Endeavour Journal*, he pictures the islanders and the island itself:

> They *appeard to us through our glasses* to be tall and to have very large heads or *possibly* much hair upon them.... Under the shade of

> these [palms] were the houses of the natives in places cleard of all
> underwood so that pleasanter groves can not be imagind, *at least so*
> *they appeard to us whose eyes had so long been unus'd* to any other
> objects than water and sky. (2006, 65; my emphasis)

Banks stresses the mediation of perception by drawing attention to
the telescopes through which the islanders were viewed. He demonstrates considerable awareness of the distortions potentially arising
from this gaze by using words like 'appeard' and 'possibly'. The
second part of the passage formulates a vision of Arcadian happiness,
but is immediately followed by a qualifying remark that stresses the
potential unreliability of the observers' eyes by admitting the possibility of their gaze being distorted by desire. Banks expresses a caution
about optical *and* cultural lenses, forging a link between the two,
admitting the *Endeavour* to be—in more than one sense—'at so
great a distance that all must be conjecture' (66), to borrow a phrase
from his description of the second island encountered in the Tuamotu
Archipelago.

Banks also demonstrates awareness of an effect commonly encountered in South Sea accounts that Porter terms a 'sense of belatedness in
a traveler, especially a traveler who decides to give a written account of
his travels' (1991, 12). Porter argues that 'there is a sense of déjà vu that
is to be understood in part through the theory of the uncanny' (12) and
that manifests itself as an 'anxiety of travel writing' (12): a sense of
inevitably following in the footsteps of previous travellers that inform
and haunt the traveller's own writing. Banks strikingly expresses this
when he describes the *Endeavour*'s arrival on the Australian east coast
on 22 April 1770:

> In the morn we stood in with the land near enough to discern 5
> people who appeard through our glasses to be enormously black: so
> far did the prejudices which we had built on Dampiers account
> influence us that we fancied we could see their Colour when we
> could scarce distinguish whether or not they were men. (2006, 260)

Again, Banks describes a doubly mediated gaze: the gaze through the
telescopes is itself shaped by previous written accounts. The explorers
are described as seeing through their predecessors' eyes, with all the
implications of racial inferiority the reference to blackness would have
carried in contemporary discourse. Even more striking, however, is

Banks's reflection on this circumstance: the use of the word 'prejudice' and the following comment on the inadequacy of their vision testify to a critical distance of the writing self from the observing self.

The scene just discussed initiated a long and intense exchange of gazes between the sailors of the *Endeavour* and the locals on shore that went on for almost a week. The early Pacific journals are full of such exchanges: long passages are devoted to the careful scanning of unknown coasts, which sometimes went on for days before landing, and the texts bespeak a heightened anxiety and a reluctance to cross the border of the island or of the ship on both sides. Before the *Dolphin* landed in Matavai Bay on 26 June 1767 'to take possession of this Beautyfull Island' (Robertson 1948, 159), Wallis and his crew slowly sailed along the shore of Tahiti, observing and speculating about the Tahitians, who in turn are described by Robertson as lined up on the shore to observe the English discovers, circling the ship in their canoes as cautiously as Wallis circled the island (135–59). This exchange of gazes was occasionally interrupted by trading activities, and on two occasions by skirmishes on water. In the first instance, a Tahitian was shot as two canoes appeared 'fully resolved to board [them]' (145); the second time, the Englishmen opened fire after the Tahitians had started a surprise attack by throwing stones at the *Dolphin*. Whatever the exact reasons for the skirmishes—mutual misunderstanding partly seems to account for it—they mark a violent infringement of the border as stones and guns replace gazes. For Smith, 'the strongest trope of the harbour welcome as described in Pacific exploration literature is incomprehension. . . . Europeans and Polynesians hold each other during arrival scenes in island harbours, bays and anchorages in the equilibrium of mutual regard' (2003, 117). James Cook's journal provides similar instances of this probing gaze: '. . . several of the Natives came off to us in their Canoes, but more to look at us then any thing else we could not prevail with any of them to come on board . . .' (1955, 73). The two outbreaks of violence between the crew of Wallis's *Dolphin* and the Tahitians broke this equilibrium as boundaries were crossed by stones and gunshots; it may be no coincidence that the second, more momentous skirmish was almost directly followed by preparations for landing.

Landing was followed by a declaration of peace on the part of the Tahitians, yet the crossing of the island's border was immediately followed by the establishment of a new border: setting up camp on one side of the river, the British carefully policed its crossing. Thus, initially only very few Tahitians were allowed to cross the river for trading purposes. The physical features of island geography thus take on symbolic dimensions as natural border zones are turned into symbolic borders across which intercultural contact is negotiated. Banks even describes the establishment of a boundary that is purely symbolic: while the British set up camp on shore, he 'drew a line before them with the butt end of [his] musquet and made signs to them to set down without it' (2006, 73).

American Re-vision of the Island: From David Porter to 1920s Hollywood Cinema

The same symbolic action is described in the journal of Captain David Porter, who was sent to the Pacific by the US government from 1812 to 1814 to 'annoy the enemy' (Porter 1822, 1), i.e. the British, during the War of 1812. Porter spent several months on the island of Nukuhiva in the Marquesas Islands, where he fought two wars with island tribes. Between the wars, Porter describes examining the coast west of the village erected for the Americans by the islanders:

> On landing, many of the natives came to the beach, who seemed disposed to treat us in the most friendly manner; but apprehensive of being troubled by their numbers, I drew a line in the sand, at some distance about the boats, and informed them they were *tabooed*.
>
> (82; emphasis original)

Yet if the journals of Robertson and Banks oscillate, often self-critically, between conflicting perceptions and assessments of the Pacific islands and their inhabitants, Porter's narrative is more closed. Suspicion is here constitutive, and the gradually attained peace with all the island tribes as described by Porter is a peace based on demonstrations of military power. While Porter often talks of the islanders in admiring terms and describes intimate friendships, his text is structured by deep-seated distrust and a conviction that the islanders would turn against the Americans should their superiority be questioned. In a sense, then, Porter never really crosses the border of the island and the line in the sand. The only way he crosses over into the cultural space of the island is by destroying it, most notably in his devastation of the Typee valley; he violently turns the island into an American space. This is in line with a development in which 'the Pacific islands and their peoples by definition became that dangerous or unpleasant other' in the nineteenth century, regarded 'with fear and loathing' by the West as the latter strove to assume economic and political control of the region (Howe 2000, 15).

Of course, this view represents a generalization and individual accounts often resist easy categorization. It also does not follow that visions of paradise had disappeared from accounts of Pacific islands. Yet by the time American vessels entered the Pacific for military purposes and for reasons of discovery and commercial exploitation, these visions had changed. Paradise found had turned into paradise lost (cf. Howe 2000, 13–21; Lyons 2006; Geiger 2007). The following excerpt is taken from Benjamin Morrell's fanciful *Narrative of Four Voyages*, in which he describes his explorations and commercial ventures from 1822 to 1831:

> [W]e counted more than seventy islands, of different sizes, situated within its circle, the appearance of which was truly paradisiacal and delightful. It was realizing, as far as the eye could judge, all that poets have dreamed of 'happy isles,' fairyland, &c.... But I could not rest contented with merely viewing these happy isles at a distance, shut out, as it were, by an envious wall impassable as adamant. (1832, 379)

This first description of a group of islands named 'Bergh's Group'[4] by Morrell in 1830 picks up on the notion of paradise, but the entire account is strangely distanced, even when Morrell describes entering the reef. As Morrell himself points out, this is paradise viewed from a distance, and the wall of adamant remains truly impassable; when Morrell records his second voyage to Bergh's Group, he describes leaving the island in haste after a stay of three days when the Americans began to suspect 'treachery and impending hostilities' (434).

---

[4] The islands of Morrell's 'Bergh's Group' are probably the Chuuk Islands in Micronesia.

The disillusioning experience of approaching a Pacific island is thematized even more directly in Charles Wilkes's account of the United States Exploring Expedition (1838–42), the first large-scale US voyage of discovery and scientific exploration to the South Seas and the Southern Ocean:

> The landing on a coral island effectually does away with all the preconceived notions of its beauty, and any previous ideas formed in its favor are immediately put to flight. That verdure which seemed from a distant view to carpet the whole island, was in reality but a few patches of wiry grass.... (1851, 127)

Referring to the Tuamotu Archipelago, Wilkes here portrays the aestheticized look at the South Sea island as a fallible vision emerging from 'preconceived notions'; this effect of seeing structured by expectation is said to occur only if the beholder is at a distance. When describing the arrival in Tahiti, Wilkes is disillusioned even with the distanced view:

> The beauty of the distant view of Tahiti has been celebrated by all navigators, but I must confess that it disappointed me. The entire outline of the island was visible for too short a time, and at too great distance to permit its boasted features to be distinctly seen.
>
> (1851, 142)

In both passages, Wilkes engages in a re-vision of the Pacific island, contesting his predecessors' gaze, which may be motivated by a desire to set himself apart from the British discoverers to establish an original American gaze.

As discussed initially, however, it was in American cinema of the 1920s that the illusory visions of the Pacific criticized by Wilkes reemerged at full tilt, coinciding with the rise of South Sea tourism. And of course these visions, though reformulated and transformed, had never disappeared. I am interested in the creation of the South Sea island-image by a complex ideological apparatus: explorers' accounts, paintings, tourist ads, travelogues, films, and newspaper articles all contributed to the production of a particular vision of island space (cf. Lefebvre 1991). The 'American Pacific archive', so termed by Paul Lyons, helped produce this space: a large body of accounts of the Pacific that formed a textual universe of its own. Dennis Porter's claim that travel writing is characterized by a textual haunting where writers posit themselves as retracing their predecessors' footsteps through whose eyes they view the islands, if only to assert their own re-vision, is possibly even more valid for this 'archive' than in the case of their British predecessors; one *NYT* review of a travelogue points out that despite 'individual coloring...even here the reader is haunted by the memory of Robert Louis Stevenson's poignant descriptions' (16 November 1930).

Lyons and Miriam Kahn argue that these aestheticized accounts also served to mask the realities of US imperialist expansion (Lyons 2006, 27; Kahn 2011, 9–17). As John R. Eperjesi points out, US imperial activity already played a crucial role throughout the nineteenth century as Pacific islands were used as refuelling and repair stations for the fur trade to China and whaling ships, and as trading centres in their own right as Americans began to exploit the islands for products such as bêche-de-mer, sandalwood, and copra (2005, 25–57). In the late nine-teenth century, American imperialism took a turn towards more direct control, beginning with the annexation of Hawai'i in 1898 and the American–Filipino War shortly after. Notions of the Pacific as an extension of the Western frontier became widespread, and the expan-sion into the Pacific was linked with myths of American exceptionalism and manifest destiny (cf. Eperjesi 25–57; Lyons 2006, 24–34); as late as 1931, a guidebook reviewed in the *NYT* referred to the South Seas as 'the last frontier' (18 October 1931). The South Sea craze of the early twentieth century partly masks these activities. A *Los Angeles Times* (*LAT*) article from 1925 entitled 'The Romance of the Island Pineapple' perfectly illustrates this mechanism: the article begins with an aesthetic vista positing an observer 'looking down at the incomparable scene spread beneath' (1 January 1925) in the typical manner of South Sea accounts. The view includes pineapple plantations, which triggers a description of the history of the pineapple industry developed by US entrepreneurs, described as 'men who had faith, courage and vision. Who says romance is dead in the islands of the Pacific?' In this way, economic activity is aestheticized and reinscribed as romance. By the 1930s, these images permeated everyday life to the extent that in 1935 a series of stamps was issued with titles like 'dancing girls', 'palm-fringed beaches', and 'cannibals' (*LAT*, 3 March 1935), and in 1937 the *LAT* advertised a lipstick 'in five new tropical shades as fascinating as the South Sea islands themselves' (*LAT*, 10 October 1937). Tourism and cinema were close allies in the promotion of these images and mutually propelled each other; it is no coincidence that during a visit to Los Angeles in 1929 Oscar G. Nordman, publisher of an American newspaper in Tahiti and president of the Pacific Tourist Bureau, was entertained in Hollywood by filmmakers whom he had met while they were shooting in Tahiti (*LAT*, 25 May 1929).

The Island as Image: *White Shadows in the South Seas* (1928)

Around the same time, MGM's *White Shadows in the South Seas* (1928), loosely based on Frederick O'Brien's bestseller travelogue of the same title and directed by W. S. Van Dyke and Robert Flaherty, was released.[5] The film opens with a series of almost still images displaying classic South Sea island iconography: an island seen from above (Figure 2.1); another high-angle, but closer shot of an island shore; a shot of an islander landing on a beach in his canoe, taken from the beach and framed by a palm tree; and finally, an eye-level shot of an island taken from the water. The shots are interrupted by intertitles describing the islands as '"for happy centuries the last remnant of an earthly paradise...', 'Islets "fresh from the touch of God"', and finally 'Memories that lingered from the Morning of Creation.' The images are closely related to the aestheticized island vistas conveyed in the newspaper article discussed above, picture postcard views of Pacific islands, and trivia such as the 1935 stamp series. Such visual prologues were a stock feature of South Sea island films of the 1920s and 1930s. In King Vidor's *Bird of Paradise* (1932), these images even—rather unusually for the time—precede the credit sequence; in *Sinners in Paradise* (1938), the credits are superimposed on the images; in *Mr. Robinson Crusoe* (1932), the superimposed credits seem to be standing on a beach through the use of three-dimensional writing and shadows, before an intertitle, against the backdrop of an island vista, announces the same fantasy of prelapsarian bliss as *White Shadows*: 'From the time Adam and Eve were banished from the Garden of Eden, man has vainly

---

[5] The following pages develop an argument first outlined in Riquet (2018, 129–34).

FIGURE 2.1   Still from *White Shadows in the South Seas* (W. S. Van Dyke, USA 1928)

sought to find solace, comfort, and earthly pleasure in an artificial world of his own creation.'[6]

These images and the fantasies they transport are the direct descendants of the island visions in the explorers' accounts of the eighteenth and nineteenth centuries. Like the latter, they stand apart from the narrative that is to follow. They are decidedly non-narrative, emphasizing an abstract principle or ideal; they present an *idea* that the films then engage with in various ways. It is therefore significant that the island first emerges as a still or almost still image. As pure surface, the island vista opens up a space for aesthetic contemplation in which the island can be taken in at a glance, constituting a pure image in the double sense of being *purely* image and offering an image *of* purity, an aesthetic idea of perfection.

---

[6] For a detailed analysis of the spatial ideologies (de)constructed in the visual prologues of contemporary South Sea island films, see Riquet (2018).

The conjunction between image and idea(l) in the visual prologues of *White Shadows* and other films opens up a revealing network of semantic associations. Etymologically, the word *idea* entered the English language through Latin, which it had in turn entered from the Greek *idéa* (appearance, form, notion) through Platonic philosophy: as the *OED* tells us, in classical Latin *idea* meant 'eternal archetype'. Interestingly, the word also meant 'form, image, likeness' in postclassical Latin ('idea, n.' 2018), thus semantically looping back to its original Greek associations with both form and the visual. But *idéa* is not the only derivative of *idein* (to see). Two further nouns are directly linked to it, and both signify 'image': *eidos* and *eídolon*. The etymologically unrelated *eikón* also means 'image', but this is image as representation, resemblance. By contrast, *eidos* (appearance, species, form) is what appears before the eye, unmediated by representation, and is thus closely linked to *idéa*. Finally, *eídolon* developed the following significations in chronological order: 'appearance, phantom, unsubstantial form, image in water or a mirror, mental image, fancy, material image, or statue' ('idol, n.' 2018). In some of its original significations, then, *eídolon* is decidedly linked to illusion and insubstantiality. It is only in its later meanings that representation (or rather reflection) and, still later, physical form come into play. Thus, *eídolon* may be the purest image, its later associations with material shapes emerging out of a kernel of the immaterial: image and nothing else.

The island vistas in the prologue of *White Shadows* are *idéa* in both its original and philosophical meanings. As pure appearance and form, they constitute an aesthetic surface at the beginning of the film. As ideal form, they are linked to the Platonic *idéa*: they clearly do *not* depict the (imperfect, colonized) island where the narrative will begin. But they do not exactly represent the same island before the arrival of white traders, either: as the intertitles make clear, they constitute a timeless, eternal ideal, a generic island against the backdrop of which the diegetic islands will be measured. As *idéa*, they are not *eikón*: they do not belong to the order of representation. The images are also *eidos*, staging the act of seeing itself: the first shot of *White Shadows* begins with a fade-in, opening the field of vision from the centre of the image through the use of an iris diaphragm (common in early cinema); after about ten seconds, the image fades out in the same way. The shot thus imitates the opening and closing of a human eye. It comments on cinema as presenting a series of images appearing before the viewer's eye: *eidos*. As this is the first image of the film, the shot also refers to an original act of seeing. Significantly, the next two shots do not fade in and out in the same way, but the iris diaphragm is again used to fade out the last shot, marking the beginning of *idéa* as *eidos*, where perception itself is as fresh as the image of the ideal island. Most importantly, the island is also *eídolon* as 'image in water or a mirror'. This is most evident in the first shot, which shows an island that can be visually taken in its entirety, surrounded by the water within which its contours emerge. The generic island of the prologue is also *eídolon* in its very insubstantiality in relation to the diegesis of the film: as pure fantasy and ideal form, it exists only as an image. The film's trajectory thus resonates with the evolution of the various meanings of *eídolon*: in *White Shadows*, too, the island moves from an insubstantial image to a material space as it develops from the initial vista into a physical location for the film's narrative. For Jacques Lacan, the completeness experienced by the subject is *imaginary* because it manifests itself as an insubstantial image, hence Lacan's insistence on the Latin *imago* and its various associations both with the immaterial and with form (2001). The visual prologues of films like *White Shadows* offer ideal images of imaginary completeness and thus speak to a collective cultural fantasy that is articulated through an aesthetic experience of the island as pure image.

The ideological underpinnings of the film's investment in the imaginary become even more apparent if the opening images are considered in relation to the overall rhetoric of the film. The initial images are followed by another intertitle: 'But the white man, in his greedy trek across the planet, cast his withering shadow over these islands.... and the business of "civilizing" them to his interests began....' After this, we enter a fallen world of sickness, death, and debauchery where white pearl traders are ruthlessly exploiting a South Sea island. A disillusioned doctor, Matthew Lloyd, whom the island experience has turned into an unkempt drunkard, picks a quarrel with a particularly greedy trader and reproaches him for destroying the island culture. The trader has him placed on a schooner full of plague victims to get rid of him. After a stormy voyage, Lloyd is shipwrecked on an island that is the unspoilt home of islanders still unaware of white civilization. He becomes part of the idealized island society and involved with a girl, Fayaway, but has a weak moment of greed for pearls during which he makes a fire that attracts the ship of the same trader. Lloyd tries to prevent the white men's contact with the islanders, but fails and is killed in the attempt. The film ends with shots of the same white debauchery we saw on the first island at the beginning of the film. In effect, then, the central part of the film, which has been interpreted as a dream sequence (Geiger 176), actualizes the nostalgic vision conjured up in the prologue. What is initially presented to us as a vanished ideal and abstract idea thus receives a location in the diegesis of the film as Lloyd sails into a mythical past. But paradise is found only to be destroyed: the whole history of the West's discovery, exploitation, and colonization of the South Seas is repeated and condensed in the rediscovery and corruption of the film's second island. At the end of the film, nothing has effectively happened: the narrative cancels itself out and we return to the beginning. We shall return to the significance of this repetition, but for the moment let us note that the film both criticizes and participates in colonial ideology. While manifestly anti-colonial, it also represents islanders as passive victims, engaging in an essentializing fantasy of a 'myth of a people frozen in time' (Geiger 2007, 1).

Throughout the film, white men are the centre of action and transformation, and drive the narrative. The islanders have no agency; while the disappearance of their culture is lamented, it is also presented as doomed to die out. In this presentation of the islanders' inherent degeneracy and weakness, the film participates in a tradition that had its beginnings already in the time of the early discoveries, took shape in the nineteenth century, and reached its peak in the 1920s (Howe 2000, 43–6): the depiction of the South Seas as 'destined for disaster with the arrival of all-powerful, restless "civilization"' (Howe 43). Howe reads this 'fatal impact' view (46) as a projection of the West's own fears of extinction or degeneration in an alien environment onto island cultures, positing Western culture as naturally dominant and active even while romanticizing the islanders. In *White Shadows*, this gesture is evident in the long central part on the second island, which is essentially without narrative development. The only eruption of narrative occurs when the son of the chief almost dies at sea and is saved by Lloyd, but this episode attains its narrative impetus only through the intercession of the white man.

Otherwise, the central island episode takes the form of an ethnographic documentary recalling Flaherty's *Moana* (1926). *Moana* was the film of which John Grierson famously said that it had 'documentary value' (qtd. in Barsam 1988, 42), for the first time applying the word 'documentary' to a film. Flaherty, who had started his career as an 'explorer, mapmaker, and prospector' (Geiger 2007, 126), took his family to live on the Samoan island of Savai'i from 1923 to 1924 to shoot *Moana*. The film evokes 'nostalgia for untouched primitive life amidst natural surroundings' (Geiger 127) in the same way as *White Shadows*' central island episode. Purporting to give a faithful account of Samoan life, Flaherty staged his own idealized vision that was part reconstruction of customs that had been out of use for a long time, part Flaherty's invention altogether (cf. Barsam 1988, 36, 118). The ethnographic episode of *White Shadows* manifests the same 'taxidermic impulse' (121) Geiger sees at work in *Moana*. Here, too, the camera explores the island, the islanders, and their customs. Abandoning narrative altogether, the film indulges in close-ups of food preparation, courtship, and dancing; in the probing gaze of the ethnographer, the camera tilts and pans, tracks forward and sideways, as though caressing its subjects. While the camera is mobile, the subjects themselves are static. At best, they are given a kind of static mobility, repeating the same actions over and over again, as when a group of islanders is swiftly climbing coconut trees.

With this in mind, there is a perverse logic to the renewed corruption of the island paradise at the end of the film, which requires the unspoilt space of the island to be annihilated in order to make it available for aesthetic consumption again. The island is reappropriated for the Western cultural imaginary as it is turned back into the image of the visual prologue. When, in the final shot of the film, we see a distraught Fayaway, dressed in a Western gown and burying her face on the ground before the image is gradually veiled and then darkened altogether in a visualization of the film's 'white shadows', this is a metaphorical rendition of the death of the island culture. But this death is only the logical conclusion to what has been implicit in the film from the visual prologue to the islanders' passivity in the ethnographic part: the mythical island and its inhabitants are never more than a static, frozen image. The circular, self-cancelling logic of the film thus returns us to the initial island vistas; once again, the island exists only as a nostalgic fantasy. But now there is no need to show these images again: they have become firmly installed in the viewer's mind.

The near stillness of the initial island vistas in *White Shadows* associates them with photographs. Susan Sontag argues that photography partly emerged out of a nostalgic fantasy of preserving an idealized world in the face of rapid technological development and human-induced transformation of the planet and its landscapes (1977, 9). As nature increasingly develops from a space of danger and threat into a space changed and controlled by human activity, photography functions as an elegiac art as the camera replaces the gun, to which it is still metaphorically linked: 'When we are afraid, we shoot. But when we are nostalgic, we take pictures' (15). As already discussed, the 1920s and 1930s island craze in Hollywood cinema coincided with a wave of South Sea island tourism: the imaginative gaze of the films was closely connected to an emerging tourist gaze that, as Lyons argues, both masked and participated in US imperialist trajectories (27). For Robert Shepherd, South Sea islands functioned as 'ground-zero' in the search for and ideological construction of Eden in both tourism and the emerging discipline of anthropology (2012, 3).

Hollywood, tourism, and anthropology are thus conjoined in a visual and imaginary appropriation of South Sea islands, and the photographic gaze lies at the heart of this project: 'Finally, the most grandiose result of the photographic enterprise is to give us the sense that we can hold the whole world in our heads—as an anthology of images' (Sontag 1977, 3). For Sontag, 'aesthetic distance seems built into the very experience of looking at photographs' (21), which, for her, differ from moving images 'because they are a neat slice of time, not a flow' (17). This reading of the photographic image fits neatly into the argument that *White Shadows* begins with and works towards an aestheticization of the island, freezing it into an image to make it available as a Western fantasy; films like *White Shadows* indeed appropriate the island as an 'anthology of images'. For Sontag, '[t]he camera makes reality atomic, manageable, and opaque. It is a view of the world which denies interconnectedness, continuity...' (23). This notion of the atomic quality of the image resonates with *White Shadows'* freezing of the island: separate, immobile, the insular image is disconnected from the world; dead, but eternally available for aesthetic contemplation.

No one has theorized the relationship between photography and death more memorably than Roland Barthes in *Camera Lucida*. For Barthes, photography is a ghostly medium and every photograph a *memento mori* as it points to a moment, object, or person that no longer exists, or at least no longer exists in the same form: 'And the person or thing photographed is the target, the referent, a kind of little simulacrum, any *eidolon* emitted by the object, which I should like to call the *Spectrum* of the Photograph...' (1981, 9; emphasis original). Here it is again, the *eídolon*, this time as the phantom or spectre that every photograph carries. Barthes's view of photography offers a way of accounting for the spectral quality of the entire episode on the second island: in terms of the narrative logic of the film, the spectrality of the initial images motivates Lloyd's journey to the second island, which is a materialization of these images. In fact, the journey itself is ghostly. Lloyd's ship, full of corpses of plague victims, is intertextually linked to other ghost ships in the South Pacific, notably those in Samuel Taylor Coleridge's 'The Rime of the Ancient Mariner' (1798) and Edgar Allan Poe's *The Narrative of Arthur Gordon Pym of Nantucket* (1838).

In the former, the ancient mariner is left to drift 'Alone on a wide wide sea!' (Coleridge 2001, 233), surrounded by the corpses of his shipmates that dropped dead at the sight of another ghost ship and soon rise up as ghosts themselves. The voice of the ancient mariner himself is a decidedly ghostly one: 'I was so light—almost / I thought that I had died in sleep, / And was a blessed ghost' (305–9), and his 'ghastly tale' (584) haunts his listener, the wedding guest, after the old man's ghostly disappearance. In *Pym*, the narrator and his companions, left without food and water on their skeletal brig, encounter a 'strange vessel' (Poe 1999, 101) seemingly sailing towards them; the entire crew of the ship turns out to be dead. Shortly before this, the narrator describes himself as being in 'a state of partial insensibility, during which the most pleasing images floated in my imagination; such as green trees, waving meadows of ripe grain, processions of dancing girls' (92–3), recalling the sailors' island fantasies expressed in the early Pacific journals. The ship of the dead, then, can be read as a phantom holding up a mirror of their own state of decay to Pym and his companions; accordingly, their second voyage on board the *Jane Grey*, bound to the South Seas, can be seen as a ghostly voyage after their improbable delivery.

But most importantly, the second voyage is ghostly because it is textually haunted: Poe's narrative participates in and parodies America's 'Oceanian imaginings' (Lyons 2006, 54) in that 'the names of characters, places, and events are linked to the American Pacific archive' (Lyons

56). *Pym* is thus haunted by the ghosts of other South Sea narratives. As Lyons argues, fact and fiction are 'hardly distinguishable' in this 'inter-textual web' (61) where both fictional and non-fictional texts refer to each other more than to any external reality encountered. Poe's narrative is thus uncanny in the specific sense outlined by Dennis, creating a textual space where different voices blend and undermine the strived-for originality of the voyage, its search for undiscovered, virginal space. As the *Jane Grey* heads for the southernmost reaches of the Pacific, where Pym and his shipmates discover the island of Tsalal, 'a country differing essentially from any hitherto visited by civilized men' (1999, 167), and encounter a 'vast chain of apparent miracles' (169) and treacherous islanders, they enter a purely textual realm. Ironically, it is the very untouched and extravagant quality of the island that marks it as a space of rewriting. Explorers and writers of fiction sought to create ever new and striking accounts of Pacific islands: 'freshness' and 'originality' themselves become the mark of repetition.

Read in this way, the 'most pleasant images float[ing] in [Pym's] imagination' (93) as he is in an impaired state of mind between waking and sleeping are hallucinations produced by the unconscious, but this unconscious is (inter)textually shaped: the narrator's fantasy springs right from the textual universe of South Sea narratives. The images proleptically announce the South Sea voyage the narrator will embark on. Arguably, Pym never fully wakes up, and the entire voyage of the *Jane Grey* can be seen as an extended version of the floating images. The real ghost ship, then, is the *Jane Grey*: if the brig encountered by Pym and his companions is uncanny because its crew seems alive but is in fact dead, the uncanniness of the *Jane Grey* stems from her quality as a ghostly ship, cruising in the waters of her textual predecessors, just as Pym's voice itself is uncanny, steeped in the voices of countless other explorers of as yet undiscovered islands.

Almost a century later, Matthew Lloyd in *White Shadows* follows in Pym's ghostly wake. As he is tied to the steering wheel, surrounded by plague victims, we see the ship sailing into the horizon before the image fades out. An intertitle announces 'Days in.... days out.... days of sun and slimy calm...days of hot and savage wind...', recalling both the blazing heat and stupor of Pym's desperate voyage and the monotony of crossing the Pacific without encountering land for weeks in the early Pacific journals. The intertitle is followed by a static shot of the silhouette of an island, apparently filmed from another island (we see a palm tree in the foreground). This shot is again followed by an intertitle: '...and then the night belt of the endless Pacific.... toward the uncharted bottom of the world.... TYPHOON!', after which we see a series of shots of Lloyd struggling to manoeuvre the ship through a storm. The second intertitle makes Lloyd's association with the early explorers moving into as yet 'uncharted' space explicit, but the voyage is also marked as ghostly. The island vista inserted between the two intertitles thereby appears curiously out of place. It serves no narrative purpose; there is no indication that it represents an island that Lloyd actually encounters (in fact, on account of the palm tree it cannot even represent his perspective). It is not announced by the intertitle immediately preceding it ('Days in.... days out....'). In fact, it is even in conflict with the latter, which leads us to expect a shot of the endlessly open sea.

But if its logic is not narrative, the shot needs to be read conceptually. On the one hand, it aesthetically recalls the initial island-images. At the same time, however, it points forward, announcing the island at the end of Lloyd's journey. In fact, it serves to link the former with the latter: it is the moment in the film where the island resurfaces as a pure idea(l). As such, the shot resonates strongly with the sailors' fantasies in their hope of 'seeing some happy place soon' (Robertson 1948, 112) during the voyage of the *Dolphin*, and with Pym's 'pleasant images' (Poe 1999, 93), both of which emerge at the moment of greatest desolation on the open sea. In all three cases, the visions represent a cultural fantasy as much as they represent the personal fantasies of the travellers. In *White Shadows*, this is particularly evident as the island vista is not marked as a subjective shot associated with Lloyd. If Pym's floating images anticipate the moving images of cinema, the island-image emerging in the middle of Lloyd's journey harks back to the images present in accounts from the beginnings of European ventures in the South Pacific as much as it harks back to the almost photographic island vistas at the beginning of the film.

Eroding the Island-Image

Unlike photographs, however, these images are not *quite* still. If they attempt to freeze the island into an abstract idea and a pure image, they do not entirely succeed. First of all, there is a tension between stasis and movement within the image itself. In the first shot (Figure 2.1), the stillness of the island is counterbalanced by the movement of the ocean. While the water in the bay on the lee side of the island is perfectly still, we see the soft movement of the breakers rolling towards the island in the distance. In the second shot, the gentle movement of the leaves in the wind in the left half of the image complements the movement of the water to the right. These movements are quite regular, but there is one moment of surprise: barely perceptible, a wave rears up before arriving on the island, just visible for a split second before the cut. Dai Vaughan suggests that the fascination of very early cinema resided in its capacity to record the spontaneity of the inanimate world, using the example of a sudden and unexpected wave briefly unbalancing the men rowing in *Barque sortant du port* and the movement of leaves in the background of *Repas de bébé* (both by Louis Lumière, 1895) as examples:

> *Boat Leaving Harbour*... survives as a reminder of that moment when... cinema seemed free, not only of its proper connotations, but of the threat of its absorption into meanings beyond it. The promise of this film remains untarnished because it is a promise which can never be kept, its every fulfilment is also its betrayal.
>
> (1990, 65–6)

The 'promise' of cinema that Vaughan is interested in is antithetical to intention as any conscious attempt at realizing this promise would necessarily undo it. What is at stake is the control of the filmic image and its meanings: Vaughan is interested in the potential of cinema to resist absorption into a cultural sign system. I would argue, then, that it is precisely in this sense that the island-images of *White Shadows* resist the cultural fantasies they are made to signify: refusing to be frozen into a fixed form and concept, the island-image is fluid on its margins.

Yet the movement within the island vistas is only the first and maybe most banal level of this resistance, still partly absorbed by the mythical signifying power of the images. But on repeating viewings, one notices that the image itself moves. Trembling continuously yet unpredictably, it duplicates the equally regular and uncontainable movement of the leaves and the water, further and more fundamentally undermining the stillness of the vistas. Of course, any image in analog cinema trembles slightly, even more so in 1920s cinema when cameras were clunkier and less steady. But the reading I propose here focuses precisely on the ways in which the apparatus *itself* participates in working against the smoothness of the images and the fantasies they transport; the physical instability of the image has the same disillusioning effect as the malfunction of the projector, temporarily displacing the image of the ideal island in the letter to the editor of the *NYT* discussed earlier ('The picture was out of frame again').

The more one watches these opening shots, the more one notices that the island-image is disturbed in yet another way, even further removed from any kind of control. The image not only trembles, it also flickers. It flickers partly because of the graininess of the analogue image, again more pronounced due to the comparatively crude film stock used in the 1920s. Furthermore, the island-image is under attack because it is in constant danger of disappearing. In the first shot, the shadows cast by the leaves of the iris diaphragm never quite disappear between fade-in and fade-out: flickering in and out on the margins, they threaten to engulf the image in blackness. In the second shot, a black triangle hovers in the top left-hand corner, while a shadow keeps moving in and out from the left margin in the third shot, partly veiling the image like a curtain. In both cases, it is not quite clear what causes the shadows; in all probability, they were present in the original film, but even this is difficult to determine with certainty.

Finally, the stability of the island visions is undermined by the disintegration of the image itself. This is the level that is furthest removed from intention and control. Just before the end of the fourth shot, a comparatively large black blotch appears for a split second in the water in the bottom right-hand corner; thin white and black lines striate the images, cutting across the horizontal shapes of the islands (a particularly prominent one nervously wanders from left to right around the centre of the island in the first shot); a tiny white thread shoots comet-like onto the island in the second shot; a thin white structure resembling a lasso shines up briefly in the sky high above the island in the fourth shot, possibly caused by a speck of dust on the film stock. Stains, white and black spots, lines, and other shapes appear everywhere; once one starts focusing on them, one cannot help noticing their effect as their abstract and random play works against and displaces the island-image. They work like Barthes's *punctum*, diverting the spectator's gaze from the balanced composition of the image:

'Hence the detail which interests me is not, or at least is not strictly, intentional, and probably must not be so; it occurs in the field of the photographed thing like a supplement...' (1981, 47). But unlike in Barthes's examples, most of this visual interference in *White Shadows* was, quite likely, not visible when the film was first screened; it is the effect of time, attacking and corroding the notoriously fragile film stock. Of course, it is impossible to determine when a given speck or blotch first appeared, and some of the interference is likely to have been present from the beginning. But what, in fact, is 'the beginning'? The premiere in New York City on 31 July 1928? The moment the images were spliced together by the editor? Or even further back, the moment when the film was developed and emerged, island-like, out of its own amniotic fluid? Or the moment when the sound was added?[7] At all of these stages, the film stock would have disintegrated through physical and chemical processes. Even in 1928, no two audiences would have seen quite the same film. But the point is precisely not that there was initially a 'pure' film which began to disintegrate after a certain amount of time. The point is that the image has been under erosion from the moment of its emergence. As such, the version of the film that has been preserved for us makes visible a process that is at the heart of the analog cinematic image. Mainly in spite of itself, the film fails to uphold the island as *idéa*, as an abstract, frozen, and pure idea, making it visible as an illusive and elusive *eídolon*.

The uncontrollable movements of the water around the island, the technological imperfections of early cinema, and the materiality of the analogue image work together to unbalance the island as image. In this, to extend Vaughan's argument to the 1920s, *White Shadows* may well exemplify a promise of cinema that has to remain unfulfilled: resisting the ideological visions expressed through its images, the film unwittingly questions its own island myth. In a film like *South Pacific* (1958), this effect has all but disappeared: this South Sea romance set in the Second World War begins with a long series (over three minutes) of still photographs of the islands and locations on them around which the film will revolve. Here, the cinematic South Sea island has been smoothed into a perfect image and frozen into a timeless myth. As

---

[7] *White Shadows* was MGM's first sound film.

such, the still photographs announce the static quality of the entire film: in a way, everything has already been said after this prologue, and the characters and actions of the film move around in these images as mere ciphers in a timeless myth. In *White Shadows*, the island-image is still impure on various levels: ever fragile, it is under constant erasure, always in danger of dissolving before the viewer's eye.

At the same time, such a reading of the visual prologue paves the way for an analysis of the difficulties the film exhibits in establishing the island as a pure space in the central narrative. Rob Wilson argues that American representations of the Pacific establish 'Asia-Pacific' as an imagined and imaginary unified region, constructing an ideology of a benevolent zone of capitalism and free trade where 'the traumas of colonial occupation, regional fracturing, and world war will be washed away in the dirty, magical waters of the Pacific' (2002, 38). In *White Shadows*, Lloyd's voyage through the typhoon indeed serves to cancel out history: as already discussed, he sails into a zone removed from history and its traumata where the encounter of white man with Pacific island cultures can be restaged. After the turbulent voyage through the storm, visually marked by an excess of movement and watery confusion, we see Lloyd swimming through the still furious water, arriving at a beach only with the utmost difficulty. He is still staggering through the water as the image fades out. The next shot shows a tiny and tidy island seen from the water (Figure 2.2), extending the series of island vistas begun in the prologue and continued in the single shot inserted into the voyage. The tint is now yellow, and the excessive motion of the voyage has made way for near stillness again. It is only now that we get a medium shot of a beach (with Lloyd just about visible in the background), followed by a shot of Lloyd waking up on the edge of (and still partly in) the water, still in the same yellow tint that will also mark large sections of the central island episode. If Lloyd's voyage was associated with death, this is his rebirth; the island becomes an anchor and a refuge. Both for Lloyd and for the Western culture he embodies, it is the site of a fresh, clean start, a move into a pure zone that is at the same time a zone for aesthetic contemplation.

However, the move into this zone is not smooth: Lloyd's rebirth is partly overshadowed by its strained and messy beginning.[8] As Lloyd

---

[8] I borrow the term from Schueller and Watts (2003).

FIGURE 2.2   Still from *White Shadows in the South Seas* (W. S. Van Dyke, USA 1928)

approaches the beach, he is overtaken and knocked down by large waves several times. When the image fades out, he is still caught in an uncertain zone between water and (is)land; the land itself here fails to demarcate itself clearly from its surrounding element. For all we know, Lloyd never leaves this in-between zone; the ellipsis between this shot and the next constitutes not only a temporal gap, but also a move into a space of fantasy. The transition is not shown; it cannot be shown because it is an impossible one. In order to establish a clean beginning for Lloyd on the island, the film requires, literally and metaphorically, a fade-out and a cut: the space Lloyd leaves behind has to be eclipsed, and the narrative transformation the voyage serves—exchanging one (corrupt, impure) island for another that is paradisiacal and pure; turning Lloyd from a degenerate and marginalized drunkard into a healthy and heroic, even God-like figure—can only be effected through an elimination and repression of the messy and impossible arrival.

The film solves this problem by letting Lloyd arrive a second time. After a while, he discovers a second, larger island at a short distance, where he sees a hut. He swims across, and this time his arrival is clean and unproblematic: the waves are gentle, and Lloyd steps onto the island without difficulties. He is now in control of his own destiny, not at the mercy of wind and water. Lloyd's second, much shorter voyage is preceded by him gazing across to the island several times, marked by point-of-view shots. Lloyd can thus truly become a discoverer: the contingency of the first voyage is replaced with the purposefulness of the second. Chance, accident, and passivity are thus displaced and transformed into meaningful and active control on the part of the white explorer. As he steps onto the beach, we see the island on which he first washed up behind him (Figure 2.3); except for Lloyd's presence, the shot is an almost exact repetition of the first shot after the storm. Only retroactively, then, does it become clear that what the earlier shot represented was indeed the island on whose beach we saw Lloyd lying two shots later. This is significant, because its initial spatial indeterminacy aligns this island even more clearly with the generic island

FIGURE 2.3   Still from *White Shadows in the South Seas* (W. S. Van Dyke, USA 1928)

vistas at the beginning of the film and during the storm. But the second composition with Lloyd in front of the island also visually reinforces the notion that the small island is a foil against whose backdrop—and *only* against it—he can successfully step onto the larger island. The small island thus marks the impossible zero point from which Lloyd can unproblematically arrive. As such, it does more than anticipate the larger one and reinforce the construction of the island as an idea and image. It is also the phantom from which the larger island can emerge and whose phantasmatic kernel it represents: like Lloyd, the film can only arrive at its central, ideal island via a detour. If islands were stepping stones on the way to the New World in Chapter 1, here the island itself can only be reached via a twisted path. Lloyd has to pass, impossibly, through the island-image as *idéa* and *eidolon*. The central island can only take shape as the destination of a deflected journey; as such the ideal island, as both fantasy and phantom, constitutes both its temporal antecedent and its condition of possibility.

We have thus seen that what I previously referred to as the second island is in fact the third diegetic island. After the film has finally, as it were, arrived at its destination, the ethnographic camera goes to great lengths to establish the island as a space without an outside. After a shot of Lloyd leaving the beach and walking towards the interior, we suddenly enter a sylvan scene of bare-breasted women bathing under a waterfall and swinging around on vines. After a moment of voyeuristic hesitation behind some ferns, the camera tracks forward into their midst. It is decidedly not associated with Lloyd's gaze: only after a minute has passed do we see him emerging from behind a screen of large leaves after another brief moment of hesitation, recalling the camera's earlier gesture. Again, Lloyd's subjective gaze is preceded by a gaze that cannot be assigned to a diegetic viewer and yet distinctly implies a viewpoint. The gaze thus becomes that of the audience which can fill this empty position; the ethnographic camera speaks to a collective cultural fantasy validated and perpetuated by the viewer. At the same time, while the camera and later Lloyd represent an external viewpoint, this externality is also masked in the abrupt movement from beach to interior. Not only are we placed in the island interior without any transition or spatial orientation, but the luxurious vegetation and the rocks around the pool create an enclosed space where even the water, so far associated with danger and death, is tamed. This sense of inwardness is repeated when we see Lloyd staggering around the endless forest, surrounded first by large trees and then by the males of the island tribe. Visually, this encounter is a far cry from Mary Louise Pratt's notion of the paradigmatic 'arrival scene' in travel narratives (2008, 77–8): swooning in their midst, Lloyd misses a substantial part of the encounter. Revived by the island girls' coconut oil massages, he is reborn a second time, apparently leaving his former degenerate self behind for good. His new, purified body, as it were, never *arrived* on the island, but emerges from its midst (we will return to the disavowal of island arrivals in Chapter 3).

As a structural operation, Lloyd's trajectory perfectly illustrates Peter Brooks's notion of narrative as transformation: the final, 'pure' island is a transformed version of the first, 'fallen' island, even if this transformation is retrogressive. It manifests itself on semantic, narrative, and aesthetic levels. On the semantic level, water is resignified as a pleasurable space in the sylvan scene discussed above: where the underwater scenes at the beginning of the film were marked by sharks and other dangerous creatures, these island waters are filled with gracious female bodies. As already discussed, the threatening ocean reemerges one more time, almost killing the chief's son; but in addition to uniting Lloyd with Fayaway, this accident neutralizes Lloyd's earlier failed attempt to save a young diver's life. If that death represented the extinction of South Sea island cultures at the hands of white man (significantly, the young man was his parents' only offspring), Lloyd's resuscitation of the boy now affirms cultural regeneration. The echo cannot be overlooked: initially, Lloyd seems to fail a second time and has already given up when the boy magically returns to life. As a direct result of his successful intervention, Lloyd's union with Fayaway reinforces this sense of fertility, significantly casting Lloyd as the agent of reproduction. This replacement of a discourse of disease, degeneration, and death with one of health, rejuvenation, and purity taps into the medical discourse that Edmond sees at work in the representation of islands as either disease-free or infected sites since the European voyages to Tahiti in the eighteenth century;[9] he further argues that islands

---

[9] Thus, the introduction of venereal disease to Tahiti by Europeans was a source of considerable debate.

themselves have often been imagined as either healthy or diseased bodies. This mechanism is certainly at work in *White Shadows*: as we have seen, the dialectic of purity/corruption structuring the representation of the film's islands is linked to the dialectic of health/disease marking the protagonists' bodies.

Aesthetically, too, the final island echoes and reverses the representation of the first island. One striking instance is a long lateral tracking shot taken from the island, following Lloyd and Fayaway paddling along the shore in a canoe. The shot is remarkable for several reasons. Firstly, it is very long, and interrupted only by two short shots of children playing in a boat. Secondly, the movement of the camera parallels the movement of the boat along the shore with only slight discrepancies, as when both the boat and the camera come to a sudden halt. As the boat starts moving slowly in the other direction, the camera lingers slightly, only to follow it again immediately; the camera continues moving in the new direction, and the boat's movements are hard to determine for a moment until we notice that it is slowly spinning before it becomes synchronized with the camera movement once again. Finally, the shot effects a subtle play of revealing and hiding its object: our vision is periodically blocked or limited by tree trunks and leaves as the camera moves behind them. This teasing of the viewer is at its most striking during the spin, quite literally the turning point of the shot: we see Fayaway standing up and taking off her clothes, but just as the boat begins to spin and we expect a frontal view of her naked body, our vision is interrupted by dense foliage.[10] When the boat reemerges, we see Fayaway holding the cloth that had covered her body in front of her, teasing Lloyd as much as the camera had teased us. The duration of the shot, the camera's slightly delayed following of the canoe's movements, and the obstruction of vision work together in constructing the sense of an observing presence. Once again, the gaze cannot be clearly assigned to any diegetic character. It is again linked with the gaze of the audience: the camera's voyeurism is implicitly our own.

[10] As *White Shadows* was made in pre-code years and naked bodies were quite commonly seen in the cinema of the time, there was no censorship that would have required this shielding of Fayaway's nakedness.

The border poetics of this shot is significant because it mirrors the first two shots of the film after the visual prologue: equally moving first from left to right and then from right to left, the camera laterally tracks along the shore of the 'fallen' island, implicitly exploring it from a boat. The tracking shot of Fayaway and Lloyd mirrors these two earlier shots quite literally as the positions are reversed: the canoe, as it were, provides the invisible vantage point of the earlier shots of the shore and vice versa, but its movement in relation to the shore is reversed although, for the viewer, the movement is from left to right and back in both cases. This structural mirroring further aligns the final island with the imaginary: if the first island is marked by lack, the final island restores the former's lost completeness, yet—as its insubstantial and impossible mirror image—it emerges from this very lack. Part of this operation is the inscription of the audience into the space of the ideal island. Along with firmly attaching Fayaway and Lloyd's canoe and the coastal sea to the island, this absorption of the viewer contributes to the overall disavowal of an outside position. At the same time, the several instances of a gaze which is not associated with a specific character haunt the space of the island by pointing to the outside position this gaze implies.

The tracking shots at the beginning of the film already negotiate this duality. Linking the initial island vistas with the film's narrative beginning, they fail to establish a smooth transition. The first shot is announced by the already cited intertitle that places it in a relation of contrast with the vistas: 'But the white man...cast his withering shadow over these islands....and the business of "civilizing" them to his interests began....' The shot itself is taken from the water and laterally tracks along the shore, showing some marks of white civilization. Then, another intertitle: 'Today — — the results of "civilization".' After the intertitle, the camera moves in the other direction, showing us a sad and decadent island corrupted by the West. Now, the water between camera and island has disappeared: the camera has moved across the border. There is no doubt as to the status of the second shot: it depicts the deplorable *status quo* of the island. Yet if it requires a separate announcement ('the results of "civilization"'), what exactly separates it from the first? If the first shot represents neither the island in its prelapsarian ideal *nor* present-day reality, what is it that we see? The answer must lie, quite literally, somewhere in between: blending the ideal island-image with the view of the fallen island, it performs the fundamental uncertainty of vision structuring the West's—and Hollywood's—perception of the South Sea island(s). It is therefore crucial that it is in this shot that the camera explores the island from the water and thus from a distance: recalling the early explorers' visions of the Pacific islands they were approaching, the shot not only operates in a similar zone of visual uncertainty, but its uncertain status is partly generated by these same accounts: themselves a blending of sight, fantasy, and earlier texts, they shape and complicate Hollywood's islandward gaze.

The invasion of the island by the white trader at the end of the film is thus the logical and necessary conclusion to the narrative as the seemingly unspoilt island has been marked by a white gaze from the outset. The film comes full circle with another tracking shot (now from left to right) of white debauchery, again in black and white. Yet although the film ends by turning the final island back into the first island, the circular narrative has effected an ideological transformation. We end up where we began, but we are given a distinct version of how we got there. The film thus ritually enacts and purges a Western sense of guilt: as the history of Western intrusion into paradise is doubled within the narrative, the white subject is split into good and evil. Even if it is Lloyd's brief moment of greedy distraction that attracts the pearl trader, the guilt for the corruption of paradise is safely located in the latter while Lloyd dies a martyr's death.

And yet, as we have seen, the film's ideological operations are not as smooth as they would be. *White Shadows*' real unsettling power does not reside in its ostensible indictment of colonial violence. It resides in the film's murky zones, in the impurities of its narrative and, especially, the island-image it conjures up. The most unsettling of the film's shadows are not the carefully fabricated ones as manifest in the veiling of the very last shot, but the shadows the film produces unwittingly, which are present from the first image. They are early cinema's analogue to the visual uncertainties structuring the explorers' accounts in the eighteenth century. Not yet quite fixed, the island-image encourages revision: framed in a new mode of vision, it returns to its earlier instability and contradictions as Hollywood rediscovers and explores the South Seas on screen.

The Tourist Gaze and Hollywood's Rediscovery of the Pacific: *The Hurricane* (1937)

Released nine years after *White Shadows*, John Ford's *The Hurricane* (1937) begins by self-reflexively commenting on Hollywood's rediscovery of the South Sea islands. The credits are superimposed on a series of maps that bear the look of the coastal survey maps issued by the Hydrographic Office of the US Navy (Figure 2.4). Several of the maps are labelled, specifying the location of the islands they depict as the Tuamotu Archipelago, the group of islands reached by Wallis, Bougainville, and Cook after weeks of crossing the Pacific. The film thus explicitly follows in these explorers' wake; fittingly enough, the first shot after the credits actually shows the wide and long wake of a ship on the ocean. Yet the maps only feign authenticity: the islands do not correspond to any existing island group in the South Pacific, let alone in the Tuamotu Archipelago. In fact, the few islands whose names can be

FIGURE 2.4   Still from *The Hurricane* (John Ford, USA 1937)

deciphered—Tutuila, Swains, and Upolu—evoke quite a different group of islands, namely the Samoan islands. All three islands had, by then, played an important part in the history of America's expansion into the Pacific.

In early 1841, Upolu was bombarded by two ships of the United States Exploring Expedition because the locals refused to hand over the murderers of an American sailor. Wilkes had already visited Upolu in 1839 and learned that several Americans had been killed by a chief named Opotuno; he had been unable to apprehend him. When the conflict escalated in 1841, the Americans burned down three villages in retribution. In his *Narrative*, Wilkes justifies the violent act by arguing that it had been 'absolutely necessary to secure the safety of the crews of such of our whaling fleet as touch at this island, as well as to restore the respect due to our flag and those who sail under it' and, finally, to demonstrate 'that they were not our equals in war...' (1844, 33). While Wilkes, who did not participate in the raid, restricts himself to evaluating the incident as a demonstration of American superiority, William Reynolds, midshipman on the *Flying Fish* in Wilkes's squadron, gives a detailed account of the attack:

> The blaze was bright among the trees, the smoke rolled upward over the green hills, and the only sound that reached our ears was the crackling of the light wood amid the flames. The boats returned, & during the rest of the day, we saw no signs of life upon the shore.
>
> (2004, 229)

Here and in other passages, Reynolds stresses the almost eerie absence of human life while the villages are 'laid waste' (229). He describes the attack as a spectacle of destruction with an aesthetic dimension, almost detached from the people involved in it on either side.

Tutuila is the largest island of American Samoa and became an overseas territory of the United States in 1900 after the Samoan islands had been divided between the United States and Germany (cf. Howe 1984, 252–4). The annexation of the Samoan islands was part of a larger, aggressive move into the Pacific on the part of the United States that also included the annexation of Hawai'i (1898), the taking of Guam from Spain during the Spanish–American War (1898), and the purchase of the Philippines from Spain (1898), followed by Philippine resistance that culminated in the Philippine–American War (cf. Eperjesi 2005, 153–9).

Swains Island, finally, a little atoll in the Tokelau group north of Samoa, was annexed by the United States as part of American Samoa in 1925.

The reference to the Samoan islands in the credits of *The Hurricane*, however, is oblique not only because of the maps' ostensible depiction of the Tuamotus, but also because the shapes of the islands do not correspond to the real shapes of Upolu, Tutuila, and Swains. At best, they vaguely resemble them, but any likeness is immediately dispelled by the surrounding islands, which bear no relation to real Samoan geography whatsoever. Lorna Fitzsimmons's claim that the credit sequence constitutes a 'paratextual *mise en abyme* of the narrative as a whole' (2003, 59) is thus true not only in that, as she points out, it anticipates the hurricane through the 'centrifugal scattering effect' created by the maps and their composition, but also in that it provides, quite literally, a map through which to read the film's narrative. If the mapping of the credit sequence is contradictory, so is, as I will argue, the mapping unfolded by the entire film. Like the novel by Charles Nordhoff and James Norman Hall (1936) on which it is based, the film has a French Polynesian setting and most of the action takes place on the fictional island of Manukura in the Tuamotu Archipelago. However, the geography of Ford's film is initially vague, and the production history further complicates its multilayered geography. Although it was originally meant to be shot entirely in the South Seas, Samuel Goldwyn, much to Ford's chagrin, changed his mind and the film was mainly shot on Goldwyn's back lot (cf. Eyman 1999, 183–5; McBride 2001, 264–6). However, a number of location shots were taken on the island of Tutuila, providing the film's ostensible French Polynesian geography with recognizable American Samoan backgrounds. At the same time, as commentators agree, many of the studio shots look blatantly artificial (cf. Gallagher 1986, 138). In Joseph McBride's view, 'Ford's Murnau-like idealization of the island paradise of Manukura is hampered by the overuse of phony studio settings' (265). Viewed as an artistic strategy, however, these shots self-reflexively refer to the film's imaginary geography where British (explicit in the maps' reference to the 'King Georges Group' in the Tuamotus), French, and American blend; where the historical, the contemporary, the 'real', the textual, and the filmic dissolve into each other and are woven together to map a landscape that does not follow the linear logic of Euclidean space, but rather the cinematic logic of montage and superimposition.

This spatial in- and overdeterminacy, already signalled by the credits, is reinforced by the frame narrative at the beginning of *The Hurricane*, which explicitly marks the voyage of the ship whose wake we see as a journey into a space that is, at least partly, cinematic. As in *White Shadows*, this uncertain geography is negotiated along and across the border of the island. The shot of the wake dissolves into a frontal long shot of a man approaching the railing and looking away from the ship. The shot dissolves into a medium long shot showing the man from behind, gazing intently at the open ocean. A barren sandspit enters the frame from the left; as we will soon learn, it is the devastated island of Manukura. Exploring the island from across the water, the shot echoes the lateral tracking shots at the beginning of *White Shadows*. In the next shot, the man (who worked as the doctor of the French administration before the island was destroyed) is joined by a young woman, an enthusiastic tourist, who happily exclaims: 'The captain told me we were actually in the South Seas now, right in the heart of them', and begins to wind up a small cine-camera. She dreamily continues: 'The South Sea islands—the last hiding place of beauty and adventure', and we see her flushed face gazing away from the ship, seemingly at the island of her dreams, as she starts to play with her camera.

Yet the next shot, again taken from behind the two characters, still shows the same barren island. The doctor immediately points to the textual nature of her fantasy, produced by her reading travel brochures, the successors of the early explorers' journals: 'That's what all the travel folders say.' For a while, she does not acknowledge the island in front of her. Only a few seconds into the frontal medium shot that follows does her face show she has noticed it at all, and she asks Doctor Kersaint: 'What's that midget-looking spot we're passing?' Even as the doctor answers 'It's one of the South Sea isles', she first rejects the reality at hand, privileging that of the tourist folders: 'Nothing like that is mentioned in the folders.' Since such an island figures in none of them, it simply cannot exist. The doctor goes on to evoke the lost beauty of the island: 'It was mentioned in all the folders once.... That was once the most beautiful of all the islands that raised their little green heads above these waters. The most beautiful and enchanting bit of paradise in all the world, Madame.'

Despite his earlier, dismissive reaction to the woman's island fantasy, then, he now launches into a nostalgic vision that is no less conventional, which is underscored by the soft romantic music that sets in during his poetic vision. His assertion that he loves the islands 'in his own way' thus becomes questionable, and this inconsistency anticipates his contradictory role as both a sharp critic of colonial law and a 'paternalistic' (Fitzsimmons 2003, 62) defender of what he perceives as the islanders' childishness and state of nature. Kersaint goes on to explain that the island was destroyed by a hurricane, whereupon the tourist excitedly takes out her camera and begins to film it. Now the same tracking shot of the island is shown a second time, beginning again on the right and moving leftward. This time, however, the observers are not shown, and accordingly what we see is marked as what the woman's camera records (cf. Fitzsimmons 60). The image of the barren island soon dissolves into a tracking shot of the island in its prime (Figure 2.5) that continues the leftward movement of the preceding shot, and the main narrative begins, relating the events leading up to the island's destruction in an 'extended analepsis' (Fitzsimmons 59).

FIGURE 2.5 Still from *The Hurricane* (John Ford, USA 1937)

The Hurricane has received very little scholarly attention, but the few critics who have written about it have drawn attention to this frame narrative. Thus, Lorna Fitzsimmons argues that 'the prologue of the film engages desire for tourism' and establishes the shot into which it dissolves as an imaginary recreation of the island (60). The use of the cine-camera marks this recreation as a cinematic fantasy. As in *White Shadows*, there is a tension between an unsatisfying present and an ideal version of the island. But this time, the nostalgic vision does not hark back to some remote and timeless past, but rather to the island's recent colonial past, and the destruction of the ideal island is not, or not explicitly, attributed to the incursion of white man but to the forces of nature. The nostalgia is thus not for some idealized pre-colonial period as in *White Shadows*, but for a version of the island as advertised by the tourist folders. Or rather, the nostalgic past has become part of the touristic present; the logic of a developed tourist industry requires the island paradise to be still available in the present.

Indeed, the tourist industry was undergoing decisive developments at the time *The Hurricane* was released. The first commercial Pan American flights from San Francisco to Hong Kong via Hawai'i, with other islands stops on the way, had just been launched, and a new line to Auckland was in preparation. The announcement of these plans caused public concern that the pristine isolation of South Sea islands would now be destroyed for good (*NYT*, 21 March 1937). The availability of airway travel was a significant step in the rapid development of the tourist industry that had begun to take shape in the nineteenth century with the introduction of steamship travel and the invention of photography (cf. Chalmers 2011, xxv–xxvi). As tourism was commercialized in the twentieth century, the development of both steamship travel and airlines went hand in hand with the emergence of travel agencies; the American Steamship and Tourist Agents Association was founded in 1931 (Chalmers 155). The well-known 'Fly to South Sea Isles' poster, depicting a Pan Am Clipper and South Sea island iconography reminiscent of Paul Gauguin's paintings, is emblematic of this link.

At the same time, the appearance on the market of amateur film cameras in the 1930s allowed tourists to take home moving images of their holiday destinations. Pacific islands were experiencing a second large wave of tourism in the late 1930s as American tourists travelled west to avoid, in the words of a *NYT* article, the 'turbulent European scenes' and the other 'war locale' (20 November 1938) in China: with the Spanish Civil War and the tensions leading up to the Second World War in Europe and the Japanese invasion of China in 1937, the Pacific islands became once again sites where Americans could 'avoid trouble and the sound of guns' (*NYT*, 20 November 1938; cf. also *NYT*, 28 January 1940). However, contemporary newspaper articles also share a remarkable awareness of the manufactured quality of the South Sea islands drawing the tourists. Abounding with references to Robert Louis Stevenson,[11] Paul Gauguin,[12] and Hollywood cinema, they talk of the islands as 'semi-mythical specks' (*NYT*, 21 March 1937) and 'dreamy Pacific isles made famous through story and picture' (*NYT*, 31 December 1939). The tourists are portrayed as 'idealists who have sought to find for themselves fragments of the dreams of the tropics, such as those woven by Paul Gauguin and Pierre Loti' (*NYT*, 21 March 1937); in this account, the South Sea islands emerge as a multilayered dreamscape constructed through text, painting, and film.

Viewed in this discursive context, the frame narrative of *The Hurricane* participates in creating this dreamscape, yet it also demonstrates an acute awareness of following in the wake not only of the early Pacific explorers, but also of the nineteenth-century writers and painters and, above all, the twentieth-century 'cinematic explorers' that rediscovered and recreated the islands in the imaginary geography of Hollywood. What results is a highly self-reflexive meditation on perception. Gazing across the border of the island-as-ruin from a distance that is more cognitive than geographical, the young woman and the doctor do not see the same island. Both islands, however, clearly emerge from the intertextual web alluded to by the newspaper articles. Furthermore, both islands are absent and initially '[raise] their little green heads' only in the observers' minds. Both see a version of the island in its full beauty

---

[11] Stevenson travelled extensively in the South Seas from 1888 onwards. He settled in Upolu with his wife in 1890, where he died four years later. On Stevenson's Pacific writings, see especially Buckton (2007) and Largeaud-Ortega (2012).

[12] Paul Gauguin first travelled to Tahiti in 1891 to escape what he perceived as the conventions and constraints of European civilization. He is best known for his primitivist paintings of Tahiti and, especially, Tahitian women, whose perceived sensuality and sexual licence he celebrated. For a discussion of Gauguin's Pacific fantasies and his paintings, see Childs (2013, 54–132).

already *before* the film makes it available to the audience. They invest the far side of its border with an aesthetic dimension despite, or rather because of, its manifest emptiness. Like the maps of the credit sequence, the imaginary geography that emerges projects a multilayered and composite space.

If space is marked by indeterminacy and overdetermination in *The Hurricane*, so is time. There are many reasons for assuming that the film, like the novel, is set in the late nineteenth century: the recent establishment of French colonial administration on the island of Manukura points to the appointment of French governors on Polynesian islands around the time when France annexed Tahiti (1880) and claimed the Tuamotus. At the same time, the frame narrative evokes the 1930s with its references to an already established and commercialized South Sea tourism and amateur filmmaking. The implied time gap between frame and main narrative cannot account for this discrepancy as the doctor appears to be of approximately the same age in both narratives; time remains as indefinite and contradictory as space. This palimpsestic chronotope characterizes the spatiotemporal relations of the entire film.

A short summary will prepare the ground for a discussion of this structure by demonstrating the crucial role of voyages to, from, and between the film's various islands. The main narrative begins by introducing us to the injustice of French colonial rule, embodied by Governor De Laage; he sentences an islander who stole a canoe to enjoy a summer night with this lover to thirty days' punishment. This curtailment of indigenous mobility is followed by an officially sanctioned voyage, the arrival of the governor's wife Germaine on Captain Nagle's ship. We are introduced to Terangi (Jon Hall), an islander working as first mate on the ship, and his lover Marama (Dorothy Lamour). We see Terangi and Marama getting married before Terangi leaves for Tahiti again. Marama secretly joins him but is discovered by Captain Nagle; again, an indigenous voyage is interrupted. In Tahiti, Terangi is unjustly imprisoned for breaking the jaw of a white man in self-defence. The film then cross-cuts between Manukura and Tahiti as we learn about Terangi's repeated attempts to escape, while De Laage remains firm in his decision not to intervene. Finally, Terangi escapes in a canoe and makes it back to Manukura. He is joined by Marama and later Chief Mehevi, who tells them to leave Manukura for a tabooed island ('the forbidden place'). Meanwhile, a storm is gathering as tensions between the governor and the islanders are mounting. De Laage gets wind of Terangi's escape and pursues him; he does not know that Terangi returns shortly after leaving on account of the storm. The hurricane destroys almost the entire island, and only two groups survive: Terangi, his family, and Germaine De Laage find shelter in a tree and drift to another small island (or rather sandspit), while Doctor Kersaint and a few islanders survive in a canoe. Meanwhile, De Laage returns to find Manukura itself reduced to a sandspit. Terangi's island is spotted by De Laage. Before he arrives, Terangi and his family depart the island for an unknown destination, leaving only Germaine behind. The film ends with De Laage spotting Terangi's canoe, but then (despite better knowledge) following his wife's urgent insistence in stating that what he sees is only a log.

Navigating a Sea of Islands: Challenging the Western Gaze

The Hurricane is thus structured around a series of sea voyages connecting a set of islands that belong to different temporal orders. While Tahiti represents fully developed colonization, Manukura is associated both with the early stages of establishing colonial order in the Pacific and, as the island is destroyed, with the end of colonial rule. This pattern is complicated by moments that present the islands in yet a different temporal order. One of Terangi's attempted escapes is triggered by him seeing Nagle's ship, the *Katopua*, emerging from behind a promontory. While the preceding shots show Terangi and others carrying heavy stones, spurred on by brutal guards, the sudden point-of-view shot of the bay evokes a very different Tahiti. In fact, the shot is an impossible one: the long shot preceding a medium close-up of Terangi shows us that the view of the bay is obstructed by other labourers and a fence. The images of colonial exploitation thus briefly make way for a more hopeful image of white presence in Tahiti, maybe even evoking the first appearance of European sails in Matavai Bay. Terangi's dreamy gaze is interrupted by a lash of the whip, but shortly after, he leaps over the fence and jumps into the sea, swimming out to the *Katopua*. However, the crew and Nagle do not—or choose not to— see him. As he collapses on the beach, the illusion of a Tahiti free of colonial violence is briefly repeated: showing only the beach, water, and Terangi's body, the framing suggests that Terangi is in his own space. This vision, too, is soon dispelled as two feet and a gun enter the frame from the right, paralleled by the intrusion of two shadows on the left. Similarly, in contrast to the bustling arrival scene at the beginning of the film, Terangi's unofficial arrival in Manukura on a beach that is not marked by the insignia of white civilization[13] after his successful escape conveys an image of a different island; Terangi enters a space that is his own, and this time no guns and white shadows intrude into the frame.

Along the same lines, the forbidden island that Terangi sets out for upon Chief Mehevi's advice is associated with pre-colonial time. At the end of the film, we enter a timeless zone both before and after white history. Paddling into an uncertain future, Terangi '[flees] the white man's gaze' (Cassano 2010, 135) and enters a world to which the (white) audience has as little access as De Laage. This world evokes the seafaring habits of Pacific peoples before European contact. Embarking on his journey in a canoe, Terangi inscribes himself in the long tradition of 'constant and deliberate voyaging' (Howe 1984, 23) that had been a central part of the lives of his ancestors since they began to explore and settle the Pacific and its islands around 3000 BP. It is therefore significant that the last image of Terangi shows him confidently navigating the ocean, an ability he had already demonstrated when sailing 600 miles from Tahiti to Manukura in a canoe without Western navigational aids. It is this intimate relationship with the sea that Howe stresses in his history of the South Sea islands: 'Broad expanses of sea, which to most Europeans are featureless (and generally full of menace), were something quite different to the trained island mariner. To him the sea was a friendly place and as full of signs as a road map is to a European' (1984, 21).

Within this complex structure of completed and interrupted as well as official and unofficial voyages, the overall trajectory of the film gradually moves from curtailment to restoration of indigenous seaborne mobility. As already pointed out, the main narrative begins with

---

[13] In the arrival scene at the beginning of the film, these insignia—e.g. the church and the French flag—are prominently displayed.

the punishment of the native canoe thief who functions as Terangi's double (Fitzsimmons 2003, 61). Although we are introduced to Terangi as an exceptionally able navigator who 'runs a ship as though it were a pair of shoes on his feet' (Nagle), in this context he has the status of an 'honorary white man' in his role as first mate (Cassano 2010, 125). After his imprisonment, his first attempted venture into the ocean fails and returns him to Tahiti; while he eventually succeeds in sailing back to Manukura, this voyage has to remain clandestine. On account of the storm Terangi's next voyage—his attempted escape to the tabooed island—is also interrupted, but so is De Laage's voyage in search of him; both have to return to Manukura without having achieved their goals. As the film moves towards its climax, its narrative dynamics reaches its anticlimax as both colonizer and colonized are blocked in their movements; both voyages are initially motivated by the other, and what results is a narrative deadlock. Terangi's next voyage on a drifting tree takes him to the sandspit, where he embarks on his last voyage. His final voyage is purposeful and brings the main narrative full circle: the forbidden canoe voyage with which it began is, as it were, completed; after the initial prohibition of movement, the entire film works towards the reestablishment of indigenous mobility.

It is significant that both canoe voyages feature a couple as the film persistently associates native mobility with sexuality and procreation, and the colonizers' desire to contain this mobility can be read as a reaction to a Western fear of cultural extinction as it emerged in nineteenth-century representations of Oceania (Howe 2000, 35–7). The nocturnal ride of the canoe thief and his lover is explicitly associated with the 'whims of love'. Terangi's first arrival from Tahiti implicitly conjoins a powerful mobility with sexuality: Terangi is seen standing on top of the mast before he jumps down into the sea to join Marama, who jumps off a tree to swim to Terangi in turn. With several shots of Terangi's strong naked torso and an extreme low-angle shot of the tall mast, the entire scene is erotically charged; the association becomes explicit when Terangi says to Marama that he is the best sailor and the best swimmer in the world, only to add that he will also be the best husband in the world on their wedding night. Terangi's two assaults on white men are also associated with a powerful virility: he breaks one man's jaw and kills another man because he 'hits too hard'; Nagle adds that he is 'too much of a man to store up any bitterness'.

Conversely, Kersaint argues that Terangi will 'not live in a cell, he'll die'. It is thus rhetorically implied that Polynesians and Europeans cannot co-exist, and that the survival of the latter can only be ensured by the confinement and death of the former. Captain Nagle takes a view similar to that of Kersaint, telling the governor of Tahiti: 'You don't know the Tuamotu natives. They're not like your Tahitians. They can't stand confinement.' While pleading for Terangi's cause, Nagle problematically represents the Tahitians as easily conquerable and fit for imprisonment; even his view of Terangi and his fellow islanders is marked by the 'fatal impact' view of a 'Pacific paradise lost' inevitably doomed by the arrival of white civilization, a view propagated by missionaries, pre-Darwinian scientists like Max Müller and Edward Tylor, and, later, salvage ethnographers like Percy Smith and Margaret Mead (cf. Howe 2000, 42–6). As Howe argues, this 'literature on the imminent extinction of Pacific islanders reached its peak in the 1920s' (46). As we have seen, this view is at the heart of the narrative logic of *White Shadows*, and *The Hurricane* still resonates with it.

However, the patronizing views expressed by Kersaint and Nagle are counteracted by a very different view first expressed by Marama. In this view, the islanders' mobility is not represented in terms of a bird-like fragility (both Kersaint and Nagle liken the islanders to birds), the curtailment of which would result in their extinction, but rather as a powerful resource enabling them to oppose their confinement. Lamenting Terangi's imprisonment, Marama poetically figures his jail as an island incapable of holding him in place: ' . . . no jail can hold Terangi very long. If it has a window in it, he'll fly away. If it has water around it, he'll swim away.' Rather than focus on the potentially fatal aspects of curtailing Terangi's mobility, Marama foregrounds the latter as a resource enabling him to cross the boundaries erected by colonial authorities. According to Gillis, 'Western thought has always preferred to assign meaning to neatly bounded, insulated things, regarding that which lies between as a void' (2004, 2). Stressing water and air as connective elements surrounding the jail as island or the island as jail, Marama dispels this Western view of the island as stronghold, anticipating the complete breakdown of colonial structures and boundaries at the end of the film.

Indeed, the view of islands that emerges in the second part of the film is much closer to that expressed by Tongan-Fijian anthropologist Epeli

Hau'ofa in his influential essay 'Our Sea of Islands', in which he attacks the widespread 'belittling view' (1994, 150) that Oceanian islands 'are much too small, too poorly endowed with resources, and too isolated from the centers of economic growth for their inhabitants ever to be able to rise above their present condition of dependence on the largess of wealthy nations' (150). To counteract this view, Hau'ofa draws attention to the complex networks of social and economic relations 'at the grass roots' (148) of Oceanic social and economic realities that cut across the territorial and economic grid imposed by colonial and neocolonial powers:

> When those who hail from continents... see a Polynesian or Micronesian island they naturally pronounce it small or tiny. Their calculation is based entirely on the extent of the land surfaces they see.
> But if we look at the myths, legends, and oral traditions, and the cosmologies of the peoples of Oceania, it becomes evident that they did not conceive of their world in such microscopic proportions....
> There is a world of difference between viewing the Pacific as "islands in a far sea" and as "a sea of islands."... Continental men, namely Europeans, on entering the Pacific after crossing huge expanses of ocean, introduced the view of "islands in a far sea." From this perspective the islands are tiny, isolated dots in a vast ocean. Later on, continental men—Europeans and Americans—drew imaginary lines across the sea, making the colonial boundaries that confined ocean peoples to tiny spaces for the first time.... Our ancestors, who had lived in the Pacific for over two thousand years, viewed their world as "a sea of islands" rather than as "islands in the sea."...
> Theirs was a large world in which peoples and cultures moved and mingled, unhindered by boundaries of the kind erected much later by imperial powers. (152-3)

I have quoted from Hau'ofa's article at some length because its implications are far-reaching. If this chapter focuses on the border of the island as an aesthetic zone, this interest grows out of and reflects a Western view of islands that segments the world into discrete units and goes hand in hand with the modern establishment of clearly demarcated nation states and territories. As we have seen, the imaginative appropriation of Oceanic islands by Europeans and Americans concentrated on their borders. Crossing them was initially fraught with uncertainty, but ultimately turned into economic and political appropriation as the islands were reimagined and subjugated as bounded colonial territories.

What prevails at the end of *The Hurricane*, however—and for this reason it is important that the film, unlike the novel, does not return to the frame narrative—is not this Western view of islands. The film's imaginative reshaping of the South Pacific into a 'sea of islands' begins with Terangi's successful voyage from Tahiti to Manukura and culminates in the hurricane sequence. As De Laage enquires about the reasons for the islanders' sudden festive spirit, a drunken Kersaint emphasizes wind as a connective medium between the islands upon De Laage's protesting that he has had 'no official report' of Terangi escaping: 'Can you hear that wind blowing? Well, it came in the wind!' Conversely, the colonial channels of communication are breaking down: as De Laage rebukes Nagle for not informing him of Terangi's escape, the captain ironically retorts that he 'saw no reason to interfere with the excellent official system of communication'. Towards the end of the film, then, the unofficial networks linking the islands prevail against the rigid and sluggish colonial administration. It is crucial that the liberation of Terangi is associated with wind and water, the elements that tear down the seemingly stable colonial structures at the end of the film; the blurred shapes of the ruins of the church, looming large in the background of the scene of De Laage's return to what remains of Manukura, are among the film's most memorable images. This literal and figurative downfall of colonial structures is anticipated by Kersaint at De Laage's dinner table. When the wind is already beginning to smash the shutters of the governor's residence, he says: 'Can you imagine Paris in a wind like this? ... Oh, I'm afraid civilization wouldn't look very pretty in a high wind.' A little later, he refers to tales of entire islands uprooted by hurricanes: 'I've heard tales of them; winds that blow the islands out of the sea. But I think Manukura is pretty well anchored.' Right after this statement, however, Kersaint's confidence in the stability of Manukura is belied as the increasing wind shakes De Laage's house, filmed in an expressionistic play of light and shadow.

The hurricane does not only temporally coincide with the return of Terangi, who functions as a model islander and allegorical figure of island culture, but is also metaphorically and metonymically associated with native revenge (Cassano 2010, 132). Along the same lines, the literal reshaping of the island by the hurricane constitutes an eradication of colonial space. Reading the climactic sequence in this way entails a view of the hurricane as destroying the island in its Western conceptualization as theorized by Gillis and Hauʻofa: the island quite literally disappears as a clearly bordered and bounded entity. After the hurricane, De Laage does not return to the same island. The island has failed as a stronghold of Western civilization; latent fears of its downfall seem realized as a few white men are left on a miniaturized version, apparently without the possibility of reproduction as the only white woman, Germaine De Laage, is thought dead. At the same time, the possibility of renewal for the islanders is implied by the baby of Marama's sister, who gives birth during the hurricane. Read belatedly with Hauʻofa in mind, Manukura indeed becomes an 'isolated [dot] in a vast ocean' from the perspective of the white men. Viewed through the lens of a 'sea of islands', however, the dissolution of the border between water and island in the hurricane magnifies a view of land and sea as connected. As waves flood the island, land vanishes into the sea, and trees are uprooted to become rafts, land and sea mingle: the border of the island loses its distinctive character and becomes fluid. From a Western perspective, the devastation and shrinking of the island means a loss of territory; for Terangi and his family, it means a renewal and reconnection with their ancestors' seafaring habits. Significantly, De Laage is left to stand on a sandspit, while Terangi continues moving. While the French governor has lost ground, Terangi fully reenters his sea of islands.

Yet it is important to note that the sandspit in question is not Manukura, and the film gives no indication as to its location. Entered by both Terangi and De Laage, but significantly not at the same time, the sandspit functions as a kind of Third Space along the lines theorized by Homi Bhabha: '... it is the "inter"—the cutting edge of translation and negotiation, the *inbetween* space—that carries the burden of the meaning of culture' (1994, 56; emphasis original). In Bhabha's account, self and other can only be articulated 'in the passage through a Third Space' (53) in which the subject of enunciation is split off from the 'subject of a proposition' (53), the *énoncé*. For Bhabha, this split undermines all cultural certainties, exposing culture as always in the making and subject to negotiation and revision. Reading the sandspit at the end of *The Hurricane* as a Third Space may be taking Bhabha all too literally, especially as he insists that the Third Space, as the ambivalent

and contradictory space from which all cultural meanings are represented, is 'unrepresentable in itself' (55). Yet Bhabha's own spatial
metaphors justify such a reading. The sandspit is truly an in-between
space: having no clear spatial location and bearing no cultural marks, it
is the space through which both groups need to pass while being unable
to meet in it. If the wasteland on Manukura represents culture unmade,
the sandspit is the space from which culture is articulated and renego-
tiated; it 'constitutes the discursive conditions of enunciation' (Bhabha
55). As such, this last island of *The Hurricane* is related to the small
island from which Matthew Lloyd reaches his fantasy island in *White
Shadows*; in a sense, both islands are phantasms and mark the conditions of possibility for cultural articulation. But *The Hurricane* reverses
the process of *White Shadows*: while the island in *White Shadows* is a
stepping stone to the larger island on which Lloyd's cultural fantasy is
actualized, the nameless island in *The Hurricane* is reached after the
physical and symbolic universes of Manukura have collapsed. This
Third Space, then, is all we are left with at the end of the film; new
configurations are yet to emerge in an uncertain future. We are left in a
state between not-anymore and not-yet.

The Hurricane and the Problem
of American Imperialism

Yet a naïve celebration of the film's anti-colonial politics would be
misplaced. Cassano is not exactly wrong when he argues that *The
Hurricane* 'evoke[s] the genesis of a decolonizing national consciousness among the natives' (2010, 131), but the islanders depicted in the
film are nonetheless largely Western constructions. Drawing on conventional South Sea iconography, the film follows in the wake of the
early explorers' diaries, the drawings of Cook's artists, anthropologists
like Margaret Mead, and earlier films like *White Shadows* in the
depiction of Polynesians in terms of classical beauty, the motif of
lovers-in-a-canoe, and the focus on an alluring native sexuality and
lightly clad bodies. The fact that the film's lead actors, Jon Hall and
Dorothy Lamour, were not Polynesian only supports this view. Hall
was born in California (cf. Monush 2003, 304) and related to James
Norman Hall; his father was born in Switzerland. While Hall partly

grew up in Tahiti, a contemporary article in *The Pittsburgh Press* makes it clear that his mother was of American, English, and French ancestry. Entitled 'He's No Native', the same article emphatically asserts these facts against rumours of Hall being of Polynesian descent: 'I am surprised, ladies, that you should ask if Jon Hall is a native Tahitian. He doesn't look like one and he doesn't act like one' (1938, par. 1). Nonetheless, rumours of Hall being Tahitian have persisted to this day: many online biographies, including the one in the *International Movie Database*, confidently assert that Hall's mother was a 'Tahitian princess'. Lamour, in turn, was born in New Orleans and had Spanish, French Louisianan, and Irish roots but came to epitomize the South Sea islands for American audiences, along with other Hispanic actresses such as Raquel Torres (who played Fayaway in *White Shadows*) and Dolores del Rio (*Bird of Paradise*) (cf. Monush 2003, 405).

Yet the film also draws attention to its own constructions by commenting on the artificial and citational quality of the representations of the island and the islanders. Two scenes on the border of the island play an important role in this: the nocturnal canoe ride and the ensuing love scene on Terangi and Marama's wedding night, and the repetition of this scene upon Terangi's return from Tahiti. The canoe ride of Terangi and Marama cites that of Matthew Lloyd and Fayaway in *White Shadows*, repeating the iconography (beach, water, canoe, palm trees), camera position (on the island), and canoe movements (left to right, spin, right to left) of the latter. With the beginning of the canoe ride, the music changes from classic orchestra to soft Hawaiian guitar, stereotypically associated with Pacific islands ever since the hugely popular Broadway production of *The Bird of Paradise* from 1912 to 1924, and one of Hollywood's stock markers of the exotic to the present day.[14] Similarly, Lamour's enticing garment, somewhat misleadingly referred to as a 'sarong' during the production of the film, is an extravagant Hollywood fantasy more than anything else.[15] Visuals, music, and clothes work together in creating an overdetermined collage of disparate markers of Polynesian 'authenticity'. Self-ironically or not, the film exposes this artificiality. As we see Terangi and Marama push off the canoe, the image dissolves into an extreme long shot of the same scene

[14] In a review of the premiere in January 1912, a *New York Times* critic commented on 'the introduction of the weirdly sensuous music of the island people' (qtd. in Balme 2005, 7).

[15] On Dorothy Lamour's 'sarong', see Brawley and Dixon (2012, 25–7).

viewed from the island, but now they are no more than silhouettes. At the exact moment of the dissolve, the music blends into the same tune in its 'Hawaiian' version. We thus move from an already artificial space into an even more stylized fantasy. The subsequent kiss against a blurry background of palm trees, sand, and sea, followed by soft-focus close-up shots of the lovers, now against an entirely indistinct background, further underscores this move into fantasy. As the lovers lie down on the ground, the camera pans away from them and tilts upwards to reveal palm trees against the moonlit sky. While motivated by censorship, this also charges the entire generic island setting erotically as it becomes metonymically associated with the sexual act.

The parallel scene, in which Terangi is found by his daughter (the result of what was not shown directly in the first scene), takes place in an almost identical setting; the lovers are seen against the same blurry background. But this time, what could still be understood as a stylized rendering of a dream shared by Terangi and Marama in the first scene is subtly marked as a cultural fantasy:

> TERANGI: Marama, I come back.
> MARAMA: I been waiting.
> TERANGI: Eight years—long time!
> MARAMA: You are the same.
> TERANGI: You?
> MARAMA: The same.

Here, both Terangi and Marama use the simple, childish, and grammatically deficient language commonly associated with natives speaking English in contemporary Hollywood films. This stands out insofar as Terangi and Marama otherwise speak impeccable English when talking both to others and to each other. The scene is thus marked as a performance of a Western construction of Polynesian-ness. The same performative gesture can be observed when Marama is discovered hiding on Captain Nagle's ship:

> MARAMA: Please, Captain Nagle, I go to Tahiti!
> NAGLE (TO TERANGI): How did she get aboard, did you bring her?
> MARAMA: No no, I come in a bag, like a coconut. What's wrong with going to Tahiti? I never been. I go just once.

In addition to deploying the same linguistic features, Marama here uses a high-pitched voice, childish gestures, and likens herself to a coconut, that epitome of the natural resources of South Sea islands, performing precisely the characteristics Nagle and Kersaint patronizingly ascribe to the islanders. She performs them to her advantage: reflecting back at Nagle his own ideal of native charm, she gets him to consent to her staying on board.[16] We thus witness a series of performances where non-Polynesian actors perform an artificial Polynesian-ness, which is self-reflexively foregrounded by being staged diegetically.

If the islanders are artificial, so is the island. The 'phony studio settings' lamented by McBride (2001, 265) point to a construction of the island that is literal (the island and the lagoon were studio constructions), ideological, and cinematic (as indicated by the tourist's cine-camera in the frame narrative). What the hurricane destroys is thus also the film's own construction of a Pacific island. By the end of the film, the island has revealed itself as a loose conglomerate of sand. If the palimpsestic geography of the film exposes its islands as conglomerates of texts, images, and maps, the full import of this imaginary geography emerges when Manukura disintegrates and a new island is created. The islands of *The Hurricane* are made, unmade, and remade. They are both material and insubstantial, made both of sand and of ideas. If *The Hurricane* offers a reflection on Hollywood's imaginary islands, it does so by revealing their multilayered and contradictory construction, and thereby challenges its own island fantasies.

Yet the question remains what exactly is dismantled at the end of the film. In order to tackle this problem, we need to return to the layering of political geographies discussed initially. The film evokes French, British, and American imperial ventures in the Pacific, but the latter are only tacitly alluded to through the use of location shots and, almost imperceptibly, the multi-referential maps in the credits. If the island and the colonial order are destroyed in the end, we need to bear in mind that it is a specific colonial order that crumbles. If British imperialism is only present in traces and the French colonial project is indicted as harsh and doomed to failure, where does this leave American imperialism? The answer is complex, not least because the United

---

[16] She leaves of her own accord, however, as her permission to stay on board is conditional upon Terangi renouncing his first mate's cap.

States has denied that it ever had an empire for most of its history.[17] George W. Bush was harping on an old string when he said in 2000 that 'America has never been an empire. We may be the only great power in history that had the chance, and refused' (qtd. in Go 2011, 1). The rhetoric of American exceptionalism insisted on portraying America in opposition to European imperialism, and on stressing its unique status as a benevolent global power. In *Empire for Liberty*, Richard H. Immerman provides an extensive discussion of the contradictions inherent in this 'national delusion' (2010, 2–3); Julian Go argues that '[d]enying empire is simply part of the... *modus operandi* of American empire itself' (2011, 2). Maintaining that even recent revisionist histories reinscribe a form of exceptionalism in arguing that the United States denied its imperial practices because they clashed with its unique values (most importantly that of liberty), Go argues that American imperialism actually underwent a development comparable to that of Britain despite important differences, and in many respects adopted Britain's imperial tactics and techniques at a later historical moment (236).

Yet if the United States has been good at disavowing and forgetting its own imperialism (Go 2), there were also moments when American imperialism became blatantly visible. One such moment occurred around the turn of the twentieth century and manifested itself in the United States' aggressive move into the Pacific. In 1899, well-known democrat William Jennings Bryan published a collection of essays, interviews, and speeches in which eminent American politicians and statesmen discuss the imperialist status of the United States; the volume is entitled *Republic or Empire? The Philippine Question*. In a speech from 1900, Senator Albert J. Beveridge leaves no doubt about his imperial ambitions: 'The Pacific is our ocean.... And the Pacific is the ocean of the commerce of the future. Most future wars will be conflicts for commerce. The power that rules the Pacific, therefore, is the power that rules the world. And, with the Philippines, that power is and will forever be the American Republic' (2008, 372). In the same year, a group of Samoan chiefs and the United States signed the Treaty of

---

[17] It was only in the wake of American reactions to the terrorist attacks of 11 September 2001 that the notion of the United States as an imperialist nation fully entered public consciousness (Immerman 2010, 1–4; Go 2011, 2–3).

Tutuila, in which the island was ceded to America; an autocratic naval government was established and the treaty was ratified by Congress in 1929. In 1930, a commission was dispatched to Samoa in response to an indigenous protest movement referred to as the Mau rebellion (cf. Go 2011, 81–90). The commission published a report in 1930, which went to great lengths to stress the benevolent intentions of the United States and convey the sense that the commission was taking the complaints seriously and viewing the chiefs as collaborative partners.

This is not the place to decide to what extent this view was accurate. What matters in the present context is the rhetorical gesture, which makes the report a useful intertext for understanding the politics of *The Hurricane*. This is how it begins:

> Always in the history of American Samoa the arrival of ships of war marked events of moment. They were the powerful hand of the great white people of the north reaching far into the South Pacific, some- times a mailed fist stretching out for the riches of the Tropics and sometimes a palm of good will extending a clasp of friendship and of helpfulness.   (Moore and Farrington 1931, 1)

While this opening paragraph recognizes the islands' history of vio- lence, it ends on a vision of benevolent colonialism. The paragraph prefigures in miniature the trajectory of the entire report, which moves through various positions and complaints to the final meeting of the commission and the chiefs, where '[n]o one was found who expressed dissatisfaction' (62). Interestingly, the first historical ship arrival the report mentions right after the opening paragraph ended in a disaster of a distinctly non-human kind: as German, British, and American warships were in the harbour of Apia in today's Independent State of Samoa, the imminent military crisis was prevented by a devastating hurricane that sank all but one of the ships; Lorna Fitzsimmons mentions this hurricane as one of the possible historical inspirations for Ford's film as well as the novel it adapts (2003, 58). The hurricane and the bombard- ment of Upolu during the Wilkes expedition form a catastrophic back- drop for *The Hurricane*;[18] significantly, one of the incidents constitutes a

---

[18] Fitzsimmons mentions the Massacre Bay incident at Tutuila of 1787, which resulted in the death of almost forty Samoans and a dozen Frenchmen, as another possible historical context for the film and the novel (2003, 57).

human threat to the islands, while the other is removed from human agency and control. The report of the commission does not mention the Upolu incident or any other outbursts of violence in its list of momentous Samoan arrivals; its emphasis is on diplomacy. Furthermore it moves, somewhat bizarrely, directly from the hurricane to the division of the islands between Germany and the United States: 'In 1889 the ships of three powers lay in menacing proximity in Apia Harbor of western Samoa only to be destroyed or driven away by the historic hurricane. The treaty of Berlin came in consequence of this visit...' (1). The transition rhetorically suggests that the division of Samoa was produced by the hurricane and thus followed a natural (or divinely ordained) path. It also reasserts white agency after the paralysis of the same by the forces of nature, but while the latter are portrayed as violent, this human agency is non-violent.

Conversely, the earlier discussed sense of detachment in midshipman Reynolds's account of the Upolu incident poetically transforms the attack into something similar to a natural disaster, but also conveys a sense that the island withdraws from the American visitors' gaze and grasp: 'There was no breath of air stirring on the water, and the shore seemed wrapt in deep repose. Occasionally and but very seldom a native was to be seen for an instant, moving amid the trees' (2004, 228). The distance to the island viewed from the water here momentarily seems unbridgeable despite the geographical proximity, and despite the attack. Similar moments of distancing run through the commission report. In the description of the approach to Tutuila, 'when the islands of American Samoa appeared to those on the *Omaha* through a drizzling rain' (13), this blurred perception finds a counterpart in perceptual difficulties that are cultural as much as sensory:

> Dense, dark green foliage covered the landscape, *made hazy* by the morning showers.... On the western side of the bay ... was the naval station, the colorless wharf, warehouses, radio towers, oil storage tanks of western civilization, and the well-kept yards of officers' homes, all of uniform frame construction. On the east side Poyer School, a low, concrete structure, once almost white, *stood out plainly*.
>
> *Where were the native homes?* Only here and there a clearing revealed a native habitation. Many others, hemmed in by the dense growth of hot, damp tropical days, were *invisible*. (13; my emphasis)

The island here resists the western gaze from the water in various ways. Vision is impaired by the hazy rain as well as by the foliage covering the landscape. While the colonial buildings are described with precision and said to stand out plainly, somewhat in contradiction to the haze asserted just before, 'the native homes' are described as nearly invisible.

Descriptions like the above are clearly intertextually shaped. In fact, the commission had an entire library on board, spending their afternoons reading texts about Samoa and the South Seas by people as diverse as Wilkes and Stevenson (Moore and Farrington 1931, 5). The description not only recalls Reynolds's diary, but also uncannily echoes Stevenson's account of his first island landfall in the South Seas in 1888:[19]

> The suffusion of vague hues deceived the eye; the shadows of clouds were confounded with the articulations of the mountain; and the isle and its unsubstantial canopy rose and shimmered before us like a single mass. There was no beacon, no smoke of towns to be expected.... Somewhere, in that pale phantasmagoria of cliff and cloud, our haven lay concealed.... These conspicuous habitations, that patch of culture, had we but known it, were a mark of the passage of whites.... It was longer ere we spied the native village, standing (in the universal fashion) close upon a curve of beach, close under a grove of palms....
>
> (1896, 3–5)

The initial perceptual uncertainty and insubstantiality, the visibility of the 'white' buildings, the difficulty to see the traces of local habitation: Stevenson's 'phantasmagoria' reverberates in the report in all of these points, as if the commission had seen the islands through Stevenson's (unseeing) eyes. The observers seem to be viewing two islands, one that is familiar (the colonial island), and another that withdraws from their gaze. If nature plays a part in shielding this second island, another passage in the commission report marks the contrast between white governance and natural forces even more pronouncedly:

> The governmental life of American Samoa, so far as it concerned the Samoan people, not only began but ended within the geographical limits of the 60 square miles of jagged, densely overgrown islands

---

[19] Stevenson's first landfall was in the Marquesas Islands.

> which were forced above the level of the Pacific Ocean by volcanic
> action centuries ago. (2)

Again, we have two sets of islands: one that is governed by the American
navy and thus produced as a colonial space, and one that was produced
by volcanic activity, separate from the former. As with the evocation of
the 1889 hurricane, and as in Reynolds's account of the attack on Upolu,
white agency and natural forces sit uneasily with each other, diametrically opposed, but also always potentially turning into each other.

A similar uncertainty surrounding the opposition between natural
and colonial forces structures the devastation of the island in *The
Hurricane*. When *The Hurricane* was produced, textual and visual
material on Pacific islands in general and on Samoa in particular was
widely circulated; Hollywood picked up on and transformed these
discourses just as the Samoan commission's perception of the islands
was shaped by previous writings. The hurricane in Ford's island 'phantasmagoria' thus resonates with Reynolds's journal and with the report
of the Samoan commission in that it is both a natural disaster and
something else; indeed, the main difference from *White Shadows* is that
the responsibility for the destruction of the island paradise is shifted
away from human agents and assigned to nature. At the same time, the
coincidence of the hurricane with the escalation of conflicts between
colonial authority and islanders marks this at least partly as an ideological operation.

But if the hurricane is also a trope, what does it represent? The wrath
of the ruthless French governor, the embodiment of colonial violence?
Or its opposite—the anti-colonial rage of the islanders—as Cassano
would have it (2010, 132)? Or God's punishment, the embodiment of
biblical apocalypse, creating a second flood, as Fitzsimmons argues
(2003, 65-7)? Then again, God's punishment for what? For human
sin? For colonial rule in general? Or only for French colonial rule? Or
does it simply represent the failure of French or European colonialism?
The hurricane is all of these things at once, and none of them fully. The
one thing it is *not* is the embodiment of American imperialism. The
film performs the same ideological operation as the Samoan commission report, the denial Immerman and Go see as characteristic of
America's relation to its own imperialism. It performs the forgetting
of America's ambitions of empire that aggressively surfaced around

1900: America, unlike Europe, is not imperialist, it is diplomatic; it is not a ruler, but a benevolent helper. Coercive force and violence are elsewhere: in the French colonial regime, say, or in nature itself. American imperialism hides in plain sight: America owns and controls its Pacific islands, yet the knowledge of this ownership cannot be shown directly, even if the location shots and the maps of the credit sequence tacitly suggest that the film is really about the American Pacific empire following in the wake of European colonial ventures.

Furthermore, the assignment of violence to nature is in itself ambivalent. If it displaces violence, it also potentially displaces human agency altogether, including American agency. If the Reynolds journal, Stevenson's account, and the Samoan commission report all betray an anxiety that the islands might elude the (American) observer's gaze, understanding, or control, the last images of Manukura in its devastation bear the same potential. On the one hand, of course, they return us to the frame narrative: the barren emptiness of the island allows its recreation as a fantasy space by the tourist and Doctor Kersaint; as a paradisiacal space, it is eroded and made present again by an aesthetic transformation associated with the film camera. Yet in their glaring artificiality, the vast expanses of sand at the end of the film also open up an alternative, more unsettling reading: they suggest that Kersaint and the tourist may in fact see nothing at all, and that their visions may emerge from a desperate desire to see the island. They hint at the possibility that the only creative and destructive power is located in nature, that islands are created by volcanic forces and destroyed or reshaped by hurricanes, and not by the American imagination. At the end of the film, Manukura becomes visible for what it is: heaps of sand and painted backgrounds in a studio, a poor substitute for an island rising out of the ocean. At the heart of *The Hurricane* lurks the fear that Hollywood may fail to imagine its islands.

Yet while challenged, the impulse to view the island is powerfully expressed in *The Hurricane*. My argument rests on the assumption that the imaginative transformation in the gaze from the water that is such an important part of eighteenth- and nineteenth-century accounts of Pacific islands is one of the reasons why cinema could so readily pick up on this tradition. These fantasies were cinematic before the advent of cinema. Albeit in different ways, both *White Shadows* and *The Hurricane* associate this imaginative act with the camera and with cinema.

Invading the Island: Ethnography, Film, and the Death of King Kong

The films share this gesture with emerging documentary film practices. Before working on *White Shadows*, Robert Flaherty had made two ethnographic films: *Nanook of the North* (1922) and the already mentioned *Moana* (1926), portraying Inuit life and life on a South Sea island, respectively. Yet in both films, Flaherty conjured up a vision that had little to do with the everyday life of the subjects he filmed, staging an imagined past and customs that had long disappeared for the camera (cf. Barsam 1992, 49–54). Flaherty left *White Shadows* before completion because the cooperation with Van Dyke did not work, but the film remains indebted to the gesture and style of his films.

This gesture was closely linked to the emerging discipline of anthropology. In *Tristes Tropiques*, a belated account of his time in the tropics in the 1930s, Claude Lévi-Strauss famously stated: 'I wished I had lived in the days of *real* journeys, when it was still possible to see the full splendour of a spectacle that had not yet been blighted, polluted and spoilt (1973, 43; emphasis original). Yet Lévi-Strauss only makes this statement in order to question it: he concludes that travellers are always doomed to miss the spectacle of the present in the search for a lost, idealized past. But the salvage anthropologists of the 1920s and 1930s often lacked Lévi-Strauss's theoretical sophistication. The first scientific anthropological studies were studies of tropical islands, such as the Torres Strait expedition of 1898 and Bronislaw Malinowski's study of the Trobriand Islands in the 1910s. Because of their apparent boundedness, islands seemed to offer ethnographers ideal field conditions (cf. Beer 1989, 22; Edmond and Smith 2003, 2–3). Desiring to grasp a culture in its totality, these anthropologists were often prone to essentializing views in their efforts to preserve vanishing cultures. It is no coincidence that, as Lyons notes (2006, 142), Mead's beginning of her 1928 study of Samoa sounds like a romantic travelogue: 'As the dawn begins to fall among the soft brown roofs and the slender palm trees stand out against a colourless, gleaming sea, lovers slip home from trysts beneath the palm trees or in shadow of beached canoes' (12). The iconography is as close as it gets to the opening images of *White Shadows*. In fact, cameras were often an integral part of ethnographers' attempts to record a foreign culture, a practice that goes back as far as the drawings of South Sea islands and islanders by the artists accompanying Cook for the purpose of visual documentation (cf. Geiger 2007, 32–8).

Released in 1933 and directed by Merian C. Cooper and Ernest B. Schoedsack, *King Kong* resonates with all of the issues addressed so far. It differs from *White Shadows* and *The Hurricane* in an important respect: its island not set in the South Pacific but in the Indian Ocean. I include it in this chapter firstly because the chapters of this book are organized neither chronologically nor geographically; as explained in the introduction, I believe it is more fruitful to map a poetics of islands by tracing links that cut across temporal and spatial continuities. More specifically, I include it because Hollywood's island geography of the 1920s and 1930s transcends geographical boundaries. Skull Island may not be in the South Pacific, but it strongly resonates with the wave of island films set in the South Seas that were made around the same time. There is no specific Indian Ocean island imaginary in the American cinema of the 1930s, and it was as good as impossible for Hollywood to imagine a tropical island outside the conventions that had formed around the countless South Sea island films,[20] although there are significant differences in the representation of the islanders, which also evokes contemporary myths of African 'savagery' and associated fantasies of human origins (see Rony 1996, 157–92).[21] *King Kong* is examined at the end of this chapter because, of the three films discussed here, it is the one that most explicitly associates the desire to see the island with cinema. It is also the film where this cinematic desire is at its most violent as it aggressively freezes the island into an image. Exploration, cinema, tourism, and ethnography are all complicit in this visual appropriation. The expedition of a film crew, led by director Carl Denham, to a hitherto undiscovered, mythical island, is both a modern

---

[20] It is no coincidence that the island of *King Kong* is sometimes mistakenly placed in the Pacific. Thus, James Snead locates it in the Pacific although he correctly states that it is west of Sumatra, notably in an article about geographical displacements (1991), and the German subtitles of the *Arthaus* DVD edition translate 'Nias Islanders' as 'Südsee-Insulaner' ('South Sea islanders'). On *King Kong*'s relation to both 'African' and 'Pacific' imaginaries, see Rony 1996, 157–92.

[21] The choice of African-American actors for the islanders also speaks to contemporary American anxieties about blackness (see Snead 1991).

cinematic enterprise and echoes the early voyages of discovery. For the unemployed Fay Wray, the voyage is an escape from Depression-era misery into the glamour of both the tropics and Hollywood.

The director's sensationalist desire is linked to travellers' yarns and tourist fantasies as well as to an ethnographic desire to record the other and the past. During the voyage to the island, it becomes clear that Denham and his crew are following in the wake of other voyages to the tropics even while purporting to make new discoveries. Shortly before the ship enters unknown waters, we see the skipper poring over his charts. Stating that they are moving to a part of the Indian Ocean that is 'way out of any waters [he] knows', although he 'know[s] the East Indies like [he] do[es his] own hand', his words suggest a possible reason for the location of the island in the Indian Ocean. Less present in American minds than the Pacific, it may have offered the imaginary possibility of discovering unknown islands at a time when the Pacific had become a highway for American steamers. Denham goes on to unfold two maps detailing the location and precise shape of the island (Figure 2.6), explaining that it cannot be found on any official map, and that he received the maps from a Norwegian skipper in Singapore, who had drawn them on the basis of the description he had received from an islander before his death, the only survivor of a storm that had blown his canoe out to sea. The pattern is familiar: a hitherto undiscovered island is accessible only through traces surviving after multiple trans-missions. Ironically, as in *White Shadows*, the very notion of the island's being undiscovered makes Denham's voyage a repetition of former voyages. Significantly, the map was drawn on the basis of words. Denham's insistence on the veracity of the map thus has an almost performative dimension; his own words bring the island into being a second time, again creating an image through words. The desire to discover the unknown translates into a desire to see: 'I tell you there's something on that island that no white man has ever seen', Denham adds, and the link between discovery, seeing, and cinema is immedi-ately understood by the skipper: 'And you expect to photograph it?' Denham makes it clear that he will film the unknown at all cost, even if he needs to use coercive force in the form of gas bombs.

At the same time, the desire to see is also linked to cinema's potential to make its viewers see what is not present. As such, the film's emphasis on unknown space has a self-reflexive dimension: there may be no

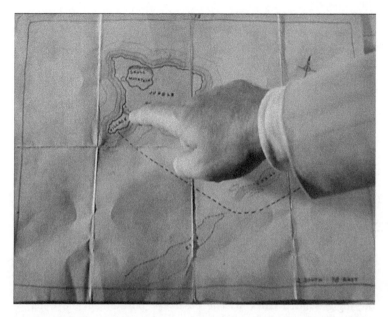

FIGURE 2.6 Still from *King Kong* (Merian C. Cooper and Ernest B. Schoedsack, USA 1933)

more unknown islands in the real world, but ever new islands can still be discovered in the imaginary geography of Hollywood. Significantly, Denham's conversation with the skipper is followed by a scene that dramatizes the cinematic gaze in its purest form as Denham has his lead actress rehearse expressions of terror in front of the camera, asking her to imagine seeing something frightening.[22] As we hear Denham's directions from off-screen space, Ann's facial expression keeps changing as she stares into imagined space, ending with a piercing scream, before a cut reveals the faces of the skipper and first mate Jack Driscoll, staring intensely at Ann in turn. We are thus faced with a series of gazes: the gaze of the diegetic film camera, associated with Denham; the gaze recorded by the camera; the gazes of Driscoll and the skipper; and,

---

[22] On the importance of the gaze in *King Kong*, see Snead (1991) and Telotte (1988).

finally, the gaze of the extradiegetic film camera and audience, gazing at Denham, the skipper, and Driscoll gazing at Ann gazing at an imagined source of terror. The camera thus ends up recording its own gaze, disseminated across the fictional universe of the film; our own gaze is reflected back at us through the various internal gazes. The original object of this series of gazes is, again, an imaginary vision triggered by words, by Carl Denham's directions.

This rehearsal of pure gazes is immediately linked back to the island as the prime imaginary object of the gaze: after a fade-out and a fade-in, we see the ship gliding through dense fog, followed by a dissolve to a shot of Denham, the skipper, and Ann gazing intently into the fog. This is followed by a series of shots of different parts of the crew staring into the fog and speculating about the island. Like Doctor Kersaint and the tourist at the beginning of *The Hurricane*, Denham, Ann, and the crew see an imaginary version of the island even though, or rather because, they cannot see anything at all. The appearance of the island marks it as a manifestation of the imaginary gaze preceding it: after the last image of the gazing faces has faded out, a view of the island from the ship after the fog has lifted fades in. The observers' position on the water is emphasized by the railings and ropes in the foreground. After a few seconds, we see the skipper stepping into the image and gazing at the island through his binoculars (Figure 2.7), which further signals the continuation of a mediated gaze. The image corresponds exactly to the descriptions and imagined versions of the island; as Denham, soon joining the skipper, says: 'There it is. Skull Mountain, the wall— everything just like on my funny little map.' The island seems to spring right from their visions and from the map.

The two scenes depicting the emergence of the island—first in Denham's narrative and map, then appearing from the fog—thus frame Ann's rehearsal of a pure gaze for the camera. Sandwiched between the two former scenes, the series of gazes around an imagined object points to the imaginary kernel at the heart of the film's con- struction of the island. The island comes into being after someone else's reputed knowledge of it has been turned into a cartographic image, reported by words, and turned into an image again. The film's mediated construction of the island thus reveals the multiple transmission of the tropical island-image from the journals of the early explorers to later travel accounts, fictional island narratives, and, finally, Hollywood's

FIGURE 2.7   Still from *King Kong* (Merian C. Cooper and Ernest B. Schoedsack, USA 1933)

imaginary islands. The gaze through the fog maximizes the phenomenal uncertainty in the perception of the island viewed from a distance. In *King Kong*, the island is not hazy as in the early Pacific journals, but initially not visible at all; it has to be imagined entirely. There is nothing unstable about this imagined island, and the cinematic gaze is undisguisedly violent.

This representational violence becomes explicit as Denham arrives on Skull Island armed with camera, guns, and gas bombs, and the impossibility of observation and recording without interference becomes apparent. A central tension that Malinowski can never quite resolve is the mutual cancelling out of two of his requirements: the ethnographer has to become part of the native community in order to record it faithfully, yet he must not enter into active relations with the locals to ensure impartial observation (see Malinowski 2002, 1–25). *King Kong* negotiates precisely this problem. The team's scopophilic

desire manifests itself again after landing as they observe a local ceremony and Ann says 'I wanna see', following Denham's 'Boy, if I could
only get a picture before they see us!' The attempt to see without being
seen in the filming of the ceremony, however, is interrupted and the
course of events irrevocably changed as the islanders notice the team: as
their shaman explains, the ceremony has been spoiled because the film
team has seen it. In what follows, guns replace cameras as Kong is
finally captured and brought to Broadway. On the island, the film team
crosses a second boundary, the high wall separating the islanders from
the realm of Kong. If the intrusive presence of the camera, both
recording and interfering in paradise, is implicit in *White Shadows*
and *The Hurricane*, its violence is explicit in *King Kong* in the analogy
between guns and camera. In fact, Malinowski himself uses a hunting
metaphor: 'But the Ethnographer has not only to spread his nets in the
right place, and wait for what will fall into them. He must be an active
huntsman, and drive his quarry into them' (2002, 8). *King Kong* seems
to suggest that the other can only be recorded objectively and trans-
parently if it is turned into a visual spectacle and thereby killed off.

As the film progresses, filmic and ethnographic gazes become more
closely linked.[23] Before Denham sets up his camera in the scene just
discussed, the extradiegetic camera explores the ceremony independently of the film crew. After a series of cuts from Denham (and, later,
the skipper) looking through the grass to a long shot of the islanders
and back, the camera suddenly disengages itself from the observers. It is
placed amidst the islanders, recording the ceremony from various
angles, some of which are entirely incompatible with the positions of
Denham and the skipper. Only the viewer is given these privileged
viewpoints, as in the depersonalized ethnographic shots of *White
Shadows* discussed earlier. After about 45 seconds, the film cuts back
to the skipper and Denham, who begins to mount his camera. In
narrative terms, the sequence is poorly motivated: there is no reason
why Denham would wait so long before beginning to film. I would
therefore argue that the spectral extradiegetic camera here functions as
a double of Denham's own camera and enacts an impossible

---

[23] For a discussion of *King Kong* in the context of ethnographic cinema, see Rony
(1996, 157–92).

ethnographic fantasy—or, read critically, points to the latter's limitations. Representing a pure and depersonalized ethnographic gaze, it can mingle with the islanders without interacting with them, record without interfering, and thus meet Malinowski's criteria for ethnographers. In doing so, however, it also contrasts with Denham's camera, thereby revealing its ideological work: as viewers, we can only enjoy its seemingly disengaged view because of the intrusive violence of the latter. Denham's camera represents the violent kernel of the apparently disinterested ethnographic gaze; as viewers, we become complicit in the ambivalent ethnographic project of both the film and Denham.

In the remainder of the film, the spectral ethnographic camera makes its presence felt at regular intervals. A particularly striking example occurs after the crew has entered the space on the far side of the wall filled with dinosaurs and other prehistoric creatures. As Kong battles a dinosaur, Ann, watching from a tree stump and screaming, acts out the previously rehearsed terrified gazes. Initially, the film cuts back and forth between a close-up view of the fighting monsters and a long shot of the fight from behind two gnarled trees that frame the scene by twisting almost entirely around it. The position is the more spectral as the remaining crew members have just been killed by the giant ape with the exception of Driscoll. I draw attention to these shots because they aesthetically repeat the first view of the island framed by railings and ropes, which we can now read as the first instance of a depersonalized vision linked to a collective desire to see the island and its inhabitants. This empty position is filled by the viewer, who becomes a ghostly presence in the film, first taking in the island in its entirety, then gradually moving into its centre and penetrating its secrets while remaining untouched by the violence of Denham's scopophilic desire.

The filming of Kong's defeat offers the most suggestive comment on the representational violence of Denham's project as the giant ape himself is turned into an image. Yet Denham's picture is never completed, at least not in the cinematic sense of the term. As the masses stream into the Broadway theatre, however, they expect a moving picture:

USHER: This is not a moving picture, Madam.
LADY: What? But Mr Denham makes those pictures of those
    darling monkeys and tigers and things.

USHER: But this is more in the nature of a personal appearance, Madam.

LADY: Well, I never! I thought I was gonna see something.

The elderly lady has clear generic expectations of seeing another of the jungle documentaries Denham usually makes.[24] Rather curiously, however, she turns away indignantly when she is promised a 'personal appearance', complaining that she had hoped to 'see something'. Should we not expect the reverse? Is there not a surplus of 'seeing' in the 'personal appearance' of Kong as opposed to the insubstantial images of film? The lady's reaction tells us much about the economy of vision in *King Kong*. She is representative of the entire audience in her dislike of a live exhibition: Kong fails to satisfy the audience's scopophilic desires as his living body interferes with the spectacle of seeing. As long as Kong is alive, there is always the possibility that he might return the gaze. This, of course, is precisely what he does: irritated by an onslaught of gazes in the form of the journalists' flashing cameras, he breaks free and scatters the audience; shortly after this, we see Kong's enormous face and roving eyes in a bedroom window. The scene is repeated when Kong's furiously blinking eyes become visible at the bottom of Ann's window higher up in the same building. Now it is Kong who has become all eyes, reflecting back at his captors their own violent gaze.

Only after he has been killed does Kong really draw the masses. The film ends with a diagonally split shot: Kong's giant body fills the bottom right half of the image, while Denham and countless bystanders fill the top left half, gazing at the black mass of flesh in awe. The final shot of Kong's dead body exposes the representational violence of cinema: Carl Denham's picture, as it were, has finally been made, but at the price of the death of its subject. Kong's death accentuates the invisible violence inherent in the spectral ethnographic camera. Observing without being observed, it presupposes the death of what is recorded. In *King Kong*, the cinematic image is ambivalent, and its ambivalence is related to the ambiguity in the word 'picture', which Denham uses as a synonym for

---

[24] On the double origins of *King Kong* in the jungle film and the travelogue, see Erb (2009, 59–119). On the two travel films made by Cooper and Schoedsack (*Grass*, 1925; *Chang*, 1927), see Barsam (1992, 54–5).

'film' (the compound nouns 'motion picture' and 'moving picture' were still commonly used when *King Kong* was made). In *King Kong*, the moving picture returns to its origins in the still image, disguised by a mere illusion of movement: the moving picture is King Kong killed and brought back to life on and as film, evident (though surely not intentionally so) in the ape's jerky half-movements caused by stop-motion technology. Echoing the static depiction of the island in *White Shadows*, the ethnographic camera of *King Kong* is caught between movement and stasis. It can record no more than a spectral movement as King Kong and, ultimately, the entire island are frozen into an image.

The Other Island: Skull Island and Mannahatta

The spatiality of the island plays a crucial role in Kong's reduction to an image. On Skull Island, his God-like control is linked to his capacity to survey the entire island; indeed, the island is defined by its mountain. In his triumph, Kong takes Ann to the highest point of the island; climbing to heights marks his power. On Skull Mountain, we are constantly reminded of the island setting as the shoreline is always in sight. Driscoll and Ann's escape route is from the mountain to the sea; Kong's defeat, in turn, is linked to his being lured from the heart of his island to its border. It is on the beach that Kong is immobilized for the first time by gas bombs; before the film cuts to the neon lights announcing Denham's Broadway show, we see Kong's body spread on the beach in a shot that anticipates the final shot of the film in its composition and camera angle.

The link between the shots points to a general spatial analogy linking the two parts of the film. There are, after all, two islands in *King Kong*, one mirroring, inverting, and replacing the other. Located on opposite sides of the globe, Skull Island and Manhattan are closely linked even while functioning as polar opposites in many ways. While the former is an island of (pre)history, the latter is an island of the future; where dark-skinned natives represented as primitive and backward populate the one, the other is the emerging centre of white civilization; where fragile bamboo huts and spears mark Skull Island, Manhattan is the site of skyscrapers and modern technology. Yet for all these differences, the two islands are at times dangerously close to each other. At the beginning of the film, when Denham's agent refuses to find an actress for him, the director replies: 'Listen, there are dozens of girls in this town tonight that are in more danger than they'll ever see with me.' When Kong roams the streets of Manhattan, the seemingly massive architecture gives way as easily as the bamboo huts on Skull Island; screaming natives running around frantically are paralleled by panicky New Yorkers doing exactly the same. The film's real source of terror lies in the possibility that Skull Island and Manhattan may not be that different from each other after all, that the glittering façade of the modern city is only a thin veneer ready to crumble at any moment. Howe is certainly right when he argues that '[t]he Pacific islands... were now seen as a safe playground for recreational sailors, travelers, tourists' (2000, 54), a claim that can be extended to tropical islands more generally. For Howe, '[i]t was a time when it was claimed that nature had been tamed. Great rivers had been diverted and dammed. Isthmuses were cut open and seas joined.... Great forests were cleared, great swamps drained' (54).

In *King Kong*, however, the old fear of Western extinction in the tropics is replayed. The natives on the shore are no obstacle and easily tamed by Denham and his crew. But the larger part of the island beyond the wall resists appropriation. Despite a series of violent incursions, the interior of the island remains out of the Americans' reach and only brings them death. The elements conspire in undoing them, and technology fails them: their guns are powerless as the impenetrable fog, the swampy lake, and the dense jungle deliver them into the hands and fangs of prehistoric monsters. The split of the island can thus also be seen in terms of the history of Western island fantasies: if the near side of the island represents the tamed island of the early twentieth century as outlined by Howe, the interior is older not only in terms of its inhabitants, but also in terms of the textual history it evokes, returning to the dangerous island of nineteenth-century representations. This is another reason why Kong must be defeated on the beach, on the edge of his territory. He needs to be brought into a zone where he can be tamed, which gives the Americans the sense of having mastered the entire island.

In Manhattan, this scenario is replayed as Kong is finally killed on another border of the island, the border of land and sky. Kong is indeed defeated by two recent inventions of Western technology: the airplane and the radio. Here, too, Kong climbs to the highest point of the island, the Empire State Building. But this time, the climb marks his defeat. Used to dominating everything on land, he is powerless in the face of an attack from the air; while he crushes a train without any difficulties in a repetition of his fight with a giant snake on his island, the airplanes do not fit into the spatial organization of the world as he knows it. While the airplanes, too, have their counterpart in the pterosaur attacking Kong on Skull Mountain, the latter poses no real threat because it can only attack Kong by entering his space. The airplanes, by contrast, can attack Kong by shooting at him from a distance and from all directions. Kong's centrally organized world is represented by a series of shots showing him against the background of Manhattan with the shoreline in view, reminiscent of the shots of the island from Skull Mountain. However, the view of Queensboro Bridge and the expanding city across the water presents Manhattan as a very different island; fully connected, it marks a contrast to the extreme remoteness of Skull Island to the point that its island status becomes insignificant or questionable. As the airplanes attack Kong, canted shots and various views of the planes against the white sky emphasize his spatial disorientation, and point-of-view shots from the perspective of the airplanes take the power of the gaze away from Kong to give it back to the Americans.

In 'The Island and the Aeroplane', Beer comments on the altered status of islands in the age of the airplane, when 'the island could be seen anew, scanned from above' (1990, 273). Beer is mainly concerned with the links between the new 'patchwork continuity of an earth seen in this style' (266) and the dissolution of nationhood in its imperial form, but a similar point can be made about the dissolution of Kong's realm. As discussed earlier, *King Kong* was made at a time when airlines were gearing up for the conquest of the oceans. The already mentioned *NYT* article titled 'Airplanes in the South Seas' speculated that this would lead to a 'drastic revision in the habits of South Sea islanders who see in such plans the final collapse of their sublime detachment from the world', and that '[t]he coming of regular airplane service... may mean the dawn of a new era in the South Seas in which semi-mythical specks shown only on the largest maps will emerge as real islands, as tourist paradises, as the fulfillment of the wealthy commuter's dreams' (21 March 1937). While masquerading as concern over impending changes in the lives of the islanders, the vision articulated here constructs the islands as remote and fragile, doomed by the 'fatal impact' of Western intrusion, reaching its apex with the coming of the airplane. Somewhat paradoxically, the article asserts a fear that 'semi-mythical specks' will become both 'real islands' and 'tourist paradises'; what is threatened by the airplane, then, is precisely *not* the islanders' islands, but America's and Hollywood's imaginary islands (alluded to in the same article). At the same time, this fantasy space is made accessible, fulfilling the dreams of all those who can afford a ticket.

King Kong enacts this ambivalence of the airplane: it kills the king of the tropical island and threatens to undo his territory, simultaneously preserving him as a static image to be gazed at. The coming of the airplane makes the seaborne voyages of discovery as depicted at the beginning of the film obsolete. It also, however, marks the final triumph over the islands, the elimination of whatever was still threatening in them. And it is not until Kong's resistance in Manhattan that the Americans realize their own technological possibilities: 'There's one thing we haven't thought of,' Driscoll, the mariner, suddenly exclaims: 'airplanes!' The trigger of this insight is another technological innovation: the radio, detailing Kong's trajectory on the island of Manhattan. Mark McGurl argues that the Empire State Building in *King Kong* can be read in relation to the radio tower depicted at the beginning of the film in the logo of the Hollywood studio RKO (Radio-Keith-Orpheum), created in the late twenties by the RCA (Radio Corporation of America). McGurl reads the film and its concerns with the visible and the invisible in relation to its corporate paternity in the radio industry or, in Lee de Forest's famous dictum, the 'Invisible Empire of the Air' (1996). I would add that the jagged radio waves emitted from the tower of the RKO logo (McGurl 1996, 418) can also be related to the airplanes whirling around the Empire State Building. Both technologies attack Kong from the air. It is with the help of the radio that his progression can be broadcast immediately to the entire city; the radio's invisible gaze keeps track of Kong's movements, depriving him of his commanding gaze along with the airplanes.

By the end of the film, then, the right to view the island has been restored to Carl Denham and his American audience. Skull Island has been superseded by the island of Manhattan, a modern island that has become fully connected to the surrounding islands and the mainland via bridges and tunnels;[25] through airplanes and radio waves, it realizes its full potential of being inserted in a continuous patchwork landscape. Manhattan represents an entirely built environment, an island fully covered by man-made constructions, extending into the mainland over and under the sea. Nature, an insuperable force for Denham and his crew while in the interior of Skull Island, has indeed been tamed and become fully manageable on the island of Manhattan. Meanwhile, the tropical island is again what it was from the start: an insubstantial image existing only in the minds of the diegetic film crew and the audience, transmitted by a series of texts and circulating in the American imaginary.

This is also why Skull Island, unlike Manhattan, is represented as remote and isolated. In order to fulfil its ideological function, it needs to be viewed from a distance. This distance is signalled by the framed image of the island when it is first seen from the ship. Despite the long island episode, the initial distance is never really bridged: as with David Porter's wars on Nukuhiva, the border is violently crossed and thus never really crossed at all. To return once again to the island vision of an operator in a movie theatre described in a letter to the editor of the *NYT*, the giant ape is, for a while, quite literally out of frame, only to be framed for good by the end of the film. At Kong's death, Denham comments that 'it was beauty killed the beast', ostensibly referring to Ann. But it is also beauty as an abstract aesthetic principle that kills King Kong. Read in this way, *King Kong* reveals the disturbing aspects lurking behind the glamorous image of the tropical island, demonstrating just how large an apparatus it takes to make palm trees and romantic pineapples mask military violence and economic exploitation, and how easily the hazy picture across the border, viewed from the water, can always fall out of frame again.

If *King Kong* dramatizes the most violent gaze of the three films discussed here, and if its island is the most distanced one in several respects, this is also, perhaps, because in a different sense Skull Island is nearest home. It may be a tropical island, but it can also serve as a reminder of Manhattan before it was settled by Europeans. In an article about the historical Manhattan, Eric W. Sanderson and Marianne

---

[25] For a discussion of the impact of fixed links on the status of islands, see Baldacchino (2007a).

Brown write that 'interest in the past ecology of the local region is almost inevitable because the modern cityscape is so markedly different from the historical landscape.... Early Dutch and English accounts overflow with fantastic descriptions of the abundant wildlife, magnificent park-like forests, and extensive marshlands of Manhattan Island and neighboring areas' (2007, 545). As director of the Wildlife Conservation Society's Mannahatta Project (1999–2009),[26] which was dedicated to a reconstruction of the ecology of Manhattan Island before the arrival of Henry Hudson in 1609 and was subsequently expanded into the Welikia Project,[27] Sanderson has been promoting an engagement with what, from a Western perspective, is indeed prehistoric Manhattan in order to articulate an ecological vision for the future, labelled Manhattan 2409:

> The goal of the project is to discover something new about a place we all know so well...and, through that discovery, to alter our way of life. New York does not lack for dystopian visions of its future; King Kong, climate change, war, and disease have all had their cinematic moments tearing the Big Apple down. But what is the vision of the future that works? Might it lie in Mannahatta, the green heart of New York, and with a new start to history, a few hours before Hudson arrived that sunny afternoon four hundred years ago? (33)

Sanderson even mentions *King Kong* in sketching his project, though he offers no further comment on the film(s). He is certainly right when he uses it to mark a contrast to his own vision, but Mannahatta is also present in *King Kong*. It is present in the swamps and jungles of Skull Island, but only as a landscape of fear that needs to be left behind. Read in this way, the story of Manhattan's transformation from a green island of hills, swamps, and dense forests into a landscape made of concrete is buried in *King Kong*, displaced almost beyond recognition. The old Manhattan has to be disavowed in the film's celebration of technological progress; it has to be located on a distant tropical island, as far away from modern Manhattan as possible. The Mannahatta

---

[26] Mannahatta was the name given to the island by the indigenous population, recorded as *Manna-hata* in the journal of Robert Juet, mate on the *Halve Maen* (2006, 516).

[27] The Welikia project examines the past ecology of the entire area of New York City (see welikia.org).

Project seeks to restore what *King Kong* would repress: its goal is to contemplate the island of the past without fear and bring it into the present—to transform Manhattan into an island for the future, utopian or otherwise.

Conclusion: The Resilience and Fragility of the Island-Image

We have travelled a long way on our journey among imaginary tropical islands. In different ways, all the islands examined in this chapter function as images, as eye-lands taking shape before the body's and the mind's eye in the perceptual effect outlined by Françoise Létoublon et al.: 'Les navigateurs qui aperçoivent de loin une île "sur la mer" la reconnaissent sans hésitation possible et la distinguent d'un continent ... ce qui permet de définir l'île comme d'étendue limitée, permettant de l'embrasser d'un seul coup d'œil à une certaine distance' (1996, 11).[28] We began with a discussion of Pitcairn as an embodiment of the mythologized Pacific island, an ideal image desired and consumed by the world, propagated by the Pitcairners themselves from the early nineteenth century onwards.[29] The Pitcairners' participation in their mythologization was mutually beneficial: they gave Mayhew Folger and later visitors what they wanted to hear, and Pitcairn received the favour of the world in return, often expressed in material goods and supplies. In a way, Pitcairn sold its own image, a practice literalized in the twentieth century when the island enjoyed a period of relative prosperity mainly due to their selling stamps with images of the island and associated motifs to collectors all over the world (see Healey 1989). Representing both self and other, home to both model subjects of the British Empire and native South Sea islanders, Pitcairn epitomizes the double bind of the tropical island in Western minds. Caught between home and the tropics, it offers the West, as Howe argues, a fantasy

---

[28] 'The navigators who perceive an island "on the sea" from afar recognize it without hesitation and distinguish it from a continent ... which allows us to define the island as being of limited extension, allowing us to embrace it at a glance from a certain distance' (my translation).

[29] See Delano (1817, 111–44); Shillibeer (1818); Beechey (1831); Brodie (1851).

ground to play through its desires, fears, and ideals. Or, in Birkett's words: 'Pitcairn soon became our island, everyone's island, anyone's island' (1997, 15).

This island-image, too, has travelled a long way. It was created in the Pacific in the late eighteenth century, with roots in the myths of classical antiquity. Taking shape as an indistinct speck on the horizon, it solidified and travelled from the European explorers' journals to nineteenth-century travelogues and fiction, from where it found its way into the heart of American culture in the early twentieth century, when Hollywood seized on the proto-cinematic visuality of its earlier written manifestations. It displayed an extraordinary resilience, transported through time and across media, serving different ideological ends at each stop. It served tourist fantasies and ethnographic desires in *White Shadows*, striving to purge colonial guilt at the same time. It served to debunk European colonialism to both promote and mask American imperialism in *The Hurricane*, blending various real and imaginary geographies. It served to herald the triumph of Western modernity, embodied by the built island of Manhattan, over the natural world, frozen into an image by cinema and kept at a distance to be contemplated as an aesthetic object.

Despite its resilience, however, the island-image always retained some of its initial fragility, and this chapter has shown different ways in which it created a space for a meditation on perception itself. The early accounts are full of moments where the gaze at the island is questioned; a simple denouncement of the ideological impulse of these texts fails to take account of the complex ways in which they subject their own visions to reflective scrutiny. In later texts, the island is frozen into a fixed image, though American writers also contest earlier (European, especially British) visions to establish a distinctly American gaze. But repeated viewing can go either way: as well as freezing the image, it can unfix it. In the reading of *White Shadows* suggested here, the island-image, despite itself, crumbles upon repeated viewing, dissolving into dancing specks and lines. In the trembling graininess of the island as captured by the new medium, something of the uncertainty in the fresh gaze of the early accounts is repeated. In *The Hurricane*, the Western conception of the island is ultimately exposed and dissolved; reading the film anachronistically through Hau'ofa's notion of a 'sea of islands' revealed a tension, an uncertainty revolving around the film's own construction of the island, a sense that the island may resist the American gaze of the audience. In *King Kong*, this gaze manifests itself in its most violent form, annihilating the object of the gaze and leaving no room for negotiation. Yet in its very violence, it points to what it tries to repress, to an earlier Manhattan that had to be radically transformed before it could be controlled by airplanes and radio waves.

In different ways, all three films reflect on and partly dismantle their own medial constructions of the island as a framed cinematic image. From the films of the twenties and thirties, the image travelled onwards, all the way to contemporary visions of the tropics, informing present-day perceptions of places like Pitcairn. It travelled, among other routes, through five films about the mutiny on the *Bounty*. Birkett's travelogue begins with the cinematic primal scene of her obsession with Pitcairn, a vision of an island seen in a movie theatre in London in the 1984 version of the film with Mel Gibson as Fletcher Christian: 'The gorgeous isle still existed, out there, somewhere, and could be visited' (1997, 5). Seeing the film impelled her to travel to Pitcairn, just as a teenage infatuation with Clark Gable's Pitcairn had driven the Norwegian Kari Boye Young, married to one of Pitcairn's sexual offenders and one of their staunchest defenders, to leave her northern home and settle on the island of her dreams: 'I saw the movie *Mutiny on the Bounty* with Clark Gable and I fell in love with him. I was thirteen years old, and I decided I had to come to Pitcairn. It represented all my ambitions and dreams' (qtd. in Birkett 1997, 27). Released in 1935, this version of the film was based on the *Bounty* trilogy by Nordhoff and Hall (1932–4), the authors who went on to write *The Hurricane* in 1936, before John Ford adapted it for the screen. The image exploded with force in the early twenty-first century when the Pitcairn scandal came to light, and the reactions suggest that what the West really saw on trial was part of its own ideals, embodied by the image itself.

The image of the mythical South Sea island, or the tropical island more generally, has not seen its last. Its pieces have already reassembled since the Pitcairn scandal.[30] It is deeply engrained in Western

---

[30] A recent history of Pitcairn by Robert W. Kirk effortlessly returns to a confident assertion of the old fantasies in its last sentences: 'They are the heirs of odyssean voyages, surging passions, of steamy romance. They are the guardians of what was once an earthly

imaginaries and will continue to travel and have effects. We should carefully examine how it is made and what ends it serves. We should not look away, but watch closely, always subject it to re-vision, allowing it to crumble and undo itself. Most importantly, we should not curse when it falls out of frame, for those are the moments that force us to reflect on the fallibilities and uncertainties of our own vision. They are, perhaps, the most revealing moments the island-image can offer us.

*   *   *

This chapter was concerned with islands as images. While the islands examined in it resist their visual appropriation, their boundedness remains a central part of the texts and films in which they appear. For their Western observers, these islands are insubstantial fantasies rather than material spaces. The third chapter will turn to a set of texts that demythologize Western conceptions of islands as closed-off and insubstantial singularities. In this sense, the ecological vision of Mannahatta discussed at the end of this chapter offers a link to the ecological island poetics examined in the next chapter. The texts examined in it open up their islands, figuring them as lived and living spaces, even while they sometimes remythologize them in other ways. This next chapter, too, has a primal scene in the Pacific; not in the tropical waters of Polynesia, but in a group of cold-water islands on the edge of the North American continent. When George Vancouver entered the Strait of Juan de Fuca in April 1792, his aim was to find the legendary Northwest Passage. Instead, he found a disorienting world of islands.

uptopia [*sic*]—and may well be again' (2008, 232). On the same page, there is a photograph of the island viewed from a ship, accompanied by a caption that reads: 'So long as the descendants of mutineers remain on "the rock" the world's greatest sea tale will remain alive' (232). It is the island seen from a distance all over again. Looking too closely might disturb the image.

From Insularity to Islandness

*Fractals, Fuzzy Borders, and the
Fourth Dimension*

In 1929 Sir Winston Churchill sailed from Vancouver to Victoria
by a Canadian Pacific steamer. He stood on the bridge and
evidenced interest in the many islands along the route. On passing
San Juan, the steamer's captain said to Sir Winston that the island
should belong to Great Britain and recounted its role in the
international boundary dispute of 1859. Mr Churchill looked at
the island and, without removing his cigar, smiled and said:
'Captain, why get worked up about it? Lord knows we have
more than enough islands already.'   (Thompson 1972, viii)

A recent novel by Lise Saffran, *Juno's Daughters* (2010), begins by
describing the arrival of a group of actors for the annual Shakespeare production and hordes of tourists on the island of San Juan,
located only a few miles from the US–Canadian border in the Salish Sea
southeast of Vancouver Island. The opening chapter is entitled 'Here
in This Island We Arriv'd', a quote from Prospero's account to his
daughter Miranda of their island arrival in the first act of Shakespeare's
The Tempest. As the narrative of Saffran's novel unfolds, Prospero's
island and the island of San Juan weave into each other; one becomes a
foil through which to read the other. Saffran's narrative is inspired by
an existing theatre company that regularly produces Shakespeare plays
in the San Juan Islands. Founded by Helen Machin-Smith and Daniel
Mayes, the company's first production in 1999 was *The Tempest*. At the

The Aesthetics of Island Space: Perception, Ideology, Geopoetics. Johannes Riquet, Oxford
University Press (2019). © Johannes Riquet.
DOI: 10.1093/oso/9780198832409.001.0001

beginning of rehearsals, Machin-Smith blindfolded the actors, separated them into groups, and led them to different places near the shore of the island, where she had them perform scenes from the play. She refers to this practice as 'magic rehearsals' and has retained them for the yearly open-air Shakespeare productions.[1] Taking the position of Prospero as dramatist and director, Machin-Smith had her actors perform *The Tempest* both in the content of the play and in the very structure of the rehearsals.

Saffran's novel may be of little literary interest, but along with Machin-Smith's 'magic rehearsals' it serves as a useful starting point to address several issues that will be of recurrent concern in this chapter. The conflation of San Juan Island with Shakespeare's island is also a conflation of history and literature; it casts an imaginative gaze on San Juan that has been diverted through the island of *The Tempest* at the same time as the play itself is relocated in the specific cultural context of the Canadian–American border zone. Although Saffran does not develop this in her novel, the histories of the two islands resonate with each other. The importance of New World contexts and discourses for *The Tempest* has been extensively discussed.[2] Thus, Meredith Anne Skura focuses on the golden world fantasies structuring both England's engagement with the New World and Shakespeare's play (1989). If the islands of Roanoke and Jamestown on the East Coast were the first islands to be settled by the English in the New World, as discussed in Chapter 1, the San Juan Islands were among the last regions of North America settled by Anglo-Americans. By that time, the golden world fantasies of the Renaissance had found a very concrete equivalent in the series of gold rushes on the West Coast in the nineteenth century (cf. Cullen 2003, 159–84). The frontier lands of the Pacific Northwest were home to one of them: according to Ficken, the 'Pacific Northwest . . . was transformed into a wet weather El Dorado, the apparent successor to the California Sierra' (2003, 1) in the mid-nineteenth century as settlers flocked to the region, spurred on by the discovery of gold in the Fraser River in 1858. Among them were the first American settlers of San Juan Island. Like Shakespeare's island, the island of San Juan was a highly contested space, the site over which

---

[1] Personal communication from Helen Machin-Smith, Friday Harbor (4 May 2013).
[2] See Chapter 1, note 20.

competing claims for the ownership of the entire archipelago were enacted. Not only were the islands the sites of various violent clashes between Anglo-Americans and Native Americans, but they were also at the heart of the territorial dispute between Britain and the United States that escalated in the 1850s, a dispute that revolved around the difficulty of drawing definite boundaries in the fluid archipelagic world of the Salish Sea. This world of land and sea—an island world in the full etymological sense of the word[3]—also helped to shape a distinctive island aesthetics that both engages with and calls into question canonical Western island representations.

A final look at *The Tempest* will help us establish some of the premises for thinking about the spatiotemporal dimensions of this aesthetics. If Shakespeare's play dramatizes 'the struggle to install a new beginning' (Lane 1995, 25) and suppresses the problematic history of the fictional island on which it is set, this is linked to a suppression of the island's border. There is an unwitting irony in the fact that the opening chapter of Saffran's novel is called 'Here in This Island We Arriv'd', for there is no real arrival scene in *The Tempest*. After the initial shipwreck, we are already on the island with Prospero and Miranda. When Prospero has told his daughter the story of his expulsion from Milan, Miranda asks the crucial question 'How came we ashore?' (Shakespeare 2000, 1. 2. 159). Prospero answers 'By Providence divine' (1. 2. 159), substituting a metaphysical category for any specification of the *how* of the arrival itself. After a digression, he asks Miranda to 'hear the last of our sea sorrow' (1. 2. 170) and goes on to state 'Here in this island we arrived' (1. 2. 171), without offering a description of the process of arriving. In Prospero's discourse as in the dramatic structure, Prospero and Miranda simply appear on the island. While the sea and its imagery are of central importance for the play (cf. Hulme 2004, 187–90), the transition from sea to land seems to pose a problem. The same is true for most of the castaways: as we return to them at the beginning of Act Two, they are already on the island. The charmed circle Prospero draws in Act Five exemplifies the spatial logic of Prospero's island. It becomes the space where Prospero subjects the castaways to his gaze and power and consolidates his own position as a

---

[3] See Introduction.

subject. Drawing a kind of map on the island, Prospero embodies the 'new cartographic impulse' Conley locates in the Renaissance: 'The self ascribes to its being the illusion of autonomy and of self-possession when it can be configured as a textual diagram' (1996, 2). In this sense, Prospero's island itself becomes a cartographic production. The island, too, is surrounded by a magical border; a border that remains invisible and assures the autonomy of what it contains. Water may surround the island, but the play gives us no sense of a shore where the island rises out of the sea, and no sense of its size. Both discrete and unlimited, both bounded and shoreless, Prospero's island is a two-dimensional space where the modern subject is drawn in all its contradictions.

Yet there is one moment where this conception of the island is called into question, and it is related to the arrival of Ferdinand, the only character whose arrival is actually described. It is in Ariel's song that the first reference to the shore of the island occurs: 'Come unto these yellow sands, / And then take hands' (1. 2. 378–9). Ariel's song is followed by Ferdinand puzzling over the source of the music that lured him onto the island: 'Sitting on a bank, / Weeping again the King my father's wreck, / This music crept by me upon the waters' (1. 2. 393–5). Ferdinand's account of his arrival on the island is unique in the play as it portrays a truly liminal zone where water and land meet. Simultaneously 'on a bank' and 'upon the waters', Ferdinand is indeed on watery land, caught in a precarious state on a small offshore island made of nothing but shifting sand; an island that is, as it were, all shore. The continuation of Ariel's song reinforces and expands this vision: 'Full fathom five thy father lies. / Of his bones are coral made. / Those are pearls that were his eyes. / Nothing of him that doth fade / But doth suffer a sea change' (1. 2. 400–4). Hulme points out that this seems to be 'the first appearance of the phrase *sea change* in English' (2004, 188; emphasis original). Arguing that 'almost all characters in *The Tempest* are castaways' (188), he relates the notion of a sea change, designating a profound transformation, to 'the new experience of circumnavigating the world' (187). However, the literal meaning of *sea change*, the 'transformations brought about by salt water' (187), should not be dismissed either. Ariel's song conjures up a vision of a human body transformed so radically that it loses its humanity altogether and points to a pre- or post-human world. As such, the vision is linked to Ferdinand's own position on his sandbank. The depth of his father's

presumed position is also the depth into which Ferdinand could potentially slide himself; just a little higher than the water around and under
him, his position is marked as precarious. While Prospero's island is a
flat space where the modern subject is mapped out, a space without
extension whose potentially dangerous liminal zone is suppressed along
with its problematic history, Ferdinand's sandbank provides a counter-
figure on the margins of the text. If only to be dismissed immediately,
for a short moment a vision opens up that radically destabilizes human
subjectivity, where history is allowed to break in and human remains
are turned into geological sediment. It is a moment where, if ever so
briefly, an ecological island poetics is sketched out.

The concept of an ecological island poetics requires some theoretical
elaboration.[4] My argument is not that *The Tempest* presents an ecological vision, at least not in any simple way. It offers glimpses of an
'ecocentric state of thinking' (Buell 1995, 21), but these only emerge
through a critical intervention. Lawrence Buell called for such ecocentric interventions in *The Environmental Imagination* (1995), one of the
foundational texts of ecological criticism. The movement took shape
rather explosively in the 1990s as an engagement with 'the relationship
between literature and the physical environment' (Glotfelty and
Fromm 1996, xviii). The initially broad and sometimes vague conceptualizations of ecocriticism (cf. Gersdorf and Mayer 2006, 9–11) were
soon challenged and revised as ecocritics found themselves accused
of being 'scholars who "would rather be hiking"' (Cohen 2004, 12).[5] In
recent years, ecocriticism has become more attentive to the linguistic,
semiotic, and aesthetic processes structuring the engagement with the
environment. Elizabeth DeLoughrey's and George B. Handley's call for
an 'aesthetics of the earth' (2011, 1–40)[6] as well as Alfred Kentigern
Siewers's attention to 'narrative and poetic ecosemiospheres' (5) are
important contributions. Of particular importance for this chapter is
the notion of ecopoetics, first advanced by Jonathan Bate in *The Song of
the Earth* (2000) and recently developed by Scott Knickerbocker, who

---

[4] Recent scholarship has revisited Shakespeare from an ecocritical perspective. See
especially Bruckner and Brayton (2011).
[5] The initial motto of the Association for the Study of Literature and Environment
(ASLE) was, in fact, 'I'd rather be hiking' (Cohen 2004, 24).
[6] DeLoughrey and Handley take the phrase from Glissant (2011, 27).

reflects on the mediating role of language in the aesthetic engagement with the earth, investigating the formal and aesthetic strategies that 'dramatize the complex relationship between the human and the non-human' (2000, 16).

This attention to textuality has been productively combined with phenomenology. According to Clark, eco-phenomenology implies an 'affirmation of the primacy of experience over those approaches that strip it of all lived qualities and leave a partial or questionable abstraction in its place' (2014, 278). This includes an alertness to the 'aesthetic of natural forms' (279; emphasis original) as 'an integral feature of the way things present themselves and are experienced' (280). Importantly, however, Clark follows Ted Toadvine in cautioning against using phenomenology 'to affirm an original oneness or kinship between the human and nature' and the 'intellectual anthropomorphism' that goes hand in hand with this: 'Instead, Toadvine postulates a kind of post-phenomenology that is sensitive to the opacity and otherness of things and does not excessively posit nature as continuous, homogeneous, predictable and assimilable' (284). This view is in line with Morton's deconstructionist critique of a nature-centred ecocriticism. For Morton, the unifying concept of nature should be abandoned altogether because it cannot be dissociated from its ideological investments: 'Just as Derrida explains how *différance* at once underlies and undermines logocentrism, I assert that the rhetorical strategies of nature writing undermine what one could call ecologocentrism' (2007, 6). For Morton, the imaginary connection of the writing I with 'nature' is bound up with a flight into figuration: 'The more I try to evoke where I am—the "I" who is writing this text—the more phrases and figures of speech I must employ.... The more convincingly I render my surroundings, the more figurative language I end up with' (2007, 30). Morton's interest, then, lies in the alterities that resist figuration, and he argues that 'our awareness of the environment contains difference—hidden dark sides that structure our experience of the side exposed to view' (2014, 291).

This chapter is not an ecocritical project, or not primarily. It is, however, influenced by the theoretical implications of the ecocritical positions outlined above. If I talk of an ecological island poetics in what follows, I will use the term to refer to the textual rendering of islands in their ecological and geological environments. The focus will be on aesthetic engagements with the experience of the (is)landscapes of the Pacific Northwest in a set of texts from different genres, with particular attention to the opacities of these islandscapes, and to the ways they challenge and transform Western visions of islands as bounded, timeless spaces available for aesthetic consumption as discussed in Chapter 2.

After a brief discussion of the destabilizing role the islands in the US–Canadian border zone had in the political struggles of drawing the border, I will develop a phenomenological perspective on the foundational text of much Northwest writing, the journal of George Vancouver. I will trace the aesthetic resistance of the unfamiliar islandscape to his attempts to order it cartographically, focusing on the moments when this ordering impulse breaks down. In a second part, we will turn to the revisionist island poetics in Pacific Northwest writing after Vancouver. While Vancouver's text strives to establish clear boundaries even if this desire is often frustrated, the set of texts that I will examine embrace the opening up of island borders and challenge the discreteness of both island and self. After a discussion of a group of memoirs that centre around island experiences in the Pacific Northwest, I will trace the development of this revisionist island poetics in a trio of texts that turn to an ecological and geological discourse to open the island up in space and time and construct it as a space where history accumulates. As we will see, the texts sometimes reinscribe a different form of totality in their visions of ecological and geological continuity and in their ideological naturalization of history. In a short final section, I will take Morton's insistence on the 'irreducible hidden dimension of things' (2014, 291) literally and turn to the interface between the island poetics examined in this chapter and late nineteenth- and early twentieth-century theories of the fourth dimension. As I will argue, the hidden dimension of the island radically destabilizes its space by moving it out of itself.

Contested Islands, Windows to History: The San Juans

In their introduction to a recent collection of essays entitled *Sea Changes: Historicizing the Ocean*, Gesa Mackenthun and Bernhard

Klein invoke Derek Walcott's poem 'The Sea is History' (1979) to announce a revisionist account of the sea as a 'transnational contact zone' (2004, 2). This chapter is informed by this notion of the sea as a historical zone and by the idea of islands as spaces flooded by history. In his monumental work on the Mediterranean at the time of Philip II, Braudel argues that islands are often windows to history:

> A precarious, restricted, and threatened life, such was the lot of the islands, their domestic life at any rate. But their external life ... far exceeds what might be expected from such poor territories. The events of history often lead to the islands.... To their ordinary day-to-day existence was added a chapter in the history of great events.
>
> (1955, 154)

Braudel here makes an important distinction between inside and outside perspectives on the Mediterranean islands. His analysis entails a view of these islands as somehow *representative* of those 'great events', providing a space where history leaves traces and becomes visible. This view is outlined when Braudel writes that 'Sardinia ... which has been described as impenetrable, had windows opening outwards from which it is sometimes possible to glimpse, as from an observatory, the general history of the sea' (151).

Braudel's reflections on Sardinia and other Mediterranean islands point to a fundamental paradox that structures the representation of islands. Islands can be characterized by both isolation and connection; for Racault, the separateness of the desert island in castaway narratives is a mirage, a structural impossibility: 'L'île déserte, île "en soi" précédant toute conscience humaine, n'est après tout qu'une hypothèse ou une impensable fiction' (1995, 13).[7] Structurally, both the castaway's narrative and the water taking him to and from the island disrupt its separateness. For the semiotician Louis Marin, islands are closed off but lack an enclosure and are thus situated at the intersection of the finiteness of their own space and the infinity of the space surrounding them (1979, 79–84). Coming into being through an interplay of the horizontality of the sea and the verticality of the relief of the earth, the

---

[7] 'The desert island, island "in itself" preceding all human consciousness, is, after all, only a hypothesis or an unthinkable fiction' (my translation).

visible discreteness of the island betrays an underlying geological continuity (1979, 79).

Environmental philosopher Kathleen Dean Moore similarly draws attention to this subterranean—or rather submarine—continuity, but extends the discussion by focusing on the shore as an indeterminate zone undermining the discreteness of islands. She points out that the precise edge of an island is impossible to determine:

> On Pine Island, . . . I push aside the rubber stems of bull kelp, searching at the edge of water for the place where the land ends and the sea begins. I can stand in the dark heart of the hemlock forest, feet planted firmly on duff, and say, 'This is Pine Island,' or slosh knee-deep into the bay and say, 'This is the Pacific Ocean.' But the disconnection doesn't hold up at the edges. The more closely I search, the more elusive the edge becomes. . . .
>
> Again and again, I face an island's paradox: Not even an island is an island. Storm-washed and rain-sodden, so hard to get to, so hard to escape, Pine Island is the very symbol of isolation and exile. But any geographer will tell you that an island is in fact only a high point in the continuous skin of the planet . . . . (2004, 3–4)

Moore's detailed description of the amphibious ecosystem of the intertidal zone reimagines the island as a trope for continuity and interconnectedness rather than isolation and autonomy. Taking issue with what she perceives as an insular bias in the history of Western philosophy, she calls into question the boundaries drawn by philosophers from Protagoras to René Descartes, Francis Bacon, Immanuel Kant, and even Henry David Thoreau (4–8). Where she sees Western philosophy separating the world into discrete, bounded units, her own project in *The Pine Island Paradox* is not to do away with the island trope, but rather to resituate it. In other words, she wants to shift the focus from the island as bounded by a magic circle drawn with Prospero's wand, the embodiment of Western learning and philosophy, to an ecological view of islands that is closer to that outlined in relation to Ferdinand's sandbank; a poetics of islandness rather than insularity (cf. Baldacchino 2006, 9).

Dean Moore's book is part of a tradition of American nature writing that goes back to the nineteenth century and writers like Thoreau. More specifically, it belongs to a tradition of Pacific Northwest writing which develops an ecological poetics through a form of writing that is part academic, part essayistic, and draws on the imaginative potential of Northwestern landscapes. Islands play a decisive role in these texts[8] as well as in a number of related literary works. With its history of contested boundaries, the San Juan Archipelago provides a particularly fertile ground for the development of a revisionist island poetics. It is to this island poetics that we shall now turn.

San Juan Island is the main island of the eponymous archipelago and county in Washington State. Any visitor will immediately notice that island consciousness is writ large: 'Islanders Bank', 'Island Bicycles', and 'Island Hearing Healthcare' are just a few examples of the innumerable shops and businesses that feature the word 'island' in their names in Friday Harbor, the principal town. The island concept has long been a central identity marker for San Juan.[9] A number of articles from the pioneering years of the local newspaper, the *San Juan Islander*, demonstrate this awareness: 'SAN JUAN COUNTY consists entirely of islands, lying north of Puget Sound proper, between the Strait of San Juan de Fuca and the Gulf of Georgia, and constituting one of the most beautiful archipelagoes in the world' (6 and 13 February 1902, 5). This is the beginning of a peculiar self-advertisement that ran in the *Islander* for some weeks in early 1902 (Figure 3.1). Followed by a long and detailed description of the islands, their population, and their economies, the article significantly begins with an emphasis on the island status of the county. In the issue of 20 February, a map of the islands appeared in the same spot where the article had been the previous weeks (Figure 3.2). A dotted line surrounds the islands of the county, and the surrounding space—in reality full of islands itself—is left blank. In a performative act of self-definition that takes insularity as a key identity marker, both text and map represent an island realm folded in upon itself. Literally in the same place as the map, the text itself engages in a form of mapping by taking its readers on an imaginary tour of their own archipelago.[10] Fifty years after the first white settlers arrived on

---

[8]   See, among others, Ricou (2002); Chamberlin (2013); Dean Moore (2004).

[9]   This phenomenon can be observed in many small island communities (cf. Royle 2001, 42–67).

[10]   The conception of the archipelago, viewed as a bounded totally, is much closer to that of a single bounded island than to that of the archipelago as a network of relations. The latter conception will be discussed in Chapter 4.

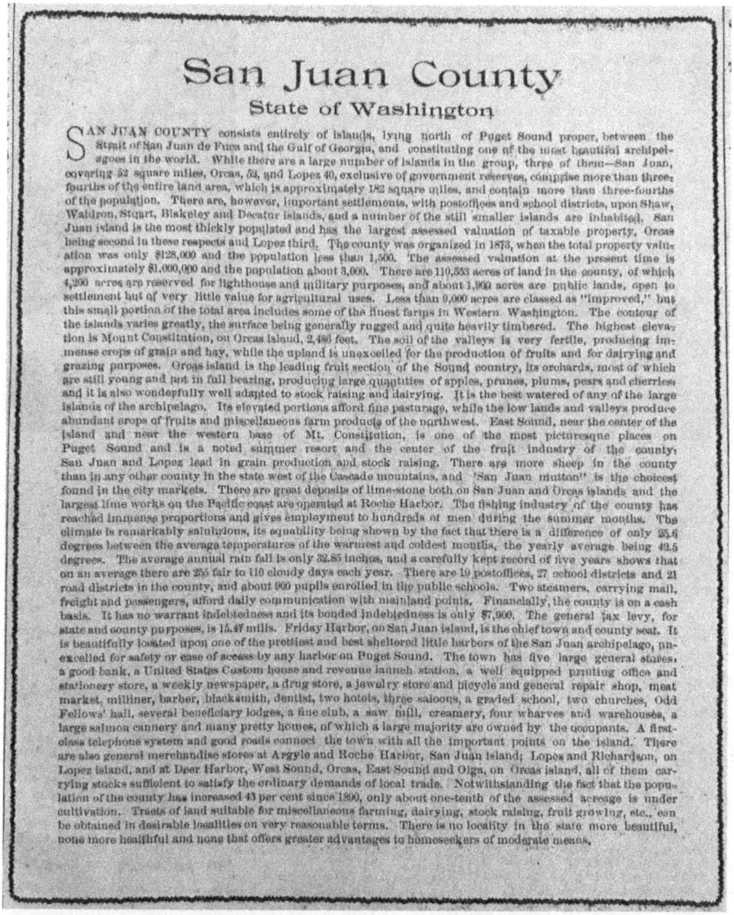

San Juan County
State of Washington

SAN JUAN COUNTY consists entirely of islands, lying north of Puget Sound proper, between the Strait of San Juan de Fuca and the Gulf of Georgia, and constituting one of the most beautiful archipelagoes in the world. While there are a large number of islands in the group, three of them—San Juan, covering 52 square miles, Orcas, 54, and Lopez 40, exclusive of government reserves, comprise more than three-fourths of the entire land area, which is approximately 182 square miles, and contain more than three-fourths of the population. There are, however, important settlements, with postoffices and school districts, upon Shaw, Waldron, Stuart, Blakeley and Decatur islands, and a number of the still smaller islands are inhabited. San Juan island is the most thickly populated and has the largest assessed valuation of taxable property, Orcas being second in these respects and Lopez third. The county was organized in 1873, when the total property valuation was only $128,000 and the population less than 1,500. The assessed valuation at the present time is approximately $1,000,000 and the population about 3,000. There are 119,553 acres of land in the county, of which 4,200 acres are reserved for lighthouse and military purposes, and about 1,900 acres are public lands, open to settlement but of very little value for agricultural uses. Less than 9,000 acres are classed as "improved," but this small portion of the total area includes some of the finest farms in Western Washington. The contour of the islands varies greatly, the surface being generally rugged and quite heavily timbered. The highest elevation is Mount Constitution, on Orcas island, 2,486 feet. The soil of the valleys is very fertile, producing immense crops of grain and hay, while the upland is unexcelled for the production of fruits and for dairying and grazing purposes. Orcas island is the leading fruit section of the Sound country, its orchards, most of which are still young and not in full bearing, producing large quantities of apples, prunes, plums, pears and cherries and it is also wonderfully well adapted to stock raising and dairying. It is the best watered of any of the large islands of the archipelago. Its elevated portions afford fine pasturage, while the low lands and valleys produce abundant crops of fruits and miscellaneous farm products of the northwest. East Sound, near the center of the island and near the western base of Mt. Constitution, is one of the most picturesque places on Puget Sound and is a noted summer resort and the center of the fruit industry of the county. San Juan and Lopez lead in grain production and stock raising. There are more sheep in the county than in any other county in the state west of the Cascade mountains, and "San Juan mutton" is the choicest found in the city markets. There are great deposits of lime-stone both on San Juan and Orcas islands and the largest lime works on the Pacific coast are operated at Roche Harbor. The fishing industry of the county has reached immense proportions and gives employment to hundreds of men during the summer months. The climate is remarkably salubrious, its equability being shown by the fact that there is a difference of only 25.6 degrees between the average temperatures of the warmest and coldest months, the yearly average being 49.5 degrees. The average annual rain fall is only 32.85 inches, and a carefully kept record of five years shows that on an average there are 255 fair to 110 cloudy days each year. There are 19 postoffices, 27 school districts and 21 road districts in the county, and about 900 pupils enrolled in the public schools. Two steamers, carrying mail, freight and passengers, afford daily communication with mainland points. Financially, the county is on a cash basis. It has no warrant indebtedness and its bonded indebtedness is only $7,000. The general tax levy, for state and county purposes, is 15.4? mills. Friday Harbor, on San Juan island, is the chief town and county seat. It is beautifully located upon one of the prettiest and best sheltered little harbors of the San Juan archipelago, unexcelled for safety or ease of access by any harbor on Puget Sound. The town has five large general stores, a good bank, a United States Custom house and revenue launch station, a well equipped printing office and stationery store, a weekly newspaper, a drug store, a jewelry store and bicycle and general repair shop, meat market, milliner, barber, blacksmith, dentist, two hotels, three saloons, a graded school, two churches, Odd Fellows' hall, several beneficial lodges, a fine club, a saw mill, creamery, four wharves and warehouses, a large salmon cannery and many pretty homes, of which a large majority are owned by the occupants. A first-class telephone system and good roads connect the town with all the important points on the island. There are also general merchandise stores at Argyle and Roche Harbor, San Juan island; Lopez and Richardson, on Lopez island, and at Deer Harbor, West Sound, Orcas, East Sound and Olga, on Orcas island, all of them carrying stocks sufficient to satisfy the ordinary demands of local trade. Notwithstanding the fact that the population of the county has increased 43 per cent since 1890, only about one-tenth of the assessed acreage is under cultivation. Tracts of land suitable for miscellaneous farming, dairying, stock raising, fruit growing, etc., can be obtained in desirable localities on very reasonable terms. There is no locality in the state more beautiful, none more healthful and none that offers greater advantages to homeseekers of moderate means.

FIGURE 3.1 'San Juan County' (article published in the *San Juan Islander* on 6 February 1902)

San Juan Island, and thirty years after the archipelago became American, the article and the map give the islanders a consciousness of themselves as islanders, like Prospero drawing an imaginary line around an island realm; a line that produces what is inside it as much as it excludes its outside.

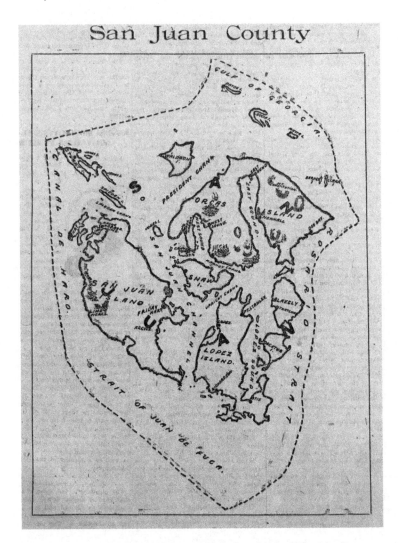

FIGURE 3.2 'San Juan County' (map published in the *San Juan Islander* on 20 February 1902)

A few months later, an *Islander* article titled 'An Island Empire' quoted lengthily from an article in the *Post-Intelligencer*, a Seattle newspaper:

> While it contains little that is new to the ISLANDER's readers, it is of interest as showing in a pleasant way how others see us. We quote the following:
>
> San Juan County, a little island empire, surrounded by winding channels and broad gulfs—arms of the sea, themselves teeming with the ocean's wealth—has been the 'land of milk and honey' for more than two hundred wanderers who left the east and middle west during the past few years and found homes within its borders. Cut off from the mainland by waters which change from deep blue to emerald green as they dance in the sunlight and again dissolve in snow-white clouds on jagged reefs and scarred brown cliffs, these islands are not in direct communication with inland points. Yet... the rich grasses... and the fat valley lands... have caught the hearts of many of the army of immigrants now invading this state.
>
> (5 June 1902, 1)

In many respects, this description shares the structure of the previous article. As the *Islander* journalist himself makes clear, the quoted article tells its readers nothing new: representing to the islanders what they already know, its only function is an affirmation of identity in the gaze of the other, even if the other is just from across the water. Yet a tension runs through the text. Sometimes focusing on the 'island empire', the utopian fantasy of a '"land of milk and honey"',[11] the 'homes within its borders', and the fact that the islands are 'cut off', then again on the winding channels and the transformative waters ultimately melting into the mainland, it freely oscillates between constructing the islands as a bounded and self-contained space and highlighting the movement of the sea, the dynamic, transformative quality of the water. The text goes on to recount the history of the islands: 'These islands are a historic spot. In the days when the first large wave of immigration came to the Pacific Northwest they were occupied by the soldiers of the world's two greatest nations' (1). Fittingly, the influx of immigrants

---

[11] The islands and coasts of Puget Sound and the Salish Sea were the site of a number of utopian communitarian settlements in the late nineteenth and early twentieth centuries (LeWarne 1975).

settling the islands is here described in terms of a wave, which links it to the restless waters described before.

At the same time, the passage demonstrates a strong historical consciousness with regard to the islands, although the events alluded to were less than half a century old when the article was written. The article refers to what is known as the Pig War, a controversy regarding the border between Great Britain and the United States that brought the two nations to the brink of war. In the aftermath of the War of 1812, Britain and the United States had agreed on joint occupation of the Oregon country in the Anglo-American Convention of 1818, which retained the spirit of the 1790 Nootka Convention between Spain and Great Britain by 'stipulating that possession of the region would be determined by "effective occupation", that is, established settlement and commerce' (Vouri 2010, 18). This meant that the sparsely populated Northwest Coast between California (42nd parallel) in the south and Russian America in the north (54th parallel) was effectively shared between Britain and the United States. With the 1846 Treaty of Oregon, after the US population of Oregon Country had increased from 300 to over 8,000 within only a few years (Vouri 21), the 49th parallel was decided upon as the continental boundary. However, things were more difficult for the water boundary. The wording of the relevant passage was imprecise and open to conflicting interpretations:

> . . . the line of boundary . . . shall be continued westward along the said forty-ninth parallel of north latitude to the middle of the channel which separates the continent from Vancouver's Island; and thence southerly through the middle of the said channel, and of Fuca's Straits to the Pacific Ocean . . . . (qtd. in Vouri 25)

The problem is that the Strait of Juan de Fuca splits off into various channels and waterways between Vancouver Island and Puget Sound on account of the many islands in this area. While the British assumed that the treaty referred to Rosario Strait, which would have given them all the islands north of Puget Sound, the Americans claimed it referred to Haro Strait, which runs northwest of the San Juan Islands and southeast of what are now the Canadian Gulf Islands.

In 1853, the governor of Vancouver Island, James Douglas, took matters into his own hands and established the Belle Vue Sheep Farm on San Juan Island for the Hudson's Bay Company (HBC), appointing

Charles J. Griffin as the local agent and hiring a group of Hawaiians as herdsmen (Vouri 35).[12] This led to several disagreements with the Americans, who treated the islands as their own, attempted to collect taxes from Griffin, and even tried to remove forty-nine sheep from the island in 1855 (see Vouri 30–49). With the influx of American settlers into the region in 1858, the conflict became acute again.[13] According to Griffin, there were at least sixteen Americans on San Juan Island by 1859,[14] the year the conflict escalated after American settler Lyman Cutler shot a pig that had strayed into his garden. General William S. Harney, the commander of Oregon, reacted by sending a dispatch of sixty-four soldiers to the island, where they set up camp near Griffin's farm.[15] Douglas, in turn, sent two British warships to the island. For a while it seemed likely that the conflict would erupt into war, but it never did. The island remained under joint military occupation until 1872, with the soldiers stationed in two camps on opposite ends of the island. In 1872, the conflict was resolved under the arbitration of the German emperor William I, who convened a three-man commission to decide on the boundary. Voting two to one, the commission decided that Haro Strait should be the boundary, thus declaring the San Juan Archipelago to be part of the United States (Vouri 224–52). The political struggle to draw the boundary was also a struggle over geography; accordingly, maps played an important role in the conflict. We will now turn to a particularly important map in the history of the region and the journal that accompanied its production. As we will see, both manifest a perceptual struggle over the ordering of the islandscape. An analysis of the latter's aesthetic resistance to cartographic absorption will prepare the ground for the ensuing discussion of literary engagements with the poetics of islands.

---

[12] The colonial administration of the region was in the hands of the Hudson's Bay Company; besides agricultural activities and trade with the indigenous population, it maintained several salmon-curing stations on and around Vancouver Island (see Ficken 2003, 1–25; Schwantes 1989, 59–66; Vouri 2013, 16–21).

[13] Ficken offers a detailed account of the conflicts surrounding the 1858 gold rush (2003, 27–70).

[14] Vouri estimates that there may have been almost thirty Americans and seven British subjects on the island at the time (2013, 263–4).

[15] The official reason given in a petition signed by twenty-two Americans was that they sought military protection from 'northern Indians' (Vouri 2013, 68).

Fuzzy Zones: Phenomenology and the Fractal Aesthetics of George Vancouver's Islands

The ambiguity in the Oregon Treaty emerged from the uncertain status of the waters surrounding the islands; flowing around and between them, the water destabilized any sure claim to the land. The performative power of maps to produce 'geographies of a space that is not always directly visible' (Ljungberg 2003, 160) played a crucial role in the fierce debate about the correct interpretation of the Treaty of Oregon. The first map of the region was published in George Vancouver's atlas of the Northwest Coast accompanying his journal; together with a map by the German cartographer Charles Preuss, it formed the basis for a map that HBC governor John H. Pelly appended to a letter in which he complained about the wording of the treaty (Vouri 2010, 25–6). J. B. Harley's work explores how 'maps—like books—became a political force in society' (1988, 279), especially since the establishment of national topographic surveys in the eighteenth century (281). In the case of Vancouver's widely circulated map (Figure 3.3), the line tracing his progress up the coast had political force in establishing Rosario Strait, often referred to as 'Vancouver's track', as the main channel— quite unlike the map from the United States Exploring Expedition commanded by Charles Wilkes (Figure 3.4), on which Haro Strait not only looks wider, but is also the only channel labelled at all (as 'Canal de Arro').[16] While the 'Canal de Arro' is labelled on Vancouver's map, it leads into a fuzzy zone where the contours of the land and the boundaries of land and sea are less clearly drawn, reflecting the fact that this area was not explored by Vancouver.

It is precisely these fuzzy zones, however, that are most interesting for the particular island aesthetics this chapter is concerned with. Unlike the sharply drawn lines of the mainland coast, these shores melt into the sea; coastlines suddenly stop and make way for indistinct zones where land and sea become indistinguishable. To a lesser extent,

---

[16] On the local map of the San Juan Islands (there named 'Archipelago of Arro') in Wilkes's *Atlas* (1844), Rosario Strait is labelled 'Ringolds Channel', but only in very small font, contrasting with the large font of the 'Canal de Arro'. The *Atlas* can be accessed online at <www.loc.gov/item/2010589747/.>

FIGURE 3.3 Excerpt from *A Chart Shewing Part of the Coast of N.W. America* (map by George Vancouver, London, G. G. & J. Robinson, 1798), David Rumsey Map Collection, www.davidrumsey.com

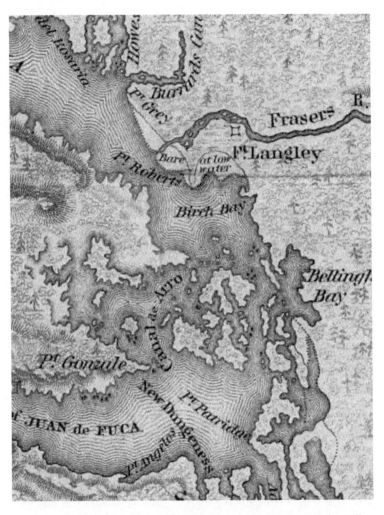

FIGURE 3.4 Excerpt from *Map of the Oregon Territory* (map by Charles Wilkes and United States Exploring Expedition, Philadelphia, Lea & Blanchard, 1841), David Rumsey Map Collection, www.davidrumsey.com

this is also true for the San Juan Archipelago, which was not entered by Vancouver himself, but by the commander of the *Chatham*, the second ship of the expedition. Thus, the east coast of San Juan Island is distinctly drawn while the western shoreline is much thinner and interrupted twice, which makes it look as though the sea were flowing into the island. Aesthetically, these islands are indefinite areas that open up to their surroundings. In a sense, these areas of the map are more 'honest' than the firmly drawn lines, albeit unwittingly so. It is the latter that are, as it were, the constitutive lie of modern cartography. Following Dean Moore's discussion of the elusiveness of the island's edge, we can say that it is the fuzzy zones, the spatial uncertainties reflecting the cartographer's own disorientation in the fresh exposure to unknown space, that are, paradoxically, more accurate, truer to the fuzzy and shifting nature of the indistinct border zone between water and (is)land.

Vancouver's journal deploys a similar aesthetics. As Nicholas O'Connell argues, it 'laid the textual foundation for Northwest literature' (2003, 18) in its aesthetic appreciation of the landscape. His claim that Vancouver's text ultimately aimed at presenting the landscape as 'subject to quantification and eventual comprehension' (17) is well founded; Vancouver repeatedly states that his objective is to '[fix] the boundaries of the continent' (1798b, 310) in his search for the legendary Northwest Passage.[17] Vancouver ultimately succeeded in fixing these boundaries with remarkable accuracy, and his text veers towards establishing complete spatial orientation in analogy to the firmly drawn lines on the map. Yet in the intermittent stages of this enterprise, an entirely different picture emerges. The most fascinating and revealing passages of the journal are those where Vancouver describes his immersion in an intricate space of coasts, islands, inlets, and channels, in a perplexing watery land he cannot yet comprehend.

Quite fittingly, Vancouver's entrance into the Strait of Juan de Fuca is marked by an emphasis on visual uncertainty when he points out that the opposite side of the straits was 'indistinctly seen in consequence of the haze' and that 'the thick rainy weather permitted [them] to see little of the country' (215). This hazy zone at the threshold of uncharted

---

[17] The most famous account was that of the Greek navigator Juan de Fuca, who allegedly discovered an inland sea in the latitude of the strait that would later receive his name, himself in search of the Northwest Passage for Spain.

territory[18] is accompanied by a phenomenal confusion of a different kind as Vancouver points out the impossibility of matching the landscape with the vague and uncertain accounts, the 'ideal reports' (216) existing of the region. What ensues is a shift from the ordered world of cartographic accuracy to a world unassimilable to represented forms:

> ...nor did we observe the Pinnacle rock, as represented by Mr. Mears and Mr. Dalrymple, in order to identify these as De Fuca's straits, or any other rock more conspicuous than thousands along the coast, *varying in form and size*; some conical, others with flat sides, flat tops, and almost *every other shape that can be figured by the imagination.* (216–17; my emphasis)

Here, the multitude of tiny islands resists categorization, and the infinity of possible shapes can only be met by the capacity of the imagination to produce innumerable forms. In his *Phenomenology of Perception*, Maurice Merleau-Ponty reminds us that our visual perception of the world is always already ordered and rectified by the brain as our primary sensory perception would show us the world upside down, calling into question categories like 'up' and 'down'. Discussing an experiment where a subject is given glasses that invert vision, he points out that the brain will re-invert the image after a while to correct the clash between tactile and visual perception. He concludes that geographical orientation presupposes a corrective intervention in perceived space:

> One cannot take the world and orientated space as given along with the contents of sense experience or with the body in itself, since experience in fact shows that the same contents can be successively orientated in one direction or another.... What we want to know is how an object can appear to us as 'the right way up' or 'inverted', and what these words mean. (2002, 288)

Merleau-Ponty is interested in situations that unsettle our corrected, normalized perception of the world, when the space surrounding us 'collapses and re-integrates before our eyes' (284), because they allow

---

[18] What Vancouver did not know at this point was that this part of the coast had already been charted by the Spaniards, though with less rigour. Vancouver admits 'no small degree of mortification in finding the external shores of the gulph had been visited' (1798b, 312) upon learning this from two Spanish vessels he encountered on 22 June.

him to describe 'what happens when these floating appearances are suddenly anchored' (287). This is also why he is interested in the spatial perceptions of schizophrenics, in the moments when they perceive the landscape as unreal, absurd, threatening, amazing, or moving. In these spatial perceptions, 'the world can no longer be taken for granted' (335) as ordered geographical perception cannot be established.

Vancouver's journal testifies to such a 'schizophrenic' vision of the world. The various emotional states he expresses—amazement, desolation, wonder, despair—are primarily registered as responses to the vivid aesthetic experience of a world temporarily unhinged from any stable spatial order. Describing the intricate network of channels and islands he would later name Puget Sound, Vancouver writes: 'From hence we made the best of our way for land, *appearing* like an island, off the other *supposed* opening; from whose summit, which *seemed* easy of access, there was little doubt of ascertaining whether the coast afforded any port within reach of the day's excursion' (1978b, 226; my emphasis). Like the fuzzy zones on the map, this and countless other passages are structured by uncertainty, a linguistic counterpart to the earlier haze. The landforms are provisional and subject to revision, which is expressed in numerous words that hedge and qualify the spatial hypotheses. At the same time, the proposed ascent to the 'supposed island' (226) counterbalances this uncertainty by already anticipating the reestablishment of geographical orientation.

Vancouver's account is structured by these two opposing forces: by the constant collapse and reintegration of the landscape, linguistically marked by an abundance of qualifiers, double negatives, and modal verbs ('it was *not impossible* a channel *might* exist . . . , which . . . *might have been* invisible to us,' 282; my emphasis) on the one hand, and a corresponding number of verbs like 'ascertain', 'fix', and 'determine', as well as their past participle forms ('fixed', 'determined'), indicating the ordering of geographical space on the other. The latter process is exemplified when Vancouver describes the examination of the coast opposite the northeast end of Vancouver Island as '*making* the land near which we were then at anchor . . . an island, or a cluster of islands of considerable extent' (322; my emphasis). In Vancouver's narrative, landforms and seascapes *become* islands, inlets, or parts of the coast; initially experienced as mutable 'floating appearances' (Merleau-Ponty 2002, 287) and living forms, they are only gradually 'anchored' and assigned a definite value. Merleau-Ponty's use of maritime metaphors ('floating'; 'anchored')[19] is suggestive in this context as it resonates with Vancouver's path through a watery land that resists cartographic fixation.

The narrative structure of the journal parallels this double impulse of fragmentation and reintegration. The more intricate the system of islands and waterways becomes, the more the channels are divided and subdivided, the more Vancouver's text breaks up into various strands as he recounts the experiences of the different officers he dispatched to explore and chart the various areas in the boats of the *Discovery* and the *Chatham*. If the map resulted from the joining of various sketches made by Vancouver and his officers, his text is equally composite in kind. The division of the landscape finds its counterpart not only in the division of the group and the narrative division of the text, but extends even to the level of syntax, producing convoluted sentences full of colons and subordinate clauses that struggle to trace the irregular and broken lines of the coast linguistically; the divided landscape writes itself into the very fabric of Vancouver's text.

The islands play a central role in figuring the landscape as 'broken', a word that recurs throughout Vancouver's account. Describing a view of the San Juan Archipelago and the surrounding islands, he writes that 'the country, occupying the northern horizon in all directions, appeared to be excessively broken, and insular' (294). The broken character of the landscape is here explicitly associated with its islands. The 'infinitely divided *appearance* of the region' (320; my emphasis) north of 'Savary's Island' in the 'Gulph of Georgia' is a direct consequence of the disintegration of the coast into 'innumerable islands' (327). Importantly, Vancouver does not say that the region *is* divided; rather, his text registers the appearance and experience of division and a resulting sense of infinity that is part of the phenomenal confusion outlined above.

This temporary unsettling of perceptual certainties can be fruitfully analysed if phenomenology is combined with Benoit Mandelbrot's fractal geometry. Mandelbrot himself provides ample justification for reading his theories alongside literary texts. In his chapter on 'Relief

[19] The French original reads 'lorsque ces apparences flottantes s'ancrent soudain' (1945, 285).

and Coastlines' in *The Fractal Geometry of Nature*, he writes that literature has long engaged with what classical geometry failed to examine and opens with a literary quotation. He makes it clear that there is a strong aesthetic interest in his work and deplores the dryness of classical geometry, the reason for which he sees in the discipline's 'inability to describe the shape of a cloud, a mountain, a coastline, or a tree. Clouds are not spheres, mountains are not cones, coastlines are not circles, and bark is not smooth . . . ' (1983, 1).

Islands are a recurrent concern in Mandelbrot's work. In 'How Long is the Coast of Britain?',[20] he demonstrates that the coast surrounding Britain can ultimately not be measured. In contrast to a circle, whose perimeter we can approximate by placing polygons with an increasing number of sides in it, a coastline becomes infinitely long if it is measured with ever smaller yardsticks. The problem resides in the irregularity of the coastline, which repeats itself at every scale: any given bay has indentures only visible at a higher resolution, which in turn have even finer irregularities, and so forth. Since the coastline can never be conclusively traced as a line, not even a curved one, this structure cannot be described by Euclidean geometry. Therefore, Mandelbrot introduces the notion of a fractal dimension, i.e. a dimension between one and two. Mandelbrot insists that the impossibility of fixing the length of an island's coastline has scientific, philosophical, and political implications (27). But the coast of an island is not only irregular; it is also fragmented. Drawing on a 1938 study by Jaromir Korčák, Mandelbrot demonstrates that the more irregular a coast is, the more it is broken and splits off smaller islands. Following an algorithm Mandelbrot terms 'island generator' (117), the coasts of these islands will in turn produce a larger number of even smaller islands, and so forth ad infinitum. He concludes that 'islands are practically infinite in numbers' (119) and that there can, from a theoretical perspective, be no continent: every island simply leads to a larger island to which it is a satellite.

---

[20] Mandelbrot's theoretical reflections were triggered by an article by Lewis Fry Richardson, who had demonstrated empirically that the length of natural borders such as coastlines increases with the enlargement of the scale of measurement. Mandelbrot's essay was originally published in *Science* in 1967. The following quotations are from the more accessible version rewritten for *The Fractal Geometry of Nature* (1983).

Mandelbrot's language is astonishingly similar to that of George Vancouver when he is trying to come to terms with a coastal world of islands. Some of Mandelbrot's more poetic subheadings, such as 'The Infinity of Islands' (119) and 'The Elusive Continent' (121), recall the latter's description of the land- and seascape as 'infinitely divided' and 'excessively broken, and insular'. Irregularity, fragmentation, disintegration, division, and infinity are terms structuring both texts. The aesthetic experience registered in Vancouver's text antici- pates Mandelbrot's revision of classical geometry on a poetic plane. As he describes the ships and boats entering ever new inlets, subdiv- ided in turn, sailing past islands and islands' islands, an aesthetics of infinite division and islandness emerges that at times appears as though it could never rest.

Merleau-Ponty's phenomenological discussion of spatial experience singles out precisely the moments where normalized, geographical perception makes way for a fresh perception. Even if this aesthetic experience is soon absorbed by a cartographic gaze, for brief moments Vancouver registers an openness in the initial encounter with the unknown:

> We seemed now to have forsaken the main direction of the gulph, being on every side encompassed by islands and small rocky islets; some lying along the continental shore, others confusedly scattered, of different forms and dimensions. . . . The very circumscribed view that we had of the country here, rendered it impossible to form the most distant idea of any circumstances relative to the situation in which we had become stationary; whether composed of islands, or of such arms of the sea as we had lately been employed in examining. . . . (2002, 319–21)

In textual moments such as this, everything disintegrates and the 'confusedly scattered' islands parallel Vancouver's phenomenal confu- sion. Islands of all forms and sizes, down to the size of mere rocks, obstruct the visual field. The status of the landforms itself is uncertain as the resulting 'circumscribed view' precludes spatiotemporal orientation.

Mandelbrot sees his fractal geometry as a response to the ideo- logically charged intervention of geographic measuring, and his writ- ings have transformed the discipline of ecology, offering a geometry that does justice to the spatial heterogeneity and complexity of eco-systems.[21] It is not surprising that these works often signal an affinity with and even indebtedness to literature and other art forms such as painting, and frequently contain numerous artistic images and ornate illustrations (cf. Seuront 2010, 1–10). While Vancouver's project is ultimately to reorder the landscape, the movement to coastal and insular infinity in his journal offers glimpses of such an ecological view of the landscape. In those moments where human control of space is surrendered and the human position loses itself by being immersed in a landscape that resists appropriation and normaliza-tion, a world opens up where geographical distinctions become blurred, where islands take and lose shape, where islets sink and re-emerge, and where the explorers are 'driven about . . . blindfolded in this labyrinth' (Vancouver 1798b, 319), an insular labyrinth of land and water.

Open Spaces: Northwest Islands
after Vancouver

While Vancouver's journal veers towards an impossible ordering of the landscape, later aesthetic engagements with the US–Canadian border region embrace the labyrinthine confusion that characterizes his text to destabilize political borders. At the beginning of the chapter entitled 'Island File' in his essayistic literary history of the region, Laurie Ricou quotes from the poem 'The Anacortes–Sydney Run' by Richard Hugo. The poem and Ricou's discussion of it read like a response to the island aesthetics of Vancouver's journal:

> Maps are hard to read. Two nations own
> these islands. The shade of green on one
> could be Canadian, but firs and grebes
> are mine. The latest run of Springs
> are far too international to claim.   (qtd. in Ricou 2002, 21)

---

[21] See, among others, Seuront (2010) and Turner et al. (2001).

In this poem, the ferry run from Anacortes on the coast of Washington through the San Juan and Gulf Islands to Sidney on Vancouver Island[22] induces a labyrinthine confusion that exposes the absurdity of the arbitrarily drawn line between the two countries. The islandscape offers what one might call an *aesthetic resistance* to the map, which becomes 'hard to read' and match with it:

> [A] passenger . . . will not be able to tell at any given moment whether she is in 'Canadian' or 'American' waters and, unless assiduously studying the marine chart . . . , whether the land masses in view are in Canada or the United States, are islands or part of the mainland, or of the nation-sized Vancouver Island. (Ricou 24)

In Ricou's reading of Hugo's poem, not only the national affiliations, but the landmasses themselves become as indistinct as those described by Vancouver. Immediately after quoting the poem, Ricou adds his own poetic vision:

> Flying over the San Juan/Gulf Islands in October 1992, I am amazed at the map below, at its complicated asymmetry (the ordered disorder of fractals, I wonder). . . . At the edge of the continent, the land looks to be breaking into pieces. Its map is a confusion of islands. (21)

Interestingly, Ricou here describes his aerial view of the islands in terms of a map, but of a map that is as 'hard to read' as that of Hugo's poem. Referring to fractal geometry to describe the aesthetics of the islandscape, he constructs a vision of a continent 'breaking into pieces' on its edge that echoes the descriptions of Vancouver.

For Ricou, this view of the landscape carries a strong political dimension. The insular confusion of the borderlands not only transcends the national boundaries between the United States and Canada, but is 'also perhaps *inter*-national in that it links peoples and cultural backgrounds: Duwamish, Vietnamese, Bella Coola, Salmon People, Finnish, Tillamook, and Chinese' (24; emphasis original). As Kornel S. Chang argues, the history of the Pacific Northwest was marked by the 'circulation of people, goods, and ideas across boundaries' (2012, 2). The fur trade transformed the region 'into a contact zone in the

---

[22] As Ricou points out, misspelling Sidney as 'Sydney' further opens up the poem's transnational geography (2002, 24).

eighteenth and nineteenth centuries' (9) as Russians, British, Spanish, French, and American traders discovered that sea otter pelts bought from Native Americans could be sold at high prices in China. Whaling and the China trade played an important role in the internationaliza-tion of the region and went hand in hand with the migration of Hawaiian, Pacific, and Asian labourers to the Pacific Northwest. The different waves of immigration[23] can be traced in the unique mixture of Spanish, English, Native American, and Hawaiian place names on both historical and present-day maps of the coastal islands near Seattle and Vancouver, including the San Juan Islands. In the second half of the nineteenth century, Japanese immigrants established themselves on Bainbridge Island in Puget Sound, where they worked at the Port Blakely Mill and later in strawberry farming (Tjossem 2013, 7, 56; see also Neiwert 2005, 47–96). Chinese immigrants on San Juan Island worked in the cannery and the San Juan Lime Company, which was established in 1860 (Vouri and Vouri 2010, 74).

After the passing of the Chinese Exclusion Act in 1882, illegal Chinese immigration to and through the Pacific Northwest kept the customs authorities on their toes and was a matter of public interest. Not only people were smuggled, but 'the natural cover afforded by the vast forested areas and by the coves and inlets of countless, heavily timbered islands' (De Lorme 1973, 77) favoured the smuggling of wool, liquor, and opium to the extent that 'naïve textbook writers credited San Juan sheep with the world's record per capita average of 150 pounds of wool' (78). James H. Hitchman points out that official trade could not account for 'the constant movement of sloops' (1976, 24) through the San Juan Islands. These smuggling activities were

---

[23] For a good overview, see Schwantes (1989). On the fur trade's role in forming an early capitalist imaginary linked to an 'American Pacific Orientalism', see Eperjesi (2005, 1–57). On the Pacific Northwest and the China trade as well as Chinese immigration to the United States, see Chang (2012). Louis Fiset and Gail M. Nomura offer perspectives on Japanese immigration (2005), while David Neiwert discusses the importance of strawberry farming for the formation of Japanese American communities in the North-west (2005). Robert H. Ruby and John A. Brown offer a survey of the Native American history of the region (1982), as does Vine Deloria Jr. (2012). Jean Barman and Bruce McIntyre Watson discuss the history of Hawaiians in the Northwest (2006). For the Russian and Scandinavian histories of the Northwest, see Kushner (1975) and Rasmussen (1993).

partly a reaction to the end of 'an era of unrestricted trade in the Pacific Northwest' (De Lorme 1973, 78) as the US–Canadian border was negotiated and established between 1846 and 1872. Both in their illicit and official manifestations, then, the region was home to multifaceted transnational flows and exchanges, and by the early twentieth century, the Pacific Northwest had become the most important hub for the Asia trade and been discursively constructed as a 'natural gateway to the Asia-Pacific' (Chang 2012, 184). Chang sees this network of trans-national border-crossing as an early form of 'cosmopolitan capitalism' (180), exemplifying its paradoxical impulses of transcending and re-inforcing national boundaries, 'the creative tensions and contradictions of a globalization born of colonial modernity' (192).[24]

The discursive construction of the Pacific Northwest as a space of global exchange is connected to visions of the insular rim of the continent as a space opening up to the world. Somewhat paradoxically, it is difficult to dissociate the economic from the ecological in many of the texts concerned. In his analysis of *Moby Dick*, Eperjesi argues that the text substitutes an 'elaborate tropography' for a 'clearly defined topography' by constructing both a 'commercial, instrumentalizing map' and an 'aesthetic map' that 'reads the Pacific as an integrative force' (2005, 48). He shows how 'excessive and extravagant similes and metaphors' (47) create connections between places as distant as the island of Manhattan and islands in the Indian Ocean, linking disparate spaces by stressing the double flow of water and economic exchange (45–56). The island 'tropography' developed by Northwest writers constructs a similar vision of global flows and interconnectedness, but it does so by drawing on the imaginative potential of North-western topographies, geologies, and ecologies. Critics agree that the figurative use of the landscape has been central to the development of a specific Northwest literature. O'Connell points out that the relationship between people and place is the single most important subject of Northwest literature (2003, x; see also Carolan 2010, 12). In

---

[24] Thus, the increasing regulation and policing of national and racial boundaries, as exemplified by the Chinese Exclusion Act, was accompanied by a 'dramatic expansion in trade and commercial relations between the North American West and the Asia-Pacific Rim' (Chang 2012, 16).

Open Spaces: Voices from the Northwest, a collection of essays from the eponymous quarterly, Penny Harrison writes that

> [*Open Spaces*] reflects a state of mind as well as a geographic entity
> ... the open spaces of the Pacific Northwest define us, inspire us,
> comfort us, and bring us together. (xix)
>   Living amidst both unpredictability and grandeur fosters a keen
> awareness of our place in a long continuum. It pushes us to transcend
> the *insularity* of our individual histories and prejudices. (xxii; my
> emphasis)

Harrison, and the entire project of *Open Spaces*, forges a link between the openness and unpredictability of the landscape and an intellectual openness; in her text, the landscape functions as both model and metaphor for an attitude she aspires to. The various essays of the collection work together in creating an 'imaginal matrix' (Daniel 2011, 3) that turns the local topography into a tropography, constructing a vision of interconnectedness, mobility, and fluidity by emphasizing geological precariousness and the instability of the mountainous landscape (Harris 2011, 108–9), the free flows of the water in rivers and the ocean (Wilkinson 2011, 80–5; Lubchenco et al. 2011, 212–13); and the restlessness of the salmon, whose migrations link the oceans with the interior of the land (Hemmingway 2011, 123–8). At the same time, despite the emphasis on openness and fluidity Harrison's assertion of the formative power of the landscape betrays a form of geographical determinism that goes against the asserted embrace of unpredictability, and the texts collected in the volume sometimes run the risk of constructing romantic or nostalgic visions of a unified and unifying nature.

Nonetheless, Harrison's collection is interesting for its aesthetic opening up of the landscape. In the above quote, however, the island appears as a counter-site to this fluid Northwest imaginary and functions as a metaphor for stasis, intellectual narrowness, and self-centredness. As such, it corresponds to the closed insularity for which Dean Moore faults Western thinking. Pointing out the 'power of the island-idea in the wider Northwest' (2002, 34), Ricou similarly starts out from an association between island and isolation, but only to deconstruct it through his readings of Northwest literature: 'When we try to own islands, or read them, the association with isolation and stasis dissolves in some interdependence of island, river, and moving ocean' (2002, 24). The interplay of islands and water creates a space 'that is neither wholly land nor wholly sea' (22), a 'confusion of islands' (21) at the edge of the continent that is linked to a 'limit of under-standing' (22), a zone where apparently stable borders and political zones '[dissolve] into a meandering hypothesis traced in water' (23), where Canada becomes intertwined with the United States and both are linked with the shores of Asia. Ricou's world of islands is a 'watery land' which undercuts all arbitrary political and geographical divisions.[25] His own text performs this fluid aesthetics in refusing to offer a conventional literary history; his poetic academic prose mean-ders from island to island, from shore to shore. By matching the textual to the geographical, Ricou's literary history engages in an 'aesthetics of the earth'. His poetic opening up of islands leads us to a close examination of the revisionist island poetics deployed in many Northwest writings. With Knickerbocker's notion of an 'ecopoetics' in mind, which draws attention to the mediating role of language in the aesthetic engagement with the earth, we shall now turn to these writings.

'These island waters': Pacific Northwest Memoirs and the Poetics of Land and Sea

While there are few notable local works of island fiction, there are a remarkable number of (semi-)autobiographical writings about the region's islands. As a physical location and figurative device, the island found a privileged genre in the memoirs of pioneering homesteaders in the US–Canadian border region.[26] Many of these texts are of high literary merit and have reached the status of local classics, though

---

[25] Ricou also mentions the Cascadia project as an alternative imagination of the Pacific Northwest cutting across arbitrary political boundaries (2002, 26–9).

[26] The memoirs that cannot be dealt with in this chapter include Frances K. Lovering's *Island Ebb & Flow: A Pioneer's Journal of Life on Waldron Island* (1985), Henry Hoff-man's *Henry's Stories: Tales of a Larger than Life Figure on a Smaller than Normal Island* (2008), Noël Murchie's *The Accidental Hermit* (2001), and Helen Troy Elmore's *This Isle of Guemes* (1973).

they are little known to wider audiences.[27] Even more strikingly, they have received practically no scholarly attention apart from a few scattered references and reviews. The emphasis on these texts gives this chapter a somewhat unique position in this book, as the other chapters focus on fictional island narratives with a largely international reach. Yet their inclusion is justified for several reasons. For one thing, they self-consciously comment on their own relationship to the genre of island fiction and thus reflect on the autobiographical impulse of much fictional island writing such as *Robinson Crusoe*, establishing links between the space of the island, the writing of the self, and—in some texts—the building of a house. At the same time, they offer alternative ways of conceiving the self and its situatedness in space by both evoking and transforming the dreamscapes of classic island fiction.

In order to do justice to the dissolution of boundaries these memoirs gesture towards, the following discussion will respect neither national borders nor textual boundaries. Rather than follow the geopolitical constructions of regions, and rather than treat each text as a discrete entity, I will trace the memoirs' island poetics by freely moving among the islands designated as 'San Juan Islands' and 'Gulf Islands', and among the individual texts. But the island concept is by no means uniform among the memoirs, or even within them. With varying emphasis, they deploy the island as a trope associated with both self-containment and interconnectedness, like the double-edged representation of the San Juans in the *Post-Intelligencer*. David Conover's *Once Upon an Island* (1967), for instance, begins by emphasizing the inward pull associated with the small island he settled with his wife Jeanne in the 1940s.[28] The opening chapter, entitled 'Island Fever', describes their one-day visit to the island. The description of their arrival constructs the island as an enclosed space:

> Two hundred yards from shore, green slopes suddenly *mirrored on the sea*. . . . The island crept closer, filling our lungs with the sweet scent of evergreens as we headed toward the slight depression among

[27] Raymond D. Gastil and Barnett Singer emphasize the frequency and importance of journals and memoirs for the local literature (2010, 5–17, 63–87). O'Connell devotes a chapter to the journals of settlers and explorers of the region (2003, 15–32).
[28] Wallace Island in the Canadian Gulf Islands.

the highest firs. Below them, a sandstone ridge honeycombed with little caves ran the length of the island *like a rampart defending its shores....*

A gap yawned in the sandstone. Then *the island closed around us,* and we were *engulfed by the forest in a motionless landlocked lagoon....*

The cove nestled between gentle wooded slopes, guarded by a *wall of firs and cedars* that grew to *enormous heights.* Madronas, maples, and alders dotted the banks like colored crayons, *their reflection creating the incredible illusion that our boat was stranded in the trees....* It was as though we had stumbled onto a *lost world....*

We glided deep into the cove, *devouring* this *unreal world* as if we were visitors from another planet, not letting a scent, a sight, or sound escape us....

We began to lose all sense of time.   (11–12, my emphasis)

In its creation of the island as a space that is both a fantasy of an originary state of nature and outside of all time, the text goes to great lengths to cut the island off from what surrounds it. The sandstone ridge is described in terms of a defensive rampart and thus figured as the enclosure islands lack. The tall firs and cedars are represented as a second wall, further underscoring the island's impenetrability.

Yet the couple are represented as, impossibly, both within and without this enclosed insular realm. Even before they land, the mirroring of the islands' 'green slopes' in the sea creates a sense of their being on the island. In what follows, the island is described as an active force closing around and 'engulfing' them as they enter the lagoon, which is described as 'motionless' and 'landlocked'; the fluid element of the water is arrested. In a series of remarkable reversals, Conover's text folds the outside of the island—the water—inward so that the island becomes a space that is both surrounded and surrounding and thus effectively an impossible space without an outside.[29] This disavowal of the connectivity of the water reaches its apex when the boat is described as impossibly stranded in the trees by a trick of vision: the outside of the island is poetically turned into its inside. The 'incredible illusion' is thus also the trick of vision performed by Conover's text itself. The fantasy is

[29] This spatial organization is reminiscent of the layout of More's island of Utopia (cf. Racault 2010, 31).

both one of being 'engulfed by' the island and 'devouring this *unreal world*' (my emphasis); of eating and of being eaten.[30] Both outside and always already within the island, the couple are represented as impossibly ingesting what eats them up. Yet the text also marks the unreality of this construction. The island is figured as a 'lost world', and the Conovers are linked to 'visitors from another planet', which turns the island into a self-contained world outside ordinary space and time. Like Prospero, Miranda, and most of the castaways in *The Tempest*, the Conovers simply *are* in this world apart without ever arriving in it, nourished by a fantasy that consumes them; the island is made to serve a desire for complete separation that is also a desire for annihilation.[31] The beginning of the narrative repeatedly marks this desire to be cut off from the world and create a new, autonomous world in chapter headings like 'Burning our Bridges' (2003, 19) and in numerous references to other self-contained or seemingly self-contained worlds like the Garden of Eden (e.g. 17, 53), Robinson Crusoe's island (e.g. 17, 26, 77, 95), and Noah's Ark (77).

At the other end of the spectrum, James Francis Tulloch emphasizes interconnectedness in an article written for the *Friday Harbor Journal* in 1934. The article, entitled 'The Sea Girt Isles of San Juan', is included as an addendum in the 1978 edition of his diary of life as a pioneer on Orcas Island from 1875 to 1910:

> From the summit of Mt. Constitution on Orcas Island...is an unparalleled *view of mountain and valley, sea and land*. The *silver winding channels among them* make up a view which can be seen nowhere else in America.
> ...The Straits of Juan de Fuca, through which passes the *commerce of the Orient*, and the magnificent Cascade range on the east

[30] My reading is influenced by Weaver-Hightower's argument that Robinson Crusoe's fear of being swallowed up by the island is compensated by his strong desire to ingest and incorporate his surroundings (2007, 12).

[31] Early on, the text gives us a hint as to the possible causes of this desire for separation and complete withdrawal: 'Then came Pearl Harbor. Guard duty, scrubbing latrines, combat photography, the South Pacific. When it was all over, we decided we owed each other a honeymoon trip' (2003, 13). While Conover lists grand reasons for leaving the world behind—among others, 'a challenge to know myself [. . .]' (24)—the seemingly casual reference to the insular war theatre of the Pacific looms over the invocation of a Northwest island paradise.

extends along the horizon from British Columbia to where it would be *lost in the distance* were it not for that grand old Mt. Rainier which refuses to be ignored as she looms heavenward. . . . The *countless salmon* by the millions throng these *island waters* on their annual *migration* to their spawning grounds at the headwaters of the *streams flowing* into Puget Sound and the Gulf of Georgia. . . .

On top of the mountain . . . , *a beautiful spring of ice-cold water boils out of the rock*. This water can have no other source than in the distant Cascade range some 40 miles to the east. *This artesian spring must therefore flow many miles beneath the sea and rise and break forth on Mt. Constitution* . . . .

This region, owing to its northern latitude and mountainous character, combined with the warm *Japan ocean current* that bathes its shores seems to be the *meeting place* of the sub-Arctic and the sub-tropical floras of North America. (1978, 117–19; my emphasis)

Tulloch did not live on the island anymore when he wrote this; the text is an imaginative recreation of the view from Mt. Constitution, the highest point of the San Juan Islands. The view is poetically reconstructed as a vision that moves outward, away from the island: the mountain, and with it the island and the imaginary observer, is merely a vantage point on which the different flows and movements from, to, and around it converge. The title already stresses the movement of the sea around the islands. In the first sentence, high and low points, sea and land, are a unit in syntactic parallelism, forming a single noun phrase twice. The 'countless salmon' and the 'silver winding channels' are described as moving restlessly among the islands and from the island into the mainland and back. The most striking image of connection is maybe that of the spring, which is claimed to establish a direct, underground connection between the island and the distant Cascades. Situated on the mountain top, the spring seems to flow directly to the observer and draw him away from the island. Moving even further outward, the description of aquatic and economic flows links the islands with the Orient and figures them as a 'meeting place' of the floras of different climate zones. Both the sea to the west and the mountains to the east, 'lost in the distance', pull the observer towards infinity. Where Conover's 'Island Fever' chapter was marked by a centripetal force, Tulloch's article displays a decidedly centrifugal gesture.

The core expression in Tulloch's description may be 'island waters', the reverse concept of Hau'ofa's 'sea of islands': in both, the island and the water infiltrate each other both metaphorically and metonymically and the two terms become inseparable. Tulloch's 'island waters' give the island back the water already contained in its etymology—'watery land'[32]—but often excluded in its conceptualization. And while Conover's *Once Upon an Island* never gives up its vision of the island as self-contained, 'rooted to the past—static and green and nearly forgotten' (2003, 34), there are glimpses of a different vision. Significantly, they are almost exclusively related either to sea journeys or to meditations on the beach. Most interestingly, Conover substitutes the term 'sea-lander' for 'islander': 'For the lonely islander leads two lives—he belongs to both the sea and the land. The word "islander" is far too nebulous. He is a sea-lander. The salt chuck is his highway and lifeline …' (63). Like 'island waters', 'sea-lander' brings out the interplay of land and water already hidden in the word 'islander' itself. The emphasis on the islander's double identity combines the two views of the island as enclosed and open.

While, somewhat ironically, the former view is predominant in Conover's narrative, the chapter 'The Desperate Voyage' is one of the moments where the island's separateness is challenged and island becomes sea-land. It opens with a cartographic view of the Gulf Islands:

> On a map of British Columbia, draw a line linking the cities of Vancouver, Nanaimo, and Victoria. In the heart of this triangle lies Wallace Island....
>
> Unspoiled by civilization's creeping hand, the islands rise from the sea.... Their names read like a history of intrepid Spanish and English explorers—Galiano, Valdez, Mayne, and Gabriola. They stretch in clusters south of the forty-ninth parallel, interlocking like a jigsaw puzzle with the American San Juan Islands, forming an unseen boundary that jogs through a great inland sea of islands toward the Straits of Juan de Fuca. (33)

Asking the reader to draw a triangle of lines on the map, the chapter starts out with a geometrical vision. In what follows, cartographic and experiential conceptions of the islands are curiously intertwined: the

---

[32] See Introduction.

emphasis on a confusing intercontinental sea of islands, again evoking Hauʻofa's use of the same term, seems to refer to an aesthetic experience similar to that of the speaker in Hugo's 'The Anacortes–Sydney Run'; the islands rising from the sea suggest a three-dimensional vision. But the reference to the imaginary lines on the map and the figuration of the islands as an interlocking jigsaw puzzle constructs a horizontal view, a distant vision tied to a cartographic gaze. It is only when Conover describes the dangerous voyage through the islands that this distant vision fully dissolves into a phenomenal confusion reminiscent of Vancouver's journal. Significantly, we are told that Conover's own chart has dissolved, marking the end of cartographic certainty: 'all that remained was bits of paper sticking like confetti to the floorboards' (47). At the same time, the islandscape has become fluid:

> The islands crept closer, each taking on a definite hue and shape of its own.... Dark patches of forest began to close around me. Like tarnished emeralds, island upon island reeled into view, etching the soft blue horizon with their black feathery crowns. Wooded shores merged and black-marbled channels sprang open, only to close as new corridors appeared. (49)

Far from constructing a distant look, the text here registers an immersion in a watery island world where land *and* water take on a life of their own. Euclidean space dissolves into lived and living space. In this world of phenomenal uncertainty, all stable reference points are lost: rather than surveying land and sea from a central vantage point, we enter a fluid world as islands reel into view, merge with each other, and split in two.

If '[e]xtension (*extensio*) is the core concept in Descartes's view of space' (Casey 1997, 153), measurable Cartesian space, exemplified by the triangular drawing of lines on the map, here dissolves into the fluid space theorized by both modern physics and phenomenological approaches. Where Einstein's theory of relativity, with its notion of a flexible spatiotemporal continuum, and Heisenberg's uncertainty principle call into questions all accounts of space as stable and measurable in absolute terms (cf. Childs 2008, 72–8), Husserl's 'critique of the mathematization of nature' (Casey 1997, 238) with its rejection of a 'single universal causality underlying an absolute, objective spatiotemporality' (222) is linked to Merleau-Ponty's focus on the body and the 'flow of experiences' in space (Merleau-Ponty 2002, 327; see also 284–347). In the above passage, space becomes fluid, and the Cartesian subject itself is overwhelmed by the spatial flux around it. Geometrical control and any sense of securely navigating a stable and immutable space make way for a disorienting experience where both the subject and space are in constant motion.

In Tulloch's text, the position of surveying the island from its highest point, the powerful vantage point of the Cartesian subject countlessly rehearsed in island fiction, is gradually decentred in the centripetal vision outlined above. The island is opened up in a poetic amalgam-ation of the various geographical elements of the space the text imaginatively surveys; what results is not only 'island waters', but more generally an island world. This entails a specific geological imaginary, exemplified by the hypothesized underground connection to the Cascade Range. Dean Moore's refiguring of islands similarly draws on the imaginative potential of geology:

> The Pacific Coast of Canada and southeast Alaska is a mountain range carved by glaciers into knife ridges and shadowed valleys. . . .
> Eventually, the whole continental shelf subsided, sinking the coastal mountains and valleys below sea level. . . .
> Standing on Pine Island, it's not hard to imagine yourself standing on the tip of a mountain, the valleys below filled, not with hemlocks and bears, but snow crabs and silt, and sea stars clinging to the kelp-draped cliffs. (2004, 11–12)

Dean Moore here draws on geology to rethink the island. Evoking its history as part of a mountain range allows her to reimagine the view from its highest point. As in Tulloch's text, this breaks up the island's separateness. In effect, her vision adds time to the three dimensions of space. The result is a remarkable blending of the spatial and the temporal through the textual. Rethinking the surrounding ocean in terms of valleys, the text asks the reader to see the landscape in its prehistoric continuity. But it also draws prehistory into the present by giving the prehistoric valleys a decidedly oceanic cast. Island and moun-tain, sea and valley, in short: 'island waters' and mountain range are collapsed. Time is inscribed in space;[33] the vision is simultaneously one

---

[33] Cf. Bakhtin (1981).

of time *and* space, or of time *as* space, effectively asking us to view the island in four dimensions.

Without disputing the value of these texts in reimagining islands and breaking up subjectivity, we should nonetheless consider the limitations of their ecopoetics. With Morton's critique of nature writing in mind, we should note that they sometimes expand rather than dissolve the self. If Conover's *Once Upon and Island*, for instance, opens up the island after an initial desire for insular autonomy and separateness, a cynical reading could argue that the text never really leaves this desire behind: in a sense, the space of the island is simply expanded beyond its borders to form an enlarged ecotopia that still excludes the world Conover wishes to escape from. Figurations of islands 'creeping closer' and wearing 'black feathery crowns' make space fluid, but also anthropomorphize it. This 'ecocentrism' is, at least in part, a form of 'anthropocentrism' in a green costume. Tulloch's 'island waters' disrupt political boundaries, but the sense of ecological interconnectedness partly naturalizes an economic vision of the free flow of a global market. Dean Moore's island in time includes the ecosystem of the past, but partly excludes that of the present.

How Hilltops Became Islands: Geology and Local Cosmogonies

Dean Moore's inclusion of geology is not coincidental: the imaginative potential of geology is exploited in much of the region's literature. Geologists tell us that the San Juan Islands are characterized by a 'remarkable geological diversity' (Orr and Orr 2006, 83). They are made up of five different *terranes*, i.e. fragments of old plates that were accreted to North America roughly between 500 and 100 million years BP (cf. Orr and Orr 2006, 81–6); the easternmost and youngest of these extends into the North Cascades. Carved into their present mountainous shapes by glaciers in the last ice ages, they were flooded due to rising sea levels as the glaciers receded and then rose out of the sea due to gradual uplifting of the land. While the detailed geological history of the region was not fully understood until the acceptance of the theory of plate tectonics in the 1960s paved the way for more precise studies, the naturalists and geologists who studied the islands in the nineteenth century already had a clear sense of its turbulence and complexity. One of the earliest of them was the American ethnologist and geologist George Gibbs, who joined the Northwest Boundary Survey in 1857 and spent some time on San Juan Island in 1858. Gibbs's journal demonstrates the way scientific, economic, and political interests were intertwined in contemporary representations of the San Juan Islands:

> Feby 26th Saty Took boat with Mr Custer & went to the terraced hill called Park Mtn. Dredged in & [word] the lagoon at its foot—mud & sand & but little *adult*. Rocks everywhere trap—The terraces on this hill [word] as horizontal as well characterized as at Mt Finlayson. Like them they [word] the south & the [word] of the hill is steep—a number of granite boulders on the south face of the hill—& others lodged on the bare rocks on the bay—As there is no granite on the islands they must have been transported from a distance, probably the northward marine range.

This entry is interesting for a number of reasons. Thematically, it expresses an awareness of the disjointed origins of the island's structure. Focusing on the conglomerate nature of the land, Gibbs presents the island as a random accretion of material. Viewed through the prism of geology, it loses its distinct identity and appears as a space where disparate materials intersect; a product of ongoing geological transformation and geomorphological transportation that challenges clear-cut notions of inside and outside.

This thematic focus on accretion is paralleled by the accretive structure of the diary itself. The different rock formations are textually separated by dashes and ampersands; the sentences are fragmentary, lack verbs, and break off abruptly. It is perhaps significant that the only finished sentence of the passage is the last one: it stands apart from the others as it marks the end of observation and offers an explanation. It moves the text from discontinuous fragments to discrete form while, rather ironically, explaining the discontinuity of the island. Of course, the disparate structure is largely explained by the diary genre and its specific formal properties, but here I am interested in the potential of the diary form as such to register discontinuous spatial experiences; in this case, it allows Gibbs to place a series of observations side by side without integrating them. If the breaking up of distinct geographical identities resonates with the form of Gibbs's text, reading the two in conjunction allows us to comment both on a view of space as shifting and on the capacity of the diary to construct fluid subjectivities.

In passages like the above, Gibbs's diary appears like a collection of a disinterested scientist's observations. But the diary jumps back and forth between geological explanation, information about the economic activities on the island, confrontations with the indigenous population, and references to the disputed boundary and the surveying activities, often moving abruptly from one to the other several times within the space of a few lines. This loose and collage-like structure is evocative of the inseparability of these different interests. The 1868 publication of the materials from the boundary commission demonstrates this inter-connectedness in its very title, *The Northwest Boundary. Discussion of the Water Boundary Question: Geographical Memoir of the Islands in Dispute: and History of the Military Occupation of San Juan Island: Accompanied by Map and Cross-Sections of Channels*. A collection of letters, geographical facts, and historical accounts, the book cuts across generic distinctions. History, geography, and politics intertwine, which becomes obvious in the discussion of Haro Strait:

> This channel is the true and natural boundary between the continent and Vancouver's Island.... Had the maps of that day represented the space between the continent and Vancouver's Island as it is now known, the Gulf of Georgia and Canal de Haro would have been designated by name in the treaty as the boundary channel, on the 'generally admitted principle' that they constitute the 'main channel'.... (80)

In this and many other instances, geography is mobilized to settle the question of the 'natural boundary'. Yet the quotation marks around 'generally admitted principle' and 'main channel' inadvertently expose these concepts as constructs. The letters and texts of the collection go to great lengths to fabricate the boundary favoured by the Americans as natural; the geographical memoir at the centre of the book laments the messiness in the nomenclature of the islands and waterways, demanding that the names chosen by Charles Wilkes and the United States Coast Survey should be retained on British maps with the exception of a few Spanish names. Faulting the British for ignoring the Wilkes map, the memoir glosses over Vancouver's map in turn. As the geologist of the Northwest Boundary Commission, Gibbs was very much part of this discourse.

Yet his unpublished diary, in contrast to the published collection,[34] resists the official account's neat production of 'natural' regions. At times, the uncertain geological interpretations seem to suggest the possibility of regions that cut across those desired by either the British or the Americans altogether, as when Gibbs wonders

> whether the tertiary deposits of the Puget Sound district including perhaps those of the coast did not form one extensive basin interior to the portions of the coast range, i.e. the Olympic & Vancouver I. mts & those of the disputed islands & the western Cascades— perhaps of the greater part of that range. The extremely distorted Portion & unusual dip would seem to indicate this . . . .

Gibbs here formulates a vision of geological continuity that runs counter to political boundaries and stretches across island, mainland, and sea. At the same time, the careful hedging of this vision with the repeatedly used 'perhaps' and 'would seem to' bespeaks a spatial uncertainty that resists easy region-making and instead allows for multiple ways of imagining regions. This ambiguity resonates with the spatial indeterminacy of the Pig War years that both sides were striving to eliminate; as such, parts of Gibbs's diary sit uneasily with the project within which he conducted his surveys. What the diary shares with Vancouver's journal is a destabilization of any rigid sense of land- and seascape. In Vancouver's case, this is linked to an immersive contemplation of as yet unstructured space; in Gibbs's, the island is broken open by an equally immersive and speculative contemplation of space with the added dimension of geological time. In both, the neat binary of land and sea is called into question by the region's islandness. In both, we enter a shifting world of islands. From a post-phenomenological perspective, both Vancouver's and Gibbs's journals register the opacity and otherness of space.

---

[34] Archibald Campbell's compilation of the material from the Northwest Boundary Commission included Gibbs's geological notes as an addendum, but they were not published.

The geology of the islands is turned into a foundational myth in a striking number of writings about the region, which often neutralize these opacities. Detailing the processes by which the San Juans became islands, these texts construct cosmogonies that ask the reader to view the islands as malleable landforms shaped by powerful forces. A striking example is Emelia L. Bave's historical pageant *San Juan Saga*, which was first shown in 1959 to commemorate the Pig War and later became a one-woman show with mannequins, running from 1965 into the late seventies. The pageant opens by quoting from the beginning of Genesis: 'The waters were gathered together into one place ... and the dry land appeared. This land was called Earth ... and the gathering together of the waters called Seas ...' (1976, 7; ellipses original). This is followed by an outline of the geological history of the islands:

> During this period, the islands we are now enjoying were part of a large continent. In time, this continent sank into the sea, leaving only the higher peaks exposed. These tops were covered by glaciers.... New lands arose around these islands, jutting sharp and tall and far above the peaks left exposed by the sunken continent. (7)

The reference to Genesis reinterprets the formation of the islands in terms of original creation. Conversely, the juxtaposition of the two narratives turns Genesis into an island story: the creation of earth is figured as the birth of an originary island.[35] If water is simply presented as given in Genesis and associated with darkness and formlessness, the creation of this island is an initial act of giving form. Yet what emerges out of the initial undifferentiated waters is the binary of earth and sea, *both* of which are linked to the creation of form. The earth island of Genesis is thus not to be thought of in opposition to a formless sea, but the initial 'waters' precede the opposition itself and as such already contain the land, but not yet as a discrete entity.

At the same time, the representation of the islands as sunken mountain tops runs counter to their figuration as spaces of origin. The

---

[35] Loxley argues that many island texts are 'reflections on origins' (1990, 3). For a sustained discussion of how literary islands project fantasies of inaccessible origins, see Racault (1989; 2010, 165–80).

beginning of the pageant thus rehearses the paradox of the island as a site of creation and 'a fragment, a part of some greater whole from which it is in exile' (Bongie 1998, 18; cf. Edmond and Smith 2003, 5). As such, Bave's geo-mythological account of the islands also evokes the description of the earth reemerging in insular form after the flood in Genesis 8:5: 'And the waters decreased continually until the tenth month: in the tenth month, on the first day of the month, were the tops of the mountains seen' (2006, 10).[36] Lucile S. McDonald's popular history of the San Juans opens by evoking another mythological apocalypse: 'Like the legendary continent of Atlantis, the San Juan Islands lie largely beneath the sea. They are peaks of a sunken mountain range which anciently joined Vancouver Island and what is now the state of Washington' (1990, 1). David Richardson's *Magic Islands: A Treasure-Trove of San Juan Island Lore* (1973) opens in almost the same way: 'Archeologically and spiritually, the San Juan Islands are a world apart. Archaeologically because the Islands actually are the last remaining mountain tops of a submerged continent, far older than the mainland of North America, now slowly receding, Atlantis-like, to a reluctant oblivion' (7). Like Dean Moore's spatiotemporal vision of Pine Island, these texts ask the reader to reimagine the islands and engage with submarine continuities: 'An inquisitive frogman would find deep valleys and subterranean mountains of long grass on the bottom' (McDonald 1990, 1).

Yet while the geo-mythology of all three texts breaks up the discreteness of the islands, it also reasserts spatial unity at a higher level. Whether as an earth island or as a sunken continent, space does not radically disintegrate. Through the Atlantis simile, the islands are imagined as fragments of a submerged whole; the reader is asked to reimagine the islandscape by filling in the pieces missing from the integrated vision of a lost continent. Evoking an ancient 'world apart' (Richardson 1973, 7), the texts reassert a closed and bounded space.

---

[36] Sam Taylor's recent island novel *The Island at the End of the World* (2009) explicitly references Genesis 8:5 as its foundational text by including it as an epigraph to the first part; in Taylor's postdiluvian vision, a deranged father leads his children to believe that they are living on a small island to which they escaped in an ark after catastrophic floods.

Islands and the Drift of History: *100 Days in the San Juans* (1946)

Gibbs's diary and the regional geo-mythology exemplify, at opposite poles, the disruptive and unifying potential of geology. By opening up the island in space *and* in time, they add a historical dimension to their island poetics. As such, they form the link to the second set of texts to be discussed in this middle section: a series of columns about the San Juans by June Burn (*100 Days in the San Juans*, 1946), a memoir about life on a lighthouse island by Helene Glidden (*The Light on the Island*, 1951), and finally a novel set on a fictional island in the San Juans by Laurie R. King (Folly, 2001). All three texts figure their islands as spaces where history accumulates as theorized by Braudel, albeit in different ways and in different genres. Whether Glidden and King were directly influenced by the earlier texts or not, the three texts are usefully examined in sequence as the later narratives develop the concerns of their predecessors.

A playful version of regional geo-mythology appears in *100 Days in the San Juans*, a compilation of articles written by June Burn for the Seattle *Post-Intelligencer* in 1946 as she sailed from island to island with her husband, camping on beaches and recording the stories of the people she met. The first two articles are entitled 'Mountain Range in the Sea':[37]

> It was back in one of these mysterious ages that a mountain range, northwest of what is now Seattle, went down like a vast ship, bits of it left sticking up. . . .
> During the ice age, glaciers gouged the valleys deeper. . . .
> Later on . . . this same mountain range rose again . . . .
> Thus in one of history's curious moments hilltops became islands. Other islands are formed by river deposits, or by tidal action. Or a reef will rise. . . . Only very distinguished islands like the San Juan Archipelago are mountain tops in the sea.
> After the hills became islands, the next thing of importance in their history was the coming of summer tourists. . . .

---

[37] The first article is titled 'A Mountain Range in the Sea' (1983, 13); its sequel removes the indefinite article from the title.

The third great event in San Juan history was the coming of
white man....

Eighteen seventy-two, finally, was the year when the great to-do
about the San Juan boundary was settled and the islands became
completely ours at last. (1983, 14–15; emphasis original)

In this short cosmogony, Burn establishes a mythical connection
between the different phases of the islands' history. In one broad
sweep, the geographical genesis of the archipelago is linked with the
different waves of immigration. The common denominator is the influx
from the islands' exterior that precedes each phase. The use of the
term 'summer tourists' for the Native Americans conflates the most
recent wave, the summer tourists from the mainland, with the first;
the history of the island is thus presented as a series of geological and
political becomings. While Burn playfully distinguishes the San
Juans from other islands, all her examples represent islands as the
product of ongoing geographical forces and movements such as tidal
action or river deposits; her islands are never final products but
always in the making. In the next article, she turns to the micro-
level of island becoming by drawing attention to the daily disappearance and reemergence of many islands: 'The actual number of
islands in the San Juan Archipelago varies with the person who
does the counting' (16).

Yet the resonance between geographical and political becomings is
ambivalent. On the one hand, the Americanness of the islands and their
boundaries is relativized as the American settlers are shown to be not
only the earlier outside folded inward, but also merely the last in a long
series of cyclical processes. The final 'the islands *became* completely
ours at last' (my emphasis) highlights the becoming that precedes all
being. Yet the sentence can also be read as 'the islands became *completely ours* at last'; this reading casts a different light on the figuration
of Native Americans as 'summer tourists', contrasting with American
ownership and legitimizing dispossession. Generally speaking, the geographical maps the historical in Burn's account: the islands are subject
to the forces of history, and at the same time the space where this
history accumulates and can be read. The remaining ninety-eight
articles perform this reading as Burn records a series of stories that
are 'a quick snapshot of island history' (15). They are often literally read
by Burn as she peruses old diaries, notebooks, letters, documents, and

even weather records kept by islanders; sometimes they are told by the islanders or the islands themselves, or contained in maps. In 'A Village of Stories', Burn talks about information about past island life derived from old notebooks, islanders' memories, and a shop selling rare old prints in the village of Eastsound on Orcas Island (100–1). In a double article on four pioneers on Lopez Island, Burn recounts going through 'a trunk full of old papers' (76) which contains records, letters, and receipts dating back to 1871. 'Never have I seen such a drift of history in one pile!' (74), Burn exclaims: 'When (if) I ever write a real book about the San Juans, I'll be going back to that old trunk' (76).

Burn never wrote this book, and appropriately so, as her conception of history is not one that could integrate it into a coherent whole. History is presented as an accidental drift; it washes up on the islands following the wind and the waves. The metaphor of drifting resonates with the Burns' own part purposeful, part accidental drifting from island to island: 'Well, shall we go to Shaw Island then, now? No, this southwest wind wouldn't take us there, either. Where is it taking us? We look around. We consult the chart. Why, we're headed straight for Guemes' (78). The connecting elements between the articles are the islands, the wind and the waves, and, of course, narrative, but narrative of a loose and episodic kind: a series of snippets spanning the various immigrant histories, pioneer life in the islands, the Wilkes expedition, the everyday realities of tax receipts and rejected proposals, beachcombing, and the loneliness of four boys operating the lighthouse on Patos Island. The texts weave in and out of the present, various layers of the past, and deep geological history, allowing their readers to relive history: 'Just in case you weren't there when we fought the Pig War in this column . . . ' (121). The very form of Burn's writing project is part of this accidental gathering of history from the beaches of the island, a series of episodic essays without an overarching frame.[38] Like the tides on which she drifts from island to island like the 'original' immigrants, Burn's narrative travels in the opposite direction, carrying the history of the islands back into the world from which it had once drifted to their shores.

---

[38] The series of articles was not published as a book until after Burn's death.

An Island of Memory: *The Light on the Island* (1951)

The notion of history as drift accumulating on the island is developed in semi-fictional form in Helene Glidden's memoir *The Light on the Island*, written in 1951, five years after Burn's column. Glidden's father was the lighthouse keeper on tiny Patos Island on the edge of the San Juans in the immediate proximity of the Canadian border from 1905 to 1913; he and his large family were the only inhabitants of the island (see McCloskey 2001, 195–200).[39] The autodiegetic narrator called Angie or Angel is a fictionalized version of the author, and the entire text mixes fact and fiction to the point that the editor of the 2001 anniversary edition begins his postscript by asking: 'Were the events described in this book historically accurate or were they just a childhood fantasy?' (McCloskey 2001, 195). A contemporary review by Verne Bright in the *Oregon Historical Quarterly* offers a brief overview of some of the central elements structuring the narrative: 'The Light on the Island is the story of every day life on Patos, which quite often becomes hectic, what with log pirates, opium smugglers, the silent vanishing Chinamen, and Spanish John, the bearded stranger, who Angie thought was God. Mrs. Glidden's story of Patos is a tale of isolation but of a happy isolation after the first shock of loneliness . . .' (327–8). Rather contra-dictorily, Bright emphasizes the isolation of the island right after referring to a series of spectacular intrusions into its space. Albeit unwittingly, Bright captures the tension between the static and inter-connected aspects of the island that runs through *The Light on the Island*, and which is linked to a tension between description and narration.

This tension is usefully examined in terms of Michel de Certeau's distinction between place and space. For de Certeau, '*space is practiced place*. Thus the street geometrically defined by urban planning is transformed into a space by walkers' (1984, 117; emphasis original). A mere description of a door represents it as a static place; if the same door is represented while someone walks through it, it becomes a space. For de Certeau, the transformation from place to space is linked to

---

[39] See also note 40.

narrative (118). In *The Light on the Island*, the account gains in narrative impulse whenever the outside world drifts into the small island world. When island life is recounted on its own, the text remains largely descriptive and the events are frequently presented as routines, recounted in the iterative mode. This tension is evident when a boat approaches the island in chapter 5:

> *One day* we were fishing in our *accustomed place*, when a boat *suddenly* appeared on the horizon. The sight of a boat was nothing unusual to us, but this one was coming toward the island. Not many boats came in so close.
>
> 'I wonder if she's coming here,' said René.
>
> 'No,' thought Lynn, 'she's out too far in the straits.... Sure coming in fast; must have a good tide.'
>
> 'Gosh,' said René, 'it sure is coming in too far. Maybe it's coming here after all.'
>
> For a short time we fished in silence....
>
> Suddenly, she veered off her course and came in quite close.
>
> 'Crack! Crack!' A bullet hit our boat. 'Crack!' (Glidden 2001, 57; my emphasis)

The opening 'one day' and the word 'accustomed' in the main clause of the first sentence paint the scene as habitual and static; the subordinate clause, reinforced by the word 'suddenly', marks a disturbance and with it the onset of narrative. The pace quickens until the unexpected shots hit the boat. The remainder of the text leaves it curiously open why the shots were fired although there is a court inquest; the scene is a pure eruption of narrative in the midst of a static description of island life. It links narrative to the movement of the boat and the bullets towards the island. Stripped of content, the scene makes visible the structure of narrative itself.

The notion of drifting is crucial in this context, and it recurs in Glidden's text. The log pirates in chapter 10 are described as 'drifting in' (2001, 118); the smuggler Spanish John, who hides on the island for years, 'drifted in at Blanchard's Harbor' (186) when he first came to the island, tied to a plank by other smugglers; even summer is described as 'lazily drifting in' (146). As visitors drift in, the island is worked upon and becomes a dynamic space. The outside world that drifts in is closely linked to the history of the region: the three most spectacular visitors— Indian Tom, Spanish John, and a certain 'Colonel Theodore Roosevelt' (the only one who does not drift; we will return to this)—represent the different phases in the discovery and settlement of the islands. The island is thus as much a historical location as a figurative site of cultural memory, a *lieu de mémoire* where the flow of history accumulates and solidifies.

A crucial character is the old historian Mr. Blanchard, who lives in a cabin on the island until his death, writing a history of the San Juan Islands:[40] 'About how the Spaniards and Indians found them; how they were named and how they finally were given to the United States' (34). Mr. Blanchard's project is to record the history that repeats itself in miniature on Patos Island. He does not live to finish his book. In a sense, it cannot be finished because Mr. Blanchard and the other characters become entangled with the island's history and thereby perform the very book he is writing. Thus, we learn of the bodies of illegal Chinese immigrants that were thrown overboard as their smugglers were discovered, washed up on the beach called Blanchard's Harbor and buried by Mr. Blanchard. Most importantly, Mr. Blanchard's friendship with the notorious smuggler Spanish John makes him a figure both participating in and recording history. In the end, as two groups of smugglers arrive on the island and Spanish John is shot, we find out that he has been hiding on Patos for years and is the same old man whom little Angie took to be God. In the violent confrontation, Angie's family become as entangled with history as Mr. Blanchard.

In the end, the island itself, and with it *The Light on the Island*, assumes the status of Mr. Blanchard's unfinished book. History becomes embedded in the topography of the island. When Mr. Blanchard tells Angie and her brothers about the incident with the Chinese immigrants, the island becomes a memoryscape:

> 'This is Frustration's Rendezvous,' he informed us.... 'These are the boys who left their homes in China....
>
> 'I found the bodies on the beaches, hands and feet tied. They were tossed overboard by the smugglers when the revenue cutters got nosy.'

[40] According to Lucile S. McDonald, there was indeed an elderly man named E. B. Blanchard living in a cabin on Patos Island; there is no mention of him having been a historian, however (1990, 165).

> Mr. Blanchard's eyes filled with tears. 'I buried them here, beneath
> these oaks—sometimes three in a single grave. There are no names—
> no markers. Only the memory of an old man to tell of their frustrated
> hopes.' (2001, 34)

The troubled history of Chinese immigration to the San Juans is, quite
literally, buried in the island, yet it is only accessible if the island can be
read. Without names and markers, the graves almost disappear into the
island, like the Native American burial site also shown to the children
by Mr. Blanchard: 'These mounds', he pointed out, 'are graves of the
Indians who died here . . .' (38). The past leaves its marks on the island,
but they require the presence of living memory to be carried into the
future. After the historian's death, Angie and her narrative keep the
past alive. Mr. Blanchard's cabin himself becomes as overgrown as the
graves: 'In a short time the weeds grew so densely around it that it was
almost forgotten by the family' (81). And yet Mr. Blanchard, like the
smugglers, Native Americans, and Chinese, becomes part of the island,
although he is not buried there, as 'one of the Patos harbors continued
to be called Blanchard's Harbor and is so called to this day' (81). With
J. Hillis Miller's reflections on the figurative transfers in the meaning
of the word 'topography' in mind (1995, 1–8), the topography of
the island consists *both* of the graves and of the place names such
as 'Blanchard's Harbor' and 'Frustration's Rendezvous'. For Miller,
topography is caught in a 'tension between creating and revealing' (5);
in *The Light of the Island*, topographic designation reveals the history
of the region as much as it creates and perpetuates a certain vision of
this history.

By the end of the narrative, Patos Island has become an island of
memory. History is inscribed on the island as a trace, just as the various
places and their names are now linked to the stories that shaped them
in Glidden's narrative. Space and place are inextricable linked:

> The day of our departure arrived. . . .
>   I stood on the stern of the *Heather, until the island was a tiny speck
> in the distance.* All the joys and sorrows of the past ten years crowded
> into my thoughts. I remembered when Patos waved a welcome to
> me, when I was five; the face in the woods; God . . . the voice of the
> island that spoke to me so often; the Chinese jewel . . . .
>   The tears were coming down fast now. 'I'll never forget you,' I said
> aloud.

'Why the tears?' asked Papa, standing beside me.
I started—then leaned on the rail again. 'Oh, Papa, it's just that *I remember Patos Island*,' I said. (192; my emphasis)

Angie here becomes the real historian of the memoir. During the whole narrative, she describes herself constantly as slightly apart from everyone else. If the island is exposed to the flow or the drift of history washing up on its shores like logs, Angie is almost magically present at all major events, often as a hidden observer. The above passage creates clear links between Angie and the island in her personification of the latter; the notion that the island spoke to her marks her as the recipient and carrier of its secrets. When the island gradually turns into a mere speck on the horizon, phenomenal experience is replaced by memories. As the physical island disappears from view, she 'remember[s] Patos Island', a rather striking statement as she has only just left it. Angie's experience becomes part of history, and her own drifting away from the island prefigures her narrative. Like Burn's newspaper column, Angie's text carries the island's history back into the world as she turns its voice into her own narrative voice. She shares this receptivity with her father: '"... I don't want to leave Patos now. It has memories—and voices." / "Papa!" I exclaimed in surprise. Do you feel like I do about Patos? Do you hear the trees, the sea, the wind, and the grasses talking?"' (189) Evoking Caliban's 'The isle is full of noises' (Shakespeare 2000, 3. 2. 130) speech in *The Tempest*, Angie here expresses a capacity to register the island in its spatial and material dimensions. The geographical elements of the island itself are said to communicate its history; this history is not merely grafted onto it, but merges with its soil and vegetation after washing up on its shores.

Significantly, Angie includes the sea and the wind when she figures the island as a talking organism: if they brought history to the island, they also carry it off again, as when Angie throws Spanish John's ashes into the sea: 'Return to the sea—the sea you loved, God of my childhood prayers. Float free with the wind and the whispering waves...' (2001, 187). Having become soil and sand himself, Spanish John leaves the island as he arrived, drifting back into the sea. This renewed emphasis on drifting coincides with Angie's recognition of the loss of her own God, the providential agency that seemed to hold the threads of everything happening on the island together and provide narrative coherence. As this structuring principle is removed, as 'God' becomes part of the island and is no longer separate from it, History with a capital H is given up and the island emerges in its capacity to register history as an accidental drift. It becomes a site where history is both in the making and recorded, both in constant flux and crystallized as a *lieu de mémoire*. The island in Glidden's text oscillates between place and space. It is transformed into a space as the world comes drifting in. It becomes a place as history thickens and crystallizes, becoming visible in the different sites of the island. It is transformed back into a space as these sites are activated and worked upon by Angie's narrative and its history is carried back into the world.

The Island in an Ocean of Becoming:
Folly (2001)

Like Burn's articles, *The Light on the Island* is not without its ambivalences. If Burn's emphasis on drifting also naturalizes the American ownership of the islands, we cannot ignore the fact that Theodore Roosevelt in *The Light on the Island* is the only representative of history who purposefully arrives on the island rather than drifting in. The difference between Indian Tom, who is almost shipwrecked in a storm and only manages to land thanks to the help of Angie's father in addition to being represented as dirty and smelly (2001, 77–81), and Roosevelt's graceful arrival as his yacht comes 'dancing into the bay' (107) could not be more pronounced. While various histories are inscribed in the island, the right to remember lies with the American narrator, who is given agency as the bearer of history. The final text in this trio, the novel *Folly* (2001) by the Californian writer Laurie R. King, figures history in terms of pressures rather than drift, reflecting on the problem of human agency within a historical force field.

If *The Light of the Island* can be seen as a semi-fictional response to Burn's *100 Days in the San Juans*, *Folly* is usefully examined as a homage to and rewriting of Glidden's text in the form of fiction. From Burn's column to King's novel, both the narratives and the islands become more and more fictional, but all three texts draw on previous writings, fictional and otherwise, to construct their islands as sites accumulating history. *Folly* is set on a fictional island in the outer reaches of the San Juans. Rae Newborn, a woman who has been mentally unstable since two traumatic events, buys a tiny uninhabited island named Folly. The island once belonged to her great-uncle Desmond, who built a house, lived, and died on Folly; Rae rebuilds the burnt-down house single-handedly. The life on the island and the building process function as a therapy and trial for her; initially startled by the slightest noise and unable to differentiate between paranoid delusions and real threats, she gradually regains control of her life. The narrative is interspersed with Rae's and her great-uncle's diaries. As the novel progresses, Rae discovers that her ancestor was murdered by his brother. In the end, the past almost repeats itself as her stepson tries to kill her, trying to burn down the house like Desmond's brother. His attempt is unsuccessful, and Rae finds out that Desmond—and not his brother—was her grandfather, the family secret that resulted in the murder.

Despite the different genres, there are striking thematic and structural parallels between *Folly* and *The Light on the Island*. Both feature a female protagonist hearing voices on the island that first appear to be delusions but turn out to have a real source; both islands are the haunts of smugglers past and present; and both establish the island as a space overflown by history. Rae digs into its past by reading Desmond's diaries and examining the traces left on the island; sometimes she literally digs into its ground. As the novel progresses, Rae is gradually confronted with the past of her family and of the island itself. This excavation of history is explicitly thematized as Rae's thirteen-year-old granddaughter Petra decides to write on Folly for her history project at school. In a letter to Petra, Rae figures the island as an archive of American history:

> Certainly a history of this 145-acre rock covers everything from Native Americans through English explorers (Cook sailed past, and Vancouver and all the rest), the Civil War period (one of the first islands of the San Juans to be colonized, other than by the various Native Americans [who didn't actually live here year-round, just fished and gathered food], was settled by a group of ex-slaves who bought their freedom in the 1850s and came here, a good long way from the South), and the late nineteenth century (when people on the islands smuggled everything from Chinese workers to whiskey), to the early twentieth century

(Desmond Newborn, for example) and WWII (those 'pillbox' bunkers watching for enemy subs), to the beginning of a new century (yours truly). (King 2001, 129; italics original)

The tiny island is here represented not only as a window to the regional past, but as a repository of North American history, distilling the core events and developments of the continent and its various populations. The syntactic structure itself replicates the intricate folds and entanglements of the history sedimented on the island. The passage consists of one single sentence with multiple brackets and brackets within brackets; history is presented as a confused and interlaced accretionary prism. It cannot be grasped in terms of a linear narrative, but only as an accumulation of intertwined material, excavated and traced in a language that follows the folds and ruptures of the debris of history. Like the characters in *The Light on the Island*, Rae and her family are folded into this general history: Desmond, who appears in one of the brackets, is presented as one of its many folds. The last bracket is reserved for Rae's granddaughter, who is given a place in the future history of the island.

The human and geological histories of the island are closely linked. In this, *Folly* draws on the region's geological imaginary. In a later letter, Rae constructs a vision of the island coming into being in a field of geological and geomorphological forces:

Dear Petra,

I wonder if you've done any research yet into the far-off, distant past of our island? Before the peoples came here, before the nomadic tribes crossed the frozen Bering Strait or paddled with the Pacific currents, when the land itself was being laid down?

A person sees everywhere the immense pressures and incomprehensible tensions that accumulated here, shoving and wrenching the landmasses around like a pizza crust. There's a layer of light-colored sandstone that runs through Folly, folded back on itself in some places, twisted in with the darker bedrock. How much pressure must it take to fold rock? ...

The other huge force acting on this placid-looking group of islands was ice. The last glaciers began to retreat up the Georgia Strait to the north around 13,000 years ago, scouring the strait, grinding and eroding the crests of the folded rock, but when they passed, the layers of sandstone and bedrock underneath them rose, jutting up into the air

sometimes nearly perpendicular to the current sea. . . . But the uneven-
ness of the postglacial rebound, following the grinding of the glaciers,
broke Folly and her neighbors away from the larger landmasses,
crumpled them as they rose, and twisted them into the shapes of
islands.
Huge tensions, incomprehensible pressures, ripping and heaving at the
land; such sweet beauty at the end.
> *Love,*
> *Gran*

(229–230; italics original)

This long account of the island's genesis provides a conceptual frame
for reading its human history. Stressing the random accumulation of
material, the pressures and tensions twisting rocks into islands, the
confused and intertwined layers of sandstone and rock, and, above all
and repeatedly, the entangled folding of the rock by forces beyond the
reach of the imagination, the text recalls the geological descriptions of
San Juan Island in Gibbs's journal; the island is unfixed and becomes
dynamic. The passage offers a set of metaphors for the accumulation
and folds of history on the island, but the link between these two force
fields is more than metaphorical. Its human history, too, is folded into
the very fabric of the island, albeit at a different scale: it becomes embedded in its soil and rock, like the Native American petroglyph carved into
the wall of a hidden cave behind Desmond's house (201; 370–1).

Engaging with the geological and human histories of her island, Rae
is linked to the history she excavates. Quite fittingly, she refers to herself
as an archaeologist:

> *. . . I was digging out the foundation . . . and almost immediately*
> *I began to find things in the soil—an old canning jar, a bunch of silver*
> *forks, the mostly rotted covers of half a dozen books, various lumps of*
> *metal. . . . —I feel like an archaeologist.* (129; italics original)

History is excavated in fragments that both demand and resist reading.
Significantly, these fragments contain a few book covers, their pages
having decayed and their texts no longer directly available. Yet the most
important object she excavates, quite literally, is Desmond's leather-
bound diary. She finds it in the breast pocket of Desmond's corpse
in the secret cave, which she refers to as 'the belly of the island' (197).
She also discovers this cave at the heart of the novel, exactly halfway

through the text. The diary will ultimately lead her to the discovery of her family's secret and allow her to read the island. Yet Desmond's diary is difficult to read—sometimes lucid, sometimes confusing and full of lists, reflecting his mental turmoil after the trauma of serving in the First World War.

Rae is a reader, but she is also a writer, keeping a leather-bound diary of her own. *Folly* is a conglomerate of texts intertwining and folding into each other, like the geological structure of the island itself and the debris of history embedded in it. Again, the link is more than metaphorical: some of *Folly*'s texts are literally embedded in the island, mingling with its soil and rocks. And like Burn's articles and Glidden's narrative, *Folly* can offer no more than the promise of a conclusive island history in the form of a book, co-authored by Rae and her granddaughter: '*Between your search engines and Internet and libraries and my actually being here, between us we could write a small book*' (129; emphasis original), a book whose completion is deferred in all three texts.

Yet Rae is not only an archaeologist and a writer. She is also, and maybe most importantly, a builder. As constructive activities, writing and building are closely associated in *Folly*, and both are shaped by the archaeological excavation of material and textual fragments of the island's past. Indeed, *Folly* persistently establishes analogies between island, house, and self. This analogy has been a standard trope of island fiction since *Robinson Crusoe*, where the island functions as an extension of Crusoe's body and self, offering the paradigm of the modern individual. Fortifying island and self, Crusoe obsessively builds structures around him. Weaver-Hightower argues that the two tents and the fence are all extensions of Crusoe's skin, with the island's border as the outermost skin (2007, 33). Yet this final skin is substantially different from the others. In fact, it is questionable whether the shifting shoreline, bounding the island without enclosing it, can be thought of as a skin at all. It might be more productive to read Crusoe's obsessive building of enclosures as a response to the *absence* of a skin around the island, to its exposure to the sea and what it carries to the land, prominently embodied in the mysterious footprint on the beach.

In *Folly*, which contains many explicit and implicit references to *Robinson Crusoe*, Rae initially fortifies the island; like Crusoe, she is terrified of incursions into body, tent, house, and island. Like him, she is thrown off balance by a single footprint: ' . . . a sharp indentation no larger than her thumb, directly in front of her fingers . . . a mark that had no business here, gouged into the soft ground at the side of her water source. The mark of a stranger's boot' (100). The scene repeats the footprint scene in *Robinson Crusoe* in that the mark is also left in soft ground, where the island's soil is responsive to human touch. In Defoe's novel, however, this sensitive zone is located on the outer fringes of the island. As it is 'very plain to be seen in the sand' (Defoe 2001, 122), it is most likely on the wet part of the beach, which Dening considers 'the true beach, the true in-between space . . . an unresolved space where things can happen' (2004, 16). In *Folly*, this zone is moved further inland, next to one of the most protected spots of the island on the side of the hill. Rae finds the footprint right after climbing the hill and taking in the view from the highest point of the island, her own monarch-of-all-I-survey scene, which gives her '[a] terrible joy' (King 2001, 97).[41] This scene of maximum spatial control is thus immediately qualified by a scene of incursion. While Crusoe fortifies his island in order to counteract the openness of its shifting border, in *Folly* the entire island becomes vulnerable and malleable: the spring is 'sand-wiched between igneous rock, cross sections of the land's stressful geological history' (98), and thus draws attention to the processes by which the island was and continues to be shaped and transformed. When Rae notices that someone has been tampering with her toolbox, this new trace of an incursion is immediately related to the former: 'The was-it-a-footprint up near the spring back in April had been bad enough; this time it was as if Crusoe had discovered Friday asleep in his bed' (311).

By this time, however, Rae has recognized and even begun to value the fact that island, house, and self can never be sealed off completely: 'And like the human body, a locked house may feel secure, but its walls are *no more impregnable than human skin*' (260; my emphasis). After a visit from a neighbour from a different island, she refers to John Donne:

---

[41] The phrase is from a 1782 poem by William Cowper: 'I am monarch of all I survey, / My right there is none to dispute; / From the centre all round to the sea' (2003, 1–3). See also Chapter 1, note 32. The notion of the monarch-of-all-I-survey scene was developed by Pratt to analyse the colonial gaze in travel writing (2008, 197–223). Weaver-Hightower picks up on Pratt in her discussion of the castaway's gaze from the highest point of the island (2007, 1–42).

'... for a hermit, she was well on her way of becoming a member of a community. No man is an island—nor, it would appear, woman' (179).[42] In this, she restates a conviction that was also gradually reached by Desmond: 'The poet has declared, No man is an island.... Here, all men are islands, linked by the touch of the sea. That which divides us is what brings us together' (330). Desmond both cites and corrects John Donne's famous words by reasserting what the latter denies, and he does so by reimagining the island trope and freeing it from the connotations of isolation and discreteness. If the island has a skin at all, *Folly* emphasizes that it is as porous as the rock through which the water seeps at the spring (98). It takes Rae a long time to abandon her fortifying impulse, but the recognition is paramount to her healing process. Her acknowledgement of her links to a larger community is thereby just as crucial as her engagement with her family history and the history of the island, which has also been marked by links to the world around it; the island thus figures the impossible autonomy of the insular self. Indeed, geological activity is initially used with negative connotations to refer to psychic disorder, shortly after the footprint scene: 'Situational psychosis. Clinical depression. Nervous breakdown. Shell shock—all names for the neurological fault line that gives way under severe pressure, a shattering, devastating internal earthquake . . .' (111). Only with time does Rae begin to develop an interest in geological pressures as productive and transformative processes, an interest that correlates with the gradual renouncement of her defensive insularity.

Unlike *The Light on the Island*, *Folly* is unambiguously fictional. Nonetheless, its form is strongly influenced by non-fictional forms of writing. As Jean M. Ward and Elaine A. Maveety have shown, memoirs and other autobiographical writings by empowered women have a strong tradition in the Pacific Northwest, and the writing process itself is often part of the authors' empowerment (1995). As discussed earlier, most of the literary classics of the region are memoirs, many of them written by women; building or renovating a house and homesteading often plays a central role in them. With Rae's and Desmond's diaries and the book Rae plans to co-author with her granddaughter (129;

---

[42] The famous line appears in Donne's 'Meditation 17' (1624): 'No man is an island, entire of itself; every man is a piece of the continent, a part of the main' (2000, 1278).

395), *Folly* inserts itself into this tradition. Building and writing become central elements of Rae's empowerment. By constructing an insular space that gives her autonomy and simultaneously learning to acknowledge the outside world and history, Rae strikes a balance between the isolation and connectedness of the islanded self. *Folly* thereby subscribes to a view of history that resonates with that of Friedrich Nietzsche, for whom '*the unhistorical and the historical are necessarily in equal measure for the health of an individual, of a people and of a culture*' (2007, 104; emphasis original). For Nietzsche, the subject must draw a line around itself and *forget* history to achieve a sense of stability; at the same time, it must *acknowledge* history, connectivity, and a constant process of exchange and becoming, or else it would be deadlocked into itself:

> Imagine the extremest power of a man who did not possess the power of forgetting at all and who was thus condemned to see everywhere a state of becoming: such a man...would see everything flowing asunder in moving points and would lose himself in a stream of becoming.... if [a living thing] is incapable of drawing a horizon around itself, and at the same time too self-centred to enclose its view within that of another, it will pine away slowly or hasten to its timely end. (103–4)

Nietzsche describes history in terms of a flow and a stream, while the limits drawn around the self to prevent it from being flooded by history are described as a boundary; the image evokes an island surrounded by the ocean. Like Nietzsche, the texts I have been discussing point, with varying emphasis, to this interplay and make a case for both the subject and culture as a watery island. Accumulating history on its shores, this island proclaims its identity and yet acknowledges the currents that never cease to shape and redefine it. Thereby the texts go beyond opening up the island and view it in a productive tension between boundedness *and* openness.

Islands in Four Dimensions

Having examined the ecological island poetics structuring a range of Pacific Northwest texts, let us return to the question addressed at the beginning of this chapter in relation to *The Tempest*, namely the question of how many dimensions are needed to make an island, or rather: how the perception of an island changes with its dimensionality. I have repeatedly intimated that the revisionist island poetics of several Northwest writers views islands in four dimensions. This assertion is more than mere metaphorical play. It is rooted in a vibrant theoretical discourse about space that preoccupied late nineteenth- and early twentieth-century scientists and intellectuals: speculations about the fourth dimension exploded in both mathematical treatises and literary works. I will end this chapter with a brief discussion of these theories of space and their potential to destabilize the island more radically by pointing to the 'hidden dark sides that structure our experience of the side exposed to view' (Morton 2014, 291).

Charles Howard Hinton's essay 'What is the Fourth Dimension?' (1880) is one of the foundational texts theorizing the fourth dimension, and many others followed suit.[43] Albert Einstein's theory of relativity (1905), which posited a spatiotemporal continuum, further spurred on the debate. At the beginning of Edwin Abbott Abbott's *Flatland: A Romance of Many Dimensions* (1884), the narrator, a square, tries to explain the effects of perception in his two-dimensional native world to the inhabitants of three-dimensional Spaceland:

> When I was in Spaceland I heard that your sailors have very similar experiences while they traverse your seas and discern some distant island or coast lying on the horizon. The far-off land may have bays, forelands, angles in and out to any number and extent; yet at a distance you see...nothing but a grey unbroken line upon the water. (16)

As the narrator explains, the two-dimensional inhabitants of Flatland (such as squares and triangles) can only perceive their world in one dimension, i.e. as lines. The island seen from afar serves the square as a comparable visual effect in Spaceland. This perceptual reduction

---

[43] Some of the more imaginative of these include Gaston de Pawlowski's *Voyage au pays de la quatrième dimension* (1912), Arthur S. Eddington's *Space Time and Gravitation: An Outline of the General Relativity Theory* (1920), and P. D. Ouspensky's *Tertium Organum* (1912). Hinton's 'What is the Fourth Dimension?' can be found in his *Scientific Romances*, a collection of writings about the fourth dimension—part scientific, part literary (1885, 3–32). See also his later *The Fourth Dimension* (1912).

suggests that islands can lend themselves to an exploration of dimensionality. Yet the hypothetical reduction of dimensions is part of a thought experiment that aims to prove the existence of the fourth dimension: '. . . it is as natural for us Flatlanders to lock up a Square for preaching the Third Dimension, as it is for you Spacelanders to lock up a Cube for preaching the Fourth' (9). If we can *perceive* an island as one- or two-dimensional, it means that we are in a world of at least one additional dimension. Islands may be perceived as one-or two-dimensional, but they cannot be *thought* without the third dimension, at least not if we take their specific spatiality and materiality seriously. Both surrounded by and rising out of water, they imply height as well as horizontal extension.

Environmental philosopher Edward S. Casey suggests as much when he argues that islands lent themselves to the representation of three-dimensional space in early modern portolan charts and *isolarii*: 'The depth in question is often most evident in the mapping of an *island*, . . . [a] circumscribed geographic entity whose bounded terrain lends itself to pictographic representation more easily than would a larger and unbounded landmass' (2002, 190–1; emphasis original). Casey's contention that islands can evoke the third dimension in two-dimensional maps is linked to his interest in modes of becoming inserted in space rather than contemplating it with a distanced cartographic gaze. I would like to suggest that reimagining islands as four-dimensional can have a similar effect in heightened form; the island in four dimensions provides a way of reimagining subjectivity and culture in terms of complex ecological and geological processes.

Before we link the speculations about the fourth dimension explicitly with Pacific Northwest writing, however, let us briefly think about islands in two and three dimensions. For Casey, island representations can facilitate an immersion in space, but this potential is often suppressed in early modern island visions. The production of a flat geometrical space in the 1516 frontispiece of More's *Utopia* and Raphael Hythlodaeus's account of the island (cf. Chapter 1) is as much part of this as the suppression of the third dimension in the service of spatial control in *The Tempest*. As I argued at the beginning of this chapter, it is only in brief moments of the play, related to the arrival of Ferdinand, that the third dimension is allowed to break in.

In *Robinson Crusoe*, this encounter with the material space of the island in its three-dimensionality receives more weight. If *The Tempest* has practically no arrival scenes, Crusoe's arrival on the island is long and painful. The entire scene is structured by an interplay between the horizontal and the vertical. Carried back and forth by the waves, Crusoe raises himself up and is pulled down again several times until he finally arrives:

> ...I *clamber'd up* the clifts of the shore, and sat me down upon the grass, free from danger, and quite out of the reach of the water.
>
> I was now landed, and safe on shore, and began to *look up* ....
>
> I walk'd about on the shore, *lifting up* my hands, and my whole being, as I may say, wrapt *up* in the contemplation of my deliverance, ... reflecting upon all my comrades that were drown'd ... for, as for them, I never saw them afterwards, or any sign of them, except three of their hats, one cap, and two shoes that were not fellows. (Defoe 2001, 38–9; my emphasis)

The final arrival is marked by a multiplication of upward movements. Washing up on the island along with the clothes of his comrades, Crusoe is initially a piece of human debris. He will gradually exploit the third dimension to raise himself further and further up, sleeping in a tree and climbing to the highest point of the island. But this assertion of his subjectivity is predicated on an initial vulnerability, on the exposure of the subject to the material space of the island where a literal 'sea change' is never far away. Crusoe's subjectivity is threatened by dissolution on the edge of the island, where he is close to becoming human sediment.

The third dimension is thus glimpsed in *The Tempest* and given more scope in *Robinson Crusoe*. These texts provide a useful foil against which to read the entirely different treatment of dimensionality in Pacific Northwest island writing. In fact, the speculations about the fourth dimension are explicitly evoked in Muriel Wylie Blanchet's *The Curve of Time* (1961). In her memoir, Blanchet returns to the watery land of Vancouver's journal. The text details her explorations of the channels and islands between Vancouver Island and the mainland in a small boat with her children, in a series of summers in the 1920s and 1930s. In the following excerpt, space itself seems to be moving:

As far as the eye could see, *islands, big and little, crowded all round us*. . . . And north, south, east, west, *among the maze of islands, winding channels lured and beckoned.* That was what we had been doing all day—just letting our little boat carry us where she pleased. . . .

Then the channels began to have some definite direction, *and the islands sorted themselves out*—the right ones *standing forward* bold and green; the others *retiring*, dim and unwanted. . . .

Yesterday, we had passed a slender Indian dugout. . . . Cliff, dugout, primitive man; all were mirrored in the still water beneath them. . . . When was it that we had watched them? Yesterday? a hundred years ago? *or just somewhere on that Curve of Time?*

Farther and farther into that Past we slipped. Down winding tortuous byways—strewn with reefs, fringed with kelp.

(2011, 73–5; my emphasis)

Space is here depicted as alive as the islands keep reshaping themselves. Like Vancouver's narrative, Blanchet paints a world where the landscape dissolves into a maze of innumerable islands, where 'everything becomes island'.[44] The text bespeaks a phenomenal experience where space is always in construction and never fully grasped. As in Vancouver's journal, the islands are malleable; they 'crowd all round them', 'sort themselves out', 'stand forward', and 'retire'. Blanchet's boat, on the other hand, is 'drift[ing] idly' (73). Unlike Vancouver, however, Blanchet does not attempt to reintegrate and fix space. Rather than manoeuvring space, the boat and its inmates are manoeuvred by space, letting themselves be carried here and there. Time is as fluid and unpredictable as space. While the vision of the 'Indian dugout' partly bespeaks a romanticized notion of 'primitive man', this vision is not safely located in an idealized past. Rather, the boat drifts not only through space, but also through time, which becomes just another dimension of space.

'That Curve of Time' refers to a book by the Belgian modernist writer Maurice Maeterlinck and his discussion of a book by the Irish aeronautical engineer and writer John W. Dunne. The importance of their

---

[44] Cf. Anne Patricia Rayner's *Everything Becomes Island: Gulf Islands Writing and the Construction of Region*. Her reading of *The Curve of Time* traces the assertion of local authority and knowledge against the authoritative texts of Vancouver's journal and the Coast Pilot (1995, 248–54).

theories for the aesthetics of her text is signalled in the very first sentences:

> On board our boat one summer we had a book by Maurice Maeter-linck called *The Fourth Dimension*, the fourth dimension being *Time*—which, according to Dunne, doesn't exist in itself, but is always relative to the person who has the idea of Time. Maeterlinck used a curve to illustrate Dunne's theory. Standing in the Present, on the highest point of the curve, you can look back and see the Past, or forward and see the Future, all in the same instant.... This was supposed to prove that Time is just a dimension of Space, and that there is no difference between the two, except that our consciousness roves along this Curve of Time. (7–8; emphasis original)

In 1928, Maeterlinck wrote a book entitled *La vie de l'espace* (*The Life of Space*). Its first part, 'The Fourth Dimension', is the text Blanchet refers to. Already the title of the book signals the spatial fluidity Blanchet's text performs. *La vie de l'espace* is an extraordinary synthesis of theories of space since Hinton. In a particularly striking section, Maeterlinck, a bit like the square in *Flatland*, draws on the writings of Peter D. Ouspensky to muse on the spatial perceptions of various organisms (81–90). Claiming that dogs perceive the world in two dimensions, he proposes the mental experiment of imagining a dog walking first around a sphere, then around a disc. While the sphere will always look like a disc to the dog, the disc will first look like a disc, then—viewed from the side—like a line, before gradually morphing into a disc again. Having no concept of the third dimension, the dog will assume the disc has actually changed its shape; it will translate the incomprehensible dimension into time. Maeterlinck claims that we do the same. Having no concept of the fourth dimension, we use time as a substitute. For Maeterlinck, the fourth dimension opens up a radically unknown field that undermines our apparent grasp of space, decentres human subjectivity, and moves it out of itself: 'We can presume that for a being superior to us ... or even for ourselves once we have sufficiently over-stepped [*outrepassés*] ourselves, there will necessarily be more than three [dimensions]' (141; my translation).

Blanchet's text performs these notions of four-dimensional space in its structure and aesthetics. Time is indeed treated as part of space; we often do not know where we are, and we never know to what summer the narration takes us. The movements of the boat from island to island go hand in hand with the text's free movement through time, and through other texts. This includes the time and text of Vancouver: 'We were inextricably associated with Captain George Vancouver. . . . / Vancouver of course had no charts—he was there to make them. But from old sources he had certain reports of a great inland sea in those latitudes . . .' (2011, 13). Vancouver's text, in turn, is portrayed as shaped by other texts, by the expectation of finding the Northwest Passage. His diary entries flow into the text of *The Curve of Time*, integrated seamlessly into Blanchet's own syntax: 'After dinner they proceed . . . "Until about five in the evening, when all our hopes vanished, by finding it terminate, as others had, in swampy low land"' (14; ellipsis original). In other places, Vancouver's voice is present in Blanchet's without quotation marks: ' . . . it seemed expedient, as Captain Vancouver would have said, to make the shore' (32). Yet if Blanchet's text is entangled with Vancouver's, she also contests it (cf. Rayner 1995, 248–54), and part of this contestation means privileging the voice of Vancouver's botanist Archibald Menzies:

> Vancouver's whole outlook on these beautiful inlets was coloured by this desire to find a seaway to the other side of the mountains. . . . Menzies, the botanist, is more enthusiastic. In his diary he notes, 'Immense cascades dashing down chasms against projecting rocks and cliffs with a furious wildness that beggars all description.' Even he doesn't say that the cascades start away up at four or five thousand feet. (2011, 15)

While Vancouver is presented as a mapmaker 'who seems to have stayed on board the *Discovery* making up his notes and maps' (55), Menzies is credited with a more thorough engagement with the landscape closer to Blanchet's own, while she also makes it clear that she has even more to offer. Given her interest in registering an exposure to and engagement with the islands and channels she explores, it is appropriate that Blanchet should privilege a botanist's voice to guide her own ecologically conscious writing. Weaving in and out of the past, the present, and even imagined futures expressed in the conditional tense (111–12), *The Curve of Time* ultimately abandons these temporal categories altogether and presents the reader with an islandscape in four dimensions.

Conclusion: Expansive Islandscapes and Ambivalent Ecologies

The Curve of Time may be the only Pacific Northwest island text that explicitly refers to the theories of the fourth dimension debated by Hinton, Maeterlinck, and their contemporaries, yet many of the texts discussed here resonate with their concerns. They foreground the edge of the island as a space where the island moves out of itself. As geological space-time is entered, human centrality is relinquished, subjectivity is broken up and dispersed. Their ecopoetic gesture is usefully examined alongside the theories of the fourth dimension of Maeterlinck and others. From different angles, they pursue the same goal of leading the subject out of its self-absorbed centrality. The insular self is broken up at the edges and makes way for a more radical islandness in multiple interconnectedness.

But the texts sometimes decentre the island only to recentre a holistic or unified ecological landscape. This tension between a de-insularization or opening up of the island and a reassertion of an idealized, harmoniously interconnected ecosystem has run through this chapter. The island memoirs examined in the middle section revisit classic island narratives to resituate the island within larger spatiotemporal continuities. They include the water in their poetic construction of a fluid islandscape, moving from closed-off islands and bounded subjectivities to notions like 'island waters' and 'sea-lander'. This re-imagination of the island disrupts arbitrarily drawn political borders, and inserts the subject in a complex ecological islandscape. Yet the texts also recentre subjectivity by placing the subject in the centre of an expansive islandscape, with the island as focal point, however border-less it may be: *eco*centrism then becomes eco*centrism*.

Burn's column, *The Light on the Island*, and *Folly* take this ecological island poetics a step further by including time in their construction of island space. *100 Days in the San Juans* figures history as drift accumulating on the islands; in *The Light on the Island*, the island oscillates between a static place and a dynamic space as history washes up on its shores and becomes inscribed in its soil. This emphasis on drifting decentres the present by resituating it within a series of historical flows. At the same time, it partly naturalizes the

American ownership of the islands and sidesteps questions of agency and responsibility. Figuring history in terms of accretion rather than drift, *Folly* locates the subject in a Nietzschean tension between becoming and self-assertion. The novel thus rewrites *Robinson Crusoe* by opening the island and the self to the pressures of history while asserting the importance of individual agency, even if it ultimately absorbs the ecology and geology of the island into a story of personal healing.

In many ways, then, the journal of George Vancouver and the geological diary of George Gibbs offer a more radical island poetics, although—or maybe because—they do so unwittingly. Rather than assert ecological and geological *continuities*, they express a struggle with *discontinuities* in spatial experience: their islands resist absorption into a unifying vision. Reading their texts in this way means following Toadvine's call for an attention to the opacities of the landscape and Morton's emphasis on the 'irreducible hidden dimension of things'. Morton does not use the word 'dimension' in its mathematical sense, but the theories of the fourth dimension we have examined can have this destabilizing effect. Yet even the fourth dimension is not necessarily unsettling. In some of the island writings examined here, it loses part of its destabilizing potential when it is presented as perfectly intelligible and observable, integrated into a unifying vision of eco-geological continuity. Conversely, the third dimension in *The Tempest* causes a rupture in the play's spatial organization. As Abbott's *Flatland* demonstrates, it is not necessarily the fourth dimension that causes such a rupture, but whatever dimension exceeds any given spatial or spatio-temporal order and imagination. It is perhaps no coincidence that Arthur S. Eddington, another of Maeterlinck's contemporaries, alludes to *Robinson Crusoe* in one of the most striking images of the world in four dimensions in the last sentence of his *Space Time and Gravitation* (1920): 'We have found a strange foot-print on the shores of the unknown. We have devised profound theories, one after another, to account for its origin. At last, we have succeeded in reconstructing the creature that made the foot-print. And Lo! it is our own' (201). The footprint that unsettles Crusoe is here refigured as the intrusion of the fourth dimension into the island, the intrusion of what is unknown about space itself. This island does not map the human subject in its self-contained autonomy. On the contrary: it is constantly confronted with the trace in itself of what moves it out of itself. It is this outward pull that marks the poetics of the island in four dimensions, or rather: in $n + 1$ dimensions.

* * *

The fourth chapter will continue the discussion of the ecology and geology of islands and further probe the poetic potential of islands in deep time, but it will go a step further. I will turn to the natural sciences themselves by examining the disruptive potential of the island poetics in the writings of Charles Darwin and Alfred Russel Wallace, and the island fictions they inspired. If this chapter has examined the opening up of the island, the last chapter will turn to a relational, archipelagic perspective to reintroduce difference, struggle, and conflict into the discussion of islands. This final chapter, too, has a primal scene. When the young Darwin embarked on his voyage around the world on HMS *Beagle* in December 1831, he probably did not know that he would write several books about islands. He certainly did not know that these writings would have a profound impact on both the natural sciences and the literary imagination. Let us join him, then, to embark on our own final voyage.

| 4 |

From Islands to Archipelagos

Volcanism, Coral, and Geopoetics

Few writers have transformed the way we think about islands as profoundly as Charles Darwin, and several critics discuss the importance of his legacy in island literature. They point to the Galápagos Islands as an evolutionary laboratory for Darwin and establish a link between Darwin's scientific laboratory and fictional islands as laboratories of ideas, playing through various (frequently dystopian) scenarios opened up by Darwin's work.[1] Beer discusses the spectre of human extinction in a text like *Robinson Crusoe*, which for her prefigures the territorial and reproductive anxieties unleashed, albeit unintentionally, by Darwin's writings (2003). Elsewhere, she examines various intersections between scientific and literary island discourses. Arguing that it is both the '*transformations* [and] the *recursiveness* of ideas that produces the significant interplay between literature and science' (5; emphasis original), she investigates the '*translatability* of concepts from one discourse to another' (2; emphasis original). Thus, she argues that the island concept has articulated specific cultural

---

[1] For general reflections on the island as laboratory, see, among others, Royle (2014, 77–101); Racault (1996, 251–3); Beer (1989, 9). On the island as an evolutionary laboratory, see Ruddick (1993, 63); Schenkel (1993, 46); Edmond and Smith (2003, 2–3); Loxley (1990, 5).

The Aesthetics of Island Space: Perception, Ideology, Geopoetics. Johannes Riquet, Oxford University Press (2019). © Johannes Riquet.
DOI: 10.1093/oso/9780198832409.001.0001

concerns across disciplinary boundaries, and evolutionary anxieties play an important role in her discussion. Beer's approach not only implies a reciprocal discursive implication of literature and science, but also hints at the possibility of reading science *as* literature.

With this conceptual framework in mind, let us take a look at the oft-cited passage from the *Ornithological Notes* that expresses Darwin's first intimation of the theory of evolution from his observation of the Galápagos birds in 1835:

> When I see these Islands in sight of each other, & possessed of but a scanty stock of animals, tenanted by these birds, but slightly differing in structure & filling the same place in Nature, I must suspect they are only varieties.... If there is the slightest foundation for these remarks the zoology of Archipelagoes will be well worth examining; for such facts would undermine the stability of Species.   (1963, 262)

The observation of slight variations in the birds on neighbouring islands here leads Darwin to suspect that they stem from a common source and have developed in different directions once geographically separated, which implies that species can change and adapt. Darwin will return to this observation more than twenty years later in *On the Origin of Species* (1859), where oceanic islands play a crucial role in providing conclusive evidence for the theory of evolution (378–96). But my main interest in the above passage lies in its aesthetic and structural dimensions, and in the semantic network it deploys. Importantly, the passage begins by emphasizing an act of seeing. Indeed, the first clause is permeated by visuality as it stresses both Darwin's own visual survey of the islands and their general visibility from other islands in the group; external and internal vantage points are conflated. This act of seeing immediately precedes and announces a vision of a different kind that requires an imaginative act. Contemplating the islands allows Darwin to re-envision them; the act of *theorein* (to look at, contemplate) here prefigures the emergence of a *theoría* (contemplation). The first contours of this *theoría* are outlined in the second part of the passage. The core term is that of stability, or rather instability: the result of Darwin's imaginative act is the undermining of species hitherto considered as discrete entities.

This is accompanied by a shift in terminology from 'Islands' to 'Archipelagoes'. This shift implies a radical change of perspective: a group of seemingly discrete islands is transformed into an archipelagic network of relations and movements. The observation of difference thus leads to a relational perspective, a perspective that traces the geographical dispersal and modification of species as much as it resituates the individual islands within the archipelago. Darwin's initial gaze from island to island prefigures this gesture. In fact, the first sentence already performs a mini-poetics of this change of perspective: if the initial act of seeing ('When I see these Islands') still allows for an outside perspective on the islands as a static group, the second ('in sight of each other') resituates the gaze itself *within* the archipelago and implicates the viewer in a network of relations.

With Beer's notion of the translatability of concepts in mind, this chapter traces the ways in which Darwin's and other scientists' re-envisioning of islands translates into a number of literary re-visions of islands. Yet my discussion will not be limited to the theory of evolution, which has been the almost exclusive focus of studies examining the interface between Darwin's writings and literature.[2] Instead, I propose that discussions of Darwin's literary legacy should take into account his other writings, notably his writings on geology. The following discussion thus outlines a poetics not just of Darwin's evolutionary island laboratories, but also of—to borrow the title of a study by geographer and ecologist Patrick H. Armstrong (2006)—Darwin's other islands. Like Armstrong, though from an entirely different perspective, the present discussion aims to go some way towards correcting the relative neglect of Darwin's writings on islands beyond Galápagos. As geneticist Steve Jones argues in *The Darwin Archipelago*, 'to remember Darwin for [*The Origin of Species*] alone would be as foolish as to celebrate Shakespeare only as the author of *Hamlet*' (2011, x). While Jones's 'archipelago' refers to the British Isles, his statement that Darwin's writings 'made sense of a whole new science and enabled its students to navigate what had been an uncharted labyrinth of shoals, reefs and remote islets of apparently unrelated facts' (x) could well be extended to those writings whose islands it metaphorically borrows: the *Beagle* diary and journal with its wealth of islands, the 1842 *The Structure and Distribution of Coral Reefs*, and its sequel, *Geological Observations*

---

[2] See especially Beer (1985) and Levine (1988).

on the Volcanic Islands (1844). Jones's evocative image turns the archipelago into a conceptual tool. We will return to the value of this conceptual tool at the end of the chapter. On the way there, we will theorize the links between material space and its textual figuration in order to discuss the island poetics in Darwin and Wallace from a geopoetic perspective. We will go on to discuss H. G. Wells's *The Island of Doctor Moreau* and 'Aepyornis Island' as imaginative responses to the evolutionary, biogeographical, and geological discourses of Darwin and Wallace. After a discussion of how these literary texts turn the island into a site of anxiety, a glance at twentieth-century biogeographical island theory will lead us to a final translation of island discourses in the archipelagic landscape of Amitav Ghosh's *The Hungry Tide*.

Material Islands, Figurative Islands: Geocriticism and Geopoetics

Before we turn to Darwin's 'other islands', then, a few reflections on the intersection of evolutionary biology, geology, and literature are necessary. The close ties between literature and the natural sciences in the nineteenth century have been well studied. In *Darwin's Plots*, Beer argued that new scientific theories require an act of imagination that 'holds the theory itself for a time within a provisional scope akin to that of fiction' (1985, 3). She points to the ambivalence of Darwin's work and the literary responses it produced: while Darwin's writings construct a world of randomness, entanglement, and extinction in which humans become just another species among animals, 'the evolutionary metaphor' has also been used to suggest 'that we inherit the world at its pinnacle of development ... ' (18; see also Page 2012, 15). But science and literature also intertwined because the generic boundaries between scientific and literary writing were not clearly defined.[3] Scientists were avid readers of fiction; Darwin took a copy of *Paradise Lost* on his voyage around the world and his *Beagle* diary is full of references to Milton and other authors. Geologists like Charles Kingsley were novelists themselves.

---

[3] The boundaries between the different disciplines of science, too, were not clearly established; Darwin was as much a geologist as he was a biologist.

H. G. Wells studied biology under Thomas Henry Huxley and his first book was not a scientific romance, but a biology textbook.

Most importantly, literary and scientific discourses borrowed each other's techniques. This is the main insight of Adelene Buckland's 2013 study *Novel Science: Fiction and the Invention of Nineteenth-Century Geology*. Arguing that geology has been treated as a stepchild in the research on the affinities between nineteenth-century science and fiction, she starts out from the observation that '[i]n nineteenth-century Britain the study of the ancient earth gripped the public imagination' (1). She discusses both how geologists drew on literary genres such as the epic, the romance, and the novel to organize their writings and the ways in which geology, in turn, provided powerful metaphors and narrative models that impacted on the very form of fiction: 'For these novelists,... the gaps and blanks of the stratigraphic column could usefully suggest dark and disturbing ruptures in the continuous flow of the plot' (27). As I shall argue, islands played a decisive role in the destabilizing impetus Buckland ascribes to the geological imagination. Evolutionary theory and geology jointly paved the way for an archipelagic, decentred conception of the world, and islands—both as real locations and as figures of thought—played a pivotal role in this.

If the island is to be thought both in its materiality and in its figurative capacities, however, the precise relationship between the two needs to be conceptualized. After the (post)structuralist rejection of the referent in favour of textuality within literary and cultural studies, recent years have seen a renewed interest in the material world. Within theories of space, the emphasis was long on socially and discursively produced space (Lefebvre 1991; Foucault 1986), the semiotic structuring of space (Lotman 1990), and the ideological implications of spatial structures (Soja 1989; Jameson 1991, 1992). Recent approaches have postulated a more thorough engagement with the links between aesthetic productions and the referential world. Among these, *geocriticism* and *geopoetics* are of particular importance for the present purposes. Both terms have taken on a life of their own, but the former is mainly associated with Bertrand Westphal and his book *Geocriticism: Real and Fictional Spaces* (2011), while *geopoetics* is closely tied to the eponymous movement started by the Scottish poet and academic Kenneth White, who founded the Institut International de la Géopoétique in Paris in 1989.

Strongly influenced by the *géophilosophie* of Gilles Deleuze and Félix Guattari and the spatial philosophy of Michel Serres, Westphal is interested in 'coupling real space and fictional space' (2011, 110). Arguing that '[t]he fictional place takes part in a variable relationship with the real' (99), he aims to chart the multiple ways in which fictional spaces are grafted onto real space. Fictional spaces with a localizable referent, or with a non-specific geographical referent, such as 'cities, islands, archipelagos, countries, mountains, rivers...' (117), are thereby of equal interest to him as entirely fictional spaces. Indeed, he argues that real and fictional spaces are necessarily implicated with each other: 'In this sense, adopting a geocentered approach amounts to arguing that literary representation is included in the world...' (116). Westphal advocates multiple textual perspectives on a given spatial referent, coupled with a polysensory attention to space and its stratigraphic layering (which includes intertextual relations). By placing geography and not the subject or individual works in the centre of analysis, Westphal aims to explore the productive interface between space and its representations. Representation is here viewed not as a copy of reality, nor as an operation that brings forth what it professes to imitate, but rather as re-presentation, as 'evolutionary and transgressive' (145). The re-presentation of space is thus accorded an active role in shaping not only the perception of space, but space itself and, importantly, our relation to it.

White's geopoetics also aims to promote a changed relation between humans and the world: 'il est question ici d'un *rapport* à la terre (énergies, rythmes, formes), non pas d'un assujettissement à la Nature, pas plus que d'un enracinement dans un terroir' (1994, 11; emphasis original).[4] Geopoetics, as both a theoretical attitude and a poetic practice, is envisaged as an ongoing activity that helps forge such a *rapport*. But where Westphal embraces postmodern theory's belief in the pervasiveness of fictionality, White has little patience for postmodernism, which for him fails to break radically with modernity and its philosophical tenets (cf. White 1994, 38–9). While sometimes understood as an ecocritic, White is quick to refute this association. For White,

---

[4] 'The question here is of a *rapport* to the earth (energies, rhythms, forms), not of a subjection to Nature, nor of being rooted in a region' (my translation).

ecology wants to understand and preserve the environment,[5] and he considers geopoetics as more radical: 'la géopoétique veut repenser radicalement le rapport de l'être humain au monde...' (1994, 38).[6] This *rapport* is not to be thought in terms of a Romantic embrace of and reverence for nature, nor as a naïve rootedness in or merging with place (both of which are present in some of the texts discussed in Chapter 3), but rather as a poetic project that values the *exposure* to the material world as opposed to its absorption and ordering by Euclidean geometry and elaborate sign systems. The poetic productivity of such an exposure is at the heart of White's project. He finds an example in a poem by Walt Whitman: 'What is at stake here for Whitman... is to elaborate a poetics that corresponds to the chaos of the rocks it contemplates. This poetics is already inherent in the world, one must first adhere to it, then try to say it' (1994, 36; my translation).

White is thus interested in drawing out the poetic potential of the material world without overlaying it with metaphysical superstructures. A precise attention to the rhythms, energies, and forms of the physical environment is seen to give rise to a poetics of space which in turn forges a *rapport* to space. This gesture of being-in-the-world,[7] observing and listening to it, implies a rethinking of subjectivity; if the modern, Cartesian subject is situated at the centre of a space it commands, the subject of geopoetics comes into being (if at all) at the intersection of force fields: 'Si l'homme moderne dit: "Je suis, et le monde est à moi", le géopoéticien dit: "Je suis au monde—j'écoute, je regarde; je ne suis pas une identité, je suis un jeu d'énergies, un réseau de facultés"' (1994, 39).[8] Being is here conceived not as autonomous, set off from the world by a comma and a conjunction ('Je suis, et...'), but as inextricably tied to the world by a preposition ('Je suis au monde'). Along with modern identity, disciplinary boundaries are called into

[5] This is not necessarily true for present-day ecocritical discourses. As Greg Garrard points out, the 'metaphor of "saving the world"' has become highly contested within eocriticism (2011, xxiii).

[6] 'Geopoetics wants to radically rethink the rapport of human beings to the world' (my translation).

[7] The term, of course, is Heidegger's in *Being and Time* (1996, see especially 49–58, 107–22).

[8] 'If modern man says: "I am, and the world is mine", the geopoetician says: "I am in the world—I listen, I watch; I am not an identity, I am a play of energies, a network of faculties"' (my translation).

question. If White is sometimes vexingly elusive about how geopoetics is to be understood, it is partly because clear-cut definitions would go against the tenets of his project. Refusing to assign geopoetics to any one field, he evokes Alexander von Humboldt's dictum that poetry, science, philosophy, and history are not fundamentally separate from each other (1994, 27). Indeed, for White a thorough engagement with all through the lens of geopoetics will lead to a better understanding of each.

The term *geopoetics* has been used in different ways since White coined it. Thus, Bouvet advocates a more practical understanding of geopoetics (2015). In an article on the geopoetics of travel writing co-authored with Marcil-Bergeron, she emphasizes the conjunction of scientific, philosophical, and poetic perspectives on the earth, and outlines some elements of geopoetic enquiry such as movement, poly-sensoriality, landscape, the elsewhere, and the unknown dimensions of space (2013). Magdalena Marszałek and Sylvia Sasse also go some way towards turning geopoetics into an analytical tool. Arguing that the main reason for the appeal of geopoetics for the study of central and eastern European literatures is to be found in the reordering of political geography after 1989 and the subsequent imaginative investment in geography, they consider Igor' Sid's geopoetic Krim-Club (Krymskij geopoétičeskij klub) the most successful application of geopoetics in its attempt to replace politics with art, geopolitics with geopoetics, and effect a shift from geopolitical power struggles towards a new aesthetic order (2010, 7–9). They also point out that the links between geography and both *poiesis* and *aisthesis* have been a matter of considerable debate (10); with varying emphasis, the concept can be understood as geo*poetics* or as *geo*poetics, and offers space for a range of interpretations:

> Geopoetics, in our view, is a suitable term for the analysis and description of different correlations and interferences between litera-ture and geography not only because the word geopoetics itself already alludes to the medial fabrication of geography, but also because this term provokes questions about the role of geographical 'attitudes', 'perceptions', or 'materialities'—regardless of whether these are culturally constructed or naturally given—in literary prac-tice and production.   (9; my translation)

This inclusive understanding of geopoetics allows for attention to both the poetic transformation of space and the aesthetic interferences of the material world in the poetic process, and thus eschews the reductive embrace of fictionality and mediality characteristic of a certain branch of postmodernism as well as the Romantic essentialism of some (not all) ecocritical discourses. Marszałek and Sasse thus admit the possibility of an aesthetic dimension in the material world without dissociating it entirely from the observing consciousness and phenomenal experience:

> Another interpretation of geopoetics draws attention to the creative element and the aisthetic element of earth or nature.... If one takes into account an aesthetic experience of world that is given by geography, it becomes clear that geopoetics is also tied to a form of geoaisthesis. (16–17)

It is with this notion of a creative interface or productive friction between the material environment and its aesthetic rendering in mind that we now turn to two geopoetic approaches to the island.

The first of these is Antonis Balasopoulos's essay 'Nesologies: Island Form and Postcolonial Geopoetics' (2008). Addressing the relation between island geography and aesthetics, he argues that 'island form has traditionally oscillated between geographical and aesthetic registers' (9) ever since the portolan charts and *isolarii* of early modernity. His second claim is that representations of islands tend towards self-reflexivity and often 'replicate in allegorical form the very operations through which [they are] discursively produced', which he sees as another reason why the island 'constitutes a privileged instance of the geopoetic imagination (10). After a *tour d'horizon* of the history of the island as a trope for colonial control and a figure for both expansiveness and imperial isolationism, Balasopoulos turns to the writings of Hau'ofa (see Chapter 2) and Glissant, opposing their 'geopoetics of postcolonial islandness' (2008, 21) to figurations of the island in colonial texts. He argues that both Hau'ofa and Glissant articulate an 'archipelagic geopoetics' despite their differences (21). Thus in Glissant's works, island form also allegorizes the textual form that produced it, yet here the result is a sense of discontinuity, of fragmentary, relational, archipelagic identity that finds its counterpart in the fragmentary and fractured nature of Glissant's writing itself. Balasopoulos concludes by hypothesizing about the possible role of islands in rethinking the geopolitical order as decentred and archipelagic (23).

Yet Balasopoulos's treatment of this 'poetic potential' of island form is limited by his understanding of geopoetics in terms of the geopolitical import of (post)colonial island writing. Balasopoulos has little interest in the material dimension of island space: what he calls 'island form' is a purely textual category. Graziadei, whose 'Geopoetics of the Island' also explicitly links geopoetics with literary islands, has similar reservations about Balasopoulos's use of the term:

> But if this 'geo' implies everything terrestrial, a mere textualisation of the metaphor might in some cases be considered too narrow. Where do we find the air, the water and the rain, the mud, the sand and the stone, where is the bird and the flower, in this texture? Their presence is a mere metaphorical or translated one, while the physical absence of the referent becomes haunting. (2011, 176)

Graziadei's dissatisfaction with Balasopoulos's essay suggests that what is lacking from the latter's understanding of island geopoetics is an engagement with the geography and physicality of islands. Influenced by the geopoetics of White, the geophilosophy of Stephan Günzel (2011), and the *geopoetica* of Federico Italiano (2009), Graziadei himself draws on ecology, physical and human geography, as well as geophysics to read the island as a figure of instability, opposed to the *terra firma* or *Festland*. He sees 'geopoetics as a possibility for using the geospheres and the biogeographical data together with the iconic and social spatialities' of the island (2011, 178) and postulates a dialectical relationship between the two parts of the word: 'Freshwater, soil, flora and fauna all form part of the geo- that allows for the poetic' (179). Graziadei finds support in the work of Guadeloupean writer Daniel Maximin, especially in his poetic essay *Les fruits du cylone: Une géopoétique de la Caraïbe* (2006). Maximin's approach to Carribean literature 'takes its examples from the tropical archipelagity of the region' (Graziadei 2011, 180) by engaging with the creative forces that shaped and continue to shape both the region's island geography and its literature, such as volcanic eruptions, cyclones, seismic activity, and tidal waves (179). Maximin shares Sid's notion of geopoetics as a counterforce to the geopolitical ordering of space: 'La Caraïbe oppose aux politiques de l'espace une poétique de l'espace' (108).[9]

---

[9] 'The Caribbean opposes to the politics of space a poetics of space' (my translation).

Graziadei's emphasis on geology and geomorphology allows us to return to both Westphal and White, for if the former's geocriticism initially seems to share little with the latter's geopoetics, there are a number of significant areas where their interests converge, and a final detour via these will take us back to Darwin's islands. Westphal and White share a frustration with the gridded order and linearity of Euclidean space, and a fascination with entropy, Albert Einstein's theory of relavity, and the philosophy of Deleuze and Guattari. They privilege the chaotic, the irregular, and the disordered over organized space, smooth space over striated space, the rhizome over the line and the root, and they adopt a stratigraphic view of space (cf. Deleuze and Guattari 1987, 2–25, 39–74, 361–74). And both find themselves attracted to geology and geomorphology. For Westphal, the shifting of tectonic plates decentres the stable and static space of Euclidean geometry. It allows him to conceptualize space in terms of transgressivity: 'Transgression is somehow the result of an oscillation, little attributable to a singular, individual responsibility but more like continental drift, the shock of geological plates' (46). White expresses a similar vision of space as heterogeneous and turbulent: 'Chance, disorder, indeterminacy... are part of the great play [*jeu*] of the universe-multiverse. One leaves the hard sciences, rigid scientism, to enter the soft or even fuzzy [*floues*] sciences, where the emphasis is on fluctuation, irregularity, complexity' (1994, 29; my translation).

This view of space is reminiscent of Buckland's description of the imaginative impact of the 'gaps and blanks of the stratigraphic column' (27). If geology gave rise to a narrative model centring around ruptures and discontinuities, it also paved the way for a corresponding theoretical discourse. Indeed, White emphasizes his debt to geology and the geopoetics of reading the landscape he finds in the writings of James Hutton, often considered the father of geology: 'It was on the basis of Hutton's tectonics, concerned with the open structure of strata and the introduction into these open structures of all kinds of heterogeneous matter, this collocation of matter being later subjected to dislocation, fracturisation, all sorts of transference and translation, that I gradually derived a style of writing, let's say... a *textonics*' (2006, 19; emphasis original). It is in this *textonics* that 'world-landscape' and 'mindscape' converge (18), that the geo- gives rise to the -poetic.

For our present purposes, it is important to note that in White's writing this *rapport* between the geo- and its -poetics finds a privileged locus in the zone where land and water meet; in particular, in the shore of the island. Already in Hutton's *Theory of the Earth*, the shore was a privileged site for 'open[ing] the book of Nature and read[ing] in her records' (qtd. in White 2006, 18). In 'strong rhythmic prose' (18), he establishes the shore as a site where 'transference and translation' can be observed: 'These movable materials, delivered into the sea, cannot, for long continuance, rest upon the shore; for, by the agitation of the winds, the tides, and currents, every moveable thing is carried farther and farther along the shelving bottom of the sea, towards the unfathomable regions of the ocean' (qtd. in White 2006, 18). The shore becomes a region where material space is unfixed and becomes visible in its mobility. White ends *Le Plateau de l'Albatros* with a similar meditation, describing a walk on the tideland of an island near his home on the coast of Brittany, with the tideland being immense thanks to a spring tide: '... one discovers a stony landscape, chaotic, normally hidden by the sea that glitters over there in the west, and murmurs' (1994, 349; my translation).

The walk becomes the starting point for a final reflection on the schematization of space in Western philosophy, accompanied by a number of diagrams, before White opposes to this his own geopoetic mapping: he first inserts a geological map of the island and its surroundings and then textually maps the region's geology. Both map and text force the reader to rethink the coastal space they represent (or re-present). In the map, island, mainland, and sea become indistinguishable and the island's shoreline loses its distinctiveness: the entire landscape becomes a play of intersecting geological formations. The poetic textual rendering of this complex geological structure has a similar effect, before White leaves the lithosphere and reaches out to include the hydrosphere and the atmosphere with their own turbulent currents, movements, and forms, accompanied by yet another map (353–5). He then cites Thoreau's reflections in *Cape Cod* on the bizarre creatures of the intertidal land, a world partly hidden and partly emerging (356). And it is this sense of a world in emergence, where literature becomes littorality, which White links to geopoetics as thought in emergence:

> I continue to walk in the tideland, not knowing very well where I am going, but in the diffuse exaltation that arises [*se produit*], that takes

place [*a lieu*] when a thought (a vision, a science) is in the process of
erupting [*surgir*] and finding...its articulation. This articulation is
not completed, it will doubtless never be. (362; my translation)

Walking, reading, and writing the earth here become intertwined:
White's text seeks to articulate a poetics that is neither fully inherent in
the material world nor a purely textual construct, but emerges in the
resonance between the two. This poetics is always in the making, like the
shifting tideland around the island, always reshaping and re-presenting
itself.

If White's book ends with an island, it also begins with one, and this
island gives the book its title:

It was when turning the globe one winter evening in my Atlantic
studio...that I chanced upon [*suis tombé sur*] the plateau of the
Albatross, off Central America on the Pacific ridge...at some 1000
nautical miles from the Galápagos Islands. This plateau barely
emerges from the water—what better symbol for a thought (that of
geopoetics) in emergence? (16; my translation)

This island is indeed all shore; barely emerging out of the sea, it figures
as an object of geopoetic thought and allows White to articulate how
he understands geopoetics. By helping to shape the very concept it
serves to illustrate, it doubly epitomizes White's geopoetic project. The
albatross plateau of the preface is a precarious island; its fragility is
emphasized. Where Hutton figured the shore as a space where the land
disappears into the sea, White's focus is on its emergence. The islands
of the preface and the epilogue frame White's geopoetic project. In
White's own terms, they are sites of geographic as well as poetic
dislocation, transference, and translation. Indeed, the figure of the
archipelago runs through White's geopoetic project (cf. Bouvet 2015,
11–23).

Darwin's Other Islands: The Aesthetics
of Geology

White must have Darwin in mind when he evokes the Galápagos
Islands in his localization of a bird rock in the Pacific, and Darwin's
writings about islands can certainly be seen as geopoetic. In what

follows, I will use the term to designate the opening up of thought that emerges through an exposure to the material world as understood by White, but without the sometimes almost esoteric pathos Marszałek and Sasse observe in his writings (2010, 7), and with Westphal's notion of re-presentation as a productive interface between real and fictional space in mind. Balasopoulos's attentiveness to island form will be complemented by a thorough engagement with the geo- and biospheres of islands as proposed by Graziadei. Let us, then, join the young Darwin at the beginning of his five-year voyage around the world (1831–6) on the *Beagle*. Early in his diary,[10] Darwin describes his experience on the island of St Jago (today's Santiago in the Cape Verde Islands): 'Geology is at present my chief pursuit & this island gives full scope for its enjoyment.—There is something in the comparative nearness of time, which is very satisfactory whilst viewing Volcanic rocks' (1988, 27). For Darwin, the volcanic oceanic islands, geological babies when compared to the continents, make it possible to imagine the seemingly solid structures of the world as perpetually shifting. Darwin expresses a strong sense of wonder in relation to this experience: 'It has been for me a glorious day, like giving to a blind man eyes' (23). In a number of poetic similes referring to an act of the imagination, Darwin constructs the island as a theatre in which geological time can be envisioned, even if not seen directly.

His treatise on the volcanic islands he visited during his voyage variously performs this imaginative act. Describing a white stratum capped by basaltic sheets on St Jago, Darwin traces its meandering course:

> I could follow it with my eye, trending away for several miles along the sea cliffs. The distance thus observed is about seven miles; but I cannot doubt...that it extends much further. In some ravines at right angles to the coast, it is seen gently dipping towards the sea, probably with the same inclination as when deposited round the ancient shores of the island. (1844, 7)

Darwin positions himself as an observer in the geological landscape. His gaze exposes the border of the island as temporary and shifting as

---

[10] The following quotations are taken from a transcription of the diary Darwin kept during his voyage, not to be confused with the published account.

he traces the rock formations that gesture towards the forces producing the island. Like White's geological map of and text about the island in Brittany, Darwin's account unfreezes the island's static insularity by inserting it within an intricate lithospheric complex; both mobilize the island on its shore. From a geopoetic perspective, it is important to note that while the passage has its origin in the close observation of the lines and forms of the landscape, it gradually emancipates itself from them; the aesthetic stimulus of the rock formations is a starting point for an imaginative *rapport* with the island and its geological history. This brief example makes it clear that geopoetics, at least as I understand it, is linked to a phenomenological approach to space. Indeed, White is indebted to phenomenology, especially to Bachelard and his interest in the materiality of space (White 1994, 61). In *La poétique de l'espace*, Bachelard comments on the mobilization of space through the imagination, clearly influenced by Merleau-Ponty's notion of lived space (cf. Merleau-Ponty 335–447): 'Space that has been seized upon by the imagination cannot remain indifferent space subject to the measures and estimates of the surveyor. It has been lived in, not in its positivity, but with all the partiality of the imagination' (Bachelard 1964, 19). The island of St Jago in Darwin's *Volcanic Islands* is indeed space seized by the imagination. Lived and experienced, it starts to live in turn, the movement of the imagination finding a counterpart in the imagined movement of the island's layers of stone and sediment.

In Darwin's imaginative engagement with the geology of volcanic islands, two recurrent metaphors stand out: the seemingly paradoxical metaphor of water, and the metaphor of war. The former appears in a description of Mauritius: 'M. Bailly boldly supposes that this enormous *gulf*, which has since been filled up to a great extent by *streams* of modern lava, was formed by the sinking in of the whole upper part of one great volcano (1844, 30–1; my emphasis). With metaphors like 'streams' and 'gulf' to describe the volcanic rock formations, the island is described in terms of the sea: solid land is linguistically turned into fluid water. A similar passage can be found in Darwin's description of Chatham Island (today's San Cristóbal) in the Galápagos Archipelago: 'The surfaces of the more recent streams were exceedingly rugged, and were crossed by great fissures; the older streams were only a little less rugged; and they were all blended and mingled together in complete confusion' (102). The island here becomes a confused intersection of flows, a site of spatiotemporal turbulence. Commenting on a formation of 'loose fragments' (39) on the island of Ascension, Darwin writes: '…I presume that a narrow-mouthed crater,…like a great air-gun, shot forth, before its final extinction, this vast accumulation of loose matter' (39). This simile figures the island as a battlefield, the product of violent forces. Taken together, the metaphors of water and war imagine the island in its ongoing production. As an imaginative tool, the island allows Darwin to reach into the future as well: discussing one of the Galápagos Islands, Darwin imagines a possible future dissolution of the island into a fragment, its rocks having been worn away by the sea. Words like 'fragment', 'decomposition', 'displacement', and 'irregularity' abound in Darwin's text, and he explicitly admits searching in vain for a centre in several places. When discussing St Helena, he recounts the impossibility of detecting a central source of its volcanic activity; in the chapter on the Galápagos Islands, he concludes by remarking that there is 'no one dominant vent' (116), no central island. As in the passage on the Galápagos birds discussed at the beginning of this chapter, the islands are reimagined in truly archipelagic terms.

Islands allow Darwin to imagine not only a world before and without humans, but a decentred world in flux, a conglomerate of criss-crossing lines. In his landscape phenomenology, Casey argues that representation as re-presentation facilitates an imaginative connection with the earth that he conceptualizes as re-implacement (2002). Similarly, Tuan advocates an experiential analysis of space, and draws attention to the etymological proximity between 'experience', 'experiment', and 'perilous': 'To experience in the active sense requires that one venture forth into the unfamiliar and experiment with the elusive and the uncertain' (1977, 9). I want to argue that Darwin's text effects a re-implacement that entails an imaginative venture into the unknown:

> When reflecting on the comparatively low coasts of many volcanic islands, which also stand *exposed* in the open ocean…, the mind recoils from an attempt to grasp the number of centuries of *exposure*, necessary to have ground into mud and to have dispersed, the enormous cubic mass of hard rock, which has been pared off the circumference of this island. (Darwin 1844, 92; my emphasis)

This passage is about various kinds of exposure. The rocks on the coast are exposed to the waves, just like the islands in their entirety are precariously exposed in the open ocean. But the exposure is also that of the observer, situated *within* this landscape rather than outside it. This exposure leads the observer into geological space and time and out of himself; the text performs and invites a daunting, but also transformative imaginative act.

The Structure and Distribution of Coral Reefs, Darwin's first geological treatise based on the *Beagle* voyage, also portrays islands as mobile spaces:

> From the limited depths at which reef-building polypifers can flourish, we are compelled to conclude...that both in atolls and barrier-reefs, the foundation on which the coral was primarily attached, has subsided; and that during this downward movement, the reefs have grown upwards. (1842, 4)

To explain the structure of coral islands, Darwin has to imagine a volcanic island sinking into the sea and a coral island simultaneously arising on its foundations; the fact that the islands are built by living organisms reinforces their malleability. Darwin's work on coral islands bridges his geological and his biological writings. As discussed initially, islands are evolutionary laboratories for Darwin as species modification and natural selection can be observed on them; they make difference visible. Islands preserve older and elsewhere extinct species as 'living fossils' (2003, 160, 395), such as the enormous Galápagos reptiles or the 'gigantic wingless birds' (338) of New Zealand.[11] They give the workings of evolution through modification free rein as there is a comparative lack of competition owing to the difficulties of immigration: '...an herbaceous plant, though it would have no chance of successfully competing in stature with a fully developed tree, when established on an island and having to compete with herbaceous plants alone, might readily gain an advantage by growing taller and taller and overtopping the other plants' (338). At the same time, words like 'migration', 'crossing barriers', 'attacks', 'compete', 'enemies', 'colonists', and 'struggle' abound in Darwin's section on oceanic islands in *On the Origin of Species* (336–47); the emphasis is on territorial struggle. As contested

---

[11] Darwin is referring to the moa, a group of ratite species endemic to New Zealand which went extinct about 500 years ago.

territories, islands make these struggles visible. From and through them, geological and evolutionary time can be imagined; they help Darwin unfix notions of geographical and biological stability. *The Structure of Coral Reefs* undermines both. It disrupts the boundary between the biological and the geological as it describes how the former is transmuted into the latter: made from fossilized organic material, coral islands are among the most imaginatively suggestive mutable landforms.

Island Life: Wallace's World of Islands

Darwin was not the only nineteenth-century scientist who turned to islands to examine the distribution and mutation of living forms as well as the geological transformations of landforms. Before we discuss *The Island of Doctor Moreau* and 'Aepyornis Island', then, we will engage with the work of Darwin's contemporary Alfred Russel Wallace as Wells's island narratives resonate with the writings of both. In his monumental *Island Life* (1880), generally regarded as the foundational work of biogeography, Wallace also combines geology and evolutionary biology to emphasize mobility and relationality over stability and stasis. Arguing that the 'full importance [of islands] in connection with the history of the earth and its inhabitants has hardly yet been recognised' (10), he breaks up the dichotomy of islands and continents altogether in a series of fascinating passages:

> By far the larger part of the islands of the globe are but portions of continents undergoing some of the various changes to which they are ever subject; and the correlative statement, that *every part of our continents have again and again passed through insular conditions*, has not been sufficiently considered.... (2013, 10–11; my emphasis)
>
> We are thus led to picture the land of the globe as a *flexible area in a state of slow and incessant change.*...In this way every part of a continent may again and again have sunk beneath the sea, and yet as a whole may never have ceased to exist as a continent or a vast *continental archipelago.* (86; my emphasis)
>
> *Seas have been changed into deserts and deserts into seas.* Volcanoes have grown into mountains, have been degraded and *sunk beneath the ocean*, have been covered with sedimentary deposits,

and again raised up into mountain ranges... and all the vegetable
forms which clothe the earth and furnish food for the various classes
of animals have been *completely changed again and again.*

(99; my emphasis)

Wallace's most important extension of Darwin's theory of species
distribution lies in his attentiveness to the malleability of the geological
landscape in relation to the horizontal movements of life forms across
it. In his view, the mutations of the inorganic world act as 'motive
power' for change and dispersal in the organic world (220–2). For
Wallace, islands with their biogeographical particularities—as natural
museums, as illustrative of various patterns of dispersal across natural
barriers—are key to understanding the dynamic complexities of the
organic and inorganic histories of the world (234). Maybe the most
interesting aspect of Wallace's islands is the figurative power they gain
in his work. Reimagining the entire surface of the earth as insular, or as
periodically passing through 'insular conditions', Wallace conjures up a
vision of all landmasses as ever mutable, continually rising out of and
sinking back into the ocean, and of living forms dispersing in space and
being modified in turn. In Wallace's epic vision, the world is in
perpetual change: islands become continents and are again broken up
into islands, deserts become seas and vice versa. He creates an insular
imaginary by foregrounding the constant interplay of land and water.

Wallace, of course, did not have it quite right. Many of his assumptions were correct, but his theory did not yet allow for the horizontal
drifting of landmasses that Alfred Wegener first postulated in 1911,
which paved the way for the theory of plate tectonics.[12] Wallace's
universe is not yet radically decentred. The very phrasing of 'a state
of slow and incessant change' points to this tension: incessant change is
reabsorbed into a 'state'. Wallace asserts the '*General Stability of Continents with Constant Change of Form*' (99; italics original), meaning
that while the landforms are in constant *transformation*, they are also in
constant transformation: the 'wonderful and repeated changes in *detail*'
are counterbalanced by the '*general* stability and permanence of our
continental areas' (99; emphasis original). Wallace only allows for

---

[12] It was not until the 1960s, when the development of marine geology had provided
evidence for seafloor spreading, that Wegener's theory was generally accepted.

endless variations of the same form. In the second quote above, 'continental archipelago' is linked to 'continent' through an inclusive 'or'; the two terms become interchangeable. Stable continental identities are not dissolved; in the last sentence of the book, Wallace stresses his 'increased confidence that the "mighty maze" of Being we see everywhere around us it "not without a plan"' (512). Wallace's planetary archipelago is not yet fully archipelagic. Darwin's islands appear more chaotic, more random, more disjointed. And yet, however limited it may be, Wallace's call for a reimagination of the world in terms of islands also asks his Victorian readership to at least partially abandon fixed notions of spatial structures and living forms. Darwin's and Wallace's island writings are a step towards Derrida's notion that '[t]here is no world, there are only islands' (2011, 9), even if—at least in Wallace—the world still looms large.

Wallace's emulation of the popular genre of travel writing exemplifies this impulse towards reimagining the world. He begins by taking the reader on an imaginary journey from one island (Great Britain) to another (Japan), bypassing many other islands along the way:

> When an Englishman travels by the nearest sea-route from Great Britain to Northern Japan he passes by countries very unlike his own....The sunny isles of the Mediterranean, the sands and date-palms of Egypt,...the cocoa groves of Ceylon...pass successively in review; till...he finds himself at Hakodadi in Japan. He is now separated from his starting-point by the whole width of Europe and Northern Asia...yet...he sees so many familiar natural objects that he can hardly help fancying he is close to his home....In the Malay Archipelago there are two islands, named Bali and Lombok... separated by a strait only fifteen miles wide at its narrowest part. Yet these islands differ far more from each other in their birds and quadrupeds than do England and Japan. (1880, 3–4)

Wallace's book begins as a deceptively simple travelogue saturated with the conventions and clichés of travel writing. But the spatial order unfolding before the imaginary traveller's and the reader's detached eyes is soon challenged as received notions of proximity and distance are overturned and Euclidean measurement of space proves useless. What masquerades as a leisurely *tour d'horizon* turns into an intricate journey in time as much as in space. *Island Life* in its entirety extends this journey and asks the reader to view the earth dynamically and plastically.

The parodic invocation of travel writing also structures two island narratives by H. G. Wells that were published little more than a decade after Wallace's *Island Life*: the short story 'Aepyornis Island' (1894) and the scientific romance *The Island of Doctor Moreau* (1896). Both also masquerade as conventional travel narratives and end up taking their protagonists and readers deep into geological and evolutionary space and time. It is these two narratives that we shall now bring into dialogue with Darwin's and Wallace's island imaginaries.

Dust on the Island-Stage: Volcanism and *The Island of Doctor Moreau* (1896)

If the imaginary voyage at the beginning of *Island Life* initially offers deceptive spatial certainties, *The Island of Doctor Moreau* similarly opens with a 'misleading attention to accuracy, precision, and narrative control' (Glendening 2007, 39). The novel is prefaced by an 'Introduction', supposedly written by the nephew of Edward Prendick, the narrator and main protagonist:

> On February the 1st, 1887, the *Lady Vain* was lost by collision with a derelict when about the latitude 1° S. and longitude 107° W.
>
> On January the 5th, 1888 ... my uncle, Edward Prendick, ... was picked up in latitude 5° 3′ S. and longitude 101° W. in a small open boat. ... He gave such a strange account of himself that he was supposed demented. Subsequently, he alleged that his mind was a blank from the moment of his escape from the *Lady Vain*. ... The following narrative was found among his papers .... (Wells 2005, 5)

While deploying the conventional authenticity markers of contemporary travel writing such as precise dates, geographical accuracy, and narrative authority, Prendick Jr simultaneously establishes the unreliability of his uncle's embedded narrative, which is 'without confirmation in its most essential particular' (5). The latter narrative thus fills a void, an unnamable gap: his reportedly blank mind after the first, discredited account (whose content we never learn) evokes a blank page waiting to be filled with text. Prendick Jr further tells us that the existence of the island of Doctor Moreau is just as impossible to ascertain as Prendick's experience: 'The only island known to exist in

the region...is Noble's Isle, a small volcanic island, and uninhabited'
(5), with no living forms beyond hogs, rabbits, and some curious moths
and rats. Moreau's island thus belongs to a tradition of untraceable
islands that; a prominent example is More's *Utopia*, where the location
of the island is lost in a cough (More 2003, 12). Existing only as a
textual trace[13] in Prendick's narrative, the island as first sighted by
Prendick emerges from a similar epistemological uncertainty: 'It was
too far to see any details; it seemed to me then simply a low-lying patch
of dim blue in the uncertain blue-grey sea. An almost vertical streak of
smoke went up from it into the sky' (18). Initially, the blue island can
barely be differentiated from the sea; it first registers as a difference in
color. The island triply emerges from smooth space (cf. Deleuze and
Guattari 1987, 361–74), space unstructured and unmarked by permanent inscriptions: Edward's blank mind, the blank page of the as-yet
unwritten text, and the 'uncertain blue-grey sea'.

Yet crucially, what assures Prendick of the island's reality is the
'vertical streak of smoke'. Itself insubstantial, it points to the island's
material existence. Read in hindsight, the smoke hints at its volcanic
nature before the island itself can be properly seen: as a reminder of the
volcanic forces producing it, the upward movement of the smoke
marks the island as a space in continual emergence. At this point,
however, the source of the smoke is unclear: it could equally point to
human habitation. This uncertainty is important for the text's oscillation between presenting the island as a setting for a human evolutionary drama and a geological space indifferent to the former. In its first
appearance, the island is all colour and smoke. The text performs the
indeterminacy and instability of the island on various levels as geology
and aesthetics intertwine. This resonance of the material and the poetic
marks the representation of the island throughout the text. It both
supports and interferes with the novel's thematic and narrative concerns. Critical interpretations of *The Island of Doctor Moreau* have
almost exclusively focused on the latter, whereas my own reading will
privilege the island itself as an object of geopoetic analysis, which is
indeed the reason why I have refrained from discussing the novel's

---

[13] For excellent discussions of the textualization of the island of Utopia, see Marin
(1973) and Racault (2010, 25–31).

overall narrative organization so far. An overview of its overall narrative and spatial dynamics, however, is now called for.

In the main narrative, Prendick is shipwrecked in the Pacific and picked up by a filthy schooner (the *Ipecacuanha*) that transports a menagerie of animals to a small, unnamed island. Prendick is made to leave the schooner by its captain. On the island, Prendick discovers that a scientist named Moreau and his helper Montgomery, both fugitives from England, are vivisecting animals to turn them into humans. Moreau never quite succeeds; one day, his creatures turn against him and kill him and, a little later, Montgomery. Prendick is left alone with the 'beast folk', who gradually revert and lose their human characteristics. As Prendick leaves in a boat that drifted to the island, he has lost faith in humanity. He thinks he is still on a larger version of the island and perceives his fellow-humans in terms of the beast folk:

> I feel as though the animal was surging up through them; that presently the degradation of the Islanders will be played over again on a larger scale.
> ... Then I would turn aside into some chapel, and even there... it seemed that the preacher gibbered Big Thinks even as the Ape Man had done.... And even it seemed that I, too, was not a reasonable creature, but only an animal tormented with some strange disorder in its brain.... (130–1)

The text thus performs an evolutionary anxiety in which the terms of the human and the non-human slide into each other and the distinctive category of the human is called into question. Structurally, the novel pits two islands, two ships, and two narratives against each other. Both are initially clearly separate: one ship (the *Lady Vain*) represents the official voyage as reported in the newspapers, the voyage of the other (the *Ipecacuanha*) is unofficial, while the ship itself is disordered and filthy; one island (Great Britain) is associated with human civilization, and the other with its dark and bestial parody; one narrative (Prendick Jr's) relies on published, official accounts, the other (his uncle's) is a self-declared supplement 'to the published story of the *Lady Vain*' (7). Yet the official spaces are barely present in the text, and Prendick Jr's narrative is only about a page long. By the end of the novel, the binary opposition has collapsed: Moreau's island becomes just a displaced or repressed version of Great Britain, and in Prendick's disillusioned vision it merges with the entire earth. In its very structure, the novel performs an evolutionary uncanny: the journey across the water to an apparently remote island turns out to be a journey to a space where unconscious fears about the stability of the human species materialize.

The evolutionary anxieties negotiated in *Moreau* have received extensive critical attention, and the allusion to Darwin's evolutionary laboratory in the Galápagos Islands is obvious: Prendick is found somewhere off the coast of Peru.[14] The most sustained discussion of the evolutionary imaginary of *Moreau* is offered by John Glendening, who argues that the text's imagery and structure revolve around confusion, entanglement, and unpredictability, thus mirroring and performing the contingency of a Darwinist universe. These evolutionary anxieties are linked to late colonial anxieties and fin-de-siècle fears of imperial decline. Indeed, the most interesting approaches are those that discuss the intersection of colonial and evolutionary imaginaries in *Moreau* (see especially Christensen 2004; Libby 2004; Ruddick 1993; Schenkel 1993). Ruddick and Elmar Schenkel explicitly focus on the island setting in their discussions of the novel's colonial and evolutionary anxieties. Ruddick reads the island as a displaced version of home where space and time are compressed (1993, 65). Schenkel reads Moreau's island as an inverted version of Prospero's island, a space that marks the demise of the project of modernity where the former had marked its beginning. Language disintegrates, regression catches up with progress, and the colonial other rises in a successful revolution. In Schenkel's reading, the dramatization of Freud's second narcissistic wound, the Darwinist insight that man is an animal among animals, and the loss of control over colonial space, epitomized by the island, become mutually expressive of each other (50–8).

Yet despite their close attention to its symbolic and metaphorical import, Ruddick and Schenkel completely ignore the geographical particularities of Moreau's island. They reach their conclusions without a single comment on the textual construction of the island in its geospheres. Their readings centre entirely around the characters and

---

[14] For a discussion of the novel in relation to evolutionary theory, see, among others, Glendening (2007); Christensen (2004); Schenkel (1993, 56–68); Philmus (1981, 7–9); Ruddick (1993, 64–7).

events *on* the island. The island itself is curiously absent from their discussions. It is perhaps no coincidence that both choose the metaphor of the stage, for this is precisely how they treat the island: like any stage, it has to be excluded from the world of the play. The island is endowed with a plethora of meanings in these accounts, but it is devoid of any material existence. Ruddick and Schenkel are in good company: the bulk of critical discussions of literary islands have taken this approach.[15] In this, they partly reproduce Prospero's attempts at symbolic absorption of the island and Moreau's project to produce the island as an ultimately superhuman (cf. Hugues 1997, 115), immaterial realm in his attempted exorcism of the material basis of human existence and culture: 'Pain and pleasure—they are for us, only so long as we wriggle in the dust' (Wells 2005, 75).

Yet dust features prominently in Prendick's first extensive description of the island in the form of volcanic debris:

> It was low, and covered with thick vegetation, chiefly of the inevitable palm-trees. From one point a thin white thread of vapour rose slantingly to an immense height, and then frayed out like a down feather.... The beach was of a dull grey sand, and sloped steeply up to a ridge, perhaps sixty or seventy feet above the sea-level, and irregularly set with trees and undergrowth. Halfway up was a square stone enclosure that I found subsequently was built partly of coral and partly of pumiceous lava. Two thatched roofs peeped from within this enclosure. (27–8)

In a continuation of the first description discussed above, this passage foregrounds the volcanic nature of the island. The dull grey colour of the sand emphasizes its volcanic origin, and the spire of smoke, now described in more detail, points to the unceasing emission of gazes from the interior of the island, maybe mixed with an imperceptible shower of volcanic ash.[16] The first feature described is the island's

---

[15] This is not to deny the importance of foundational works like Loxley's *Problematic Shores* (1990), Gillis's *Islands of the Mind* (2004), and Weaver-Hightower's *Empire Islands* (2007); they deserve the highest respect for their groundbreaking analyses of the importance of islands in Western culture. I offer a complementary perspective that pays more attention to islands in their materiality.

[16] Prendick sometimes refers to a spire of smoke, at other times a spire of vapour, which leaves some ambiguity as to its precise composition.

lowness, marking its precarious position as an ephemeral volcanic product. The vegetation is merely a secondary feature: the 'inevitable palm-trees' are ironically marked as a stock feature of the tropical island as represented in the travelogues *Moreau* parodies. It has been argued that literary islands become increasingly artificial in the passage from early to late modernity.[17] I disagree with this view. If anything (and I would resist any generalizing narrative), I would argue the reverse: Utopia is an entirely constructed island; it is all fortification and built environment. The island of *The Tempest* is largely an aesthetic production, with significant exceptions (see Chapters 1 and 3). Robinson Crusoe is constantly confronted with the geographical environment and the geological forces of the island while managing to fortify and cultivate it. In *Moreau*, the built environment is fleeting and transitory at best. Its building materials, part lava and part coral, are the same as that of the island and its surrounding reefs: ironically, Prendick's description of the enclosure turns into a description of the island's geological constituents. The island's only artificial structure reveals itself as thoroughly natural, and the human habitations peeping from within it seem engulfed by the island itself, buried, as it were, in its lava. And this will indeed be their fate. When Prendick accidentally overturns a lamp, the enclosure burns down: 'Against the warm dawn great tumultuous masses of black smoke were boiling up out of the enclosure.... A spurt of fire jetted from the window of my room' (111). Prendick's description evokes a volcanic eruption; the enclosure becomes a vent spurting fire and smoke.

I insist on the geological descriptions of Moreau's island because they recur at crucial moments in the narrative. After the initial descriptions upon Prendick's arrival, the island is not described in its entirety until some fifty pages later, when Prendick decides to give the reader 'a few general facts about the island':

---

[17] Christopher Palmer argued this in his paper at the conference *Navigating Cultural Spaces: Images of Coast and Sea* (Kiel University, 1–3 October 2010); his book on castaway fiction, however, presents a somewhat different argument that traces the development 'from practical reason directly engaged with material things, to a more abstract and abstracting reason' in the castaway's relationship with the island (2016, 182). His starting point is *Robinson Crusoe*.

> The island, which was of irregular outline and lay low upon the wide sea, had a total area, I suppose, of seven or eight square miles. It was volcanic in origin, and was now fringed on three sides by coral reefs. Some fumaroles to the northward, and a hot spring, were the only vestiges of the forces that had long since originated it. Now and then a faint quiver of earthquake would be sensible, and sometimes the ascent of the spire of smoke would be rendered tumultuous by gusts of steam. But that was all. (81)

Significantly, Prendick gives this description right after narrating how he learned about Moreau's experiments, but before proceeding to the catastrophe. The renewed reference to the lowness of the island and the coral reefs implies that the island used to be larger and is now sinking into the sea while coral reefs are growing on its volcanic foundations; the 'now' in 'was now fringed' marks the reefs as a recent development. The island is described as comparatively still ('But that was all'), yet Prendick focuses on the traces of the geological forces that 'long since' shaped it: the fumaroles, the hot spring, the faint quiver, and the ubiquitous spire of smoke evoke latent powers that could erupt at any moment. And they do erupt metaphorically as Prendick goes on to narrate the beginning of Moreau's downfall. It is perhaps significant that the fatal meeting with the beast folk, the novel's turning point, takes place in 'a wide area covered over with a thick powdery yellow substance which I believe was sulphur' (89). No other scene is equally insistent on the island's volcanic activity. The island is indeed a stage here: 'We came to a kind of shallow amphitheatre' (89), with Moreau as its director, yet the island-stage refuses to go unnoticed in its materiality: 'Imagine the scene if you can. We three blue-clad men, with our misshapen black-faced attendant, standing in a wide expanse of sunlit yellow dust under the blazing blue sky, and surrounded by this circle or crouching and gesticulating monstrosities...' (89). Flung about by the beast folk ('the Satyr...tossed the dust with his hoofs'; 'they...began flinging the white dust upon their heads'; 'the dust-throwing circle', 89), the dusty stage interferes with Moreau's play.

The sulphurous dust, of course, does not impede Moreau's control in any concrete way. In fact, it has no narrative function at all. But this is precisely the point: through the repeated insistence on the traces of volcanic activity, the text, if ever so briefly, draws our attention away from the narrative. It underscores the failure of Moreau's project;

ironically, Moreau's creatures now quite literally 'wriggle in the dust' (75). Yet the dust also interferes with the narrative in another, more fundamental sense that goes beyond metaphorical reinforcement. Glendening's enlightening reading of the 'green confusion' (Wells 2005, 43) abundant in Wells's text is attentive to the aesthetics of the island's biosphere and the ways in which it intersects and resonates with the evolutionary narrative. To my knowledge, no one has engaged with the island's geology in a similar way. Yet the latter is possibly even more substantial in putting Moreau's project into perspective and destabilizing the human position. If evolution is figured as a random force indifferent to human aspirations, the geology of the island is indifferent to all forms of life. The novel's evolutionary imagination remains tied to a strong cultural anxiety: as long as Moreau's island is read uniquely in terms of the Galápagos Islands, it will be expressive of this anxiety. Yet once Darwin's 'other islands' are included in the discussion, a more complicated picture emerges. I would like to return to the calmness implicit in the description of the island's volcanic activity, and offer an alternative to my own earlier reading of it. While I would maintain that it points to the island's potential eruptive force, we can also take it seriously in its own right. Once we do so, geological change becomes a mere given, open to contemplation rather than a source of anxiety. Read this way, the island's geology takes on an expansive poetic force that resonates with Darwin's engagement with islands. Once we allow these moments in the text to suspend the narrative, its human and half-human actors fade, and the island itself moves into the foreground. Human subjectivity does not disappear, but it yields its neurotic centrality. However brief, these moments gesture towards a geopoetic *rapport* between the reader and the island.

It is important to insist at this point that the island is still a textually produced object. If I have drawn attention to its topography, I have done so with Miller's discussion of the word in mind (see also Chapter 3):

> 'Topography' originally meant the creation of a metaphorical equivalent in words of a landscape. Then, by another transfer, it came to mean representation of a landscape according to the conventional signs of some system of mapping. Finally, by a third transfer, the name of the map was carried over to name what is mapped. (1995, 4)

For Miller, the very notion of topography points to an undecidability inherent in any landscape description: '[the] terrain... always seems to have been there already when we move into it, though the text and its reading, it may be, are performative speech acts bringing the terrain into existence' (3). Importantly, Miller refrains from dogmatically asserting the absorption of the landscape by the text. His ambiguous, even contradictory wording ('it may be, are') allows for a more complex relationship between text and terrain where the latter is allowed to enter the former, a 'tension between creating and revealing' (5) that we might conceptualize as a form of geopoetic resonance. Like the first appearance of the island in *Moreau*, its last description performs this resonance. By the end of the narrative, the island has become a site of Darwinian territorial struggle: Prendick, the human, has been pushed to the beach, where he spends his time in paranoid anxiety. Although the beast folk are reverting, it is the human who is pushed to the border of the island-as-territory and is threatened with extinction. Prendick and the human species, like the island itself, are literally losing ground. This is Prendick's final description of the island as seen during his escape: '... the island grew smaller and smaller, and the lank spire of smoke dwindled to a finer and finer line against the hot sunset. The ocean rose up around me, hiding that low dark patch from my eyes' (129). Phenomenally and aesthetically, the island sinks back into the sea, paralleling its geological downward movement. In contrast, and rather curiously, the ocean is said to rise up. This is less readily intelligible in terms of phenomenal experience, but it poetically emphasizes the sense that the island is swallowed by the sea. As solid ground, as human territory, the island disappears, and the last thing that remains visible is again the spire of smoke: in this last vision, the island is again pure eruptive energy. While the island in its entirety is sinking into the sea, the smoke rises out of it. As Moreau's laboratory, it disappears never to return. Yet as a field of geological and poetic energy, the island retains its force.

To grasp the full significance of this, we need to come to terms with the text's final blending of island and earth. Critics have noted that Moreau's island functions as a trope for the planet, but they have failed to discuss the textual mechanism that produces this association. Thus, Ruddick argues that '[Moreau's island is] no more an island than the continent near which or than the planet on which it is situated.... Science

has placed them all...in the same boat adrift in the cosmic ocean...'
(1993, 71). Ruddick is rather careless in his use of metaphors, which are
taken straight out of the novel itself. Prendick, of course, is repeatedly
adrift in a boat, and the novel's emphasis on drifting underscores the
aimlessness and randomness of its Darwinian vision (Glendening
2007, 43). Yet in Ruddick's text, the island, the drifting boat, the
continent, and the earth all become interchangeable. Against this,
I would argue that the island *morphs into* the earth for Prendick in
his drifting boat as soon as it has disappeared:

> The ocean rose up around me, hiding that low dark patch from my
> eyes. The daylight...was drawn aside like some luminous curtain,
> and at last I looked into that blue gulf of immensity that the sunshine
> hides, and saw the floating hosts of the stars.   (2005, 129)

The disappearance of the island is immediately followed by the phenomenal disappearance of the entire earth, and the emergence of the
nocturnal sky in its stead. The sky is metaphorically figured as an
ocean, a second 'blue gulf of immensity' replacing the sea towards
which Prendick had wistfully turned, sitting on the beach of the
island.[18] This latter vision, hidden by the sunlight, is now privileged
over that of the earth. At the very end of the novel, Prendick returns to
this cosmic vision, stating that he seeks solace in the study of 'the
glittering hosts of heaven' (131). Prendick turns to the heavens,
which he perceives as stable and eternal. They are also, of course,
entirely out of reach, like the sea had been before he had a boat.
Prendick seems to prefer an imaginative investment in the loftiness of
a space he cannot enter.

Prendick's failure to dwell on the island is thus also his failure to
inhabit the world. If he uses a theatrical simile by figuring the disappearing sunlight as a curtain that both hides the earth and reveals the
starry sky, it is because like so many critics of the novel, he chooses to
read space in theatrical terms; to observe space rather than inhabit it.
He prefers a transcendent vision over an engagement with space in its
materiality. The island could have offered him a heightened experience

---

[18] Prendick here reminds us of Odysseus 'looking out with streaming eyes across the
watery wilderness' (Homer 2006, 67) when held captive on the island of Ogygia by
Calypso.

of being-in-the-world, even if this would have entailed a renunciation of his privileged position as a human subject. Drawing on Martin Heidegger, Merleau-Ponty, and Tim Ingold, Wylie advances a view of space that emphasizes the entanglement of body and landscape as an interplay of active forces (2007, 159). In its volcanic and seismic productivity, the island conveys such a view of landscape as an active force. As a character, Prendick fails to engage with this aspect of the island. Yet it surfaces at crucial moments of the narrative, interfering with its evolutionary drama. In those moments, the possibility of a *rapport* of subject and space emerges in the resonance between geology and the poetics of the island. It is present in the interstices of the text, yet it is quietly powerful, always ready to erupt.

Living Fossils: Bones and Coral in 'Aepyornis Island' (1894)

Darwin's works on volcanic islands write themselves into the text of *Moreau*, both supporting and interfering with its narrative. If I have brought *Moreau* into dialogue with Darwin's *Geological Observations on the Volcanic Islands*, the geological intertext for 'Aepyornis Island' is *The Structure and Distribution of Coral Reefs*. Written two years before *Moreau* and published in the *Pall Mall Budget*, this short evolutionary fantasy has received less critical attention. The few discussions of the story usually refer to it as a kind of textual testing ground where the concerns of *Moreau* are rehearsed before they are fully developed (cf. Bowen 1976, 325; Ruddick 1993, 62–3). The story is indeed a miniature version of *Moreau* in various ways: the narrative is scant, the set of characters is much smaller, and the island itself is a mere speck of coral, tiny and barren in comparison to the more complex spatial dispos-ition of Moreau's island. The story appears like a sketch containing the building blocks from which the more fleshed-out novel could develop. But this perspective is misleading: if anything, the precariousness and instability of the island is heightened by its skeletal quality. If 'Aepyornis Island' and Aepyornis Island are a text and an island in construction, this only affirms the provisional quality of the island and accentuates that both islands embody construction, reconstruction, and destruction.

Like *Moreau*, 'Aepyornis Island' is a narrative of a journey to an island of which only textual traces remain. The story is told to the nameless narrator by a scar-faced Englishman named Butcher, whose unpolished and sometimes ungrammatical language reveals him to be uneducated. His rash, violent, and instinct-driven disposition soon becomes apparent. In his story, Butcher is looking for Aepyornis eggs preserved in a swamp on the coast of Madagascar for a London museum (the Aepyornis was a giant wingless ratite bird that became extinct at some point in the last thousand years). He is deserted by his local helpers after beating one of them. Left without oars in a tiny boat, Butcher is cast away on a coral atoll with one Aepyornis egg left. An Aepyornis is hatched from the egg. He names it Man Friday, and for a while the two coexist in harmony, but soon Friday grows and wants more food than Butcher can provide, and a fierce territorial struggle begins. In the end, Butcher manages to kill the bird, before he is found and picked up by a yacht.

Like *Moreau*, 'Aepyornis Island' effects a displacement from a familiar island to its unofficial and untraceable double. In fact, the displacement is a twofold one, as the narrator moves from Britain to Madagascar and, finally, the atoll. The text thus presents us with three islands corresponding to the three types of islands distinguished by Wallace: continental, ancient continental, and oceanic islands. Butcher emphasizes the barrenness of the island right after his chance arrival:

> It was just a common atoll about four miles round, with a few trees growing and a spring in one place, and the lagoon full of parrot-fish.... It's rum how dull an atoll is. As soon as I had found a spring all the interest seemed to vanish. When I was a kid I thought nothing could be finer or more adventurous than the Robinson Crusoe business, but that place was as monotonous as a book of sermons.
>
> (1911, 79)

This is indeed a minimal island. If Moreau's island is 'covered with thick vegetation' (27), albeit in ironic reference to other island narratives, Aepyornis Island sports no more than a few trees; where the former is marked by 'green confusion' (Wells 2005, 43), the latter is decidedly not green, and a far cry from the inexhaustible profusion of that most popular coral island of nineteenth-century literature in

R. M. Ballantyne's *The Coral Island* (1858). The island is devoid of interest to Butcher and contrasts with his island fantasies derived from reading *Robinson Crusoe*, which 'Aepyornis Island' ironizes. If Crusoe never ceases to discover new parts and aspects of his island, Butcher has seen it all after a day. The island bores him as soon as there is nothing left to discover, and as soon as he realizes that the experience does not correspond to his expectations shaped by fiction.

The barrenness of the island and the self-referential rejection of earlier island fictions are linked to the story's evolutionary imaginary. The few critical engagements with 'Aepyornis Island' have discussed its Darwinian themes. Roger Bowen notes that Butcher's struggle with the bird marks the 'spectre of prehistory' and challenges 'man's sovereign position in nature' (1976, 325). He explicitly links this to the general disenchantment of the island in Wells's texts: 'In this light the blessed isle, that *locus amoenus*, becomes an arena for struggle and survival...' (322–3). In 'Aepyornis Island', this struggle is linked to the very barrenness of the island, which fails to produce sufficient food to sustain the two competing species, echoing the difficulty of survival on islands discussed by Darwin and Wallace. More recently, Richard Pearson has examined the short story in the context of late nineteenth-century anthropological and sociological discourses, arguing that 'Aepyornis Island' is an imaginative response to the bones and fossils that were dug out of the earth in large numbers and a source of immense cultural interest (2007, 66). He concludes that the story negotiates the reassessment of man's position in the world brought about by science (74).[19]

A close look at the different geospheres of the island adds a spatial dimension to the story's evolutionary imaginary. The proximity of water, land, and trees allows the stability of species to be unsettled to a heightened degree:

> I made for the lagoon, and went in up to my neck....He started strutting up and down the beach. I'll admit I felt small to see this blessed fossil lording it there....

---

[19] The connection of this aspect of Wells's fiction to the theories of his contemporary, Sigmund Freud, are unmistakable (cf. Freud 1918; 2005).

> I decided to swim across the lagoon and leave him alone for a bit,
> until the affair blew over. I shinned up the tallest palm-tree, and sat
> there thinking of it all. (1911, 83)

If Prendick is driven to the border of the land at the end of his stay
there, Butcher is even temporarily pushed off it. The distinctiveness of
species is unsettled as the terms of human and non-human are
unhinged and substitute for each other: while the narrator is forced
to occupy the spaces usually reserved for fish and birds—water and
trees—the bird struts around on the island, like the Crusoe Butcher fails
to be. The story here offers an extreme version of the increased variation and species modification that attracted biogeographers like Darwin and Wallace to islands. Like Darwin's herbaceous island plants
growing into trees, the Aepyornis evolves fast, finding an ecological
niche by picking worms on the beach and thus proving his survival
skills even when no longer fed, while Butcher regresses and is deprived
of his human prerogatives:[20] 'Here was this extinct animal mooning
about my island like a sulky duke, and me not allowed to rest the sole of
my foot on the place' (1911, 84). Butcher is losing ground literally and
metaphorically: his inability to keep his feet on the land points to his
impending loss of one of the distinguishing characteristics of the
human species, the ability to walk erect;[21] the island becomes the
beleaguered territory of humanity. Meanwhile, Butcher emphasizes
the menacingly erect appearance of the bird with disgust, having
stressed its beauty only paragraphs earlier: 'Great ugly bird, all legs
and neck!' (84). Referred to as a 'damned anachronism' by Butcher
(84), the Aepyornis literalizes Darwin's notion of 'living fossils' inhabiting oceanic islands.

As mentioned above, however, 'Aepyornis Island' also includes the
third type of islands that Wallace added to Darwin's distinction

---

[20] Darwinism is here mixed with the Lamarckian variety of evolutionary theory; where
Darwin's model is based on modification through selection, Jean-Baptiste de Lamarck
allows for willed modification in the span of a single lifetime (cf. his 1809 *Philosophie
zoologique*). On the entanglement of Darwinism and Lamarckism in *Moreau*, see
Glendening 2007, 46–52.
[21] As a flightless and very tall bird, the Aepyornis inherently disturbs neat biological
categories.

between continental and oceanic islands: ancient continental islands. The Madagascar group is Wallace's prime example:

> We have now to consider ... those [islands] which, although once forming part of a continent, have been separated from it at a remote epoch when its animal forms were very unlike what they are now. Such islands preserve to us the record of a by-gone world.... The problem presented by these ancient islands is often complicated by the changes they themselves have undergone since the period of their separation. A partial subsidence will have led to the extinction of some of the types that were originally preserved.... (2013, 383–4)

Wallace is even more interested in the Madagascar group than in oceanic islands because they seem to offer still more anomalies. Once connected to the continent and considerably older than oceanic islands, they preserve a flora and fauna long extinct on the continent. Noticing that Madagascar has two distinct floras and faunas, Wallace discusses the numerous shoals and coral reefs between India and Madagascar and concludes that there must have been several now submerged islands facilitating the migration of species from India to the Mascarene Islands and Madagascar. Aepyornis Island clearly resonates with these theories. Situated somewhere east of Madagascar, it 'reveals Europeans' fascination with Madagascar as a biogeographical anachronism' (Sodikoff 2013, 140). Being an oceanic island, it also evokes Wallace's conjectured migration routes between Madagascar and India. In fact, as we will see, it can be read as a phantasmagoric version of one of Wallace's submerged islands.

The changes in the islands themselves, such as the repeated subsidence and elevation of Madagascar, are an important aspect of Wallace's theory, and they are present in 'Aepyornis Island' as well. The threat of human extinction at the hands of an extinct species is present before the bird is even hatched:

> [T]he very day I landed the weather changed. A thunderstorm went by to the north and flicked its wing over the island....
>
> I was sleeping under the canoe ... and the first thing I remember was a sound like a hundred pebbles hitting the boat at once, and a rush of water over my body.... Then I remembered where I was. There were phosphorescent waves rolling up as if they meant to eat me....
> (1911, 79–80)

In the storm, the low-lying island itself threatens to be swallowed by the waves in the vertical movement Darwin describes in relation to coral islands. The metaphor of being eaten thus extends to both the island and the narrator. It also proleptically announces the threat of being eaten by the Aepyornis; the metaphor of the wing for the thunderstorm underscores this, albeit ironically as the Aepyornis was a flightless bird (it had tiny wings). The elements seem to conspire in attacking Butcher as the wind slaps him, pebbles pelt against his canoe as though the island itself were disintegrating, and the waves rush over him. By evoking the phosphorescent marine plankton, the text portrays the ocean as a living space with an appetite of its own. The possibility of the island sinking into the sea is also hinted at in relation to the yacht rescuing Butcher: 'Then one day a chap cruising about in a yacht had a fancy to see if my atoll still existed' (85). Resonating with both Darwin's writings on coral islands and Wallace's submerged reefs, Aepyornis Island has a fragile life of its own.

The idea that the island is alive reveals its intimate connection to the Aepyornis and, eventually, Butcher. The specific materiality of the island is evoked several times. All of these moments are linked to the Aepyornis, or more specifically, to its death. If Butcher was attacked by pebbles himself, throwing lumps of coral at the Aepyornis is his first violent attempt to 'get that bird round again' (84), but the Aepyornis merely swallows the lumps. Butcher eventually captures the Aepyornis by attaching two lumps of coral to a string and whirling it around the bird before he saws through its neck. When the bird is dead, the omnipresence of coral is emphasized as Butcher laments the fact that he cannot bury it: 'If I'd had any means of digging into the coral rock I'd have buried him' (85). Yet the bird's blood mingles with the coral sand: 'I stood over him and saw him bleeding on the white sand' (85). Coral both helps and resists Butcher: it serves him as a weapon and interferes with his intentions. Butcher can master coral as little as he can master the Aepyornis. And indeed, they are linked: if the Aepyornis is a living fossil, coral is fossilized life.

Darwin's *Coral Reefs* reveals a fascination with coral islands as living organisms caught in an ongoing process of living matter turning into stone:

> [E]very one must be struck with astonishment, when he first beholds one of these vast rings of coral-rock, often many leagues in

diameter.... The naturalist will feel this astonishment more deeply after having examined the soft and almost gelatinous bodies of these apparently insignificant creatures, and when he knows that the solid reef increases only on the outer edge, which day and night is lashed by the breakers of an ocean never at rest. (1)

The description oscillates between the fragility and softness of the living corals and the solid rock consisting of their fossilized skeletons. The poetic appeal of the islands Darwin expresses here is distinctly related to this interplay between organic growth and solidification, to their peculiar mixture of fragility and resilience. When the Aepyornis bleeds into the sand and its bones, picked clean by the fish, settle in the lagoon, the 'blessed fossil' (83) mingles again with what it has been all along, dead matter whose life has been extended into the present. It is appropriate that the story should begin and end with a discussion of various Aepyornis bones found by Butcher and others, for the island itself is nothing but a conglomerate of skeletons.

This takes us back to the island as a phantasm. Such a reading is supported by its first appearance when Butcher is paralysed by the infernal blaze: 'Then came the atoll. Came out of the sunrise, as it were, suddenly, close up to me' (79). Coupled with Butcher's altered state of mind due to heat and starvation, the sudden appearance of the island marks it as a chimera. Like Moreau's island, Aepyornis Island is a fictional laboratory onto which latent cultural anxieties are displaced. If the Aepyornis gives flesh to the bones filling the display cabinets of British museums, the island has a similar function: it seems to spring right from the writings of Darwin and Wallace. Its submerged coral reefs, as it were, grow upwards and attain new life in Wells's text as an imaginative site. And indeed, Pearson's argument that the bones dug up by anthropologists and archaeologists forced Western man to recognize his own 'modernity as being beyond humanity' (2007, 74) can be extended to the island itself: if the Aepyornis bones point to humanity's own status as a transient species, an examination of Wallace's work on recent continental islands suggests that Aepyornis Island can also be read as a displaced version of Britain. The British Isles are Wallace's main example of these islands. Starting by referring to them as 'the very reverse of the "oceanic" class' (2013, 312), he discusses the peculiarities of the British fauna and flora and concludes that 'the idea so generally entertained as to the biological identity of the British Isles with the adjacent continent is not altogether correct' (345). He goes on to state that the biogeographical difference between the island types is a matter of degree rather than kind as all islands develop endemic species and are a refuge for species extinct elsewhere (346). Oceanic and ancient continental islands make the workings of evolution more visible than recent continental islands, but the same processes can be observed in all islands, and ultimately in the whole word reimagined as insular. Islands for Wallace are a key and an imaginative tool to chart the instability of landforms and species, to register processes of dispersal, mutation, and extinction.

With Wallace's three island types as its settings, 'Aepyornis Island' offers a reflection on these processes that ultimately returns us to the heart of European civilization. Anthropologist Genese Marie Sodikoff uses 'Aepyornis Island' as an example to discuss the concept of extinction debt, which refers to the time lag between the habitat perturbation eventually leading to the extinction of a species and the moment when its last representatives die, having lived as a 'living dead species' doomed to extinction in between. Starting out from the observation that the story 'plays with the mutability of time and the specter of extinction' (2013, 140), Sodikoff argues that it 'offers an entrée into the ... terrible reckoning that happens when living beings are "out of time" ... ' (140). Drawing on Dipesh Chakrabarty, she maintains that '[t]hought experiments about a world bereft of *Homo sapiens*' can productively transform contemporary subjectivities in a world where we need to come to terms with our function not only as 'devastating biological agents ... but also as geological agents capable of disrupting geophysical processes on a planetary scale' (141)—capable of inducing or accelerating the submergence of low-lying coral islands, we might add.[22] In this reading, Butcher is as much a 'living fossil' as the Aepyornis. After the storm at the beginning of his stay, the canoe, under which he had been sleeping, has become a 'disarticulated skeleton' (80) scattered on the beach. The choice of metaphor is evocative: having used the canoe as a protective shell or skin to fortify his body, Butcher is, as it were, contemplating the possibility of his own skeleton

---

[22] Environmental anthropologist Peter Rudiak-Gould analyses the response of the Marshall Islanders to the imminent threat of their islands disappearing (2013).

on the beach, mingling with the fragmented coral skeletons like the bones of the Aepyornis in the lagoon.

For Butcher, however, this contemplation is not a transformative experience. This becomes clear in the development of the island from a utopian fantasy to a dystopian vision of extinction. When recounting his two happy years with the young Aepyornis, Butcher describes the island as an ecological utopia:

> I amused myself, too, by decorating the island with designs worked in sea-urchins and fancy shells of various kinds. I put AEPYORNIS ISLAND all round the place very nearly, in big letters, like what you see done with coloured stones at railway stations in the old country, and mathematical calculations and drawings of various sorts. And I used to... think how I could make a living out of him by showing him about if I ever got taken off.... And after a storm we would go round the island together to see if there was any drift.... It was a kind of idyll, you might say.   (Wells 1911, 81–2)

For a short time, the island is a site of perfect ecological balance and symbiotic coexistence. Like Robinson Crusoe, Butcher is writing on the island, but he is doing so quite literally. Where Robinson could only write in his diary until his ink, an emblem of Western civilization, ran out, Butcher's book is the island itself. Gathering drift accumulating on the island, he uses an ink that will never run out. Decorating the island not only with words, but also with calculations and drawings, Butcher is a writer, an artist, and a scientist at the same time. If writing for Crusoe manifested the same impulse as his excessive desire to control, measure, and master his island, Butcher's writing and drawing follows no agenda. Made of sea urchins and shells, his island art is both the epitome of culture *and* the product of nature; indeed, the distinction becomes irrelevant. For a brief time, Butcher is the ideal geopoetic artist as conceptualized by White, bringing out the poetry inherent in the earth itself.

This vision of ecological balance, however, is soon disturbed as it becomes clear that the island cannot sustain two fully-grown representatives of different vertebrate species. In fact, the line that precedes the above passage already suggests that the island is not fully removed from the capitalist logic of circulation and exchange. Butcher's peace of mind and disinterested artistic autonomy depend on his awareness of his collector's 'salary...mounting up' (81) at home without his doing anything precisely *because* he is cast away on a desert island. 'Aepyornis Island' thus also expresses a capitalist fantasy. In this, the story is close to *Robinson Crusoe* despite its ostensible contestation of the parent text, although we also learn that Butcher's financial demands are not met by his employer.[23] Butcher also ponders how he could make money out of the Aepyornis once off the island; their future relationship is not envisaged as purely symbiotic but as hierarchical, with one species dominating and living on the other. The story builds up to the logical consequence of this imagined instrumentalization of the Aepyornis: it ends with one species contemplating its dead counterpart, selling its bones to survive.

The ecological utopia is also compromised from the start because it emerges as a compensatory fantasy after the ecological dystopia of the Madagascar episode. Decay and death structure Butcher's descriptions of the landscape in this part of the narrative. The 'rotten, black beach' (75) contrasts with the white coral beach of Aepyornis Island. Butcher generally emphasizes darkness: the word 'black' alone occurs five times in this section (and not once in the Aepyornis Island episode). The 'black and blood-red' sunset contrasts with the bright sunrise out of which the latter island emerges; the lethal centipede bite that turns one of his local helpers into a bloated corpse adds to this general sense of doom and decline. In this threatening landscape, the only things that do not decay are the things that should: 'And somehow there's something in the water that keeps things from decaying' (72–3). At the same time, Butcher himself is, as it were, fossilized alive: 'we were all covered with beastly black mud' (73). Nothing and nobody is properly alive in this landscape.

By the end of the narrative, we have not quite returned to this decaying world, but we have certainly left the ecological utopia of the middle section behind. Instead, we are presented with multiple forms of coexistence between the various organisms of the island. Symbiosis and its frustration, domination and territorial rivalry coexist, with no single mode being privileged over the other, encapsulated in Butcher's

---

[23] Crusoe's fortune from his plantation in Brazil accumulates during his stay on the island. Hulme offers an enlightening reading of Crusoe's division into a spiritual and an economic self, and the deceptiveness of the island's autonomy (1986, 175–224).

ambivalent relationship with the coral of the island itself. Butcher is too threatened by the biological and geological contingency of this landscape to survive in it. He has to leave the island behind and return to the apparent stability of England. As in *Moreau*, the frame narrative removes the island even further. The killing of the bird and the narrative containment of the island experience strive to reestablish control and human uniqueness, but the threat remains. In both narratives, the emphasis on chance and drifting, including the narrators' frequent divergences from their stories, creates a Darwinian world of aimlessness and mutability. Darwin's and Wallace's writings celebrate this instability as a liberating concept; in Wells's fiction, the island is an imaginative site for working through the anxieties generated by their writings, but it fails to contain them fully. Alternatives to these threatening visions have a faint presence in the stories, but they are not allowed to come to the fore.

The Ecology of Islands

Twentieth- and twenty-first-century biogeographers and ecologists have expanded the island studies of Darwin and Wallace and form an important link between the nineteenth-century texts discussed above and Ghosh's *The Hungry Tide* (2004), the final text of this chapter. In their landmark study *The Theory of Island Biogeography* (1967), Robert MacArthur and Edward O. Wilson further open up the island concept. The opening chapter, titled 'The Importance of Islands', makes a passionate case for the study of islands as a key to the study of the world:

> An island is certainly an intrinsically appealing study object. It is simpler than a continent or an ocean, a visible discrete object that can be labelled with a name and its resident populations identified thereby. In the science of biogeography, the island is the first unit that the mind can pick out and begin to comprehend.... By their very multiplicity, and variation in shape, size, degree of isolation, and ecology, islands provide the necessary replications in natural 'experiments' by which evolutionary hypotheses can be tested.
>
> Insularity is moreover a universal feature of biogeography. Many of the principles displayed in the Galápagos Islands and other remote

> archipelagos apply in lesser or greater degree to all natural habitats. Consider, for example, the insular nature of streams, caves, gallery forest, tide pools.... (3–4)

These introductory remarks express two contrasting conceptions of islands. The text begins by stating a general fascination for the island as a discrete and simple study object, resonating with fictional and non-fictional discourses which establish the island as a singularity that can be easily overlooked and managed.[24] By moving from 'the island' to islands in their multiplicity, however, Wilson and MacArthur abandon this notion. Thought of in the plural, islands come to embody variation and diversity rather than simplicity. In the remainder of the passage, this diversity explodes as the island condition is seen as universal. Caves and tide pools here qualify as islands as much as land surrounded by water. Wilson and MacArthur stress the difficulty of establishing a permanent population and the frequency of extinction on islands, yet their tone is not elegiac. For Wilson and MacArthur, islands make the shifting processes of evolution visible without conveying a sense of threat. Struggle and extinction are a constitutive part of the processes they analyse.

In *Mountain Islands and Desert Seas*, Frederick R. Gehlbach also adopts an ecological view of islands, now detached from the definition of land surrounded by water, in his discussion of forested mountain tops in the desert of the US–Mexican borderlands. Like Wallace, he starts by taking the reader on a 'brief mental excursion' (1981, 3) through geological space and time:

> The Border landscape is a carpet of interacting plants and animals deftly woven on a geological loom....
> Cool-wet mountain islands and warm-dry desert seas give me the initial feel of the Borderlands. The living landscape depends primarily on the lay of the land plus climate and the nature of parent rock— the shape and materials of the loom. (3)

---

[24] The island as a discrete object available for visual control played a crucial role especially in nineteenth-century island fiction (Loxley 1990; Weaver-Hightower 2007). See Ralph in Ballantyne's *The Coral Island* (1858): 'We found this to be the highest point of the island, and from it we saw our kingdom lying, as it were, like a map around us' (1995, 56).

> North of the arc…high mountain islands float in flat desert or grassland seas.…it is so hot at midday in the summer that travelers head for the cool mountain islands like shipwrecked sailors. (5)

Gehlbach asks the reader to imagine his islands as shifting, sinking into and rising out of the desert sea in response to geological and climatic change. The image of the geological loom underscores the zooming out of the gaze from the present to resituate the landscape within a larger timeframe. Gehlbach's 'living landscape' is in perpetual reconstruction. Like Wilson and MacArthur, he views islands as part of a larger ecosystem, situated in a web of dynamic relations, movements, and metamorphoses.

Islands Made and Unmade in Days: *The Hungry Tide* (2004)

Such an ecological view of islands as a living landscape is strikingly performed in Amitav Ghosh's *The Hungry Tide*. Written more than a hundred years after Wells's island narratives, the novel offers a very different response to the challenges posed by evolution, biogeography, and geo(morpho)logy. Though the novel refers neither to Darwin and Wallace nor to twentieth-century island biogeographers and ecologists explicitly, its archipelagic universe resonates with and expands their archipelagic thought. *The Hungry Tide* has produced a wealth of critical responses from postcolonial ecocritics, who have celebrated its multi-layered and multiperspectival approach to politically charged ecological questions, examining especially its engagement with the human–nature nexus in the context of development policies and conservation practices in postcolonial India.[25] The novel centres around the experiences of Piya, an American cetologist with Indian roots who has come to the

---

[25] Graham Huggan and Helen Tiffin discuss the novel in their introduction to *Green Postcolonialism* (2007, 4–5) and in *Postcolonial Ecocriticism* (2010, 185–91). Pablo Mukherjee discusses the novel in terms of a resurfacing of the material and the social in what he considers a second wave in both postcolonial studies and ecocriticism (2006). Divya Anand (2008), Rajender Kaur (2007), Malcolm Sen (2009), and Robert P. Marzec (2009) engage with the conflict of human and ecological interests, and the appropriation of the latter by postcolonial models of development at the expense of subaltern populations.

Indian Sundarbans to observe a rare species of dolphin, and Kanai, a mundane Delhi translator. Kanai's aunt Nilima, founder of a cooperative trust to support the poor and a hospital, has asked him to come to the island of Lusibari in the Sundarbans to read a notebook written by her deceased husband Nirmal, a Marxist idealist and former schoolmaster of Lusibari. A central character is Fokir, a local fisherman who does not speak English and acts as a guide for Piya. From Nirmal's notebook we learn that Fokir is the son of Kusum, whom Kanai met as a child and who was killed in the historical massacre of Morichjhāpi, an island settled by Bengali refugees in the 1970s. They were forcefully evicted by the left-wing government although the CPI(M) had championed their cause before it came to power. Towards the end of the novel, the Sundarbans is hit by a devastating cyclone. Fokir dies in the cyclone but saves Piya's life, and she returns to Lusibari to start a dolphin conservation project with the participation of the local population.

But the real protagonist of the novel is 'the landscape, in its epic mutability' (Ghosh 2001, 128), which is given at least the same attention as the characters. Or rather, the characters are themselves presented as part of the landscape, both as active agents and in their exposure to its unpredictable transformations. Critics have not failed to notice the importance of the setting as an integral part of *The Hungry Tide* both in its materiality and in its metaphorical resonance with the concerns of the novel (see esp. Thieme 2009, 33–9; Anand 2008, 25–8; White 2013, 519–29; Mukherjee 2010, 116–30). The Sundarbans is an immense mangrove forest in an archipelago situated between land and sea, in the giant delta produced by the confluence of the Ganges, Meghna, and Brahmaputra rivers in the Bay of Bengal. Due to tidal action, the landscape is constantly reshaped; while some islands have existed for centuries, others appear and disappear on a daily basis. Nirmal's description of the tide country, read by Kanai in the first chapter, gives a striking account of this living landscape:

> *Until you behold it for yourself, it is almost impossible to believe that here, interposed between the sea and the plains of Bengal, lies an immense archipelago of islands....*
>
> *The islands are the trailing threads of India's fabric, the ragged fringe of her sari, the* āchol *that follows her, half wetted by the sea.*

> *They number in the thousands, these islands. Some are immense and*
> *some no larger than sandbars; some have lasted through recorded history*
> *while others were washed into being just a year or two ago.... The rivers'*
> *channels are spread across the land like a fine-mesh net, creating a*
> *terrain where the boundaries between land and water are always mutat-*
> *ing, always unpredictable....*
>
> *There are no borders here to divide fresh water from salt, river from*
> *sea.... The currents are so powerful as to reshape the islands almost*
> *daily—some days the water tears away entire promontories and pen-*
> *insulas; at other times it throws up new shelves and sandbanks where*
> *there were none before.* (2004, 6–7; italics original)

In this archipelagic universe, there is no room for stable structures. Even more extremely than those discussed by Darwin and Wallace, the islands of the tide country embody instability and metamorphosis. They, or parts of them, cyclically emerge and disappear through the movements of the tide, and they keep being reshaped by the strong currents. In fact, the time scales for both processes, usually differing massively, come to coincide. In their multiplicity of shapes and sizes, the islands of the tide country embody variation and diversity to a degree envisioned not even by Wilson and MacArthur.

Crucially, Nirmal begins his description by emphasizing the importance of lived experience for an understanding of the archipelago ('Until you behold it for yourself...'). Laura A. White argues that the novel challenges colonial visual practices and suggests alternative ways of knowing the Sundarbans based on partial knowledge and embodied experience (2013, 528). She finds this impetus at work from the very first pages when a map of the Sundarbans, representing colonial forms of knowing, is followed and contrasted by an account of Piya and Kanai orienting themselves at the train station of Kolkata without the narrator giving the readers any distanced spatial overview (518–19). Nirmal's account of the Sundarbans further ironizes the use of the map and questions its authority, not only because it can offer no more than a schematic overview of the land breaking up (it shows, perhaps, a few dozen islands), but also because any attempt to represent the Sundarbans on a map is necessarily frustrated by the always shifting topography.

At the same time as advocating the necessity of lived experience, however, Nirmal's text immediately makes it clear that the Sundarbans is also a metaphorical landscape. Figuring the islands as 'the trailing threads of India's fabric' and 'the ragged fringe of her sari', it announces the double function of the islands as both material and figurative. Importantly, the metaphors themselves are grounded in materiality: the islands are represented as the zone where the very fabric of the country becomes visible, where the texture of the threads from which it is woven trail off and are exposed, where the inchoate and messy substances on which the appearance of integrity and coherence is based becomes visible. Returning to the physical geography of the islands, Nirmal stresses the impossibility of establishing clear borders in the Sundarbans. Land and sea, freshwater and saltwater intersect; furthermore, the Sundarbans stretches across two countries, India and Bangladesh. Political and cultural boundaries are questioned along with physical ones.

A useful model for describing the spatiality of *The Hungry Tide* is Deleuze and Guattari's already invoked notion of smooth space. As opposed to striated space, smooth space is not broken up into lines and grids, whether on a map or by roads and power lines. The imaginative model for Deleuze and Guattari is the space of nomads, whose tracks in the sand are temporary and erased in the next sandstorm. The Sundarbans offers such a vision of space. When Nirmal teaches the young Kanai about the islands, he stresses their constant erasure of all traces of human activity: '...almost every island in the tide country has been inhabited at some time or another. But to look at them you would never know: the speciality of the mangroves is that they do not merely recolonize land; they erase time' (2004, 43). He restates the same point in his diary: '*No one knows better than I how skillful the tide country is in silting over its past*' (59; italics original). Again, the use of 'silting over' is both literal and metaphorical; the figurative erasure of history is effected through the very material process of silt deposited by the tides. This does not, however, mean that the Sundarbans is a space devoid of history, as a later entry in Nirmal's notebook emphasizes:

> *To me, a townsman, the tide country's jungle was an emptiness, a place where time stood still. I saw now that this was an illusion, that exactly the opposite was true. What was happening here, I realized, was that the wheel of time was spinning too fast to be seen. In other places it took decades, even centuries, for a river to change course; it took an*

epoch for an island to appear. But here in the tide country, transform-
ation is the rule of life: rivers stray from week to week, and islands are
made and unmade in days. (186; italics original)

At first sight, Nirmal's metaphor of the fast-spinning and thus invisible
wheel of time seems to clash with his description of the extreme
visibility of landscape change. However, it is the very hyper-visibility
of the *effects* of time that makes time itself invisible, makes it escape
from the observer's grasp as an abstract entity within which human
activity can be traced. Like the islands themselves, the human endeav-
ours on them are subject to erasure, and cultural identity is portrayed as
shifting. For Darwin and Wallace, studying islands helps to unfix
seemingly stable entities. In *The Hungry Tide*, the islands of the tide
country are distinguished from other islands, which further heightens
their transformative potential.

This conception of the archipelago as a network of relations in flux,
however, is not the only figuration of islands in the novel, for the
Sundarbans of Ghosh's novel are also home to a number of visions
that rely on a conception of the island inflected by the utopian tradition. The utopian appeal of the Sundarbans is signalled early in the
novel, when Kanai remembers Nirmal telling him about the Scotsman
Sir Daniel Hamilton, a historical figure who played an active role in the
settlement of the Sundarbans in the early twentieth century, introducing
cooperatives to relieve the poverty and misery of the population: 'What
he wanted was to build a new society, a new kind of country.... Here
people wouldn't exploit each other and everyone would have a share in
the land' (2004, 45). A Marxist visionary and a poet, Nirmal is drawn to
this utopian vision despite its failure: '"What he wanted was no different
from what dreamers have always wanted. He wanted to build a place
where no one would exploit anyone and people would live together
without petty social distinctions and differences. He dreamed of a place
where men and women could be farmers in the morning, poets in the
afternoon and carpenters in the evening"' (46). Here, Nirmal's vision of
Hamilton's vision unmistakably evokes More's *Utopia*, where all citizens are farmers and learn one of four additional jobs, one of which is
carpentry (More 2003, 55); lunch and supper are begun with a reading
of literature (63). Nirmal's depiction of Hamilton's dream as timeless
and universal inserts it in a long line of utopian visions dreamt up in

different times and places. The Sundarbans is viewed from the outside; not as lived space, but in terms of a timeless and static island dream. This dream is marked as a patronizing vision of the ruling class on behalf of the poor: 'The bourgeoisie all agreed with S'Daniel that this place could be a model for all of India; it could be a new kind of country' (45). However benevolent in intention, Hamilton's project is portrayed as unmistakably imperialist (Zullo 104; Mukherjee 2006, 152), and its failure is encapsulated in young Kanai's cynical response to his uncle's story: '"And look what he ended up with", he said. "These rat-eaten islands"' (46).

If the historical account of Hamilton's vision establishes the Sundarbans in its entirety as a utopian landscape, two islands stand out in the novel's utopian topography: the already mentioned island of Morichjhāpi, site of the 1979 massacre,[26] and the fictional island of Garjontola, where Piya makes her first important discoveries about the tide country dolphins' special patterns of migration. Evelyne Hanquart-Turner argues that while Morichjhāpi embodies 'the utopian vision of a possible perfect society on earth' (77), Garjontola functions as 'a privileged place where dolphins communicate with mankind in trusting harmony...' (75). Both islands, however, are ambivalent in their representation, and in their function as idealized islands for Nirmal and Piya both are conceived in opposition to the complex and shifting archipelagic world of the Sundarbans. Pablo Mukherjee correctly points out that '[t]he problem with Piya's environmentalism and Nirmal's would-be Marxism is that in their own ways they remain wedded to idealist notions of "universal progress" and their ignorance of local ecologies' (2006, 151). While Morichjhāpi functions as a political utopia for Nirmal, Garjontola is an ecological utopia for Piya. It is in the juxtaposition of the two islands that the problems of each become apparent.

Nirmal's description of his first sighting of Morichjhāpi makes its links to Hamilton's project explicit:

> *Taking in these sights, I felt the onrush of a strange, heady excitement: suddenly it dawned on me that I was watching the birth of something*

---

[26] For a discussion of the portrayal of Morichjhāpi in relation to More's *Utopia*, see Singh (2011); on the historical massacre, see Mallick (1999) and Jalais (2005).

new, something hitherto unseen. This, I thought, is what Daniel
Hamilton must have felt when he stood upon the deck of his launch
and watched the mangroves being shorn from the islands. But...this
was not one man's vision. This dream had been dreamt by the very
people who were trying to make it real.

    I could walk no more. I stood transfixed on the still wet pathway,
leaning on my umbrella while the wind snatched at my crumple dhoti.
I felt something changing within me: how astonishing it was that I, an
aging, bookish schoolmaster, should live to see this, an experiment,
imagined not by those with learning and power, but by those without!

                             (Ghosh 2004b, 141; italics original)

Nirmal's assertion that he is witnessing 'the birth of something new' is
immediately qualified as he perceives it in terms of something old,
namely Hamilton's timeless vision, even though he is quick to point out
the difference between the two dreams. In his very embrace of Morichjhāpi as the dream of the poor, he ascribes his own revolutionary
idealism to them (cf. Mukherjee 2006, 151). It becomes clear that the
dream is really Nirmal's own: 'transfixed' by the view, he turns the
island into an imaginary landscape where the refugees come to embody
the possibility of revolution. Like Nirmal himself, the island is frozen in
his gaze to embody an abstract principle: taking it in visually, he fills it
with an idea, like the islands examined in Chapter 2. He becomes a
double of Hamilton standing on his boat and watching the islands from
the outside. In Nirmal's account, the writers, intellectuals, and journalists from Kolkata invited by the settlers share his utopian vision: 'It was
universally agreed that the significance of Morichjhāpi extended far
beyond the island itself. Was it possible that in Morichjhāpi had been
planted the seeds of what might become... a place of true freedom for
the country's most oppressed?' (159). Like Hamilton's project, this
island utopia is also viewed as a model, as a representative idea, rather
than in its situated specificity.

    If Morichjhāpi comes to represent a social experiment, Garjontola is
an island without human inhabitants. Although it seems diametrically
opposed to the former island, it is utopian in a different way. When
Fokir takes Piya there to observe dolphins in a tidal pool, she perceives the
landscape as a field for detached observation. She reflects on this when
thinking about the impossibility of an involvement with Fokir: 'She was
out on an assignment, working in the field—it was the exclusion of

intimate involvements that made a place into a field and the line between the two was marked by a taboo...' (94). Like Nirmal, Piya watches her island from a distance; it embodies an ideal. Her utopia is a scientific one which allows her to observe the dolphins without interference, even from herself. Treating the island as a 'field' rather than a 'place', she draws boundaries around Garjontola, insisting on the exclusion of personal involvement with the object of study. This exclusionary gesture becomes apparent when she decides to ignore what Fokir leads her to believe is the mark of a tiger's paw in the mud of the island's shore: 'Then she heard the sound of an exhalation, and all thought of the tiger was banished from her mind. Picking up her binoculars, she spotted two humps breaking the river's surface: it was the adult Orcaella swimming in tandem with the calf' (127–8). Focusing all her attention on the dolphins, she dismisses everything else. The tiger's mark on the beach resonates with the footprint scene in *Robinson Crusoe*: Crusoe's fear of incursion into his island kingdom here translates into the tiger's incursion into her field of study.

Yet it is precisely the tiger which forms the disavowed link between Morichjhāpi and Garjontola. Already the narrative structure suggests that the two islands should be read in relation to each other. In the first part of the novel, chapters alternate between Piya's and Kanai's experiences (Hanquart–Turner 2011, 77). The initial descriptions of Morichjhāpi and Garjontola run parallel; the account of Piya's observations of dolphins by the latter island is interspersed with Nirmal's narrative of how he first came to the former, read by Kanai. Thematically, the tiger connects the two islands because it is the historical reason why the settlers were evicted from Morichjhāpi, or at least the official reason, as the settlers were said to be 'in unauthorised occupation of Marichjhapi which is a part of the Sundarbans Government Reserve Forest' (qtd. in Mallick 1999, 107). *The Hungry Tide* points to the problematic history of conservation projects in area of 'mass migration of refugees from Bangladesh and resultant political and social unrest' (Sen 2009, 46). Indira Gandhi's Project Tiger 'was also a means of winning international approval and raising India's profile and diplomatic strength' (Kaur 2007, 129); the Indian Sundarbans became a Tiger Reserve in 1973 and was declared a national park in 1984, becoming a UNESCO World Heritage Site and a Biosphere Reserve within a few years (Anand 2008, 25).

A large-scale ecotourism project by the Sahara Group with plans for a luxury resort in the Sundarbans formed the immediate historical context for The Hungry Tide (cf. Anand 29; Sen 372; White 2013, 515). Like many critics of the project, Ghosh was alarmed at the possible dangers to the region's population and ecosystem and campaigned against it (Ghosh 2004a). The publication of The Hungry Tide led to worldwide protests against the project, which was finally terminated by the government (Anand 2008, 39). Anand maintains that the novel offers a reflection on 'the violence inscribed within western conservation discourses when arbitrarily implemented in the Third World' (38). For several critics, The Hungry Tide exposes the problems of a misguided environmentalism where 'humans become the expendable species in favor of the treasured tiger' (Kaur 2007, 131), and the poor inhabitants of places like the tide country are 'figured as a threat to the environment' (White 2013, 515) rather than viewed as an integral part of it (cf. Sen 2009, 372–3; Anand 2008, 33). The conflict between the local population and the man-eating tigers is latently present throughout the novel, and openly breaks out when the inhabitants of a village torture and burn a tiger to the dismay of Piya (Ghosh 2004b, 238–44). Graham Huggan and Helen Tiffin argue that this is the unresolved real conflict of the novel; it must be displaced for the final resolution to be possible, which only works 'because the local people have no particular problem with the dolphins' (2007, 5). What adds to the dilemma is that the conservationist efforts have also masked economic interests, notably in the case of Morichjhāpi, where the state had planned the establishment of 'revenue-generating coconut and tamarisk plantations' (Anand 2008, 31).

If Garjontola seems to offers a peaceful and harmonious counter-space to Morichjhāpi, free from the conflict and bloodshed with which the latter's utopian project ends, it is also a spectral version of that other island, a kind of nature reserve from which human activity has withdrawn. Indeed, Piya discovers the traces of a former human settlement on the island; read cynically, Garjontola represents Morichjhāpi after eviction, a pristine environment embodying the vision of the Sundarbans as 'empty space' (White 2013, 516). According to White, this vision has been propagated by developers and conservationists (2013, 515–16). Indeed, even a cursory glance at the websites of the nature reserves in the Sundarbans reveals the conspicuous absence of humans from most of the glossy photographs, which emphasize instead the majesty of the tigers and capture beautiful views of the mangrove forests.[27] Garjontola represents a similar vision of a thriving ecosystem which depends on the exclusion of human settler presence. Indeed, Garjontola is closely associated with tigers: Kusum tells Nirmal that her father was saved from a near encounter with a tiger by Bon Bibi, a local goddess, while caught in a storm on the island; left on Garjontola by Fokir, Kanai finds himself face to face with a tiger without being harmed, although it is not clear whether he is hallucinating or not; Piya and Fokir see a tiger from the tree where they sit out the cyclone. Garjontola is thus also a sacred space where tigers do humans no harm; where they are perceived in sounds and smells,[28] seen from a distance or as hallucinatory images, or present in a mere imprint left in the mud.

This, then, is the ecological utopia of Garjontola: it is the realm of the tiger, but without the tiger's threatening presence. In a thoughtful essay on the Morichjhãpi incident, Annu Jalais discusses local responses to the eviction, among which a theory about the tigers' sudden proclivity for human flesh stands out: 'The brutality and rhetoric with which the refugees had been chased away, coupled with measures for safeguarding tigers..., had, explained the villagers, gradually made tigers "self-important". With this increased conviction of their self-worth, tigers had grown to see poorer people as "tiger-food"' (2005, 1758). The harmonious semi-encounters between humans and tigers stand in marked contrast to this figurative expression of the sacrificing of human lives for the preservation of tigers, similarly expressed by Kusum (Ghosh 2004b, 216–17; cf. Kaur 2007, 130–1), and to the novel's repeated references to humans killed by tigers. In the juxtaposition of Morichjhãpi and Garjontala, the latter island represents the problematic environmental vision upon which the failure of the former is predicated.

Beyond the Island: The Geopoetic Archipelago

While Nirmal and Piya are closely linked to the utopian visions of Morichjhãpi and Garjontola, they also learn to give them up. As

[27] See, for instance, <whc.unesco.org/en/list/798>.
[28] Kusum's father does not actually see the tiger; he merely hears it in the mangroves and smells it (Ghosh 2004b, 193).

Mukherjee argues, they and Kanai learn to view themselves through the eyes of others and absorb local knowledge: they 'are all trans- formed through their encounters with radically different texts and contexts—songs, folk tales, folk theatre performances, oral historical narratives, and above all, the complex networks of everyday lives' (2006, 152). We should add that the encounters with the material space of the islands play an important part in interfering with their utopian dimensions. Nirmal's first daylight view of Morichjhāpi makes him dream, but it also covers him in mud: while he describes nothing but the 'brilliant sunshine' (Ghosh 2004b, 141), we learn that Kusum is alarmed upon his return: 'Why are your clothes muddy, your face red?' (142). Piya, too, mingles with the mud of Garjontola when stepping off the boat at Fokir's behest: 'The mud parted under her weight, sucking her feet in with a wet slurping sound. She was taken completely by surprise.... Suddenly she was tipping over, fall- ing face forward, extending her arm to keep herself from slamming into the mud' (126). Piya's distance and disengagement from the island is suddenly and unexpectedly cut short as she is pulled into its muddy ground.

Even before she steps onto the island, the temporary relaxation of her observing gaze makes way for an observation of a different kind:

> ... for the first time in hours, Piya went 'off effort', dropping her binoculars and resting her eyes on the greenery of the shore. Pres- ently her gaze was drawn to what seemed to be a fragment of brick lying in the mud. She looked more closely ...: this was indeed a bit of broken brick, and it was not the only one—the shore was littered with them. Examining the tangled greenery, she discovered that some of the mangroves were growing out of mud walls, while others had chunks of brick entwined in their roots. (124)

It is precisely when Piya goes 'off effort' that she becomes most receptive to the complexities of the environment. Mud, mangroves, and the remains of human settlement intertwine; litho-, bio-, and anthroposphere are here intricately interwoven. Mud walls and frag- mented brick become interchangeable; all form part of the island's ecosystem. The island, seemingly devoid of human presence, is in fact 'littered' with debris from human activity. The image we get is one of entanglement, reminiscent of Darwin's 'entangled bank' at the very end of *On the Origin of Species*:

It is interesting to contemplate an entangled bank, clothed with many plants of many kinds, with birds singing on the bushes, with various insects flitting about, and with worms crawling through the damp earth, and to reflect that these elaborately constructed forms, so different from each other, and dependent on each other in so complex a manner, have all been produced by laws acting around us.

(2003, 397)

The scene viewed by Piya speaks to an even more radical vision than that offered by Darwin because it folds traces of human culture into its 'tangled greenery'. Mud and brick, made of the same materials, are worked into the soil of the island. They exist side by side without becoming indistinguishable. Embedding the human element in the very material of the island, the image works against Piya's detached scientific observation of the island as a space undisturbed by humans, and is thus linked to her own inadvertent immersion in the mud.

It is precisely in the moments when the text itself goes 'off effort' that its archipelagic island poetics fully emerges. While the narrative cannot resolve the various struggles and conflicts it portrays, the poetic engagements with the landscape offer a non-narrative counterstrategy. Unlike in Wells, they are more than brief interferences; they take centre stage in the novel. Without offering a solution, they sketch and perform a way of inhabiting the landscape that is neither politically utopian nor ecologically naïve, working against visions of the islands frozen into ideas. When Kanai returns to Lusibari, his perception of the island is first guided by a cartographic gaze, recalling the map at the beginning of the novel: '... suddenly it was as if his memory had rolled out a map so that the whole island lay spread out before his eyes' (Ghosh 2004b, 31). The stability of this vision is immediately qualified, however, by another memory:

At low tide, when the embankment, or *bādh*, was riding high on the water, Lusibari looked like some giant earthen ark, floating serenely above its surroundings. Only at high tide was it evident that the interior of the island lay well below the level of the water. At such times the unsinkable ship of a few hours before took on the appearance of a flimsy saucer that could tip over at any moment....

(32; emphasis original)

Variously figuring the island as an 'unsinkable ship' and a 'flimsy saucer', this view of Lusibari outlines a perceptual acknowledgement of space in its fragility. Kanai experiences a similar perceptual transformation of the islandscape when contemplating it from the roof of Nilima's house:

> ... the landscape, in its epic mutability, had undergone yet another transformation: the moonlight had turned it into a silvery negative of its daytime image. Now it was the darkened islands that looked like lakes of liquid, while the water lay spread across the earth like a vast slick of solid metal. (128)

Islands here poetically turn into water and water solidifies into islands, parallelling the physical reshaping of the islandscape.

It is in this resonance of the material with the poetic that *The Hungry Tide* develops its force. Struck by the linguistic and cultural hybridity of the 'tattered old pamphlet' (205) in which the legend of Bon Bibi is written down, Nirmal reads the booklet in relation to the materiality of the archipelago: '... the mudbanks of the tide country are shaped not only by rivers of silt, but also by rivers of language. Bengali, English, Arabic, Hindi, Arakanese and who knows what else? Flowing into one another they create a proliferation of small worlds that hang suspended in the flow' (205). Language is here conceived in terms of sediment deposited in the confluence of rivers, always subject to erosion, flows, and resedimentation. The booklet is an example of such a confluence, its pages opening to the right as in Arabic texts, yet written in the prosody of Bangla folklore and marked by generic instability: '[the lines] flowed into each other, being broken only by slashes and asterisks. In other words they looked like prose and read like verse...' (205). Flowing like rivers, arrested by asterisks and slashes, the language of the booklet is described in its materiality, like the book itself, whose physical features are part of its significance. Nirmal forges a similar metaphorical connection between landscape and language when he explains the etymology of *badabon*, the Bengali word for mangrove. The first part of the word deriving from the Arabic word for desert, 'our Bangla word joins Arabic to Sanskrit—*bada* to *bon*, or "forest." It is as though the word itself were an island, born of the meeting of two great rivers of language—just as the tide country is begotten of the Ganga's

union with the Brahmaputra' (69). This is a very different notion of
islands than that implicit in the utopian visions discussed above.
Although also partly figurative, the island here does not represent a
timeless idea in isolation but is the product of intersecting flows, linked
to the formation of words in the confluence of languages. Viewed in
this way, the island is necessarily one of many islands rather than a
singular entity. As such, the material and textual islands of the tide
country cannot be destroyed. The materials from which they are
formed can only be rearranged; like a rhizome, they may change their
layout but will always reform in new configurations (cf. Deleuze and
Guattari 1987, 30).

Rejecting a conception of the island as singular and static, *The
Hungry Tide* maps an archipelagic landscape. Recent island scholarship
has advanced the notion of the archipelago as a useful concept for
counteracting static notions of insularity and reimagining islands as
situated in a network of relations. Thus, Elizabeth DeLoughrey argues
that

> a system of archipelagraphy—that is, a historiography that considers
> chains of islands in fluctuating relationship to their surrounding seas,
> islands and continents—provides a more appropriate metaphor for
> reading island cultures. Not surprisingly, writers from the Caribbean
> and Pacific such as Edouard Glissant, Epeli Hau'ofa, and Derek
> Walcott have called for a cartography of archipelagoes that maps
> the complex ebb and flow of immigration, arrival, and of island
> settlement. (2001, 23)

Similarly, Elaine Stratford et al. call for a rethinking of islands in terms
of flows and exchanges: '...islands *qua* archipelagos invite us to
recover a history and a practice of what Brathwaite called tidalectics;
of tossings, across and between seas, of people, things, processes and
affects' (124).

The islands of *The Hungry Tide* are archipelagic in the sense conceptualized by DeLoughrey and Stratford et al. They are shaped by a
number of different flows and currents, some of them material, others
metaphorical. They come to be at the confluence of silt, language, and
people. Early in the novel, Nirmal comments on the Sundarbans
archipelago as a site of migration flows: 'Everyone who has ever taken
the eastern route into the Gangetic heartland has had to pass through

it—the Arakanese, the Khmer, the Javanese, the Dutch, the Malays, the Chinese, the Portuguese, the English' (43). This pattern of migration to and from the islands, and from island to island, is repeated by the characters of the novel. It is perhaps most evidently embodied by Kusum, who moves to Lusibari from a nearby island named Satjelia after the death of her father, goes to the mainland in search of her mother, and returns to the Sundarbans as a refugee settling on Morichjhãpi. As Mukherjee argues, '[m]obility, migrancy, uprootedness permeate the world of the novel' (2006, 150).[29] Sailing from island to island, Piya and later also Kanai enact this flow at a smaller scale, first as detached observers, later as a more integral part of the archipelagic landscape, sometimes immersed in it quite literally.

The concept of geopoetics is useful for thinking about the archipelago of *The Hungry Tide* because the novel's metaphors for the cultural sphere are developed out of the landscape itself, and this landscape already includes the human element. It would not be entirely accurate to say that the geomorphological sphere is metaphorically related to the cultural and textual sphere. It is, but the latter is also a material part of the former (cf. Rath and Malshe 2010, 31–2). A potent image for the interpenetration of geography and textuality is offered at the end of the novel, when Kanai loses Nirmal's notebook as he steps onto Lusibari at the end of the storm:

> And then it was as if the wind had been waiting for this one unguarded moment: it spun him around and knocked him sideways into the water. He thrust his hands into the mud and came up spluttering. He scrambled to his feet just in time to see the notebook bobbing in the current some thirty feet away. It stayed on the surface for a couple of minutes before sinking out of sight.
>
> (Ghosh 2004b, 310)

If the landscape entered Nirmal's notebook, the latter now enters the landscape again. As Kanai arrives on one island of the archipelago, it drifts on to the next, before its pages dissolve in the water and mingle with the silt, maybe to form parts of new islands one day. Like the brick

---

[29] At the same time, Mukherjee argues that the different characters' conditions of migrancy differ significantly, contrasting the cosmopolitanism of Piya and Kanai with the forced migration of the dispossessed (2006, 157).

fragments Piya spots on Garjontola, it is woven into the very fabric of the archipelago. The mixed geography of the novel, where 'real' islands like Morichjhãpi exist side by side with fictional ones like Garjontola and Lusibari, also includes the textual in the geographical. Together they form an archipelagic landscape made up of real and imagined islands, of soil and words, of mangroves and people. The loss of the notebook gives Kanai responsibility and a place in this landscape: in the end, we learn that he will return to the Sundarbans to 'write the story of Nirmal's notebook' (329) and participate in the ongoing story of the islands. The archipelago, already inhabited by language, will in turn inhabit language one more time. Human history is precarious in *The Hungry Tide*, but the novel's vision of a world of ever-changing islands, or of islands without a world, also gives those islands and their inhabitants a certain immediacy and presence, and allows for the creation of ever new forms. Humans may lose ground in these shifting islands. But in this fragility, they also gain a certain dignity; not the grand pathos of making a world, but the quiet dignity of making and inhabiting many small worlds. With this, we return to Derrida's take on islands discussed at the beginning of Chapter 1, and mentioned again at the beginning of this chapter: 'There is no world, there are only islands' (2011, 9).

Conclusion: Archipelagic Struggle, Difference, and Discontinuity

We have come full circle. We began with an examination of the importance of islands for Darwin and Wallace. Their thinking, too, is archipelagic: they are not interested in islands in isolation, but their groundbreaking insights depend on a relational perspective, on thinking about islands in terms of their links to and differences from both the mainland and other islands. They mobilize the imaginative potential of the geology and biogeography of islands to challenge received notions of the stability and fixity of species and of geographical space, and decentre the human position by imagining deep geological time. The central insight of *Island Life* is that the adaptations and transformations of living forms can only be understood in relation to horizontal dispersal on the surface of the earth, in turn bound up with the fluidity of geological structures. The assumption of the vertical movements of landforms prompts Wallace to assert a universal island condition. While he ultimately reinscribes stability by postulating an overall constancy of form, his view of a planetary archipelago prepares the ground for a relational view of space. Darwin, on the whole, is more radical. His islands are sites of geological pressures and ecological struggles, and there is little room for unifying principles. I started this chapter with an emphasis on the translatability of concepts from scientific to literary discourses. As the analysis of the writings of Darwin and Wallace has shown, an aesthetic engagement with islands is part of their projects. The literariness of their texts is more than a mere byproduct; their challenges to received ways of thinking about space and the position of human and non-human life within it are brought about by a poetic response to the materiality of islands.

Beer emphasizes that the translatability of concepts and ideas is tied to both their resilience and their transformation. *The Island of Doctor Moreau* and 'Aepyornis Island' transform the island poetics developed in Darwin's and Wallace's writings by turning the island into a dystopian site. While their own writings are not marked by anxiety, Wells's narratives negotiate the anxieties generated by their thinking. They centre around single islands that are beleaguered territories haunted by the spectre of (human) extinction. In both texts, the geological materiality of the island resonates with the narrative played out on it, but is also important in its own right, interfering with the latter's evolutionary drama and putting it into perspective. In their physicality, both islands offer alternative forms of inhabiting the island and the planet that can be considered geopoetic, yet they remain a faint presence. In *Moreau*, this potential resides in the engagement with the volcanic forces shaping the island; in 'Aepyornis Island', in the imaginative fossilization of all living forms, including the coral skeletons forming the island itself.

Reading Wells's islands in this way does not mean asserting a unified vision of geological continuity and ecological harmony, a danger that sometimes characterized the revisionist island poetics discussed in Chapter 3. On the contrary: it means facing the inevitability of struggle and difference. With a century of biogeographical thinking about islands in between, *The Hungry Tide* offers what *Moreau* and

'Aepyornis Island' suppress. It moves beyond the island as an isolated singularity, revisiting and expanding the relational archipelagic universe explored by Darwin and Wallace. The human element intersects with other living forms and the physical geography to form a landscape shaped by conflicts. Both material and poetic, the islands of the novel take global pressures and environmental concerns seriously while resisting utopian solutions and angst-ridden visions of decline and extinction. They mobilize the poetic as an alternative to the political— or rather, as a political stance in itself. It is appropriate, perhaps, that the islands discussed in this last chapter are always in danger of disappearing. If the first chapter began with hopeful arrivals, we end with the dissolution of islands. This should not be a source of despair. It points to the possibility of new beginnings.

Epilogue

The Life on/of Islands

In the frame narrative of Michael Powell's 1937 film *The Edge of the World*, we see a tourist yacht approaching the island of Hirta in the Outer Hebrides.[1] At least, this is the diegetic island of the film: the boat is actually approaching the island of Foula in the Shetlands. Powell did not receive permission to film on Hirta, also known as St Kilda, whose tiny population had asked to be removed to the Scottish mainland in 1930. *The Edge of the World* is a fictionalized account of their story. Foula, on the other hand, was (and is) inhabited by humans, and its population participated in the film. The tourists approaching the island after the evacuation are accompanied by Andrew Gray, one of its former inhabitants and a central character in the film. The tourists' gazes alternate between the island and its representations as they attempt to match the former with the latter. While the man looks at the island on a large chart (Figure E.1), the woman reads about it in a guidebook. But the island and its representations do not match: the tourists are surprised to learn that the island is deserted although their guidebook states that it is inhabited. Andrew reacts by saying: 'Your

[1] I am grateful to Daniel Graziadei, Britta Hartmann, and Michel Bodmer for an inspiring discussion of the film at the Zurich Filmpodium on 5 August 2014.

The Aesthetics of Island Space: Perception, Ideology, Geopoetics. Johannes Riquet, Oxford University Press (2019). © Johannes Riquet.
DOI: 10.1093/oso/9780198832409.001.0001

FIGURE E.1   Still from *The Edge of the World* (Michael Powell, UK 1937)

book was right when it was published, Mr Graham. But you were wrong when you said that nothing changes on these islands.' Ironically, the evacuation represents a form of life and figures the island as a dynamic environment rather than a static, immutable space as suggested by the guidebook and the map.

But in a different sense, the map also matches the island, although in a way certainly not intended by the mapmakers. One of its most striking features are the contour lines, which cut across the border of land and sea. A second set of lines form concentric circles around the island, possibly suggesting the waves. Taken together, all these lines portray the island as a field of force. After the map, we see the steep cliffs on the shore (Figure E.2), whose layered sandstone is also traversed by countless lines, pointing to the forces that shaped the island. Read in conjunction, the lines on paper and stone belie the assertion of the island as a lifeless space, and establish it as a site of multiple energies. The map and the island are thus in a relation of productive friction, both opposed to and resonating with each other. In fact, the

FIGURE E.2   Still from *The Edge of the World* (Michael Powell, UK 1937)

map shows the outline of the island of Foula, but designates it as Hirta while otherwise retaining the toponyms of the former island; this referential hybridity underscores the ambivalences in the map's negotiation of the island's geography.

The frame narrative of *The Edge of the World* figures the island in various ways. In fact, the frame itself is framed in the opening titles: 'When the Roman Fleet first sailed round Britain they saw from the Orkneys a distant island, like a blue haze across a hundred miles of sea. They called it—"ULTIMA THULE"'. This reference to the fabled last island at the edge of the world adds a mythical extradiegetic frame to the narrative frame discussed above. It also ties the island to the discourse of exploration that framed the four chapters of this book. Referred to as an uncertain object of perception, a 'blue haze', it is situated at the outer edge of European knowledge and understanding. The film thus begins with multiple approaches to the island in various media and registers.

The opening minutes of *The Edge of the World* encapsulate what *The Aesthetics of Island Space* has been about. I have traced a range of approaches to islands that are in productive friction both with each other and with the islands themselves. I believe we have much to gain from such a multilayered and multimedial engagement with islands: the islands examined in this book attain their life in the oscillations between their various figurations, between geography and text, and between matter and idea. Approaching an island does not necessarily mean getting closer to it: confronted with various conflicting versions of the island, the tourists landing on Hirta in *The Edge of the World* find themselves more and more distanced from it despite their increasing geographical proximity. But grappling with distance is also a form of engagement, and, as (post-)phenomenological approaches suggest, may be more productive than one which seeks complete understanding of or fusion with a given space. The island lives in its multiple figurations, in the interplay of its various textual layers, which parallel the stratigraphic layers of its material existence.

This difficulty of matching the experience of islands with various forms of actual and conceptual maps has been a central interest of this book. In different ways, each of its chapters has been concerned with the productive friction between the islands as encountered and experienced by narrators, protagonists, readers, and viewers, and the expectations brought to them. Islands have fascinated mapmakers and cartographers since early modernity, and played an equally important role in imaginative cartographies. These cartographies have turned islands into figures for comprehensible, abstract, and ideal spatialities, from early modern texts and maps to present-day island fantasies. Yet my discussions of island texts have privileged a different, no less important story. If the aesthetics of islands in these texts is tied to a series of ruptures in the modern experience of space, it is linked to a different form of imaginative cartographies as well: the perceptual uncertainties and the breakdown of spatial orders in the aesthetic experience of islands call for a remapping of space that is expansive rather than reductive. In this view, the perceptual challenges experienced by narrators, protagonists, readers, and viewers stimulate an active engagement with the physical environment and the space of the planet. As in *The Edge of the World*, the mismatch between island

and (real or conceptual) map generates new, unexpected resonances between the textual and the material.

These considerations imply a more inclusive understanding of geopoetics according to which geography guides and shapes both poetic practice and aesthetic experience. Rather than subscribing to geographical determinism, such a perspective allows for bidirectional exchanges between the material world, poetic production, and phenomenal experience—indeed, ecocritical and geocritical positions consider texts as part of the material world, and phenomenology implies an embodied view of human perception and understanding. Paying more attention to the material world than (post-)structuralist approaches does not mean sidestepping textuality and ideological appropriations of space. Rather, it means that these should not be considered independently of their material bases. There is perhaps no other landform that has been assigned as many ideologically charged meanings in Western modernity as the island, but my discussions of poetic and aesthetic responses to islands have shown an equally important story of challenged perceptions and disrupted conceptions in the attempt to map and remap the world. Combining (post-)phenomenology with geopoetic and geocritical perspectives can alert us to the aesthetic activity that emerges from these perceptual struggles on the part of writers, protagonists, and narrators on the one hand, and readers and viewers on the other.

The islands examined in this book are thus not just alive through their complex ecosystems and their geographical and textual mobility. They are also alive in the minds of their narrators and protagonists, as well as those of their readers and viewers; finally, they are alive in a critical dialogue that reshapes and remaps them. This returns us to *The Edge of the World* and its multiple geological and textual layers. As stated in the introduction, the life of islands is linked to the life on islands. Bearing in mind Beer's contention that '[t]he decision to call an island uninhabited is always a cultural choice' (2003, 40), we should challenge the island's asserted function as a site of death in *The Edge of the World*:

FIRST TOURIST (WOMAN): Hirta's the old name of the island, isn't it?
SECOND TOURIST (MAN): Do you know what it means, Andrew?
ANDREW: It means—death.

Immediately after the word 'death', we see a bird of prey on the island, followed by a shot of a sheep and a lamb. After a shot-reverse exchange between the animals, we see the bird fly off to pursue the lamb, evoking Nietzsche's parable of the lamb and the bird of prey.[2] The film cross-cuts between the bird and the lamb, until we see the tourists ascending the grassy slopes. The man raises his rifle, fires a shot, says 'got him', and the bird falls to the ground. From the moment the tourists step ashore, then, they participate in the balance of life on the island, however one evaluates the man's action: does he save the lamb from the bird? Does he shoot the bird for mere pleasure? Does he reclaim the island for humans after Andrew has told them that its original owners, the birds, have taken possession of it again? The island is not a harmonious and transparent space—neither before nor after the tourists' arrival. But in its various conflicts and struggles, it is thoroughly alive, and life on the island necessarily includes death.

At the end of the film, we briefly return to the frame as we see the tombstone of an islander who fell down the cliffs at the end of the main narrative. The tombstone dissolves into an extreme long shot of the island. We see the tourists and Andrew in the bottom left-hand corner, on the edge of the cliffs. Tiny and barely recognizable, they almost merge with the landscape. As the camera pans right, they disappear from view, and the hard edge of the cliffs makes way for a soft edge as the film ends with a view of the island blending into the sea. This last shot is similar to the final shot of *Letters from Iwo Jima* (2006), with which I began: at the end of both films, we are left with the island. But in *The Edge of the World*, the humans are part of the island, however insignificant they may appear, and however temporary their visit may be. The frame flows into the main narrative: where the latter emptied the island of its human population, the former offers a tentative and inconclusive vision of renewed inhabitation. Barely noticeable and merely hinted at, this vision is only available to an attentive and active viewer. It emerges on the edge of the island and at the limits of perception; it requires an expansive understanding of the island and a flexible mind.

* * *

[2] 'There is nothing strange about the fact that lambs bear a grudge towards large birds of prey: but that is no reason to blame the large birds of prey for carrying off the little lambs' (Nietzsche 2006, 25–6).

All islands are framed. They are framed in spatial terms, and—in literature and film—they are often framed in narrative terms.[3] But the islands interact with their frames. For Godfrey Baldacchino, '[i]sland studies is very much about the implications of permeable borders' (2007, 5). The islands examined in this study are framed in multiple ways, but they only become alive and dynamic if their frames are considered as part of their space. It is fitting, therefore, that *The Aesthetics of Island Space* ends with a discussion of a narrative frame that is also an epilogue, for this epilogue about the last island at the edge of the world is not a conclusion. It is a frame, hopefully in productive friction with the rest of the book. Rather than freeze the islands examined in it by offering a set of conclusive comments, I wish to keep them alive.

---

[3] Among countless examples, one could list the frames in *The Hurricane* (Chapter 2), *The Island of Doctor Moreau* and 'Aepyornis Island' (Chapter 4), and Bernardin de Saint-Pierre's *Paul et Virginie* (1788).

REFERENCES

Abbott, Edwin A. 2006. *Flatland*. Oxford: Oxford University Press.

Adamic, Louis. 1940. *Plymouth Rock and Ellis Island*. New York: Common Council for American Unity.

Adams, Samuel, 1999. 'American Independence'. In *The World's Great Speeches*, edited by Lewis Copeland et al., fourth enlarged edition, pp. 234–5. New York: Dover.

'Airplanes in South Seas'. 1937. *The New York Times*, 21 March.

'aesthesis | esthesis, n.' June 2018. *OED Online*. Oxford University Press. <www.oed.com/view/Entry/3234>.

'aesthetics, n.' June 2018. *OED Online*. Oxford University Press. <www.oed.com/view/Entry/293508>.

Anand, Divya. 2008. 'Words on Water: Nature and Agency in Amitav Ghosh's *The Hungry Tide*'. *Concentric: Literary and Cultural Studies* 34 (1): pp. 21–44.

André, Bénédicte. 2016. *Îléité: Perspectives sur le vécu insulaire*. Paris: Pétra.

Appelbaum, Robert. 2005. 'Hunger in Early Virginia: Indians and English Facing Off over Excess, Want, and Need'. In *Envisioning an English Empire: Jamestown and the Making of the North Atlantic World*, edited by Robert Appelbaum and John Wood Sweet, pp. 195–216. Philadelphia: University of Pennsylvania Press.

Arapoglou Eleftheria, Mónika Fodor, and Jopi Nyman. 2014. *Mobile Narratives: Travel, Migration, and Transculturation*. New York: Routledge.

Armstrong, Patrick H. 2006. *Darwin's Other Islands*. London: Continuum.

Bachelard, Gaston. 1964 [1958]. *The Poetics of Space*. Translated by Maria Jolas. New York: Penguin.

Bakhtin, Mikhail M. 1981 [1975]. 'Forms of Time and of the Chronotope in the Novel'. In *The Dialogic Imagination*, translated by Caryl Emerson and Michael Holquist, pp. 84–258. Austin: University of Texas Press.

Balasopoulos, Antonis. 2008. 'Nesologies: Island Form and Postcolonial Geopoetics'. *Postcolonial Studies* 11 (1): pp. 9–26.

Baldacchino, Godfrey. 2006. 'Islands, Island Studies, Island Studies Journal'. *Island Studies Journal* 1 (1): pp. 3–18.

Baldacchino, Godfrey (ed.). 2007a. *Bridging Islands: The Impact of 'Fixed Links'*. Charlottetown: Acorn Press.

Baldacchino, Godfrey. 2007b. 'Introducing a World of Islands'. In *A World of Islands: An Island Studies Reader*, edited by Godfrey Baldacchino, pp. 1–29. Charlottetown: Institute of Island Studies and Agenda Academic.

Baldacchino, Godfrey (ed.). 2007c. *A World of Islands: An Island Studies Reader*. Charlottetown: Institute of Island Studies and Agenda Academic.

Baldacchino, Godfrey. 2008. 'Studying Islands: On Whose Terms? Some Epistemological and Methodological Challenges to the Pursuit of Island Studies'. *Island Studies Journal* 3 (1): pp. 37–56.

Ballantyne, R. M. 1995 [1858]. *The Coral Island*. London: Penguin.

Ballard, J. G. 1973. *Concrete Island*. London: Harper Perennial.

Balme, Christopher B. 2005. 'Selling the Bird: Richard Walton Tully's *The Bird of Paradise* and the Dynamics of Theatrical Commodification'. *Theatre Journal* 57 (1): pp. 1–20.

Bancroft, Hubert Howe. 1886. *The Works of Hubert Howe Bancroft, Volume XX: History of California, Vol. III: 1825–1840*. San Francisco: A. L. Bancroft.

Banks, Joseph. 2006 [1768–1771]. *The Endeavour Journal of Sir Joseph Banks*. Teddington: The Echo Library.

Barker, Francis and Peter Hulme. 2000. 'Nymphs and Reapers Heavily Vanish: The Discursive Contexts of *The Tempest*'. In *The Tempest: A Case Study in Critical Controversy*, edited by Gerald Graff and James Phelan, pp. 205–29. Boston: Bedford/St. Martin's.

Barlowe, Arthur. 1955. *Arthur Barlowe's Discourse of the First Voyage. 1584–1585*. In *The Roanoke Voyages: 1584–1590*, volume one, edited by David Beers Quinn, pp. 91–116. London: The Hakluyt Society.

Barman, Jean and Bruce McIntyre Watson. 2006. *Leaving Paradise: Indigenous Hawaiians in the Pacific Northwest, 1787–1898*. Honolulu: University of Hawai'i Press.

Barque sortant du port. 1895. Directed by Louis Lumière. France: Lumière.

Barrie, J. M. 1955 [1902]. *The Admirable Crichton. In Peter Pan and Other Plays*. New York: Oxford University Press.

Barrie, J. M. 1995 [1904]. *Peter Pan. In Peter Pan and Other Plays*. New York: Oxford University Press.

Barron, W. R. J. 2002. *The Voyage of Saint Brendan: Representative Versions of the Legend in English Translation*. Exeter: Exeter University Press.

Barsam, Richard M. 1988. *The Vision of Robert Flaherty: The Artist as Myth and Filmmaker*. Bloomington: Indiana University Press.

Barsam, Richard M. 1992. *Nonfiction Film: A Critical History*. Revised and expanded edition. Bloomington: Indiana University Press.

Barthes, Roland. 1981. *Camera Lucida: Reflections on Photography*. Translated by Richard Howard. New York: Hill and Wang.

Bate, Jonathan. 2000. *The Song of the Earth*. Basingstoke: Picador.

Bauer, Ralph. 2003. *The Cultural Geography of Colonial American Literatures: Empire, Travel, Modernity*. Cambridge: Cambridge University Press.

Bave, Emelia L. 1976. *San Juan Saga*. Revised and enlarged third edition. Friday Harbor: self-published.

Bazin, André. 2005. 'Cinema and Exploration'. In *What is Cinema?*, volume one, translated by Hugh Gray. Berkeley and Los Angeles: University of California Press.

Beechey, F. W. 1831. *Narrative of a Voyage to the Pacific and Beering's Strait*. London: Henry Colburn and Richard Bentley.

Beer, Gillian. 1985. *Darwin's Plots: Evolutionary Narrative in Darwin, George Eliot and Nineteenth-Century Fiction*. London: Ark.

Beer, Gillian. 1989. 'Discourses of the Island'. In *Literature and Science as Modes of Expression*, edited by Frederick Amrine, pp. 1–27. Dordrecht: Kluwer.

Beer, Gillian. 1990. 'The Island and the Aeroplane: The Case of Virginia Woolf'. In *Nation and Narration*, edited by Homi K. Bhabha, pp. 265–90. London: Routledge.

Beer, Gillian. 2003. 'Island Bounds'. In *Islands in History and Representation*, edited by Rod Edmond and Vanessa Smith, pp. 32–42. London: Routledge.

Bell, James B. and Richard I. Abrams. 1984. *In Search of Liberty: The Story of the Statue of Liberty and Ellis Island*. New York: Doubleday & Company.

Benítez-Rojo, Antonio. 1996. *The Repeating Island: The Caribbean and the Postmodern Perspective*. Durham: Duke University Press.

Berman, John S. 2003. *Ellis Island*. New York: Barnes & Noble.

Beveridge, Albert J. 2008. 'The Philippine Question'. In *Voices of the American Past: Documents in U.S. History*, volume two, edited by Raymond M. Hyser and J. Chris Arndt, fourth edition, pp. 371–4. Boston: Thomson.

The Bible. 2006. Edited by David Norton. London: Penguin.

Birchard, Robert S. 2004. *Cecil B. DeMille's Hollywood*. Lexington: The University Press of Kentucky.

Bird of Paradise. 1932. Directed by King Vidor. USA: RKO Radio Pictures.

Birkett, Dea. 1997. *Serpent in Paradise*. New York: Anchor Books.

Birkett, Dea. 2004. '"You don't know what lonely is"'. In *The Telegraph*, 1 October. <www.telegraph.co.uk/news/1473039/You-dont-know-what-lonely-is.html>.

Bhabha, Homi. 1994. *The Location of Culture*. Routledge: Abingdon.

Blanchet, Muriel Wylie. 2011 [1961]. *The Curve of Time*. Fiftieth anniversary edition. Vancouver: Whitecap Books.

Bongie, Chris. 1998. *Islands and Exiles*. Stanford: Stanford University Press.

Bougainville, Louis Antoine de. 2002. *The Pacific Journal of Louis-Antoine de Bougainville, 1767–1768*. London: The Hakluyt Society.

Bouvet, Rachel. 2015. *Vers une approche géopoétique: Lectures de Kenneth White, Victor Segalen, J.-M. G. Le Clézio*. Québec: Presses de l'Université du Québec.

Bouvet, Rachel and Myriam Marcil-Bergeron. 2013. 'Pour une approche géopoétique du récit de voyage'. *Arborescences* 3: pp. 4–23.

Bowen, Roger. 1976. 'Science, Myth, and Fiction in H. G. Well's *Island of Dr. Moreau*'. *Studies in the Novel* 8 (3): pp. 318–35.

Brandon, M. T., D. S. Cowan, and J. A. Vance. 1988. *The Late Cretaceous San Juan Thrust System, San Juan Islands, Washington*. Geological Society of America, Special Paper 221.

Braudel, Fernand. 1995 [1949]. *The Mediterranean and the Mediterranean World in the Age of Philip II*. Volume one. Berkeley: University of California Press.

Brawley, Jean and Chris Dixon. 2012. *Hollywood's South Seas and the Pacific War: Searching for Dorothy Lamour*. New York: Palgrave.

Bright, Verne. 1953. '*The Light on the Island*, by Helene Glidden'. In *Oregon Historical Quarterly* 54 (4): pp. 327–8.

Brodie, Walter. 1851. *Pitcairn's Island, and the Islanders*. London: Whittaker & Co.

Brooks, Peter. 2000. *Reading for the Plot: Design and Intention in Narrative*. Cambridge, MA: Harvard University Press.

Brown, Charles S. and Ted Toadvine. 2003. *Eco-Phenomenology: Back to the Earth Itself*. Albany: State University of New York Press.

Brown, Paul. 2000. '"This Thing of Darkness I Acknowledge Mine": *The Tempest* and the Discourse of Colonialism'. In *The Tempest: A Case Study in Critical Controversy*, edited by Gerald Graff and James Phelan, pp. 205–29. Boston: Bedford/St Martin's.

Brownstone, David M. et al. 1979. *Island of Hope, Island of Tears: The Story of Those Who Entered the New World through Ellis Island—in Their Own Words*. New York: Sterling.

Bruckner, Lynne and Dan Brayton. 2011. *Ecocritical Shakespeare*. Farnham: Ashgate.

Bryan, William Jennings. 1899. *Republic or Empire? The Philippine Question*. Chicago: The Independence Company.

Buckland, Adelene. 2013. *Novel Science: Fiction and the Invention of Nineteenth-Century Geology*. Chicago: University of Chicago Press.

Buckton, Oliver S. 2007. *Cruising with Robert Louis Stevenson: Travel, Narrative, and the Colonial Body*. Athens: Ohio University Press.

Buell, Lawrence. 1995. *The Environmental Imagination*. Cambridge, MA: Harvard University Press.

Burn, June. 1983 [1946]. *100 Days in the San Juans*. Friday Harbor: Long House.

Bustard, Bruce I. 2012. *Attachments: Faces and Stories from America's Gates*. London: Giles.

Campbell, Archibald. 1868. *The Northwest Boundary. Discussion of the Water Boundary Question: Geographical Memoir of the Islands in Dispute: and History of the Military Occupation of San Juan Island: Accompanied by Map and Cross-Sections of Channels*. Washington: Government Printing Office.

Carolan, Trevor. 2010. 'Introduction'. In *Making Waves: Reading B.C. and Pacific Northwest Literature*. Abbotsford: UFV Press/Anvil Press.

Carson, Rachel. 1951. *The Sea Around Us*. Oxford: Oxford University Press.

Casey, Edward S. 1997. *The Fate of Place: A Philosophical History*. Berkeley: University of California Press.

Casey, Edward S. 2002. *Representing Place: Landscape Painting and Maps*. Minneapolis: University of Minnesota Press.

Cassano, Graham. 2010. '"The Last of the World's Afflicted Race of Humans Who Believe in Freedom": Race, Colonial Whiteness and Imperialism in John Ford and Dudley Nichols's *The Hurricane* (1937)'. *Journal of American Studies* 44: pp. 117–36.

Cast Away. 2000. Directed by Robert Zemeckis. USA: Twentieth Century Fox and DreamWorks.

Castles, Stephen and Mark J. Miller. 2009. *The Age of Migration: International Population Movements in the Modern World*. Fourth edition. Basingstoke: Palgrave.

Cauchi, Maurice N. 2002. *Worlds Apart: Migration in Modern English Literature*. Victoria: Europe–Australia Institute.

Certeau, Michel de. 1984. *The Practice of Everyday Life*. Translated by Steven Rendall. Berkeley: University of California Press.

Chalmers, William D. 2011. *On the Origin of the Species Homo Touristicus: The Evolution of Travel from Greek Spas to Space Tourism*. Bloomington: iUniverse.

Chamberlin, J. Edward. 2013. *Island: How Islands Transform the World*. Toronto: Cormorant Books.

Chang, Kornel S. 2012. *Pacific Connections: The Making of the U.S.-Canadian Borderlands*. Berkeley: University of California Press.

Cheyfitz, Eric. 1997. *The Poetics of Imperialism: Translation and Colonization from The Tempest to Tarzan*. Expanded edition. Philadelphia: University of Pennsylvania Press.

Childs, Elizabeth C. 2013. *Vanishing Paradise: Art and Exoticism in Colonial Tahiti*. Berkeley: University of California Press.

Childs, Peter. 2008. *Modernism*. Second edition. Abingdon: Routledge.

Christensen, Timothy. 2004. 'The "Bestial Mark" of Race in *The Island of Dr. Moreau*'. *Criticism* 46 (4): pp. 575–94.

Christian, Jacqui. 2012. 'Pitcairn Islands: Back to the Future', 21 August. <www.youtube.com/watch?v=VKrol9oX530>.

Christie, Agatha. 1939. *And Then There Were None*. London: Harper.

Clark, Timothy. 2014. 'Phenomenology'. In *The Oxford Handbook of Ecocriticism*, edited by Greg Garrard, pp. 276–90. Oxford: Oxford University Press.

Cohen, Michael P. 2004. 'Blues in the Green: Ecocriticism under Critique'. *Environmental History* 9 (1): pp. 9–36.

Coleridge, Samuel T. 2001 [1798]. 'The Rime of the Ancient Mariner'. In *The Norton Anthology of English Literature, volume two*, edited by M. H. Abrams et al., seventh edition, pp. 1580–95. New York: Norton.

Columbus, Christopher. 1870 [1493]. 'A Letter sent by Columbus to [Luis de Santagel] Chancellor of the Exchequer [of Aragon], respecting the Islands found in the Indies, enclosing another for their Highnesses'. In *Select Letters of Christopher Columbus*, translated and edited by R. H. Major, second edition, pp. 1–18. London: The Hakluyt Society.

Conley, Tom. 1996. *The Self-Made Map: Cartographic Writing in Early Modern France*. Minneapolis: University of Minnesota Press.

Connor, Steven. 2008. 'Introduction'. In *The Five Senses: A Philosophy of Mingled Bodies*, by Michel Serres, pp. 1–16. London: Continuum.

Conover, David. 2003 [1967]. *Once Upon an Island*. Second edition. Woodinville: San Juan Publishing.

Conrich, Ian, Kseniia Kalugina, Laura Sedgwick, and Roy Smith (eds.). 2018. Special issue: *Islands and Film. Post Script: Essays in Film and the Humanities* 37 (2 & 3).

Cook, James. 1955. *The Voyage of the Endeavour, 1768–1771*. Edited by J. C. Beaglehole. Cambridge: Cambridge University Press.

Corsi, Edward. 1937. *In the Shadow of Liberty: The Chronicle of Ellis Island*. New York: The Macmillan Company.

Cosgrove, Denis. 2001. *Apollo's Eye: A Cartographic Genealogy of the Earth in the Western Imagination*. Baltimore: Johns Hopkins University Press.

Cowper, William. 2003 [1782]. 'Verses Supposed to Be Written by Alexander Selkirk, during His Solitary Abode in the Island of Juan Fernandez'. In *Selected Poems*, pp. 38–40. New York: Routledge.

'Cruising Among Tropic Isles'. 1930. *The New York Times*, 16 November.

Cullen, Jim. 2003. *The American Dream: A Short History of an Idea that Shaped a Nation*. New York: Oxford University Press.

Daniel, John. 2011. 'Writing West'. In *Open Spaces: Voices from the Northwest*, edited by Penny Harrison, pp. 3–5. Seattle: University of Washington Press.

Darwin, Charles. 1842. *The Structure and Distribution of Coral Reefs*. London: Smith, Elder and Co.

Darwin, Charles. 1844. *Geological Observations on the Volcanic Islands*. London: Smith, Elder and Co.

Darwin, Charles. 1963 [1832–6]. *Darwin's Ornithological Notes*. Edited by Nora Barlow. London: British Museum.

Darwin, Charles. 1988 [1831–6]. *Charles Darwin's Beagle Diary*. Edited by R. D. Keynes. Cambridge: Cambridge University Press.

Darwin, Charles. 2003 [1859]. *On the Origin of Species*. Peterborough: Broadview Press.

Davies, Lizzy. 2013. 'Why Lampedusa Remains an Island of Hope for Migrants'. In *The Guardian*, 16 October. <www.theguardian.com/world/2013/oct/16/lampedusa-island-of-hope>.

Dean Moore, Kathleen. 2004. *The Pine Island Paradox*. Minneapolis: Milkweed Editions.

de Bry, Theodor (after John White). 1590. 'The Arriual of the Englishemen in Virginia'. In *A Briefe and True Report*, by Thomas Hariot. Frankfurt: Iohn Wechel.

de Bry, Theodor. 1955. 'The Arriual of the Englishemen in Virginia'. In *The Roanoke Voyages: 1584–1590*, ed. David Beers Quinn, volume one, pp. 413–15. London: The Hakluyt Society.

Defoe, Daniel. 2001 [1719]. *Robinson Crusoe*. London: Penguin.

Delano, Amasa. 1817. *Narrative of Voyages and Travels*. Boston: E. G. House.

Deleuze, Gilles. 2004. 'Desert Islands'. In *'Desert Islands' and Other Texts, 1953–1974*, edited by David Lapoujade and translated by Michael Taormina. Los Angeles: Semiotext(e).

Deleuze, Gilles and Félix Guattari. 1987. *A Thousand Plateaus: Capitalism and Schizophrenia*. Translated by Brian Massumi. Minneapolis: University of Minnesota Press.

Deloria, Vine Jr. 2012. *Indians of the Pacific Northwest: From the Coming of the White Man to the Present Day*. Golden: Fulcrum.

DeLoughrey, Elizabeth. 2001. '"The litany of islands, the rosary of archipelagos": Pacific and Carribean Archipelagraphy'. *ARIEL: A Review of International English Literature* 32 (1): pp. 21–51.

DeLoughrey, Elizabeth. 2007. *Routes and Roots: Navigating Caribbean and Pacific Island Literatures*. Honolulu: University of Hawai'i Press.

DeLoughrey, Elizabeth and George B. Handley. 2011. *Postcolonial Ecologies: Literatures of the Environment*. Oxford: Oxford University Press.

De Lorme, Roland L. 1973. 'The United States Bureau of Customs and Smuggling on Puget Sound, 1851 to 1913'. *Prologue: The Journal of the National Archives* 5: pp. 77–99.

Dening, Greg. 1980. *Islands and Beaches*. Honolulu: The University Press of Hawaii.

Dening, Greg. 1992. *Mr Bligh's Bad Language: Passion, Power and Theatre on the Bounty*. Cambridge: Cambridge University Press.

Dening, Greg. 2003. 'Afterword'. In *Islands in History and Representation*, edited by Rod Edmond and Vanessa Smith, pp. 203–6. London: Routledge.

Dening, Greg. 2004. *Beach Crossings*. Philadelphia: University of Pennsylvania Press.

Depraetere, Christian and Arthur L. Dahl. 2007. 'Island Locations and Classifications'. In *A World of Islands: An Island Studies Reader*, edited by Godfrey Baldacchino, pp. 57–105. Charlottetown: Institute of Island Studies and Agenda Academic.

Derrida, Jacques. 1974. *Of Grammatology*. Translated by Gayatri Chatravorty Spivak. Baltimore: Johns Hopkins University Press.

Derrida, Jacques. 2011. *The Beast and the Sovereign*. Volume two. Edited by Michel Lisse et al. and translated by Geoffrey Bennington. Chicago: University of Chicago Press.

'desert, n.2'. June 2018. *OED Online*. Oxford University Press. <www.oed.com/view/Entry/50774>.

Desjardins, Mary. 2010. 'An Appetite for Living: Gloria Swanson, Coleen Moore, and Clara Bow'. In *Idols of Modernity: Movie Stars of the 1920s*, edited by Patrice Petro, pp. 109–36. New Brunswick: Rutgers University Press.

Donne, John. 2000 [1624]. 'Meditation 17'. In *The Norton Anthology of English Literature*, volume one, edited by M. H. Abrams et al., seventh edition. New York: Norton.

Dr. No. 1962. Directed by Terence Young. UK: Eon Productions.

Eagleton, Terry. 1990. *The Ideology of the Aesthetic*. Oxford: Blackwell.

Eddington, Arthur S. 1920. *Space Time and Gravitation: An Outline of the General Relativity Theory*. Cambridge: Cambridge University Press.

The Edge of the World. 1937. Directed by Michael Powell. UK: Joe Rock Productions.

Edmond, Rod. 2006. 'Writing Islands'. In *Literature and Place 1800–2000*, edited by Peter Brown and Michael Irwin, pp. 199–218. Bern: Peter Lang.

Edmond, Rod and Vanessa Smith. 2003. 'Editors' Introduction'. In *Islands in History and Representation*, pp. 1–18. London: Routledge.

Elmore, Helen Troy. 1973. *This Isle of Guemes*. Caldwell: Caxton.

Emerson, Ralph Waldo. 2003 [1836]. *Nature*. In *Nature and Selected Writings*, pp. 35–82. London: Penguin.

Eperjesi, John R. 2005. *The Imperialist Imaginary: Visions of Asia and the Pacific in American Culture*. Hanover: Dartmouth Press.

Erb, Cynthia. 2009. *Tracking King Kong: A Hollywood Icon in World Culture*. Second edition. Detroit: Wayne State University Press.

'Exotic Stamps from the South Sea Islands'. 1935. *Los Angeles Times*, 3 March.

Ewen, Elizabeth. 1980. 'City Lights: Immigrant Women and the Rise of the Movies'. *Signs: Journal of Women in Culture and Society* 5 (S3): pp. S45–S66.

Eyman, Scott. 1999. *Print the Legend: The Life and Times of John Ford*. New York: Simon & Schuster.

Eyman, Scott. 2010. *Empire of Dreams: The Epic Life of Cecil B. DeMille*. New York: Simon & Schuster.

Ficken, Robert E. 2003. *Unsettled Boundaries: Fraser Gold and the British–American Northwest*. Pullman: Washington State University Press.

Fiset, Louis and Gail M. Nomura. 2005. *Nikkei in the Pacific Northwest: Japanese Americans and Japanese Canadians in the Twentieth Century*. Seattle: University of Washington Press.

Fitzsimmons, Lorna. 2003. 'Contra Colonialism: Turning the Edge in Ford's *The Hurricane*'. *Literature/Film Quarterly* 31 (1): pp. 57–68.

Foley, Edna. 1919–20. 'On a Typical, Tropical Isle'. *Picture-Play*, pp. 43–4.

Foner, Nancy. 2000. *From Ellis Island to JFK: New York's Two Great Waves of Immigration*. New Haven: Yale University Press.

Foucault, Michel. 1986 [1967]. 'Of Other Spaces'. Translated by Jay Mis-
kowiec. *Diacritics* 16 (1): pp. 22–7.

Frenzel, Elisabeth. 1980. 'Inseldasein'. In *Motive der Weltliteratur*,
pp. 383–401. Stuttgart: Kröner.

Freud, Sigmund. 1918. *Reflections on War and Death*. Translated by
A. A. Brill and Alfred B. Kuttner. New York: Moffat Yard.

Freud, Sigmund. 2005 [1930]. *Civilization and Its Discontents*. Translated
by James Strachey. New York: London.

Frey, Charles. 1979. '*The Tempest* and the New World'. In *Shakespeare
Quarterly* 30: pp. 29–41.

'From South Seas'. 1920. *The New York Times*, 25 April.

Fuller, Mary C. 1995. *Voyages in Print: English Travel to America
1576–1624*. Cambridge: Cambridge University Press.

Fuson, Robert H. 1995. *Legendary Islands of the Ocean Sea*. Sarasota:
Pineapple Press.

Gabler, Neal. 1988. *An Empire of Their Own: How the Jews Invented
Hollywood*. New York: Crown.

Gallagher, Tag. 1986. *John Ford: The Man and His Films*. Berkeley: University of California Press.

Garland, Alex. 1996. *The Beach*. London: Penguin.

Garrard, Greg. 2011. 'Foreword'. In *Ecocritical Shakespeare*, edited by
Lynne Dickson Bruckner and Daniel Brayton, pp. xvii–xxiv. Farnham:
Ashgate.

Gastil, Raymond D. and Barnett Singer. 2010. *The Pacific Northwest:
Growth of a Regional Identity*. Jefferson: McFarland.

Gehlbach, Frederick R. 1981. *Mountain Islands and Desert Seas: A Natural
History of the U.S.–Mexican Borderlands*. College Station: Texas A&M
University Press.

Geiger, Jeffrey. 2007. *Facing the Pacific: Polynesia and the U.S. Imperial
Imagination*. Honolulu: University of Hawai'i Press.

Gersdorf, Catrin and Sylvia Mayer (eds.). 2006. *Nature in Literary and
Cultural Studies: Transatlantic Conversations on Ecocriticism*. Amsterdam: Rodopi.

Ghosh, Amitav. 2004a. 'Folly in the Sundarbans'. Website of Amitav
Ghosh. November 2004. <www.amitavghosh.com/essays/folly.html>.

Ghosh, Amitav. 2004b. *The Hungry Tide*. Boston and New York: Mariner
Book.

Gibbs, George. [1858]. Journal. Unpublished appendix to Campbell (see
above). Translated by Tom Schroeder (November 1999) from photocopy

of Mike Vouri, National Park Service, San Juan Island, October 1999, of original located in National Archives, College Park, MD: Record Group (RG) 76, Entry (E)–1978, Box 3.

Gillis, John R. 2003. 'Taking History Offshore: Atlantic Islands in European Minds, 1400–1800'. In *Islands in History and Representation*, edited by Rod Edmond and Vanessa Smith, pp. 19–31. London: Routledge.

Gillis, John R. 2004. *Islands of the Mind: How the Human Imagination Created the Atlantic World*. New York: Palgrave.

Glendening, John. 2007. *The Evolutionary Imagination in Late-Victorian Novels: An Entangled Bank*. Aldershot: Ashgate.

Glidden, Helen. 2001 [1951]. *The Light on the Island*. Second edition. Woodinville: San Juan Publishing.

Glissant, Édouard. 2007 [1990]. *Poetics of Relation*. Translated by Betsy Wing. Ann Arbor: University of Michigan Press.

Glotfelty, Cheryll and Harold Fromm (eds.). 1996. *The Ecocriticism Reader: Landmarks in Literary Ecology*. Athens, GA: University of Georgia Press.

Go, Julian. 2011. *Patterns of Empire: The British and American Empires, 1688 to the Present*. New York: Cambridge University Press.

Goldie, Matthew Boyd. 2011. 'Island Theory: The Antipodes'. In *Islanded Identities: Constructions of Postcolonial Cultural Insularity*, edited by Maeve McCusker and Anthony Soares, pp. 1–40. Amsterdam: Rodopi.

Golding, William. 1954. *The Lord of the Flies*. New York: Penguin.

Graves, Robert. 1925. *Poetic Unreason: And Other Studies*. New York: Biblio and Tannen.

Graziadei, Daniel. 2011. 'Geopoetics of the Island'. In *Geopoetiche: Studi di geografia e letteratura*, edited by Federico Italiano and Marco Mastronunzio, pp. 163–81. Milano: Unicopli.

Graziadei, Daniel. 2017. *Insel(n) im Archipel: Zur Verwendung einer Raumfigur in den zeitgenössischen anglo-, franko- und hispanophonen Literaturen der Karibik*. München: Fink.

Greenblatt, Stephen. 1991. *Marvelous Possessions: The Wonder of the New World*. Chicago: University of Chicago Press.

Greenblatt, Stephen. 1988. *Shakespearean Negotiations: The Circulation of Social Energy in Renaissance England*. Berkeley: University of California Press.

Gundle, Stephen. 2008. *Glamour: A History*. New York: Oxford University Press.

Günzel, Stephan. 2011. *Geophilosophie: Nietzsches philosophische Geographie*. Berlin: Akademie Verlag.

Guterson, David. 1994. *Snow Falling on Cedars*. New York: Vintage.

Hakluyt, Richard. 1955. 'Dedication by Richard Hakluyt to Raleigh'. 10/20 February 1587. In *The Roanoke Voyages: 1584–1590, volume two*, edited by David Beers Quinn, pp. 513–15. London: The Hakluyt Society.

Hanquart-Turner, Evelyne. 2011. 'The Search for Paradise: Amitav Ghosh's *The Hungry Tide*'. In *Projections of Paradise: Ideal Elsewheres in Post-colonial Migrant Literature*, edited by Helga Ramsey-Kurtz and Geetha Ganapathy-Doré, pp. 73–81 Amsterdam: Rodopi.

Harding, Georgina. 2007. *The Solitude of Thomas Cave*. London: Bloomsbury.

Hariot, Thomas. 1955. *A Briefe and True Report*. 1588. In *The Roanoke Voyages: 1584–1590*, volume one, edited by David Beers Quinn, pp. 317–87. London: The Hakluyt Society.

Harley, J. B. 1988. 'Maps, Knowledge, and Power'. In *The Iconography of Landscape*, edited by Denis Cosgrove and Stephen Daniels, pp. 277–312. New York: Cambridge University Press.

Harris, Stephen L. 2011. 'Volcanoes and Superquakes: Living with Geologic Hazards in the Pacific Northwest'. In *Open Spaces: Voices from the Northwest*, edited by Penny Harrison, pp. 108–21. Seattle: University of Washington Press.

Harrison, Penny. 2011. 'Groundtruthing: An Introduction'. In *Open Spaces: Voices from the Northwest*, edited by Penny Harrison, pp. xvii–xxiii. Seattle: University of Washington Press.

Harrison, Penny (ed.). 2011. *Open Spaces: Voices from the Northwest*. Seattle: University of Washington Press.

Hart, Jonathan. 2003. *Columbus, Shakespeare, and the Interpretation of the New World*. New York: Palgrave.

Hartmann, Britta. 2018. 'Two Centuries of Spatial "Island" Assumptions: *The Swiss Family Robinson* and the *Robinson Crusoe* Legacy'. In *Spatial Modernities: Geography, Narrative, Imaginaries*, edited by Johannes Riquet and Elizabeth Kollmann, pp. 103–18. London: Routledge.

Hauʻofa, Epeli. 1994 [1993]. 'Our Sea of Islands'. In *The Contemporary Pacific* 6 (1): pp. 147–61.

Hayes, Derek. 1999. *Historical Atlas of the Pacific Northwest: Exploration and Discovery*. Seattle: Sasquatch Books.

Healey, Barth. 1989. 'Stamps: Big Issues from a Small Volcanic Island in the Pacific'. In *The New York Times*, 5 February. <www.nytimes.com/1989/02/05/style/stamps-big-issues-from-a-small-volcanic-island-in-the-pacific.html>.

Heidegger, Martin. 1996 [1927]. *Being and Time*. Translated by Joan Stambaugh. Albany: State University of New York Press.

Hemmingway, Roy. 2011. 'Salmon and the Northwest'. In *Open Spaces: Voices from the Northwest*, edited by Penny Harrison, pp. 123–37. Seattle: University of Washington Press.

'He's No Native'. 1938. *In The Pittsburgh Press*, 30 January.

Higginson, Thomas Wentworth. 2006. *Tales of the Enchanted Islands of the Atlantic*. Middlesex: The Echo Library.

Hillstrom, Kevin. 2009. *The Dream of America: Immigration 1870–1920*. Detroit: Omnigraphics.

Hinton, Charles Howard. 1885. 'What is the Fourth Dimension?' In *Scientific Romances*, pp. 3–32. London: Swan Sonnenschein & Co.

Hinton, Charles Howard. 1912. *The Fourth Dimension*. Third edition. London: George Allen & Co.

Hirt, Paul W. 1998. 'Foreword: Terry Pacifica'. In *Terra Pacifica: People and Place in the Northwest States and Western Canada*. Pullman: Washington State University Press.

Hitchman, James H. 1976. *The Waterborne Commerce of British Columbia and Washington, 1850–1970*. *Occasional Paper # 7*. Bellingham: Center for Pacific Northwest Studies, Western Washington State College.

Hoffman, Henry. 2008. *Henry's Stories: Tales of a Larger than Life Figure on a Smaller than Normal Island*. Shaw Island: Kitchen Garden Press.

Homer. 2006 [*c*.8th century BC]. *The Odyssey*. Edited by Peter Jones and translated by E. V. Rieu, revised by D. C. H. Rieu. London: Penguin.

Horn, James. 2005. 'The Conquest of Eden: Possession and Dominion in Early Virginia'. In *Envisioning an English Empire: Jamestown and the Making of the North Atlantic World*, edited by Robert Appelbaum and John Wood Sweet, pp. 25–48. Philadelphia: University of Pennsylvania Press.

Horn, James. 2010. *A Kingdom Strange: The Brief and Tragic History of the Lost Colony of Roanoke*. New York: Basic Books.

Howe, K. R. 1984. *Where the Waves Fall: A New South Sea Islands History from First Settlement to Colonial Rule*. Sydney: George Allen & Unwin.

Howe, K. R. 2000. *Nature, Culture, and History: The 'Knowing' of Oceania*. Honolulu: University of Hawai'i Press.

Huggan, Graham and Helen Tiffin. 2007. 'Green Postcolonialism'. *Interventions: International Journal of Postcolonial Studies* 9 (1): pp. 1–11.

Huggan, Graham and Helen Tiffin. 2010. *Postcolonial Ecocriticism: Literature, Animals, Environment*. London: Routledge.

Hugues, David Y. 1997. 'The Doctor Vivisected'. *Science Fiction Studies* 24 (1): pp. 109–18.

Hulme, Peter. 1986. *Colonial Encounters: Europe and the Native Caribbean, 1492–1797*. London: Methuen.

Hulme, Peter. 2004. 'Cast Away: The Uttermost Parts of the Earth'. In *Sea Changes: Historicizing the Ocean*, edited by Bernhard Klein and Gesa Mackenthun, pp. 187–201. New York: Routledge.

The Hurricane. 1937. Directed by John Ford. USA: Samuel Goldwyn.

'idea, n.' June 2018. *OED Online*. Oxford University Press. <www.oed.com/view/Entry/90954>.

'idol, n.' June 2018. *OED Online*. Oxford University Press. <www.oed.com/view/Entry/91087>.

Immerman, Richard H. 2010. *Empire for Liberty: A History of American Imperialism from Benjamin Franklin to Paul Wolfowitz*. Princeton: Princeton University Press.

Immigrant Family Looking at New York Skyline. 1925. Photograph. Bettmann Archive, retrieved from Getty Images. <www.gettyimages.ch/license/517213446>.

Immigrants Waiting to Be Transferred, Ellis Island, October 30, 1912. 1912. Photograph. New York: Underwood & Underwood. Retrieved from the Library of Congress. <www.loc.gov/item/97501083/>.

'An Island Empire'. 1902. *San Juan Islander*, 5 June.

Island of Hope, Island of Tears. 1989. Directed by Charles Guggenheim. USA: Guggenheim Productions.

Italiano, Federico. 2009. *Tra miele e pietra: Aspetti di geopoetica in Montale e Celan*. Milano: Mimesis.

It Happened One Night. 1934. Directed by Frank Capra. USA: Columbia Pictures.

Jalais, Annu. 2005. 'Dwelling on Morichjhãpi: When Tigers Became "Citizens", Refugees "Tiger–Food"'. *Economic and Political Weekly* 40 (17): pp. 1757–62.

Jameson, Fredric. 1991. *Postmodernism, or the Cultural Logic of Late Capitalism*. Durham: Duke University Press.

Jameson, Fredric. 1992. *The Geopolitical Aesthetic: Cinema and Space in the World System*. Bloomington: Indiana University Press.

Jarvis, Michael J. 2010. *In the Eye of All Trade: Bermuda, Bermudians, and the Maritime Atlantic World, 1680–1783*. Chapel Hill: University of North Carolina Press.

Jones, Steve. 2011. *The Darwin Archipelago: The Naturalist's Career Beyond Origin of Species*. New Haven: Yale University Press.

Juet, Robert. 2006. *Juet's Journal of Hudson's 1609 Voyage, from the 1625 Edition of Purchas His Pilgrimes*. Transcribed by Brea Barthel. New Netherland Museum/Half Moon.

Kahn, Miriam. 2011. *Tahiti Beyond the Postcard: Power, Place, and Everyday Life*. Seattle: University of Washington Press.

Kaur, Rajender. 2007. ' "Home is Where the Oracella [*sic*] Are": Toward a New Paradigm of Transcultural Ecocritical Engagement in Amitav Ghosh's *The Hungry Tide*'. *Interdisciplinary Studies in Literature and the Environment* 14 (1): pp. 125–41.

Kiening, Christian. 2006. *Das wilde Subjekt. Kleine Poetik der Neuen Welt*. Göttingen: Vandenhoeck & Ruprecht.

Kinane, Ian. 2017. *Theorising Literary Islands: The Island Trope in Contemporary Robinsonade Narratives*. London: Rowman & Littlefield.

King, Laurie R. 2001. *Folly*. New York: Bantam.

King Kong. 1933. Directed by Merian C. Cooper and Ernest B. Schoedsack. USA: RKO Radio Pictures.

Kirk, Robert W. 2008. *Pitcairn Islands, the Bounty Mutineers and Their Descendants*. Jefferson: McFarland & Company.

Klein, Bernhard and Gesa Mackenthun (eds.). 2004. *Sea Changes: Historicizing the Ocean*. New York: Routledge.

Knapp, Jeffrey. 1992. *An Empire Nowhere: England, America, and Literature from Utopia to The Tempest*. Berkeley: University of California Press.

Knickerbocker, Scott. 2012. *Ecopoetics: The Language of Nature, the Nature of Language*. Amherst: University of Massachussetts Press.

Kreis, Bernadine. 1951. 'At the Gateway of America Bedloe—Ellis—Governors—3 Islands in New York Harbor'. *Timesquare Reporter*, 3–9 March.

Kupperman, Karen Ordahl. 2007. *Roanoke: The Abandoned Colony*. Lanham: Rowman & Littlefield.

Kushner, Howard I. 1975. *Conflict on the Northwest Coast: American-Russian Rivalry in the Pacific Northwest, 1790–1867*. Westport: Greenwood Press.

Lacan, Jacques. 2001 [1949]. 'The Mirror Stage as Formative of the I as Revealed in Psychoanalytic Experience'. In *The Norton Anthology of Theory and Criticism*, edited by Vincent B. Leitch et al., seventh edition, pp. 1285–90. New York: Norton.

The Lady from Shanghai. 1947. Directed by Orson Welles. USA: Columbia Pictures and Mercury Productions.

Lai, Him Mark, Genny Lim, and Judy Yung. 1980. *Island: Poetry and History of Chinese Immigrants on Angel Island, 1910–1940*. Seattle: University of Washington Press.

Lamarck, Jean-Baptiste de. 1968 [1809]. *Philosophie zoologique*. Paris: Union générale d'éditions.

Lane, Dorothy F. 1995. *The Island as Site of Resistance*. New York: Peter Lang.

Lane, Ralph. 1955a. *Ralph Lane's Discourse on the First Colony*. 17 August 1585–18 June 1586. In *The Roanoke Voyages: 1584–1590*, volume one, edited by David Beers Quinn, pp. 255–94. London: The Hakluyt Society, 1955.

Lane, Ralph. 1955b. 'Ralph Lane to Sir Francis Walsingham'. Letter from 12 August 1585. In *The Roanoke Voyages: 1584–1590, volume one*, edited by David Beers Quinn, pp. 199–204. London: The Hakluyt Society.

Langman, Larry. 1998. *Return to Paradise: A Guide to South Sea Island Films*. Lanham: Scarecrow Press.

Largeaud-Ortega, Sylvie. 2012. *Ainsi Soit-Île: Littérature et anthropologie dans les* Contes des mers du sud *de Robert Louis Stevenson*. Paris: Champion.

Lawrence, D. H. 2007 [1927]. 'The Man Who Loved Islands'. In *Selected Stories*, pp. 286–312. London: Penguin.

Lee, Erika and Judy Yung. 2010. *Angel Island: Immigrant Gateway to America*. New York: Oxford University Press.

Lefebvre, Henri. 1991 [1974]. *The Production of Space*. Translated by Donald Nicholson-Smith. Oxford: Blackwell.

Lestringant, Frank. 2002. *Le livre des îles*. Genève: Librairie Droz.

Létoublon, Françoise, Paola Ceccarelli, and Jean Sgard. 1996. 'Qu'est–ce qu'une île?' In *Impressions d'îles*, edited by Françoise Létoublon, pp. 9–27. Toulouse: Presses Universitaires du Mirail.

Letters from Iwo Jima. 2006. Directed by Clint Eastwood. USA: Dream-Works and Warner Bros.

Levine, George. 1988. *Darwin and the Novelists: Patterns of Science in Victorian Fiction*. Cambridge, MA: Harvard University Press.

Lévi-Strauss, Claude. 1973 [1955]. *Tristes Tropiques*. Translated by John Weightman. London: Penguin.

LeWarne, Charles Pierce. 1975. *Utopias on Puget Sound, 1885–1915*. Seattle: University of Washington Press.

Libby, Andrew. 2004. 'The Aesthetics of Adventure: The Dark Sublime and the Rise of the Colonial Anti-Hero'. *Victorian Newsletter* 105: pp. 7–15.

Ljungberg, Christina. 2003. 'Constructing New "Realities": The Performative Function of Maps in Contemporary Fiction'. In *Representing Realities: Essays on American Literature, Art and Culture*, edited by Beverly Maeder, pp. 159–76. Tübingen: Gunter Narr.

Lotman, Yuri M. 1990. *Universe of the Mind: A Semiotic Theory of Culture*. Translated by Ann Shukman. London: I.B. Tauris.

Louvish, Simon. 2007. *Cecil B. DeMille: A Life in Art*. New York: St. Martin's Press.

Lovering, Frances K. 2008 [1985]. *Island Ebb & Flow: A Pioneer's Journal of Life on Waldron Island*. Second edition. Friday Harbor: Illumina Publishing.

Loxley, Diana. 1990. *Problematic Shores: The Literature of Islands*. New York: St. Martin's Press.

Lubchenco, Jane, Renee Davis–Born, and Brooke Simler. 2011. 'Lessons from the Land for Protection in the See: The Need for a New Ocean Ethic'. Updated by Kirsten Grorud–Colvert. In *Open Spaces: Voices from the Northwest*, edited by Penny Harrison, pp. 197–213. Seattle: University of Washington Press.

Lukács, Georg. 1971 [1914–15]. *The Theory of the Novel*. Translated by Anna Bostock. Cambridge, MA: MIT Press.

'Lure of South Seas Gaining'. 1929. *Los Angeles Times*, 25 May.

Lyons, Paul. 2006. *American Pacificism: Oceania in the U.S. Imagination*. New York: Routledge.

MacArthur, Robert and Edward O. Wilson. 1967. *The Theory of Island Biogeography*. Princeton: Princeton University Press.

Macherey, Pierre. 2006 [1966]. *A Theory of Literary Production*. Translated by Geoffrey Wall. Abingdon: Routledge.

Mackay Brown, George. 2005 [1994]. *Beside the Ocean of Time*. Edinburgh: Polygon.

Mackenthun, Gesa. 1997. *Metaphors of Dispossession: American Beginnings and the Translation of Empire, 1492–1637*. Norman: University of Oklahoma Press.

Maeterlinck, Maurice. 1928. *La vie de l'espace*. Paris: Bibliothèque-Charpentier.

Male and Female. 1919. Directed by Cecil B. DeMille. USA: Paramount Pictures.

Maleuvre, Didier. 2011. *The Horizon: A History of Our Infinite Longing*. Berkeley: University of California Press.

Malinowski, Bronislaw. 2002 [1922]. *Argonauts of the Western Pacific*. Collected Works, volume two. London: Routledge.

Mallick, Ross. 1999. 'Refugee Resettlement in Forest Reserves: West Bengal Policy Reversal and the Marichjhapi Massacre'. *The Journal of Asian Studies* 58 (1): pp. 104–25.

Mandelbrot, Benoit B. 1983. *The Fractal Geometry of Nature*. New York: W. H. Freeman & Company.

Mandeville, John. 2005 [c.1356]. *The Travels of Sir John Mandeville*. Translated by C. W. R. D. Moseley. London: Penguin.

Marin, Louis. 1973. *Utopiques: Jeux d'espaces*. Paris: Minuit.

Marin, Louis. 1979. 'Archipels'. *Silex* 14 (4): pp. 79–87.

Marks, Kathy. *Lost Paradise*. 2009. New York: Free Press.

Marryat, Frederick. 1841. *Masterman Ready; or, the Wreck of the 'Pacific'*. New York: A. L. Burt.

Marszałek, Magdalena and Sylvia Sasse (eds.). 2010. *Geopoetiken. Geographische Entwürfe in den mittel- und osteuropäischen Literaturen*. Berlin: Kulturverlag Kadmos.

Marzec, Robert P. 2009. 'Speaking before the Environment: Modern Fiction and the Ecological'. *Modern Fiction Studies* 55 (3): pp. 419–42.

Maximin, Daniel. 2006. *Les fruits du cyclone: Une géopoétique de la Caraïbe*. Paris: Seuil.

McBride, Joseph. 2001. *Searching for John Ford: A Life*. New York: St. Martin's Press.

McCloskey, Michael D. 2001. 'Postscript'. In *The Light on the Island*, by Helene Glidden, pp. 195–200. Second edition. Woodinville: San Juan Publishing.

McCusker, Maeve and Anthony Soares (eds.). 2011. *Islanded Identities: Constructions of Postcolonial Cultural Insularity*. Amsterdam: Rodopi.

McDonald, Lucile S. 1990. *Making History: The People Who Shaped the San Juan Islands*. Friday Harbor: Harbor Press.

McDonald, Russ. 1991. 'Reading *The Tempest*'. *Shakespeare Survey* 43: pp. 15–28.

McGurl, Mark. 1996. 'Making it Big: Picturing the Radio Age in *King Kong*'. *Critical Inquiry* 22 (3): pp. 415–45.

McLeod, Judyth A. 2009. *The Atlas of Legendary Lands: Fabled Kingdoms, Phantom Islands, Lost Continents and Other Mythical Worlds*. Millers Point: Pier 9.

Mead, Margaret. 2001 [1928]. *Coming of Age in Samoa*. New York: Harper Perennial.

Melville, Herman. 1996 [1846]. *Typee: A Peep at Polynesian Life*. New York: Penguin.

Merleau-Ponty, Maurice. 1945. *Phénomenologie de la perception*. Paris: Gallimard.

Merleau-Ponty, Maurice. 2002 [1945]. *Phenomenology of Perception*. Translated by Colin Smith. London: Routledge.

Miller, Lee. 2000. *Roanoke: Solving the Mystery of the Lost Colony*. New York: Penguin.

Miller, J. Hillis. 1995. *Topographies*. Stanford: Stanford University Press.

Moana. 1926. Directed by Robert Flaherty. USA: Famous Players-Lasky.

Monush, Barry. 2003. *The Encyclopedia of Hollywood Film Actors: From the Silent Era to 1965*. New York: Applause Theatre & Cinema Books.

Moore, Reuel S. and Joseph R. Farrington. 1931. *The American Samoan Commission's Visit to Samoa, September–October 1930*. Washington: United States Government Printing Office.

More, Thomas. 2003 [1516]. *Utopia*. Translated by Paul Turner. London: Penguin.

Moretti, Franco. 1998. *Atlas of the European Novel, 1800–1900*. London: Verso.

Morrell, Benjamin. 1832. *A Narrative of Four Voyages to the South Sea, North and South Pacific Ocean, Chinese Sea, Ethiopic and Southern Atlantic Ocean, Indian and Antarctic Ocean, from the Year 1822 to 1831*. New York: J. & J. Harper.

Morton, Timothy. 2007. *Ecology without Nature: Rethinking Environmental Aesthetics*. Cambridge, MA: Harvard University Press.

Morton, Timothy. 2014. 'Deconstruction and/as Ecology'. In *The Oxford Handbook of Ecocriticism*, edited by Greg Garrard, pp. 291–304. Oxford: Oxford University Press.

Moseley, C. W. R. D. 2005. 'Introduction'. In *The Travels of Sir John Mandeville*, pp. 9–41. London: Penguin.

Mr. Robinson Crusoe. 1932. Directed by A. Edward Sutherland. USA: Elton Productions.

Mukherjee, Pablo. 2006. 'Surfing the Second Waves: Amitav Ghosh's Tide Country'. *New Formations* 59 (1): pp. 144–57.

Mukherjee, Upamanyu Pablo. 2010. *Postcolonial Environments: Nature, Culture and the Contemporary Indian Novel in English*. Basingstoke: Palgrave.

Munz, Georg Christoph. 2004 [1711]. *Exercitatio academica de insulis natantibus*. In *Floating Islands: A Global Bibliography*, edited by Chet Van Duzer, pp. 1–68. Los Altos Hills: Cantor Press.

Murchie, Noël. 2001. *The Accidental Hermit*. Orcas: Nine Toes Press.

Nanook of the North. 1922. Directed by Robert Flaherty. USA/France: Les Frères Revillon and Pathé Exchange.

Naughton, Momilani. *Hawaiians in the Fur Trade: Cultural Influence on the Northwest Coast, 1811–1875*. Unpublished MA thesis.

Neiwert, David. 2005. *Strawberry Days: How Internment Destroyed a Japanese American Community*. New York: St. Martin's Press.

'Newly Discovered South Sea Islands'. 1921. The New York Times, 21 August.

The New World. Extended Cut. 2008 [2005]. Directed by Terrence Malick. USA/UK: New Line Cinema et al.

Nicol, David. 2011. 'Understanding Virginia: Quoting the Sources in Terrence Malick's *The New World*'. *Screening the Past 32*. <http://www.screeningthepast.com/2011/11/understanding-virginia-quoting-the-sources-in-terrence-malick%E2%80%99s-the-new-world/>.

Nietzsche, Friedrich. 2006 [1887]. *On the Genealogy of Morality*. Translated by Carol Diethe. Cambridge: Cambridge University Press.

Nietzsche, Friedrich. 2007 [1874]. 'On the Uses and Disadvantages of History for Life'. In *Theories of Memory: A Reader*, edited by Michael Rossington and Anne Whitehead, pp. 102–8. Edinburgh: Edinburgh University Press.

Nora, Pierre. 2007 [1989]. 'Between Memory and History: *Les Lieux de Mémoire*', translated by Marc Roudebush. In *Theories of Memory: A Reader*, edited by Michael Rossington and Anne Whitehead, pp. 144–9. Edinburgh: Edinburgh University Press.

Nordhoff, Charles and James Norman Hall. 1989 [1932]. *Mutiny on the Bounty*. Boston: Little, Brown and Company.

Nordquist, Myron H., Shabtai Rosenne, and Satya N. Nandan. 1995. *United Nations Convention on the Law of the Sea: A Commentary*. Volume three. The Hague: Nijhoff.

O'Connell, Nicholas. 2003. *On Sacred Ground: The Spirit of Place in Pacific Northwest Literature*. Seattle: University of Washington Press.

O'Connor, Ralph. 2007. *The Earth on Show: Fossils and the Poetics of Popular Science, 1802–1856*. Chicago: University of Chicago Press.

Orgel, Stephen. 1975. *The Illusion of Power: Political Theater in the English Renaissance*. Berkeley: University of California Press.

Orr, William N. and Elizabeth L. Orr. 2006. *Geology of the Pacific Northwest*. Second edition. Long Grove: Waveland Press.

Ouspensky, P. D. 1920 [1912]. *Tertium Organum: A Key to the Enigmas of the World*. Translated by Nicholas Bessaraboff and Claude Bragdon. Manas Press: New York.

Øverland, Orm. 2000. *Immigrant Minds, American Identities: Making the United States Home, 1870–1930*. Urbana: University of Illinois Press.

Page, Michael R. 2012. *The Literary Imagination from Erasmus Darwin to H. G. Wells: Science, Evolution, and Ecology*. Farnham: Ashgate.

Palmer, Christopher. 2016. *Castaway Tales: From Robinson Crusoe to Life of Pi*. Middletown: Wesleyan University Press.

Paul, Heike. 2014. *The Myths That Made America: An Introduction to American Studies*. Bielefeld: transcript.

Pawlowski, Gaston de. 2004 [1912]. *Voyage au pays de la quatrième dimension*. Paris: Images Modernes.

Pearson, Richard. 2007. 'Primitive Modernity: H. G. Wells and the Prehistoric Man of the 1890s'. *The Yearbook of English Studies* 37 (1): 58–74.

Philmus, Robert M. 1981. 'The Satiric Ambivalence of *The Island of Dr Moreau*'. *Science-Fiction Studies* 8 (1): 2–11.

Poe, Edgar Allan. 1999 [1838]. *The Narrative of Arthur Gordon Pym of Nantucket*. New York: Penguin.

'poetics, n.' June 2018. *OED Online*. Oxford University Press. <www.oed.com/view/Entry/318383>.

Polo, Marco. 1958 [c.1300]. *The Travels*. Translated by Ronald Latham. London: Penguin.

Porter, David. 1822. *Journal of a Cruise Made to the Pacific Ocean, by Captain David Porter, in the United States Frigate Essex, in the Years 1812, 1813, and 1814*. Second edition. New York: J. & J. Harper.

Porter, Dennis. 1991. *Haunted Journeys: Desire and Transgression in European Travel Writing*. Princeton: Princeton University Press.

Pratt, Mary Louise. 2008. *Imperial Eyes: Travel Writing and Transculturation*. Second edition. New York: Routledge.

'The Primrose Journal of Drake's Voyage. Florida and Virginia'. 1955 [1586]. In *The Roanoke Voyages: 1584–1590*, volume one, edited by David Beers Quinn, pp. 303–8. London: The Hakluyt Society.

Quinn, David Beers. 1955. *The Roanoke Voyages: 1584–1590*. Two volumes. London: The Hakluyt Society.

Quinn, David Beers. 1984. *The Lost Colonists: Their Fortune and Probable Fate*. Collingdale: Diane Publishing.

Quinn, David Beers. 1985. *Set Fair for Roanoke: Voyages and Coonies, 1584–1606*. Chapel Hill: University of North Carolina Press.

Racault, Jean-Michel. 1989. 'Insularité et origine'. *Corps Écrit* 32: pp. 111–23.

Racault, Jean-Michel. 1995. 'Avant-Propos: De la définition de l'île à la thématique insulaire'. In *L'insularité: Thématique et représentations*, edited by Jean-Claude Marimoutou and Jean-Michel Racault, pp. 9–13. Paris: L'Harmattan.

Racault, Jean-Michel. 1996. 'Géographie et topographie de l'espace insulaire dans l'utopie narrative classique'. In *Impressions d'îles*, edited by Françoise Létoublon, pp. 247–57. Toulouse: Presses Universitaires du Mirail.

Racault, Jean-Michel. 2007. *Mémoires du Grand Océan: Des relations de voyages aux littératures francophones de l'océan Indien*. Paris: Presses de l'Université Paris-Sorbonne.

Racault, Jean-Michel. 2010. *Robinson & compagnie: Aspects de l'insularité politique de Thomas More à Michel Tournier*. Paris: Éditions Pétra.

Racusin, M. Jay. 1947. 'Drab Ellis Island Has Fulfilled Elysian Dreams of 30,000,000'. *New York Herald Tribune*, 25 May.

Rasmussen, Janet E. 1993. *New Land, New Lives: Scandinavian Immigrants to the Pacific Northwest*. Northfield: Norwegian–American Historical Association.

Rath, Arnapurna and Milind Malshe. 2010. 'Chronotopes of "Places" and "Non-places": Ecopoetics of Amitav Ghosh's *The Hungry Tide*'. *Asiatic* 4 (2): pp. 14–33.

Rayner, Anne Patricia. 1995. *Everything Becomes Island: Gulf Islands Writing and the Construction of Region*. Unpublished doctoral dissertation. University of British Columbia.

Redmon, Michael. 2013. 'Prisoners Harbor: Santa Cruz Island's Infamous Port'. In *Santa Barbara Independent*, 12 February. Reproduced in *National Park Service* (website), 10 June 2016. <https://www.nps.gov/chis/learn/historyculture/prisoners.htm>.

Reeves, Pamela. 1991. *Ellis Island: Gateway to the American Dream*. New York: Dorset Press.

Repas de bébé. 1895. Directed by Louis Lumière. France: Lumière.

Reynolds, William. 2004. *The Private Journals of William Reynolds: United States Exploring Expedition, 1838–1842*. New York: Penguin.

Richardson, David. 1973. *Magic Islands: A Treasure-Trove of San Juan Islands Lore*. Eastsound: Orcas Publishing Company.

Ricou, Laurie. 2002. *The Arbutus/Madrone Files: Reading the Pacific Northwest*. Corvallis: Oregon State University Press.

Riquet, Johannes. 2014. 'Killing King Kong: The Camera at the Borders of the Tropical Island, 1767–1937'. *Nordlit* 31: pp. 133–49.

Riquet, Johannes. 2016. 'Islands as Shifting Territories: Evolution, Geology and the Island Poetics of Darwin, Wallace, Wells and Ghosh'. In

Insularity: Representations of Small Worlds, edited by Katrin Dautel and Kathrin Schödel, pp. 223–36. Würzburg: Königshausen & Neumann.

Riquet, Johannes. 2018. 'Island Stills and Island Movements: Un/freezing the Island in 1920s and 1930s Hollywood Cinema'. In *Spatial Modernities: Geography, Narrative, Imaginaries*, edited by Johannes Riquet and Elizabeth Kollmann, pp. 119–36. London: Routledge.

Robertson, George. 1948. *The Discovery of Tahiti: A Journal of the Second Voyage of H.M.S. Dolphin Round the World, Under the Command of Captain Wallis, R.N., in the Years 1766, 1767 and 1768*. London: The Hakluyt Society.

Robinson, Tim. 1991 [1976]. 'Islands and Images'. In *Setting Foot on the Shores of Connemara & Other Writings*, pp. 1–17. Dublin: The Lilliput Press.

'The Romance of the Island Pineapple'. 1925. *Los Angeles Times*, 1 January.

Rony, Fatimah Tobing. 1996. *The Third Eye: Race, Cinema, and Ethnographic Spectacle*. Durham: Duke University Press.

Royle, Stephen A. 2001. *A Geography of Islands: Small Island Insularity*. London: Routledge.

Royle, Stephen A. 2007. 'Island Definitions and Typologies'. In *A World of Islands: An Island Studies Reader*, edited by Godfrey Baldacchino, pp. 33–56. Charlottetown: Institute of Island Studies and Agenda Academic.

Royle, Stephen A. 2014. *Islands: Nature and Culture*. London: Reaktion Books.

Ruby, Robert H. and John A. Brown. 1982. *Indians of the Pacific Northwest: A History*. Norman: University of Nebraska Press.

Ruddick, Nicholas. 1993. *Ultimate Island: On the Nature of British Science Fiction*. Westport: Greenwood.

Rudiak-Gould, Peter. 2013. *Climate Change and Tradition in a Small Island State: The Rising Tide*. New York: Routledge.

Saffran, Lise. 2010. *Juno's Daughters*. New York: Plume.

Sailor in Philippines. 1908. USA: Kalem.

Saint-Pierre, Bernardin de. 2008 [1788]. *Paul et Virginie*. Paris: LGF.

Samson, Barney. 2020 (forthcoming). *Desert Islands and the Liquid Modern*. Basingstoke: Palgrave.

Sanderson, Eric W. 2009. *Mannahatta: A Natural History of New York City*. New York: Abrams.

Sanderson, Eric W. and Marianne Brown. 2007. 'Mannahatta: An Ecological First Look at the Manhattan Landscape Prior to Henry Hudson'. *Northeastern Naturalist* 14 (4): pp. 545–70.

'San Jan County'. 1902. *San Juan Islander*, 6 and 13 February.

'San Jan County'. 1902. *San Juan Islander*, 20 February.

'Santa Cruz Island History and Culture'. June 2016. Website of the National Park Service. <www.nps.gov/chis/historyculture/santacruzisland.htm>.

Schalansky, Judith. 2010. *Atlas of Remote Islands: Fifty Islands I Have Never Set Foot on and Never Will*. London: Penguin.

Schenkel, Elmar. 1993. 'Die verkehrte Insel: *The Tempest* und H. G. Wells' *The Island of Dr Moreau*'. *Anglia* 111: pp. 39–58.

Schneider, Dorothee. 2011. *Crossing Borders: Migration and Citizenship in the Twentieth-Century United States*. Cambridge, MA: Harvard University Press.

Schueller, Malini Johar and Edward Watts (eds.). 2003. *Messy Beginnings: Postcoloniality and Early American Beginnings*. New Brunswick: Rutgers University Press.

Schwantes, Carlos A. 1989. *The Pacific Northwest: An Interpretive History*. Lincoln: University of Nebraska Press.

Scotte, Jason Mark. 2007. '"Give My Love to the Sunrise": *The Lady from Shanghai*'. *Bright Lights Film Journal* 58. <brightlightsfilm.com/58/58lady.php#.U9UzokDVfSg>.

Sen, Malcolm. 2009. 'Spatial Justice: The Ecological Imperative and Postcolonial Development'. *Journal of Postcolonial Writing* 45 (4): pp. 365–77.

Serres, Michel. 2008 [1985]. *The Five Senses: A Philosophy of Mingled Bodies*. Translated by Margaret Sankey and Peter Cowley. London: Continuum.

Seuront, Laurent. 2010. *Fractals and Multifractals in Ecology and Aquatic Science*. Boca Raton: Taylor & Francis.

Shakespeare, William. 1623. *The Tempest*. In *Mr William Shakespeares Comedies, Histories, & Tragedies. Published according to the True Originall Copies*, pp. 1–19. London: Isaac Iaggard and Ed. Blount.

Shakespeare, William. 2000 [1611]. *The Tempest*. Edited by Gerald Graff and James Phelan. Boston: Bedford/St. Martin's.

Shepherd, Robert. 2012. *Partners in Paradise: Tourism Practices, Heritage Policies, and Anthropological Sites*. New York: Peter Lang.

Shillibeer, John. 1818. *A Narrative of the Briton's Voyage to Pitcairn's Island*. London: Law and Whittaker.

Siewers, Alfred Kentigern (ed.). 2014. *Re-Imagining Nature: Environmental Humanities and Ecosemiotics*. Plymouth: Bucknell University Press.

Singh, Omendra Kumar. 2011. '"Nation" within the Nation: Revisiting the Failed Revolution of Morichjhāpi in Amitav Ghosh's The Hungry Tide'. *South Asian Review* 32 (2): pp. 241–57.

Sinners in Paradise. 1938. Directed by James Whale. USA: James Whale Productions and Universal Pictures.

Skura, Meredith Anne. 1989. 'Discourse and the Individual: The Case of Colonialism in *The Tempest*'. *Shakespeare Quarterly* 40 (1): pp. 42–69.

Skyfall. 2012. Directed by Sam Mendes. UK/USA: Eon Productions.

Smith, Vanessa. 2003. 'Pitairn's 'Guilty Stock''. In *Islands in History and Representation*, edited by Rod Edmond and Vanessa Smith, pp. 116–32. London: Routledge.

Snead, James. 1991. 'Spectatorship and Capture in *King Kong*: The Guilty Look'. *Critical Quarterly* 33 (1): pp. 53–69.

Sodikoff, Genese Marie. 2013. 'The Time of Living Dead Species: Extinction Debt and Futurity in Madagascar'. In *Debt: Ethics, the Environment, and the Economy*, edited by Peter Y. Paik and Merry Wiesner-Hanks, pp. 140–63. Bloomington: Indiana University Press.

Soja, Edward W. 1989. *Postmodern Geographies: The Reassertion of Space in Critical Social Theory.* London: Verso.

Sokol, B. J. 1998. '"Text-in-History": *The Tempest* and New World Cultural Encounter'. *George Herbert Journal* 22 (1): pp. 21–40.

Sontag, Susan. 1977. 'In Plato's Cave'. In *On Photography*, pp. 3–26. London: Penguin.

South Pacific. 1958. Directed by Joshua Logan. USA: Magna Theatre and South Pacific Enterprises.

'South Sea Idyl'. 1926. *The New York Times*, 25 March.

'The South Seas'. 1931. *The New York Times*, 18 October.

The Statue of Liberty from Ellis Island. c.1930. Photograph. Retrieved from the Library of Congress. <www.loc.gov/item/97502760/>.

Stevenson, Robert Louis. 1896. *In the South Seas.* New York: Charles Scribner's Sons.

Stevenson, Robert Louis. 1985 [1883]. *Treasure Island.* Oxford: Oxford University Press.

Strahler, Alan H. and Arthur N. Strahler. 2002. *Physische Geographie.* Second revised and enlarged edition. Stuttgart: Eugen Ulmer.

Stratford, Elaine, Godfrey Baldacchino, Elizabeth McMahon, Carol Farbotko, and Andrew Harwood. 2011. 'Envisioning the Archipelago'. *Island Studies Journal* 6 (2): pp. 113–30.

'The Sundarbans'. 1992–2018. Website of the UNESCO World Heritage Convention. <whc.unesco.org/en/list/798>.

Superman Returns. 2006. Directed by Bryan Singer. USA: Warner Bros.

Sweet, John Wood. 2005. 'Introduction: Sea Changes'. In *Envisioning an English Empire: Jamestown and the Making of the North Atlantic World*, edited by Robert Appelbaum and John Wood Sweet, pp. 1–21. Philadelphia: University of Pennsylvania Press.

Swift, Jonathan. 2001. *Gulliver's Travels*. London: Penguin.

'Tattoo Lipstick'. 1937. *Los Angeles Times*, 10 October.

Taylor, Sam. 2009. *The Island at the End of the World*. New York: Penguin.

Telotte, J. P. 1988. 'The Movies as Monster: Seeing in *King Kong*'. *The Georgia Review* 42 (2): pp. 388–98.

Thieme, John. 2009. 'Out of Place? The Poetics of Space in Amitav Ghosh's *The Hungry Tide* and Michael Ondaatje's *Anil's Ghost*'. *Commonwealth* 31 (2): pp. 32–43.

Thompson, Erwin N. 1972. *Historic Resource Study: San Juan Island National Historical Park*. Denver: National Park Service.

Tjossem, Donald R. 2013. *Bainbridge Island*. Charleston: Arcadia.

Tocqueville, Alexis de. 1840. *Democracy in America: Part the Second, The Social Influence of Democracy*. Translated by Henry Reeve. New York: J. & H. G. Langley.

Tournier, Michel. 1967. *Vendredi ou les limbes du Pacifique*. Paris: Gallimard.

Tuan, Yi-Fu. 1977. *Space and Place: The Perspective of Experience*. Minneapolis: University of Minnesota Press.

Tuan, Yi-Fu. 1990. *Topophilia: A Study of Environmental Perception, Attitudes, and Values*. New York: Columbia University Press.

Tulloch, James Francis. 1978. *The James Francis Tulloch Diary, 1875–1910*. Edited by Gordon Keith. Portland: Binford & Mort.

Turner, Monica G., Robert H. Gardner, and Robert V. O'Neill. 2001. *Landscape Ecology in Theory and Practice: Pattern and Process*. New York: Springer.

United Nations Convention on the Law of the Sea. 1982. United Nations: Oceans and Law of the Sea. <www.un.org/depts/los/convention_agree ments/texts/unclos/unclos_e.pdf>.

Vancouver, George. 1798a. *A Chart Shewing Part of the Coast of N. W. America*. London: G. G. & J. Robinson. Retrieved from David Rumsey Map Collection. <www.davidrumsey.com/maps1495.html>.

Vancouver, George. 1798b. *A Voyage of Discovery to the North Pacific Ocean and round the World. Three volumes.* London: G. G. and J. Robinson and J. Edward.

Van Duzer, Chet. 2004. *Floating Islands: A Global Bibliography.* Los Altos Hills: Cantor Press.

Van Duzer, Chet. 2006. 'From Odysseus to Robinson Crusoe: A Survey of Early Western Island Literature'. *Island Studies Journal* 1 (1): pp. 143–62.

Vann, David. 2011. *Caribou Island.* London: Penguin.

Vaughan, Dai. 1990. 'Let There Be Lumière'. *Early Cinema: Space, Frame, Narrative,* edited by Thomas Elsaesser and Adam Barker, pp. 63–7. London: British Film Institute.

Verne, Jules. 2002 [1875]. *L'île mystérieuse.* Paris: Le Livre de Poche.

Vouri, Mike. 2013. *The Pig War: Standoff at Griffin Bay.* Seattle: Discover Your Northwest.

Vouri, Mike and Julia Vouri. 2010. *San Juan Island.* Charleston: Arcadia.

Waldseemüller, Martin. 1507. *Universalis Cosmographia Secundum Ptholomaei Traditionem et Americi Vespucii Alioru[m]que Lustrationes.* Retrieved from the Library of Congress. [Strasbourg, France? : s.n]. <https://www.loc.gov/item/2003626426/>.

Wallace, Alfred Russel. 2013 [1880]. *Island Life.* Chicago: University of Chicago Press.

Walsh, Jill Paton. 1994. *Knowledge of Angels.* London: Black Swan.

Ward, Jean M. and Elaine A. Maveety. 1995. *Pacific Northwest Women, 1815–1925: Lives, Memories, and Writings.* Corvallis: Oregon State University Press.

Weaver-Hightower, Rebecca. 2007. *Empire Islands: Castaways, Cannibals, and Fantasies of Conquest.* Minneapolis: University of Minnesota Press.

Wegener, Alfred. 1915. *Die Entstehung der Kontinente und Ozeane.* Braunschweig: Druck und Verlag von Friedrich Vieweg.

Wells, H. G. 1911 [1894]. 'Aepyornis Island'. In *The Country of the Blind, and Other Stories,* pp. 71–86. London: T. Nelson & Sons.

Wells, H. G. 2005 [1896]. *The Island of Doctor Moreau.* London: Penguin.

Werner, Emmy E. 2009. *Passages to America: Oral Histories of Child Immigrants from Ellis Island and Angel Island.* Washington: Potomac Books.

Westphal, Bertrand. 2011. *Geocriticism: Real and Fictional Spaces.* Translated by Robert T. Tally Jr. New York: Palgrave.

White, John. 1955. *John White's Narrative of the 1590 Voyage to Virginia.* In *The Roanoke Voyages: 1584–1590,* volume two, edited by David Beers Quinn, pp. 598–622. London: The Hakluyt Society.

White, Kenneth. 1994. *Le Plateau de l'Albatros: Introduction à la géopoé-tique*. Paris: Grasset & Fasquelle.

White, Kenneth. 2006. *On the Atlantic Edge: A Geopoetics Project*. Dingwall: Sandstone Press.

White, Laura A. 2013. 'Novel Vision: Seeing the Sundarbans through Amitav Ghosh's *The Hungry Tide*'. *Interdisciplinary Studies in Literature and Environment* 20 (3): pp. 513–31.

White, Paul. 1995. 'Geography, Literature and Migration'. In *Writing Across Worlds: Literature and Migration*, edited by Russell King, John Connell, and Paul White, pp. 1–19. London: Routledge.

White, Richard. 1991. *The Middle Ground*. Cambridge: Cambridge University Press.

White Shadows in the South Seas. 1928. Directed by W. S. Van Dyke and Robert Flaherty (uncredited). USA: Metro Goldwyn-Mayer.

Wilkes, Charles and United States Exploring Expedition. 1841. *Map of the Oregon Territory*. Philadelphia: Lea & Blanchard. Retrieved from David Rumsey Map Collection. <http://www.davidrumsey.com/maps890027-24331.html>.

Wilkes, Charles and United States Exploring Expedition. 1844. *Atlas of the Narrative of the United States Exploring Expedition*. Philadelphia: C. Sherman. Retrieved from the Library of Congress. <www.loc.gov/item/2010589747/>.

Wilkes, Charles. 1851. *Voyage Round the World, Embracing the Principal Events of the Narrative of the United States Exploring Expedition*. New York: George P. Putnam.

Wilkinson, Charles. 2011. 'Water in the West'. In *Open Spaces: Voices from the Northwest*, edited by Penny Harrison, pp. 72–85. Seattle: University of Washington Press.

Wilson, Rob. 2000. *Reimagining the American Pacific: From South Pacific to Bamboo Ridge and Beyond*. Durham: Duke University Press.

Wingfield, Andrew. 2005. 'Approaching the Island'. *Interdisciplinary Studies in Literature and Environment* 12 (1): pp. 147–58.

Wooding, Jonathan M. 2002. 'The Latin Version'. In *The Voyage of Saint Brendan: Representative Versions of the Legend in English Translation*, edited by W. R. J. Barron, pp. 13–25. Exeter: Exeter University Press.

Wylie, John. 2007. *Landscape*. Abingdon: Routledge.

Wylie, John. 2012. 'Dwelling and Displacement: Tim Robinson and the Questions of Landscape'. *Cultural Geographies* 19 (3): pp. 365–83.

Wylie, John. 2013. 'Landscape and Phenomenology'. In *The Routledge Companion to Landscape Studies*, edited by Peter Howard et al., pp. 54–65. London: Routledge.

Wyss, Johan David. 2006 [1812]. *The Swiss Family Robinson*. New York: Sterling.

Zullo, Federica. 2012. 'Amitav Ghosh's "Imagined Communities": *The Hungry Tide* as a Possible "Other" World'. In *History, Narrative, and Testimony in Amitav Ghosh's Fiction*, edited by Chitra Sankaran, pp. 95–108. Albany: State University of New York Press.

INDEX

Note: Figures are indicated by an italic "*f*" and notes are indicated by an "n" following the page numbers.

For the benefit of digital users, indexed terms that span two pages (e.g., 52–53) may, on occasion, appear on only one of those pages.